BARBADOS

JUST BEYOND YOUR IMAGINATION

Edited by Arif Ali

HANSIB

Tent Bay and Bathsheba

Grand Kadooment

Cannon and Clock Tower at Garrison Savannah

Published in 1996 by Hansib Caribbean
PO Box 2773, St John's, Antigua, Westindies

Distributed in Barbados by Cedolph H Kennedy, President
Enterprise, 1 Villa Park, Britton Hill, St Michael. Tel/Fax: (246)
436 0068 or Fax: (246) 438 1003

Editor: Arif Ali; Project Manager: John Hughes; Production:
Shareef Ali; Marketing: Jennifer Francis & Joy Ann Haigh;
Bulk photographs: Willie Alleyne Associates Photography Ltd.

Colour origination by Graphic Ideas Studios, London
& The Harrington Consultancy, London.
Printed in the United Kingdom by Caledonian International Book
Manufacturing, Glasgow.

British Library Cataloguing in Publication Data. A catalogue
record for this book is available from the British Library.

ISBN 1-870518-54-3

PUBLISHER'S NOTE: Readers unfamiliar with Hansib's
publications may note the use of 'Westindies' (not 'West Indies').
This has been used in all Hansib publications since 1973 in a
tribute to the formation of the Caribbean Community (CariCom) at
Chaguaramas, Trinidad, on 4 July 1973 and as an appropriation of
the name given by the "discoverers" to assert the region's united,
unique and distinctive identity.

Bibliography

A True and Exact History of the Island of Barbados,
   Richard Ligon, Second edition, 1673.
Glimpses of Old Barbados, E A Stoute, serialised in
   the Advocate News.
Barbados, George Hunte, 1974.
The Barbados Book, Louis Lynch, 1972.
Insight Guide: Barbados, 1988.
Barbados - Insight Guide, Apa Publications, 1994.
The History of Barbados, Robert H Schomburgk, 1971.
The Bajan, ed. George Hunte, November 1958.
The Bridge Barbados, Patrick Roach, c. 1970.
The Life and Times of Errol Barrow, Peter Morgan.
1995 Pamphlets from Energy Division, Ministry of
   Finance and Economy.
Barbados Advocate-News, July 9 - 18, 1970.
*Barbados: A History from the Amerindians to
Independence,* F A Hoyos, 1978.
A-Z of Barbados Heritage, Henry Fraser, Sean
   Carrington, Addinton Forde, John Gilmore, 1990.
The Barbados-Carolina Connection, Warren Alleyne
   and Henry Fraser, 1988.
De mortar-pestle: A collection of Barbadian Proverbs,
   G Addinton Forde, 1993.
Folk Beliefs of Barbados, G Addinton Forde, 1988.
Tribute to Landship, Winston Farrel, 1996.
Historic Churches of Barbados, Barbara Hill, 1984.
Some Early Barbadian History, P F Campbell, 1993.
Barbados Our Island Home, F A Hoyos, 1989.
A History of Barbados, Hilary Beckles, 1990.
Barbados: The Visitor Guide, F A Hoyos, 1982.
Heritage Sites of Barbados, The Barbados Tourism
   Authority.
The Rise of West Indian Cricket: From Colony to Nation,
   Frank Birbalsingh, 1996.
Caribbean Story: Book Two - The Inheritors, William
   Claypole and John Robottom, 1989.
Historic Houses of Barbados, Henry Fraser and Ronnie
   Hughes, 1982.
Treasures of Barbados, Henry S Fraser, 1990.
Caribbean Companion - The A to Z Reference, Brian
   Dyde, 1992.
A Short History of the West Indies, J H Parry, Philip
   Sherlock and Anthony Maingot, 4th Edition, 1994.
Prehistoric Barbados, Peter L Drewett, 1991.
The Barbados Railway, W E L Fletcher, 1961 .

The support of the following companies was given when this project was on the drawing board.
For their commitment and confidence we are sincerely grateful.

American Airlines
Frank B Armstrong Ltd
Arrow Developers Ltd
Atlantic Manufacturing Co Ltd
Bamboo Culture Shop
Banks (Barbados) Breweries Ltd
The Bank of Nova Scotia
Barbados Chamber of Commerce & Industry
Barbados Dairy Industries Ltd
Barbados Fire & Commercial Insurance Co
Barbados Flight Kitchen Ltd
Barbados Hilton
Barbados Investment Development Corporation
Barbados Mills Ltd
Barbados Mutual Life Assurance Society
Barbados Tourism Investment Corporation
Barclays Bank Plc
A S Bryden & Sons
B S & T Co Ltd
Capital Life Insurance Co
Caribbean Graphics Production Ltd
Casuarina Beach Club
Cave Shepherd & Co Ltd

CCS Information Technology Ltd
CIBC Caribbean Ltd
Coopers Lybrand
Courtesy Rent-A-Car
C L Gibbs & Co Ltd
Discovery Bay Beach Hotel
Doyle Offshore Sails
Fujitsu - ICL Caribbean (Barbados) Ltd
Geddes Grant (Barbados) Ltd
General Finance Corporation Ltd
Goddard Shipping & Tours Ltd
Harrison's
Island Inn Hotel
Interamericana Trading Corporation
Jolly Roger Cruises Inc
Jason H Jones & Co Ltd
Life of Barbados Ltd
Liquid Carbonic (Barbados) Ltd
Mango Bay Hotel & Beach Club
Moore Paragon (Caribbean) Ltd
Mount Gay Distilleries Ltd
National Cultural Foundation
National Petroleum Corporation

Neal & Massy (Barbados) Ltd
N E M (West Indies) Insurance Ltd
Pelican Pride Craft and Cottage Industries Co
Pemberton Princess Hotel
Photo Finish One Hour Lab
Pine Hill Marketing
Plantation Restaurant
Plantrac Engineering Ltd
Port St Charles Development Ltd
Purity Bakeries
Regional Business Systems Inc
Royal Bank of Canada
Sea Breeze Beach Hotel
Sea Freight Agencies (B'dos) Ltd
Securicor Barbados Ltd
The Shipping Association of Barbados
Simpson Motors
Stansfeld Scott & Co Ltd
United Insurance Company Ltd
Williams Industries Inc
Windsurf Village Barbados

BARBADOS

JUST BEYOND YOUR IMAGINATION

Contents

*B*ARBADOS

JUST BEYOND YOUR IMAGINATION

Foreword

The publication of *'Barbados: Just Beyond Your Imagination'* represents the culmination of an ambition - even a dream - that dates back some 20 years. I am truly delighted that this dream has now become a reality.

In turn, we hope that this present volume can do justice to a magnificent country. In a volatile and precarious world, Barbados has grappled with dependence on tourism and a host of related challenges and always managed to stay one step ahead. From what I have been privileged to see in the course of numerous visits to the country, I believe that this can be ascribed to a number of factors, among them:

- a patriotism that holds true whether Barbadians are at home or living in some distant corner of the globe
- a democracy that is engraved deep into the national psyche and therefore ensures accountability
- a press and media which is as proud of its freedom as it is of its quality and which therefore serves to underpin and reinforce both democracy and development

- a modern, efficient and professional approach to infrastructure, utilities and human development.

These factors and more combine to make Barbados a veritable hub of the entire Caribbean.

Fortunately, for the region, the leaders, opinion-formers and people of Barbados are aware of the fact that small nations can best advance their interests in today's world if they abide by the motto that 'unity is strength'. Their commitment to regional integration can only serve to benefit the common good.

Whatever your interest in Barbados, be it as a tourist, a potential investor or a national at home or abroad, we are sure this book will serve to reflect what first attracted you to this land 'just beyond your imagination'.

Arif Ali
Barbados, September 1996

Contributors

Warren Alleyne: Rachel Pringle Polgreen, Historical Bridgetown, High Court, St Michael's Cathedral, Queen's Park, Nelson's Statue, The Parliament Buildings, The Synagogue, The Public Library Bridgetown, Government House, Fountain, St Mary's Church, Bridgetown Harbour.
Barclays Bank Plc.: 150 Years of Caribbean Banking.
Leslie Barker: The Geology and Landscape of Barbados.
Dan Carter: Oistins Festival.
Dr Sean Carrington: Green Barbados, Barbadian Fauna, Photos.
Karin Dear: The Newspapers
Brian Dyde: The West India Regiment.

Winston Farrell: Tribute to Landship.
Addinton Forde: The Landship, Warri, Tuk Bands, Sticklicking, Road Tennis, Marble Cricket, Dialect, Proverbs, Legends.
Henry Fraser: Architectural Heritage of Barbados, Great Houses, Historical Churches of Barbados, Chattel Houses, Photos.
John Gilmore: Rastafarianism in Barbados, Not 'Sundays Only' Religion.
Michael L Goddard: Sports Paradise, Photos.
Major M Hartland: National Cannon Collection, Volunteer Force.
Colin Hudson: Joshua Steele.
Ronnie Hughes: BS&T Co Limited.

Arti Meyers: Mount Gay.
Velma Newton: Law and the Legal System, Emigration from Barbados.
Mike Seale: Diving, Photos.
H E Peter Simmons: Redlegs.
Margaret Waithe: Barbados Hilton.
Dr Karl Watson: Social History of Barbados, The Birds of Barbados.
Robert Weekes: Oil and Natural Gas
Andrea Wells: Arts, Crafts, Handcrafts, Photos.
John Wickham: Barbados is Bajan, The Story of the Press in Barbados.
Sarah Venable: St Lucy, Sea Eggs, Future Centre, Alternative Energy, Aloe Vera, Barbados-Egyptian Connection.

BARBADOS

JUST BEYOND YOUR IMAGINATION

Message

From the Hon Billie A Miller, MP

Deputy Prime Minister, Minister of Foreign Affairs, Tourism and International Transport

It is with pleasure that I welcome and invite the readers of this publication to what I believe will prove a journey of true discovery. A journey which will reveal in detail the undiscovered secrets of our island paradise, Barbados.

We believe that the Barbados tourist product possesses every attribute necessary to be characterized as the best year-round warm weather destination in the Caribbean and beyond. We wish therefore to share the facts with you, our readers, that you may judge for yourselves.

From our beautiful beaches to the friendly smiling faces; from luxury resorts to intimate budget-priced accommodations; from century old historical landmarks to the most exotic in land and watersports; from the best in gastonomic delights to the pulsating and captivating nightlife, we offer our visitors the most imaginable tropical pleasures. I believe they have all been captured in the text and photographs.

The publishers therefore have accomplished their mission in producing a comprehensive guidebook capturing succinctly every subject of relevance to the casual reader, the curious academic, the searching student or the visitor planning a holiday and seeking information on the island.

I am therefore pleased to note that the focus of the book puts in perspective the policy of the Government of Barbados to continue to promote tourism as the major engine of growth of the economy. It also highlights the commendable efforts that are being taken to enhance and preserve the unique attractiveness of Barbados as we prepare to meet the challenges of competing with other emerging destinations in the year 2000 and beyond.

I am proud to welcome this publication to an already impressive inventory of literature which seeks to share the charms of Barbados with the world. I hope that the colourful and informative pages of this book capture for the reader the essence of what Barbados has to offer - the warmth and friendliness of our people, the social and economic stability of the country, the tranquil and scenic beauty of the landscape and its exciting and diverse attractions.

Congratulations to Hansib Caribbean on the publication of the sixth volume in its Caribbean Nations series. We are delighted to have been selected for this edition.

Billie A Miller

Billie A Miller, MP

BARBADOS

JUST BEYOND YOUR IMAGINATION

Acknowledgements

The Publisher wishes to thank the following individuals, companies and organisations for providing assistance, advice and support for this project. Our apologies to those we have inadvertently omitted.

Judith Allsopp
Cavendish Atwell
Lesley Barrow-Whattley
Jean Baulu
Keith Bennett
Tony Best
Laura Blackman
Jennifer Braithwaite
Michael Brown
Gaston Browne
Claudio Bordin
Debbie Buckmaster
Ken Campbell
P F Campbell
Alexia Carr
Richard Cheltenham QC
Ray Chee-A-Tow
Emerson Clarke
Alan Cross
Deidre Cumberbatch
Ingrid Cumberbatch
Jennifer Cummings
Alisandra Cummings
William Cummins
Pierra & Franca De Bono
Drucilla Daley
Charles Davies
Brenda P Edwards
Lorna Edwards
Philip Edwards
Owen Eversley
Abigail Fortin
Hugh Foster
Paul Foster
Kristian Francis
Joyce Gibbons
Joyce Gibson
Avril Gollop
Wendy Goddard
Rosalind Green
Villeneuve Greaves
Pauline Henry
Thomas Hill
Harry Hines
Margaret Hope

Julia Horrocks
Sir Alexander Hoyos
Ronnie Hughes
James Hunte
Molly Hunter
Penelope Hynan-Roach
Ibo and Team
Nicholas Jones
Hazel Ann and Trevor Kent
Ernest King and Staff
John King
Geoff Kinch
Senator Noel Lynch
Marcia Manning
Karen Many
Trevor Marshall
Judith Mayers
Marcelle Millar
Randy Moore
Amy Moore
Robert Morris
Peggy McGreary
Dr Patrick McConney
Zarina Mc Culloch
Dr Leonard Nurse
Freida Nichols
Peter Odle
Nigel Parker
Vino Patel
Isha Persaud
Christine Piggott
Cecil & Cita Pilgrim
Steve Prescott
Amory Philips
Bernard Philips
Angella Phillips
Henderson Riley
Victor Roach
H E Ronald Sanders
Dr Hugh Sealy
Percival Sealy
Phil Sealy
H E Peter Simmons
Donna Simmonds
Bolanle Simmons

Joyce Simmons
Jill Shepherd
Leroy Sisnet
Brian Smurthwaite
Corrie Scott
John Stevenson
Joy Kim Thorpe
Aaron Truss
Mark Vicker
Michael Walcott
Barbara Walters
Laura Ward
Hildegarde Weekes
Magnus Whitehead
David Williams
Cynthia Wilson
Emily Wood

**Management and staff of
the following hotels:**
Asta Beach Hotel
Coconut Court Beach Hotel
Coconut Creek Hotel
Discovery Bay Hotel
Island Inn Hotel
Mango Bay Hotel
Oasis Hotel
Ocean View Hotel
Sea Breeze Beach Hotel

**Companies and
Organisations**:
Advocate Co Ltd
American Airlines
Atlantis Submarines
Banks (Barbados) Breweries
    Ltd
Bamboo Culture Shop
Bajan Helicopters
Barbados Archives
Barbados Agriculture &
    Marketing Development
    Corporation
Barbados Bottling Co Ltd

Barbados Government
    Information Service
Barbados High Commission
    (London)
Barbados Hotel &Tourism
    Association
Barbados Investment &
    Development
    Corporation
Barbados Museum &
    Historical Society
Barbados National Trust
Barbados Philatelic Society
Barbados Port Authority
Barbados Tourism
    Authority (Airport)
Barbados Tourism
    Authority (Head office)
Barbados Tourism
    Authority (London)
Barbados Turf Club
Britannia Airways
British Airways
Caribbean Export
    Development Project
Caribbean Reunion Club
CIBC Caribbean Ltd
Courtesy Rent-A-Car
Cydex (Barbados)
Crocodile's Den
Ernst & Young
Hilton Hotel
LIAT Airways
Mount Gay Rum Distilleries
Land & Surveys
    Department
Nation Publishing Co Ltd
National Cultural
    Foundation
Swiss American Bank

The National Flag of Barbados

The National Flag of Barbados is composed of three equal vertical panels - the outer panels of ultramarine and the centre panel of gold. A broken trident in black is in the centre of the flag. The British standard colour code numbers for the colours of the flag are as follows - Ultramarine - BCC 148, Gold - BS 0/002. The flag is designed in the proportion 3:2. The description of the flag - Blue for the sea and sky of Barbados; Gold for the sand of its beaches.

The symbol in the centre panel is the Trident of the mythical sea god, Neptune. This symbol appears in the Seal of the colony which was replaced by the Barbados Coat of Arms. The shaft of the Trident is broken indicating Barbados' break with its historical and constitutional ties as a former colony.

THE DESIGNER. The National Flag was designed by Grantley W Prescod. His design was chosen from 1029 entries in an open competition organised by the government of Barbados. Prescod was awarded a Gold Medal, an inscribed scroll from the government and $500 which was donated by the Advocate Company Limited. The judges of the competition were Bruce St John, Chairman, Major Leonard Banfield, Maurice Cave, Neville Connell, Enid Lynch and Mrs B Ward.

Prescod attended St Barnabas Boys School. He taught before undertaking a one-year course at the West of England College of Art for Specialist Teachers of Art in 1962-63. He also attained a certificate in Education from Bristol University. Between 1970-72 he studied for the Master of Education degree majoring in Art Education at Temple University, Philadelphia, US.

Prescod has taught at the Parkinson Secondary School. He served as an Education Officer from September 1977 until retiring in Februry 1987.

The National Emblems and the Law

The Regulation of the National Emblems falls under the portfolio of the prime minister. The Act cited as the National Emblems and National Anthem of Barbados (Regulation) Act - Chapter 300A of the Laws of Barbados regulates the use of the National Emblems and National Anthem of Barbados.

National Emblems means The Broken Trident, the Coat of Arms, the National Flag, the National Flower and any of the National Colours when used together. This Act clearly defines the Coat of Arms and the National Flag in Parts I and II of the First Schedule. The National Anthem means the words and music recognised by the Government as the National Anthem of Barbados. The minister responsible for the National Emblems may declare by order The National Flower, The National Prayer, and The National Song of Barbados.

The copyright in the words and music of the National Anthem and the design of the National Emblems is vested in the Crown in perpetuity.

A person who desires to import into Barbados, manufacture for sale, offer for sale or sell any articles, goods or things that represent or on which is reproduced or represented any of the National Emblems must apply to the minister responsible for his approval and the grant of a licence for the purpose. This is also necessary when it is intended to use or displaying any of the National Emblems in connection with a business, trade, profession or calling, or with the activities of a body of persons, whether corporate or unincorporate.

Where an applicant for a licence pursuant to Section 4 of the Act is a government department, a statutory body or any other similar body or a charitable organisation the minister may waive all or such part of the fees as he thinks fit.

Under Section 5 of the Act any person who

(a) not being the holder of a valid licence granted under this Act

(i) uses or displays in connection with the carrying on of any business, trade, profession or calling or with the activity of any body of persons whether corporate or unincorporate, or

(ii) sells or offers for sale any article or thing which represents or on which is reproduced or represented any National Emblem or any emblem so nearly resembling a National Emblem as to be calculated to deceive; or

(b) being the holder of a valid licence granted under this Act, fails to comply with, or contravenes, any of the terms or conditions subject to which the licence is granted is guilty of an offence and liable on summary conviction to a fine of BDS$1,000 or to imprisonment for one year, and in the case of a continuing offence, to a fine not exceeding BDS$100 for each day or part thereof during which the offence continues after day on which a conviction under this section was obtained.

It is also an offence to mutilate, cut, tear or in any other way deface any of the National Emblems. In addition, the consent of the minister given in writing must be obtained before anyone can print or write on, affix a stamp to or otherwise mark any of the National Emblems. This carries on summary conviction a fine of BDS$1,000 or imprisonment for one year or both.

The Barbados Coat of Arms

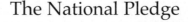

The Grant of Arms conveyed by royal warrant was presented by Her Majesty the Queen to the President of the Senate of the island on 14 February, 1966 on the occasion of the royal visit to Barbados.

Prior to this Grant of Arms the only other heraldic device was the seal of the colony. It represented the British Sovereign in a shell chariot being drawn by two sea horses through foaming waves. The seal was changed when there was a new monarch. Kings sit in the chariot while Queens stand.

The Golden Shield of the Arms carries two Pride of Barbados flowers (the National Flower) and the Bearded Fig Tree (*Ficus Citrifolia*) which was common on the island at the time of its settlement. On either side of the shield are the supporters - on the right (dexter) is a dolphin symbolic of the fishing industry and on the left (sinister) is a pelican. The association is made with a small island named Pelican Island which existed off Barbados and which was incorporated into the Deep Water Harbour development.

Above the shield is a helmet and mantling and on a wreath is the arm and hand of a Barbadian holding two crossed pieces of sugar cane symbolic of the sugar industry. This is a saltire cross, the cross upon which Saint Andrew was crucified. Independence Day in Barbados is celebrated on 30 November, Saint Andrews Day.

The Coat of Arms carries the motto "Pride and Industry".

THE DESIGNER: The Barbados Coat of Arms was designed by Neville Clarke Connell who was a director of the Barbados Museum for almost 24 years. He was a prolific writer and contributed a great number of articles for the museum journals, local newspapers as well as publications overseas.

He was educated at Harrison College, Barbados and Fitzwilliam College, Cambridge. He was called to the Bar at Gray's Inn. He served in the Royal Artillery on the outbreak of war. On being discharged he worked in an antique dealer's business and was also assistant secretary of the Institute of Incorporated Practitioners in Advertising.

The design of the Barbados Coat of Arms was the result of extensive research conducted by Connell who was a student of heraldry. He was assisted in this work by the artist, Hilda Ince (now deceased). The development sketches of the Coat of Arms remain in the possession of the Barbados Museum and Historical Society.

Connell died on 19 January, 1973, aged 66.

The National Pledge

I pledge allegiance to my country Barbados
and to my flag,
To uphold and defend their honour,
And by my living to do credit
to my nation wherever I go.

The National Pledge was written by Lester Vaughan a former teacher and education officer of primary schools. Vaughan was born in 1910 at St Simons in the parish of St Andrew. He started his career as a teacher and between 1928 - 1944 he taught at a number of primary schools in St Andrew. He was trained at the Rawi Training Institute, forerunner of Erdiston College 1933-1935.

In 1944 he emigrated to St Lucia and continued his career as a teacher until 1954 when he entered the Tuskeegee Institute Alabama, USA, where he pursued a course in primary education. He returned to St Lucia in 1952 and served there until 1954 before he returned home to Barbados.

He taught at St John the Baptist Boys School, served as headmaster of Holy Innocents and then acted as an education officer for six years. He retired in November 1970. He was recalled from retirement in 1973 to the '14 plus' scheme which was designed to assist those children who had left school aged 14.

The choice of the National Pledge was announced on 2 April 1973 by the Honorable Erskine Sandiford, then Minister of Education, Youth Affairs, Community Development and Sport.

In a competition which attracted 167 entrants Vaughan's composition was chosen as the National Pledge. He was awarded a prize of BDS$100.

The National Anthem of Barbados

In plenty and in time of need
When this fair land was young
Our brave forefathers sowed the seed
From which our pride is sprung,
A pride that makes no wanton boast
Of what is has withstood
That binds our hearts from coast to coast -
The pride of nationhood

Chorus:
We loyal sons and daughters all
Do hereby make it known
These fields and hills beyond recall
Are now our very own.
We write our names on history's page
With expectations great
Strict guardians of our heritage
Firm craftsmen of our fate

The Lord has been the people's guide
For past three hundred years
With him still on the people's side
We have no doubts or fears
Upward and onward we shall go
Inspired, exulting, free
And greater will our nation grow
In strength and unity

THE MUSIC. When C Van Roland Edwards composed the music for the National Anthem he was partly blind. Edwards was born in 1912 and had been writing music from his school days as a pupil of St Peter's Church Boy's School. Although he had no formal training he had been a member of the British Song Society since 1933. Because of the partial blindness he was assisted in his work by his two daughters Nanette and Eullia.

Edwards was known for his compositions 'The St Andrew Murder', 'The Goodman Song' and 'The Federation Song'. He also composed 'Welcome to Her Majesty The Queen Elizabeth II' which was sung in the presence of the Queen when she opened the St Elizabeth School in St Joseph during the official visit to the island in February, 1966.

A committee which comprised, Bruce St John, Frank Collymore, Enid Lynch, George Lamming, Gerald Hudson and John Fletcher was appointed to oversee the selection of the National Anthem. Edwards was awarded $500 for his efforts.

He died on April 22, 1985.

In 1967 the music of the National Anthem was rearranged. This work was undertaken by Inspector Prince Cave of the Royal Barbados Police Band. He had earlier that year returned from a three year Band Masters course at the Royal Military School of Music, Kneller Hall. The Anthem was given a more sustained harmony while at the same time retaining the original tune.

THE LYRICS. The lyrics of the National Anthem of Barbados were written by Irving Burgie who was born in Brooklyn, New York, US, of a Barbadian mother and American father. Burgie whose stage name was Lord Burgess was born in 1926. He served in India and after his return to the US he entered the University of Southern California and studied music and performed in many cities of the US.

Burgie has composed works for 'Ballad for Bimshire' and 'Island in the Sun', he has also written for a number of internationally famous artistes. Among his works is 'The West Indian Song Book'. He is a Life Member of the National Association for the Advancement of Coloured People.

Burgie who is a frequent visitor to Barbados has instituted the Irving Burgie Literary Award for Barbadian school children.

National Emblems

Code of Etiquette

The National Flag

The dimensions of the National Flag shall be in the following proportions: For flags flown on land and at sea: three to two (3: 2).

How to display the flag

(i) The flag should be of regulation appearance. It should not be faded or bleached and a torn flag should be repaired before being hoisted.

(ii) The flag-mast, when erected on land, should be placed upright and should be in a central or conspicuous place. On buildings, however, the flag-mast may either be placed in an upright position on the roof or fixed at an angle on the front of the building or from a balcony.

(iii) The flag-mast should be painted white.

(iv) No other flag may be flown above the Barbados flag. When several flags are flown on one halliard the Barbados flag is placed at the peak. When the flags of two or more nations are displayed together they are to be flown from separate staffs of the same height and all the flags should be, as far as possible, of the same size. The flag of one nation should not be displayed above that of another.

(v) No other flag, colour, standard, ensign or other emblem should be displayed above or to the right of the National Flag, i.e. the observer's left facing it.

(vi) When two flags are placed against a wall with crossed staffs, the Barbados flag should be at the right - i.e. to the observer's left facing the flags - and its staff should be in front of the staff of the other flag. When a number of flags are grouped and displayed from staffs the Barbados flag should be at the centre and at the highest point of the group.

(vii) When the National Flag is flown with other flags it should be the first to be hoisted and the last to be lowered. It should never be lowered while the other flags are flying or being hoisted.

(viii) The flag may be displayed flat above and behind the speaker in a church or in a auditorium. If on a staff, it should be at the right of the speaker as he/she faces the congregation or audience. Other flags should be at the speaker's left. If the flag is displayed on a staff elsewhere, than on a platform or chancel, it should be at the right of the audience or congregation as they face the speaker. It should not cover a speaker's desk or be draped in front of a platform.

(ix) Except on a day of special significance the National Flag shall not be flown on a motor car without the permission of the minister.

(x) Where the National Flag is flown on a motor car in accordance with paragraph (ix) it shall be affixed to a small staff erected on the right front fender of the motor car so the flag should be above the bonnet or at the centre and to the front of the bonnet of that motor car.

(xi) A citizen may fly the flag on a day of special significance provided he flies the flag from an upright staff on or in front of his dwelling or place of business.

When to display the flag

(i) The National Flag will be flown every day from the public buildings, Trafalgar Square, from 6.00 am to 6.00 pm. It may be flown daily from government buildings and schools when they are in session, and places of business.

(ii) The National Flag should not be flown after 6.00 pm except inside a building. However, on important ceremonial occasions the flag may be flown in the open after 6.00 pm when it should be floodlit if possible.

The flag in a parade

When carried with another flag or flags, the flag of Barbados should be held on the marching right or in front of the centre of the line of flags. When the flag is passing in a parade or in a review or during the ceremony of hoisting or lowering the flag, all persons present should face the flag and stand at attention.

The flag at half-staff

(i) The National Flag is flown at half-staff in mourning.

(ii) When flown at half-staff the flag should first be raised to the peak and then lowered to half-staff. The

Code of Etiquette

flag should again be raised to the peak before it is lowered.

(iii) By half-staff is meant lowering the flag by its own depth from the peak of the staff. The decision on the occasions on which the flag should be flown at half-staff would rest with the Cabinet.

Prohibited uses of the flag

(i) The flag should not be dipped to any person or thing, except in accordance with maritime practice.

(ii) The flag should never be flown with the trident inverted except as a signal of distress.

(iii) The flag should not be displayed on a float, motorcar or other vehicle or on a boat, except from a staff or masthead.

(iv) The flag should not have placed on it or attached to it any mark, insignia, letter, word, figure, design, picture or drawing.

(v) The flag should never be used as a receptacle. It should not be used to cover a statue or monument.

(vi) The flag should not be used for purposes of adornment or advertising. It should not be printed on, or reproduced on, articles of clothing or furniture.

(vii) The flag when on display should not be allowed to touch anything beneath it such as furniture, floors, trees, plants, vehicles, buildings, water or the earth.

The National Anthem

1. Whenever the National Anthem is played all civilians present should stand at attention, men with bared heads. Persons in uniform should act in accordance with instructions.

2. Normally one verse only and the chorus will be played. Where a shortened version of the National Anthem is played, it shall consist of the first twelve bars of the verse and the last four bars of the chorus.

The National Anthem shall be played:

(a) for the purposes of a salute on ceremonial or official occasions, on the arrival and departure of

(i) the Governor-General

(ii) the Sovereign or a member of the Royal Family.

(iii) a foreign Sovereign, Head of State or member of a reigning foreign Imperial or Royal Family.

(iv) Governors-General of Independent Commonwealth countries.

(v) Governors of the Associated States, and

(vi) Governors, High Commissioners or Officers administering the Government of a dependent territory within the Commonwealth; and

(b) at the beginning of all public performances in a cinema house.

3. The National Anthem may be played

(a) at the completion of any public function, or

(b) when toasts are proposed at official functions.

4. The National Anthem should not be parodied in verse or in song, neither should it be played in any tempo other than that officially recognised (eighty-eight crotchets to the minute). Particularly, the tune should not be used as a dance number or for the purposes of advertisement. When more than one anthem is played the Barbados anthem should be played last.

The Coat of Arms

The Coat of Arms of Barbados is the official seal of the Government of Barbados. It may not be used or reproduced in any form without the approval of the Government.

It should be noted that any person who contravenes or fails to comply with regulations 3, 8, 9, 10, 12, 14, 17, 18, or 21 of the National Emblems and National Anthem of Barbados (Regulations) 1976, CAP, 300A of the Laws of Barbados, is guilty of an offence and liable on summary conviction to a fine not exceeding BDS$500 or imprisonment for a term not exceeding six months, or both.

The National Flower

The National Flower of Barbados is the Pride of Barbados *(Dwarf Poinciana or Flower Fence)*

Poinciana pulcherrima LINNAEUS
Syn. Caesalpinia pulcherrima (L) SWARTZ

References to this flower were recorded as early as 1657. It is a shrub and is often pruned into a low hedge. If untrimmed it grows to a height of 10 to 15 feet. It is a member of the Legume family and can be found in other tropical countries.

The Pride of Barbados blooms most of the year, the more common varieties are a fiery red and yellow although other colour variations can be found. The flower has five petals with a yellow margin in a pyramidal inflorescence. Each flower is about one and a half inches across with five sepals. The ten stamens are long and the pistils project from the centre of the flower. The fifth petal is far smaller than the other four. The stamens have coloured filaments with anthers at the tips however, the eleventh filament bears a stigma and is the style.

The branches are prickly and the leaves are large and doubly compound about one foot long and six inches wide with many small leaflets.

The National Flower is accepted as the red variety with the yellow margin on the petals. It appears on the Coat of Arms.

The Nation State

National Honours and Decorations

A local system of national awards and honours which gives special recognition to citizens of Barbados who distinguish themselves in various fields of endeavour was instituted in November 1980.

The system provides for:

1. The Order of Barbados - in which there are four classes of awards

(a) Knight or Dame of St Andrew (KA) or (DA): for extraordinary and outstanding contribution in service to Barbados or to humanity at large.

(b) Companion of Honour of Barbados (CHB): for distinguished national achievement and merit.

(c) The Crown of Merit - which is made in two grades: the Gold Crown of Merit (GCM) and the Silver Crown of Merit (SCM): for high meritorious service or achievement in Science, the Arts, Literature, Sport, Civic duties or any other endeavour worthy of national recognition.

(d) The Barbados Services Award - which is made in two grades: the Barbados Service Star (BSS) and the Barbados Service Medal (BSM): for meritorious work in the civil, fire, military, police, prison or other protective services or in any similar field or endeavour.

2. Bravery Decorations
(a) The Barbados Star of Gallantry (SG) - for an act of conspicuous courage in circumstances of extreme peril.
(b) The Barbados Bravery Medal (BM) - for an act of bravery in hazardous circumstances.

3. Services Medal of Honour
This is exclusively for members of the Barbados Defence Force, the Royal Barbados Police Force, the Barbados Fire Service and the Prisons Service, in recognition of long and faithful service.
Services Medal of Honour - 15-25 years' service
1 clasp and Services Medal of Honour: 25-30 years' service
2 clasp and Services Medal of Honour: 30-35 years' service
3 clasp and Services Medal of Honour: over 35 years' service.

Regional and International Links

Barbados recognises that it must co-operate with other countries in order to overcome those limitations imposed by its small size and scarce resources. To this end, Barbados is a member of several regional and international organisations.

There is a strong commitment to regional integration and some of the regional bodies whose headquarters are based on the island are: Caribbean Examinations Council (CXC), Caribbean Export Development Project (CEDP), Caribbean Development Bank (CDB), Caribbean Conference of Churches (CCC), the Caribbean Association of Industry and Commerce (CAIC) and the Caribbean Tourism Organisation (CTO).

Barbados is also a founding member of the Caribbean Community (CariCom). This body is a trade and economic grouping of 13 English-speaking countries in the Caribbean.

In the international arena, Barbados is a member of the United Nations and its specialised agencies, the Organisation of American States (OAS) and other agencies, of the Inter-American system, the Commonwealth, the group of African, Caribbean and Pacific states (ACP) as well as the Non-Aligned Movement.

Foreign Affairs

The Barbados Ministry of Foreign Affairs along with its overseas missions, is the key agency in the development and maintenance of its external relations.

Its main objectives are:
• Promotion of beneficial trading relationships with third states and economic groupings, and protection of Barbados' interests within the framework of international, commercial and economic policy making;
• Procurement of concessionary financing for Barbados' development effort;
• Attraction of investment capital for industrial development in prescribed sectors of the economy and the promotion of Barbados as an offshore financial sector;
• Promotion and expansion of tourism and connected hospitality services;
• Preservation and protection of national sovereignty and security;
• Strengthening the regional integration movement and promoting the concept of Caribbean unity;
• Strengthening ties with traditional allies and fastening new ties with friendly countries based on the principles of peaceful co-existence and of the sovereign equality of states;
• Collaborating with like-minded countries to advance the concepts of morality, justice and respect for human rights in international affairs;
• Pursuing in its international behaviour, the goal of peaceful relations among states and seeking to create, through constructive, collective action, a new social, political and economic order;
• Protection and promotion of the interests and welfare of Barbadian nationals abroad.

These objectives represent the Barbados government's commitment to economic and social betterment of its people without compromising those fundamental principles and rights necessary for its survival as a free sovereign and democratic nation.

Constitution and Administration

The present constitution provides for the separation of powers under the governor-general, parliament, the executive, the judicature and the public service.

The Governor-General

The country is a constitutional monarchy with a parliamentary system of government. Therefore, at the helm is the monarchy and acting on its behalf is the governor-general.

Parliament

This consists of Her Majesty the Queen, a Senate and a House of Assembly.

The Senate is the Upper nominated House. The Constitution provides for twenty-one persons. Twelve of these are government senators, appointed by the governor-general on the advice of the prime minister, two are the opposition's choice and seven are appointed to represent various interest groups. The House of Assembly is the Lower House. There are now twenty-seven members elected for a maximum of five years.

Anyone over twenty-one-years is eligible for election to the House of Assembly.

Executive Powers

Under this area the Constitution lists, Her Majesty, the Cabinet, the Leader of the Opposition and the Privy Council and a Director of Public Prosecutions.

The Cabinet - this consists of the prime minister and not fewer than five other ministers.

The Privy Council - members of this body are appointed by the governor-general after consultation with the prime minister. According to the provision of the Constitution no person can serve on the body for more than fifteen years.

The Council advises the governor-general in the exercise of the Royal Perogative of Mercy and in the exercise of disciplinary powers over members of the public and policy services, who may appeal to the Council in cases of disciplinary actions against them.

Director of Public Prosecutions - is a public office free of political interference.

The Judiciary - this is free from executive interference and comprises the magistrate courts, a high court and a court of appeal.

Public Service

The Services Commissions is made up of the judicial, legal and public service commissions. These commissions have executive powers to deal with the appointment, dismissal and discipline of members of the services for which they are respectively responsible.

The Prime Minister

The Rt Hon Owen Seymour Arthur

Prime Minister of Barbados

The Rt Hon Owen Seymour Arthur assumed office on 7 September 1994, as Barbados' fifth Prime Minister.

Mr Arthur, who was born in Barbados on 17 October 1949, became one of the youngest Barbadian politicians elected to that office, at age 44.

He successfully led the Barbados Labour Party (BLP) to victory in the General Elections held on 6 September 1994, when it won 19 of the 28 seats in the House of Assembly.

The Prime Minister's political career began when he was appointed a member of the Barbados Senate in 1983. He became a Member of Parliament in 1984 and was appointed Leader of the Opposition in 1993. He remains Chairman of the Barbados Labour Party.

The Prime Minister was educated at All Saints' Boys' School, Coleridge and Parry School on a government scholarship, Harrison College and the University of the West Indies, Cave Hill Campus and Mona Campuses, the latter on a UWI postgraduate scholarship.

The holder of a Bachelor of Arts (BA) degree in Economics and History, and a Master of Science MSC degree in Economics, Mr Arthur began his working career in Jamaica, as a research assistant in the Department of Management of the Mona Campus.

In 1974 he took up the post of Assistant Economic Planner at the National Planning Agency in Jamaica. Within five years he attained the top post of Chief Economic Planner.

Mr Arthur's next appointment was that of Director of Economics, from 1971 to 1981, at the Jamaica Bauxite Institute.

As director, his responsibilities included the management of the Division of Economics and Financial Affairs which monitored production of bauxite in Jamaica, the payment of levies and taxes by bauxite companies and all other aspects of the economic performance and affairs of the Jamaican bauxite industry.

He represented Jamaica on UNCTAD's Inter-Governmental Group of Exports on the Transer of Technology in 1975 and 1976, was a member of the OAS Task Force on Technology Transfer in the Caribbean and a member of the Caribbean Technology Policy Studies Project between 1977 and 1978. In addition, Mr Arthur also served as a member of the Board of Directors of Jamaica's Scientific Research Council.

In 1981, the Prime Minister returned to Barbados and took up the post of Chief Project Analyst in the Ministry of Finance and Planning, where he assisted with the preparation and review of pre-feasibility studies in relation to Barbados' public investment programme.

He also coordinated the preparation of Barbados' 1983-88 Development Plan and participated in the negotiation of Barbados' 1982 programme with the International Monetary Fund.

Mr Arthur joined the Institute of Social and Economic Research, Cave Hill Campus, UWI in 1983 and undertook research for publication into the balance of payments stabilisation policies in Barbados. He also reviewed and edited articles submitted to the institute for publication.

He returned to the Ministry of Finance and Planning as a parliamentary secretary in 1985 for one year, before joining the Department of Management, UWI as a part-time lecturer.

He has served as a member of the Board of Directors of the Barbados Industrial Development Corporation; a member of the Board of Directors of the Central Bank of Barbados, and Chairman of the Barbados Agricultural Corporation.

The Prime Minister also has wide experience as a consultant. He was consultant to the Organisation of American States (OAS) in 1975; to the Ministry of Housing and Lands, Barbados, from 1983 to 1984 and to CariCom, 1992.

His publications include 'The Commercialisation of Technology in Jamaica' 1979; 'Energy and Mineral Resource Development in the Jamaica Bauxite Industry' 1981; and 'The IMF and Economic Stabilisation Polices in Barbados' 1984.

He has been a member of the Barbados Economic Society and is an active member of the Barbados External Communications (BET) Sports Club. His hobbies include gardening and cooking. Mr Arthur is married to the former Beverley Jeane Batchelor.

The Legal System

by Velma Newton

The date on which English law was received in Barbados has been regarded as 25 February 1628 - when the English sovereign recognised the settlement.[1] With regard to extent of the reception, according to dicta in *Terrell v. Secretary of State for the Colonies*[2] and *Campbell v. Hall*,[3] at the date of the establishment of a settlement, so much of the common law of England and English statutes of general application prior to that date as was applicable to the situation of the inhabitants *"and the conditions of the infant colony"* applied.

As in the United Kingdom and most of the Commonwealth Caribbean, the main historical sources of law in Barbados are the common law, equity and the law merchant.[4] The authority for any proposition of law is its legal source. At present, the Constitution, followed by legislation and judicial precedent are the two most important legal sources.

Historical Sources

(a) Common Law
This is the main historical source of English law introduced into the Caribbean. The term 'common law' as used in the time of King Edward I was that part of the law common to the whole of England which was not statute law, local custom and royal prerogative. It was strongly influenced by Canon Law, or the law of the Catholic Church from which a number of common law concepts such as the nature of criminal law and its close association with moral fault developed and Roman Law. Today, it often means that part of English law which is contained in the decisions of the courts, as opposed to Acts of Parliament and subordinate legislation. Judicial precedent, or the common law as found in the decisions of courts are one of the main legal sources, and therefore it is important to be aware of the development of the common law.[5]

(b) Equity
Like legislation, equity evolved as a 'gloss' on the common law. The basic nature of equity is expressed in the famous maxims of equity - that it provides new remedies where a remedy at common law is deficient, on the basis that 'equity does not suffer a wrong to be without a remedy,' that 'equity will not assist a volunteer,' i.e. that it will not allow specific performance to be granted to a person who has given no consideration in return for the obligation which he seeks to have enforced, and similarly, that equity does not provide a remedy to a person who has behaved unconscionably since 'he who comes to equity must come with clean hands.' In Barbados as in England, the effect of equity has been felt mainly in the areas of contract and property law.[6]

(c) The Law Merchant
The Law Merchant was a set of rules which evolved in the 13th Century to regulate commercial transactions.[7]

Legal Sources

(d) Legislation
A body of English legislation would have been 'received' by Barbados at the time of settlement, and from then until 1966 when the island became independent, all the English navigation, revenue and trade acts and English legislation which stated that it applied to the Westindies in particular, or to the colonies in general, would have extended to Barbados. A corpus of local legislation, most of it based on English models, was added over the centuries, for example, the general principles of criminal law, laws relating to contracts, real property and torts, to mention a few areas. However, since the 1970s Barbados has been increasingly basing its legislation on models from Commonwealth countries other than the United Kingdom. For instance, its tax law is based on Canadian, its evidence and family law legislation on Australian, its company law on a mixture of Canadian and US models and its charities legislation on that of New Zealand.[8]

The latest revised edition of laws of Barbados was published in 1971 in loose-leaf format which is kept up to date by annual supplements.

(e) The Constitution
From 1627 until 1652 the island was under the general overlordship of the Earl of Carlisle to whom a charter for establishing a government in the island had been given by the British sovereign.[9] From 1652 a system of government known as 'the Old Representative System', which comprised the governor, nominated Legislative Council and elected House of Assembly, all of which were provided for in Letters Patent, the Queen's Commission and Royal Instructions issued to the Governor, was in place.[10] An Executive Committee was introduced in 1881[11] and this became the main instrument of policy until 1958 when it was replaced by the Cabinet system.[12] In 1966 provision of Barbados' independence was made under the *Barbados Independence Act*.[13] The Constitution was passed as an appendix to the *Barbados Independence Order*, a British Order in Council issued under the Act.[14]

In Barbados and the Commonwealth countries their written constitutions take precedence over legislation and judicial precedence as legal sources. Article 1 of the Constitution states that it is the supreme law of the land and that any law which is inconsistent with its provision is void to the extent of the inconsistency.[14]

The Constitution established a parliamentary system of government based on the Westminster model, and contains the framework of government, providing for the head of state, who is the English sovereign, represented locally by the governor-general, parliament, the prime minister and cabinet, the courts, civil service, police, armed forces, the party system, elections, citizenship, the human rights to be guaranteed every citizen and for judicial review of legislation and administrative acts.

Courts and Special Tribunals

Justice is administered in a system comprising magistrates courts, a high court, divisional court, a divisional court which has exclusive jurisdiction to hear appeals from decisions of magistrates, a Court of Appeal and the Judicial Committee of the Privy Council which is at the apex.[15]

Special tribunals include the Income Tax Appeal Board, the Land Valuation Board, the National Insurance Board, the Public Utilities Board and various tribunals established as part of the national insurance scheme such as the Benefits and Severance Payments Tribunals.[16]

The most important decisions of the higher courts are published in the *Barbados Law Reports*, (1948 onward) but, at present, the only tribunals which publish their decisions are the National Insurance Benefits Tribunal and the Severance Payments Tribunal.[17]

The Legal Profession

Prior to 1970 when a Westindian system of legal education was established, lawyers were trained in the United Kingdom. Since 1970 most are products of a system under which the LL.B. is awarded by the University of the West Indies after three years of study in the Faculty of Law, followed by a two year practical course leading to the Legal Education Certificate. The certificate is offered at two law schools, the Hugh Wooding Law School in Trinidad and Tobago and the Norman Manley Law School in Jamaica.[18]

The legal profession in Barbados is fused, and lawyers are styled attorneys-at-law, and not barristers and solicitors. At the end of 1995 there were 374 attorneys-at-law in an island with a population of approximately 264,000.[19]

Notes
1. Keith Patchett. *Reception of law in the West Indies* (1973) April *West Indian Law Journal*, 17 at 20.
2. [1953] 2 All E.R. 490.
3. 20 State Tr. 239.
4. Edward Laing. *Introduction to law and legal systems of the Commonwealth Caribbean.* - Cave Hill, Barbados: 1973, 2 vols., P. 47 (Unpublished work).
5. RJ. Walker. *The English Legal System.* - London: Butterworths, 1985, p. 64.
6. E.H.T. Snell, *Principles of Equity.* 27th ed. - London: Sweet and Maxwell, 1973, p. 27 et seq.
7. See Note 5.
8. *Laws of Barbados*, 1667/1-1971/44. - London: Sweet and Maxwell; Bridgetown: Government Printer, 1973. - Bridgetown: 7 vols originally, now 9 (Loose-leaf).
9. Peter Campbell. *An Outline of Barbados History.* - Bridgetown: The Author, 1973, p. 5.
10. See Hume Wrong. *Government of the West Indies.* - Oxford: Clarendon Press, 1923.
11. Executive Committee Act, *Laws of Barbados*, 1880/81, c. 32.
12. *Cabinet Instrument of Delegation Regulations*, 1958.
13. *Barbados Independence Act*, 1966 (UK).
14. *Barbados Independence Order*, 1966 (S.L. 1966 No. 1455) (UK).
15. See *The Barbados Constitution*, s. 85; *The Supreme Court of Judicature Act*, Cap. 117 and *The Magistrates Jurisdiction and Procedure Act*, Cap. 116.
16. *Administrative Appeal Tribunal Act*, 1981-18. First Schedule.
17. Barbados National Insurance Board. Barbados National Insurance Tribunal Reports: one volume of cases decided by the Benefits Tribunal between 1968-1990 and three volumes of cases decided by the Severance Payments Tribunals between 1982-1993 published to date.
18. Velma Newton. *Commonwealth Caribbean Legal Systems.* - Bridgetown, Barbados: Triumph Publications, 1988/9. Reprinted Wm. Gaunt & Sons, Inc., 1989, pp. 119-142.
19. Information supplied by Bar Association Office.

Education

The foundation of education in Barbados was laid by the "philanthropic efforts" of private individuals and the humanitarian interests of the churches. Government aid goes back to 1835 when the British Government made an annual grant to the Westindian colonies for the education of former slaves. The present system provides for education at three levels: primary, secondary and tertiary.

There are three kinds of primary and secondary schools: Government-owned or maintained; assisted private and non-assisted or independent schools. Government assisted private schools are at the secondary level only.

Mindful of the importance of education to a country, the government offers assistance in a number of ways: in the government schools, expenditure is met from the public coffers; the private assisted schools receive grants for covering the salaries for some of the teachers, subventions to include specialised subjects on the curriculum and bursaries to assist some children.

Furthermore, pupils attending government-approved secondary schools receive books under the Textbook Loan Scheme.

Tertiary education also receives a boost since the economic costs of Barbadian students attending the University of the West Indies, is paid by the government.

Primary Schools

The term 'primary' describes education for children from four - eleven years and therefore includes nursery (under five years) and junior (seven - eleven years).

There are 85 primary schools with an enrolment of approximately 28,000 pupils and about 1,400 teachers in Barbados which provide the quality education crucial to the further development of the country's human resources. At all these schools children from all social and economic backgrounds benefit from a government policy of providing low cost school meals throughout the primary school system.

Government has sought to upgrade the primary school plants with the assistance of the Inter-American Development Bank. Newly amalgamated and more cost effective schools have been built to replace older ones to achieve greater efficiency in the utilisation of educational facilities and resources.

Secondary Schools

Secondary education is provided for children eleven - eighteen years. In the government-owned schools, the trend is towards a co-educational system.

There are presently 22 government secondary schools with an enrolment of 21,510 students and 12 approved private secondary schools with a student population of just over 3,000. There are 1,382 teachers in these schools, with 1,196 at the government secondary and under 200 at private secondary schools.

Free education is available to all students attending the island's government secondary schools, where the quality of instruction is enhanced by an even distribution of trained and graduate teachers.

Both private and government schools help Barbados to proudly boast of compulsory education for all children up to the age of 16 and a 98 percent literacy rate.

Senior Schools

There are presently two senior schools on the island, St Mark's and St Giles, which provide training for slow learners over the age of 11 in technical and vocational subjects. Government hopes to phase out all senior schools and incorporate secondary school age students into the mainstream system utilising a progressive remedial programme.

Special Schools

There are special schools catering for the blind, the deaf, the mentally retarded and the juvenile delinquent. In addition, a number of private institutions offer courses in secretarial and commercial subjects and language studies.

Over the next few years government intends to accelerate the process of integrating slow learners, mentally retarded and the learning and physically disabled into the mainstream of the school system.

Tertiary Institutions

Erdiston Teachers' Training College
The college opened in 1948 with 32 students. It is co-educational and provides training for non-graduate and graduate teachers.

The college has been restructured to enhance the quality of education through the delivery of pre-service, in-service and continuing education programmes for teachers and other people interested in education and training. Part of the strategy will involve an expanded mandate to allow students to pursue the Diploma of Education, Certificate of Educational Management and Administration and Bachelor of Education conferments.

Samuel Jackman Prescod Polytechnic
The Samuel Jackman Prescod Polytechnic was opened in January 1970 with both day and evening classes. The Institution now has over 2,000 students and provides courses in electrical, building and engineering trades,

Education

commerce, agriculture and garment studies. The campus opened at Wildey, St Michael in May 1982 with an additional faculty for human ecology including cosmetology and home economics.

In addition to its regular students, the polytechnic provides institutional training for apprentices of the National Training Board.

Barbados Community College

The Barbados Community College is a tertiary educational institution offering a wide range of programmes in academic, vocational and technical areas.

An Associate Degree programme was started in September 1987 and offers qualifications in areas pursued in eight divisions at the college.

The programmes offered in these divisions include: Fine arts, health sciences, hospitality studies, liberal arts, science, technology which leads to various professional and vocational qualifications through appropriate examinations.

The college has established mechanisms to strengthen linkages with other tertiary level institutions and as part of its institutional strengthening will be offering a Bachelor of Arts degree in fine arts and a programme leading to the Bachelors Degree and Diploma in education in technical and vocational studies.

University of the West Indies

The University of the West Indies on three campuses, in Barbados, Jamaica and Trinidad and Tobago, caters to students from the English-speaking Caribbean. However, it serves Guyana in the faculties of medicine and law only.

The university offers a number of degrees and certificate courses at the three campuses, but the Faculty of Law is located in Barbados, at the Cave Hill Campus. There is, however, a law school in each of the other campuses.

In 1985 the University created the Office of University Services with a director at Cave Hill. Its objective is to serve the needs of the non-campus territories.

Affiliated bodies include two located in Barbados: The Theological Institute, Codrington College, which offers the BA and L.Th.; the Caribbean Meteorological Institute which offers the B.Sc., meteorological component of the B.Sc., in meteorology, under agreement with the Caribbean Meteorological Council.

In an effort to create a pool of highly efficient and effective managers in the public and private sectors who would lead the economic recovery in the various territories, the University of the West Indies launched the Centre for Management Development (CMD) at the Cave Hill Campus. The CMD is a semi-autonomous institution which provides training for executive management leading to the conferment of the Executive MBA degree.

UWIDITE is a telecommunications network linking the three campuses and some of the other non-campus territories. UWIDITE provides tele-conferencing and allows for distance teaching to name but two advantages. The Cave Hill Campus is a link in the UWIDITE network.

Barbados Institute of Management and Productivity (BIMAP)

BIMAP was established in 1971 by the joint efforts of government and private sector to improve the efficiency and effectiveness of management - public and private, and to increase national productivity.

BIMAP offers a comprehensive range of services in the areas of management training, consulting, research and small business development to its members and clients. The training programme is oriented towards the needs of personnel at the operational, supervisory and management levels.

The institute has refocussed its objectives to include the expansion of the BIMAP Entrepreneurial Development Programme to provide greater opportunities for self-employment, as well as the introduction of new areas of specialisation in the Diploma in Management Studies programme.

Skills Training Programme

Government established the Skills Training Programme in 1979 to provide short, intensive training - 'decentralised' and community based - using light equipment to reach young people in or near the place where they live and where they may use the skills. The programme caters for skills such as auto-mechanics; electrical installation; horticulture; key punch operation; leather work, masonry; needlecraft; plumbing; steel-bending; upholstery and woodwork. The Skills Training Programme is also serving as a feeder to the National Training Board's Apprenticeship Programme, in general, the project when measured by the objectives set, has been very successful.

Health

The island's population has easy access to a comprehensive health care system which offers preventative and curative services.

There are eight polyclinics throughout the island. Services offered include maternal and child care, family planning, health education, school health services, communicable diseases and environmental health. Specialised services which include an X-ray facility, yellow fever surveillance, an eye clinic, bacteriological analysis, food testing and a skin disease facility are offered at the island's largest polyclinic, Sir Winston Scott.

One general hospital known as the Queen Elizabeth Hospital services the island. It is located in St Michael and offers specialised care in areas such as gynaecology, paediatrics, obstetrics, cardiac surgery, plastic surgery, pyschotherapy, radiology, radiography and opthalmology.

The island also boasts a fully serviced government owned hospital in St Peter called the St Joseph Hospital, as well as the ultra modern private Bay View Hospital in St Michael. Part of the island's health care system is supported by the Barbados Drug Service (BDS) which was brought into operation in April 1980. A system of "walk in" clinics was started at the polyclinics in September 1985 which allows all Barbadians to be seen and to receive medication free of cost irrespective of whether they are on welfare or not.

Unique Barbados

Crop Over - more than a carnival

IT IS important that one remembers this when one thinks of Barbados' major national festival. Ours is simply not a display of music and dance and general revelry. Crop Over provides an opportunity for Barbadians to demonstrate the full range of their creative ability. Music is indeed a very important part of Crop Over, and our musicians and entertainers, both young and old, come into their own, as evidenced by the extremely high standard of our calypso Pic O De Crop Competition and the Party Monarch Competition.

But music and dance are only part of what we offer. There are opportunities to enjoy a wide range of other products of Barbados' rich cultural heritage.

The Fine Craft Exhibition at the Queen's Park Gallery features the work of a number of craft producers; the Crop Over Promenade focuses on local fashion and floral arranging; the Bajan Culture Village offers a trip back in time, to the days of the village rum shop, traditional village games and crafts. These are but a few!

Barbados is a unique island. The creativity, the resourcefulness, the resilience of our people are unbelievable - given the small size of our country. We have something special to share with the rest of the world and what better place to start with than with our Crop Over festival.

Those of you who may never had the pleasure of participating in this cultural wonder, come and share it with us. Come and see what makes Barbados so special. Barbadians living overseas should come and recapture what it means to be a Barbadian - relive experiences, bring memories alive again.
• **The Honourable Mia Mottley, MP, Minister of Education, Youth Affairs and Culture' message for Crop Over 1996. Courtesy** *Crop Over Traveller* **July/August**

Corporate Responsibility

IN 1981, Barbados' largest company, Barbados Shipping and Trading Company (BS&T) and members of the private sector agreed to contribute on a voluntary basis 3 percent of pre-tax profits to an entity named the Tourism Development Corporation (TDC). Successive governments allocated on an annual basis very significant sums for the development and marketing of tourism, but the majority of the funds appeared to go into administration and not enough were earmarked for hard advertising. Against this background, TDC was formed and would use the funds collected for the promotion of Barbados abroad, as it was envisaged that the island needed a 'shot in the arm' and tourism was identified as the catalyst.

The project proved to be successful and the contributions, originally guaranteed for three years in the first instance still continue, although now stabilized at 2 percent. The Minister of Finance, in recognising the contribution of the TDC to the Barbados tourism effort, has encouraged the initiative by allowing expenses to be written off against tax at a rate of 150 percent

Over the next decade, BS&T envisages two main areas of growth in Barbados - tourism and services generally, including financial. BS&T looks to the future with confidence and with the expectation that during the course of the next 75 years the company will meet its challenges and far surpass its achievements to date.

CariCom Heads of Government 17th meeting in Barbados

CariCom, Heads of Government held their 17th meeting at the Sherbourne Conference Centre, Barbados, 1996. At the opening ceremony, Allyson Riley, a physical education teacher and personal fitness trainer, entertained the Honorable guests with a solo performance of a dance entitled 'Caribbean Fantasy' which she also choreographed.

Sam Lord's is Bajan

A 24-year association with Sam Lord's Castle ended in August 1996 when the Marriott International Hotels Incorporation sold the 234-room, four star hotel complex to local Grant Hotels Incorporated, thus becoming the first Barbadian to own the famous property.

Sir Garfield Sobers - National hero

SIR GARFIELD SOBERS is a national hero and international cricket celebrity, who created incredible cricket records during his long career - few of these have been broken and many never will. Sir Garfield is best described as an original hero: a boy from the back streets who became a shining example to all. Rising to become captain of the West Indies cricket team, and a veritable, consummate all-rounder, accepted by all in the cricket world as the greatest cricketer of his generation and, an unrivalled ambassador for his countrymen and women and his sport. All of this achieved with genuine modesty and simple dignity

Sir Garfield's potential genius was recognised from his early days when he was representing Barbados at the tender age of 16. After one year of first class cricket he was selected for the West Indies. In 1958, he scored his first Test century which resulted in a world record of 365 Not Out against Pakistan in Jamaica - the record stood for 36 years. Brian Lara, in 1994, scored 375 in Antigua and Sir Garfield who witnessed this magnificent feat was the first to rush on the field to congratulate Lara.

In a Test cricket career which ran from 1954 to 1974 Sir Garfield had a batting aggregate of 8,032 runs - a world record at the time. He made 26 Test centuries and an average of 57.78, a spectacular achievement for a player who batted only 160 innings. In all first class cricket, Sir Garfield made a total of 28,315 runs and averaged 54.67 per innings, blasting an incredible 86 centuries. He had 235 Test wickets and a total of 1,043 first class victims, distinguishing himself as one of the most successful Westindian bowlers of all time.

Sir Garfield Sobers retired from the game in 1974 and was knighted by Queen Elizabeth in 1975, in recognition of his outstanding contribution to world cricket - a most appropriate honour to this cricketing genius

Dame Ruth Nita Barrow

HER EXCELLENCY Dame Ruth Nita Barrow, GCMG, DA, the first woman to be appointed Governor-General of Barbados, was born on 15 November, 1916 at Nessfield, St Lucy. Prior to her appointment as Governor-General, she was Ambassador Extraordinary and Plenipotentiary, Permanent Representative of Barbados to the United Nations.

Dame Nita had a long and distinguished career as a nurse and healthcare administrator. After she qualified as a registered nurse in Barbados in 1941 she became a registered midwife in Trinidad the following year. She later obtained a Public Health Diploma from the University of Toronto, a Nursing Education Diploma from Edinburgh University, Scotland, and a BSc (Nursing) degree from Columbia University, New York.

Dame Nita also worked for many years in Jamaica where she was successively Sister Tutor at the Kingston Hospital of Nursing, Matron of the University College Hospital and Principal Nursing Officer.

Dame Nita had been, among other things, nursing advisor to the Pan American Health Organization (PAHO); President of the World Council of Churches; and Health Consultant with the World Health Organisation (WHO).

Dame Nita was highly respected internationally for her community service, her work in the women's movement and her involvement in the struggle against apartheid. She had a long association with the Young Women's Christian Association (YWCA), culminating with her appointment as President of the World YWCA, from 1975 to 1983. She was Convenor of Forum '85, held in conjunction with the Nairobi World Conference of Non-Government Women's Organisations to review and appraise the United Nations Decade for Women. Dame Nita was a member of the Commonwealth Group of Eminent Persons' mission to South Africa in 1986.

Dame Nita's work has been recognised in many countries. Her awards include an Honorary Doctor of Law degree from the University of the West Indies as well as a similar degree in science from McMaster University, Canada; Fellowship of the Royal College of Nursing; Gamaliel Chair Lecturer, University of Wisconsin, Milwaukee: CariCom Award for Women and the Caribbean Prize for Peace through the Struggle for Justice. Dame Ruth Nita Barrow passed away on 19 December 1995

Notable dates in Barbados' history

1000 -	
500 BC	First stone age Arawak settlers arrive.
100 AD	Second culture group arrived from South America.
500-600	Third settlement by Troumassoid people
1300	Fourth culture group, the Suazoids arrive.
1500-20	Arawak occupation mysteriously comes to an end.
1625	English took possession in the name of James 1.
1627	Founding of the colony - first colonists settled.
1628	Rival settlement established in Barbados.
1629	Barbados divided into six parishes.
1631	Sir Henry Colt visited the island.
1635	Tobacco market prices collapses. Cotton, ginger and indigo introduced.
1639	Birth of Parliament.
1640	Manufacture of sugar started in early 1640s.
1645	The island divided into eleven parishes.
1647	An epidemic of yellow fever kills 6,000 people.
1649	First open revolt of slaves
1651	Declaration of Independence of the Commonwealth.
1652	'Rights of the People' Agreement signed.
1663	Postal agency established to handle overseas mail.
1675	Second open revolt of slaves
1680	Over 90 percent of land under cultivation.
1692	Third open revolt of slaves
1694	Slave-planned uprising.
1698	Act declares the rights and powers of Assembly.
1710	Codrington bequeaths his plantations to a Society for the Propagation of the Gospel
1731	First Caribbean newspaper, *The Barbados Gazette*.
1745	Codrington College established.
1750	Slave population - 65,000. White population - 18,000.
1751	George Washington visits Barbados.
1765	First Moravian missionaries arrive.
1766	Bridgetown destroyed by fire.
1780	Hurricane killed 4,326 people.
1784	Bridgetown slave market was established.
1816	Fourth slave uprising led by Bussa and Washington Franklin.
1817	Free coloured people allowed to give court evidence.
1818	Gun Hill Station erected.
1826	Amelioration legislation laws are passed. The first verdict to establish the right of a slave to protection under common law when Chief Justice Renn Hampden sentenced John Archer, a white man, to a years imprisonment for manslaughter.
1831	Free coloured people given the right to vote. Hurricane destroys homes and churches.
1834	1st August, slavery abolished. Enforced Apprenticeship established. 155 charity schools compared to eight in 1825.
1835	Police Force was established.
1838	1st August. Emancipation Day.
1840	Legislation allows coloured people to sit in Assembly.
1843	Bridgetown became a constituency. First coloured person elected to Assembly.
1847	Founding of the public library.
1850	First Education Act.
1851	Inland mail service authorised.
1852	First Barbados postage stamps issued .
1854	Cholera epidemic - 20,000 deaths
1861	Waterworks established in Bridgetown.
1871	Census - 104,904 black people, 39,578 coloureds and 16,560 whites.
1876	Confederation riots.
1878	Elementary education introduced.
1881	Executive Committee Act passed.
1884	Vote Franchise - £50 property requirement.
1885	Separation from Government of the Windward islands.
1886	Piped water extended to rural districts.
1889	Police Force Band established.
1891	Executive Committee (Consolidation) Act passed. Masters and Servants Act was repealed.
1898	Hurricane kills 80 people - destroying 18,000 homes.
1924	Charles Duncan O'Neal founds Democratic League, the first organised black political group.
1934	Grantley Adams elected to the House of Assembly.
1937	Bridgetown riots - 14 dead, 47 wounded - 400 arrested.
1938	Birth of the Barbados Labour Party.
1940	The Trade Union Act, 1 August.
1941	Barbados Workers Union registered on 4th October.

Notable dates in Barbados' history

1944	Vote Franchise lowered from £50 - £20. Women allowed to vote.
1946	'Bushe Experiment' - the birth of party politics.
1950	Universal Adult Suffrage introduced.
1954	Ministerial government established. Grantley Adams became first Premier.
1955	Democratic Labour Party formed.
1958	Barbados part of the Federation of the West Indies. Grantley Adams the first Federation Prime Minister. The cabinet system of government was instituted.
1959	Common entrance examination for secondary schools.
1961	Full internal self-government achieved. Errol Barrow of DLP becomes Premier.
1962	Dissolution of the West Indies Federation.
1963	Voting age reduced from 21 - 18 years of age. Abolition of fees in government Secondary schools.
1964	Senate of 21 members replaced Legislation Council. Legislation was passed permitting peaceful picketing.
1966	Archaeologists unearth Arawak and Carib settlements. H M Queen Elizabeth II visits. Independence Order laid before Parliament. 30 November - Independence. Right Honourable Errol Barrow first Prime Minister.
1967	System of Local Government Council dissolved, replaced by Interim Commissioner for Local Government. First native Governor-General, Sir Winston Scott. National Insurance and Social Security Scheme.
1968	Caribbean Free Trade Association (CARIFTA) established.
1969	Local government services transferred to central government. Barbados Development Bank established.
1970	Caribbean Development Bank founded. Large slave burial ground excavated
1971	Democratic Labour Party win General Election.
1972	Central Bank of Barbados established.
1973	CariCom treaty signed by four founding members.
1976	Tom J M G M Adams wins General Election.
1978	State-owned Insurance Company established. Barbados Defence formally established.
1979	New BDS $29 million airport complex opened.
1980	Constituencies increased to 27.
1981	Transport Levy introduced. Rt Hon Tom J M G M Adams, Prime Minister, re-elected. Hosting of Carifesta - 2000 artists from 33 countries.
1982	US President Ronald Reagan - official visit. Bridgetown sewerage treatment plant opened.
1983	Oistins Fish Terminal opened. May 26 - Spring Garden Highway opened. Length of St Barnabas Highway opened.
1984	Heywood's Holiday Village, St Peter, opened. Heywood's - Government's largest tourism project to date.
1985	New General Post Office opened. March 11 - Prime Minister Rt Hon Tom J M G M Adams died. Harold Bernard 'Bree' St John, sworn in as Prime Minister. XIV CARIFTA Games held at the National Stadium.
1986	Democratic Labour Party win General Election.
1987	Prime Minister Errol Barrow died. Lloyd Erskine Sandiford sworn in as Prime Minister.
1989	350 years of unbroken Parliamentary rule
1990	Dame Nita Barrow first female Governor General
1991	Election - Prime Minister Sandiford returned to office.
1993	Owen Arthur appointed Leader of the Opposition.
1994	General Election - Owen Arthur became Prime Minister. Barbados hosts United Nations Conference.
1995	Bridgetown wins Port of the Year award.
1996	Barbados hosts 20th Caribbean Tourism Conference.

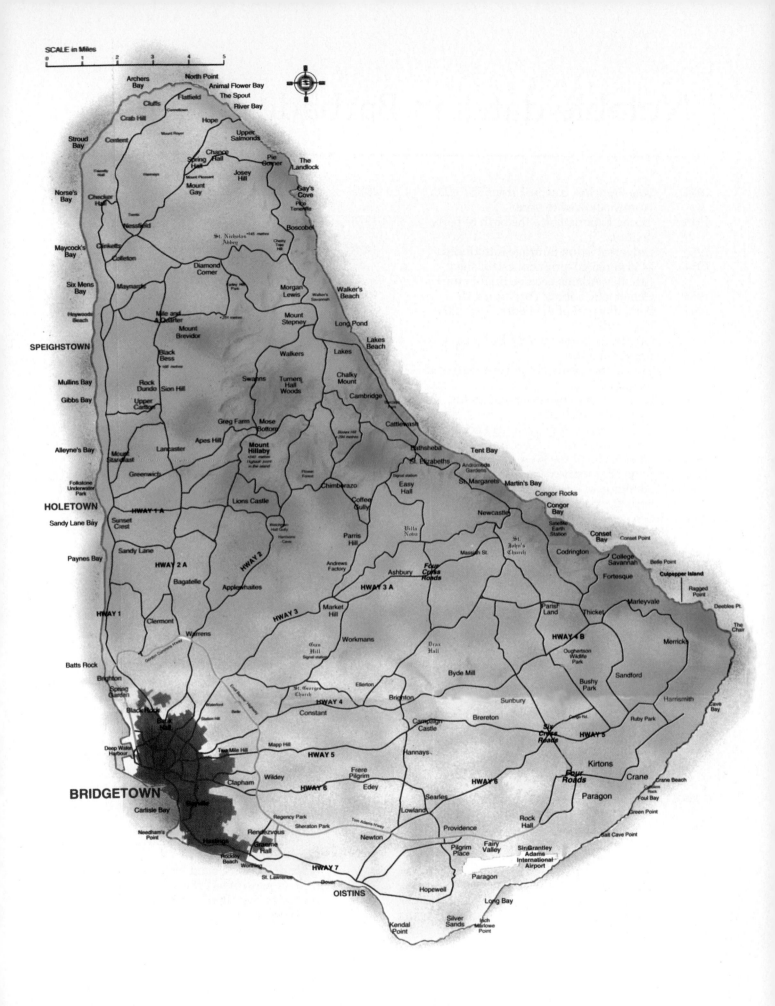

A brief history of Barbados

by Karl Watson, PhD

Barbados is the Crown and Front of all the Caribbee Islands towards the rising sun, being the most east of any and lies more conveniently than any of the rest for a seat of war, being most healthful, fruitful and stored with all things necessary of its own innate growth which are necessary for life. The greatest mart of trade, not only of the Caribbees, but of any island in the West Indies, being inhabited with many wealthy planters and merchants, and hath very great conveniency for a hole where ships might hide amongst the houses as in Amsterdam and Venice, of great conveniency for trade and in the time of war free from the danger of any enemy, except so powerful as to invade the island, which well managed would be too great a task for any Prince in Europe.

Major John Scott
Description of Barbados (c. 1667)

Shell tools of the Suazoid culture made from the conch

Two adornos, one a dog's head the other a finely modelled face, from the Suazoid culture

In spite of its small size, Barbados has had an interesting and varied history, both in its own right and within the context of British imperial politics.

The settlement of Barbados, by English colonists and Africans taken from a slave ship in mid-Atlantic occurred in the year 1627. However, settlement by Arawak peoples moving north from the Orinoco and Guyana region of South America, had occurred some 2,000 years previously. The exact date of their arrival is unknown and archaeological discoveries keep pushing back that date. What is known, however, is that four distinct culture groups inhabited the island at varying points in time and for yet to be determined periods of occupation. First to arrive were a pre-ceramic people, a true Stone Age people, who had not yet discovered the secret of firing clay to make pottery. Archaeological excavations at Heywoods, on the west side of the island immediately north of Speightstown, have revealed traces of their presence. Very little is known of their life-style, which certainly was based on hunting and gathering. They made tools from the large conch (*Stombus gigas*) and many examples of these have been found at Heywoods.

Sometime around 100 AD, a second culture group arrived from South America. They occupied the islands of the Eastern Caribbean and were characterized by a highly-developed ceramic assemblage which included thin, finely made wares, well fired and often decorated, either with

33

incised abstract designs or exterior paint, most frequently comprising abstract or geometric patterns painted in red and white. This ceramic tradition is given the name Saladoid, a derivative of a place name from the Orinoco River region in Venezuela, from where it is believed these people originated.

Several hundred years later, a third culture group appeared on the island whose ceramic patterns differed sufficiently from the Saladoid tradition to be assigned to a separate category. This group is known by archaeologists as the Troumassoid culture. Their ceramics were also well made but without much of the decorative techniques of the Saladoid peoples, including an absence of polychromatic wares. They also tended to incorporate footed vessels in their assemblages.

Around 1300 AD, the fourth culture group, known as the Suazoids, entered the island. Their occupation lasted until the early part of the 16th Century, when they either abandoned the island or were removed by Spanish slave-raiding expeditions.

The Suazoid ceramic tradition was cruder than that of the preceding groups with a preponderance of thick, unslipped, undecorated wares, many of which are footed griddle forms used to prepare cassava bread. An interesting feature of their potting tradition, however, is the inclusion of lugs or handles to bowls, frequently shaped in animal or human forms. These are called adornos. More than any of the preceding culture groups, the Suazoids tended to use shell tools made from large conchs. Barbados is a coral island and possesses no hard volcanic material used elsewhere in the Caribbean to make tools. The early people living on Barbados had two choices - either, to bring in volcanic material from other islands, or secondly, to use the material at hand. For convenience, if not durability, they chose the latter alternative, though one occasionally finds a basalt hatchet or petaloid celt transported from neighbouring islands.

The social and economic lifestyle of the Amerindians of Barbados did not vary markedly during their 2,000-3,000 year occupation of the island. They left no written records, coming closest to this is the petroglyphs carved in Springhead Cave, St James. Reconstruction of their lifestyle has had to depend heavily on the archaeological record, supplemented by ethnographic data from the Guianas, Venezuela and Brazil. Thus far, an incomplete picture has emerged. Excavations have been too few in number to make accurate generalizations and the nature of the evidence relating to material culture is skewed in favour of the inorganic materials which survive in great numbers: for example, one thinks about the large

A pot from the Saladoid culture, c. 300 AD

Salaloid vessel recently discovered in the course of marine development at Port St Charles, c. 300 AD

OPPOSITE: Petroglyphs carved in Springhead Cave, St James, are the closest to a written record of Barbados' earliest settlers

34

quantity of Amerindian ceramic shards scattered across the face of Barbados. Yet, we know from comparative ethnographic evidence that much Amerindian material culture derived from the use of organic materials such as wood, cotton, leaves, gourds, lianas, feathers and other highly perishable materials which have simply not survived the harsh tropical elements, negative soil conditions and the passage of time.

Despite these negative factors, we still know enough about the Amerindians to offer the following broad picture.

They had many settlements on the island. Known ones amount to 50, located mostly on the coast with a few inland. The concensus is that at peak settlement, there may have been as many as 150 settlements on the island.

The size of the population is subject to considerable debate. It obviously fluctuated, but a low estimate places the number of Amerindians on the island at any given time as less than 1,000 individuals, while a high estimate places the figure closer to 8,000 individuals.

There are three areas in particular which had large settlements. The Bridgetown area, with settlements stretching back to the Batts Rock region, Heywoods in the north of the island and Chancery Lane in the south. They have all been partially excavated and show traces of the communal long houses used by the Amerindians.

For food resources, both the sea and land were used. The Amerindians were adept fishermen, practising both inshore or reef fishing and deep sea fishing. They built fish traps, used leaves and vines with poisonous properties to stun fish and used lines and nets as well as spears. They caught fish of all sizes and species, ranging from sharks to flying fish. Their middens or refuse heaps also show that the Amerindians had a fondness for shell fish, especially conchs and whelks, crabs, lobsters and turtles. They also consumed many species of birds, and not just water fowl either, since warblers and mockingbirds were also eaten.

In their garden plots, they planted cassava which was a major source of carbohydrate and assorted squashes, beans and peppers. They also cultivated cotton which they spun for use as clothing, nets, carrying sacks, rope and fishing lines and roucou for making red dyes and body paint.

Their material culture shows evidence of a sense of balance, proportion and overall harmony of design in the objects which they made and their finest ceramics, particularly from the Saladoid culture, are outstanding examples of artistic achievement.

The Amerindians were adept fishermen, practising both inshore and reef fishing. Settlements on Barbados' south eastern coast near Sam Lord's Castle would probably have fished Cobbler's Reef and the shores it protects (pictured opposite)

Their political and social organisation was loose, centred around the extended family and the leader or cacique. Some families may have been accorded higher status than others, but it would not seem as if a true elite existed.

Higher status usually derived from a combination of economic, military and religious considerations. Ownership of an ocean-going canoe with its related knowledge of sea currents and the geography of the islands was important, as were valour, and leadership qualities. A good relationship with a shaman or the possession of shamanic qualities was also very important, since the Amerindians had a profound understanding of the harmony and inter-relationships of the natural world with the supernatural. They had polytheistic, animistic beliefs and the shaman knew the correct rituals which opened lines of communication between the natural and the supernatural world. Their world vision was based on the concept of a balance of forces and energy in which their society existed and it was essential that harmony among these forces be maintained in order to guarantee continuity.

Excavation of their graves provides us with some clues about the nature of their belief in the afterlife. Grave goods were often interred with the dead. These included the three pointed stones or zemis which facilitated movement to the spirit world. Dogs were sometimes sacrificed to accompany their owners to the spirit world, and since the idea of the ancestor was integral to the family unit of the Amerindian, bones were at times disinterred, hung in the long house for a period and then reburied, a practice which gave rise to the charge of cannibalism, although it is entirely possible that the Amerindians practised ritual cannibalism.

The Arawak occupation of Barbados seems to have come to an end sometime before 1520. This may be related to a 1512 cedula issued by Ferdinand of Spain authorising Spanish subjects in the Greater Antilles to raid islands in the Lesser Antilles including Barbados and to capture and enslave inhabitants found there.

Thus far, there is no evidence that the people known as Caribs (though they referred to themselves as Kalinago) ever permanently occupied Barbados, though they often visited it, paddling their canoes from the neighbouring islands of St Vincent and St Lucia. These visits continued into the 17th Century after English settlement, for contemporary observers saw and recorded some of these visits. The Carib name for Barbados was Ichirouganaim, which has been translated as red stone island with teeth outside (reefs).

Ferdinand & Isabella
"In 1492, a triple process of national unification took place in Spain, through the marriage of Isabella of Castille and Ferdinand of Aragon, the expulsion of the Moors, and the conquest and subsequent colonisation of the new American territories. The unification of the country's political power and the creation of the kingdom of Spain were carried out at the expense of the Moors and Jews (and members of other cultures), who were expelled from Spain after having lived there for many centuries"

OPPOSITE: The early settlers on Barbados would have found a lush, forested island with ample fruit-bearing trees and a rich soil. The nature trail at Codrington College, St John maintains some of the feeling of this early time

Late 16th Century Spanish accounts refer to the island as uninhabited and the first English contacts also reported the absence of inhabitants. Until evidence to the contrary is established, the conclusion must stand that Barbados was uninhabited when colonized by the English in 1627.

The first decades of the 17th Century saw a shift in English and French attitudes to the New World. Earlier voyages of exploration and contact by English and French explorers and privateers had confirmed the limits of Spanish power, identified the weak areas in their claim to hemispheric hegemony and provided their respective European crowned heads with sufficient intelligence to embolden them to mount a challenge to a once powerful Spain, now declining through internal social decay, inflation and over commitment on several European fronts.

Lack of effective occupation on lands claimed by Spain, it was believed, gave other European powers legal justification to establish a physical presence and claim that land as their own. Of course, this was a thoroughly Eurocentric view, but in the early jostling for positions from

ABOVE: The east coast settlements were protected by off-shore reefs and rugged coastlines

Privateers

A term used to describe the privately-owned, armed ships, and also the commanders of such vessels, employed by various European nations in the Caribbean from the 16th Century onwards. A privateer was issued with letters of marque.

40

which later empires would evolve, no one was willing to acknowledge any rights of earlier native peoples who were regarded as mere obstacles to European overseas expansion.

These early ventures were privately financed with the tacit approval of the respective monarchs. It had been easily discerned by English, French and Dutch planners that the islands of the Lesser Antilles constituted a weak, but vital link in the Spanish-American empire. Their geographic position cut Spanish lines of communication and at the same time provided bases from which contact could be made with Spanish towns on the mainland, which had been systematically starved of commerce through the existence of antiquated custom rules, irregular sailing schedules, monopolistic ideas and high levels of multiple taxation. Furthermore, the Portuguese had earlier demonstrated, by the example of sugar cane cultivation in their Atlantic islands and in the North Eastern region of Brazil, that colonies in the Americas did not require deposits of gold and silver to be successful, but that tropical export

The islands of the Caribbean

agriculture could make them viable propositions.

It is against this background therefore, that one must view the early settlement and development of Barbados in the 17th Century to what rapidly became England's wealthiest colony and, according to contemporary observers, *"the richest spote of groundell in the world."*

A number of factors have influenced the patterns of Barbadian history and should be mentioned here. The island's geographic location is one of these. Barbados is the most easterly of the Lesser Antilles and is well situated in terms of the north easterly trade-winds and ocean currents to receive shipping from Europe. On the other hand, her relative isolation out of sight of the other islands and the difficulties of sailing against the tradewinds, plus the protection afforded by encircling coral reefs, gave her a degree of security and immunity during periods of intense European rivalry, when Caribbean islands changed colonial masters over and over again.

The topography of the island was also advantageous for her early development, since the absence of mountain barriers permitted the rapid creation of a road system which covered the entire island and provided the catalyst for almost complete utilization of the island's surface area for human settlement and economic activities. The complete network of roads which Barbados possesses today - a stunning 1,500 kilometres of roads on an island 21 miles long by 14 across, derives in large part from road building activities carried out in the first 40 years of settlement.

The Barbadian landscape in 1627 was dominated by extensive forest cover. The northern, eastern and southern sections of the island almost certainly were characterized by dense scrub with patches of grassland, but otherwise the island was covered with true rainforest of at least three canopies and the western and southern coasts of the island had extensive stretches of coastal mangrove.

All of this would change with an astonishing rapidity under the aegis of English colonization. By 1660, just 33 years after settlement, the island had been completely deforested and the Barbadian ideal had emerged - that of a garden. The natural world of the tropics had given way to a controlled world of artificial husbandry, where in excess of 90 per cent of the island's total surface area was devoted to growing crops of the one kind or another, although sugar cane was the dominant crop.

The arrival of the ship *William and John* in February 1627 with some 60 odd settlers and six Africans taken en route marked the beginning of formal colonization. This first effort was financed by a London-based

A monument to commemorate the first landing of Englishmen, at Holetown, St James

The Restoration

The restoration of the Stuart monarchy in Britain with the return of Charles II to the throne in 1660. After the death of Oliver Cromwell in 1658, his son Richard proved incapable of maintaining the Protectorate, and with no other viable form of government possible, a faction led by General Monck organised the King's return from exile.

OPPOSITE: The absence of mountain barriers permitted the rapid creation of a road system for complete utilization of the island

42

mercantile partnership of two brothers, Sir William and Sir Peter Courteen. The settlers, who from early accounts were an all male group, established themselves at what is today, Holetown on the west coast of the island. They immediately set about the arduous task of forest clearance in order to plant their first crops of vegetables, corn and root crops for subsistence and tobacco and cotton for export. In this venture the novices were helped by 40 Arawaks brought expressly from Guiana for this purpose.

The political situation on the island, however, quickly became confused and acrimonious since the Earl of Carlisle had made an application to King Charles I for a proprietary grant for the Lesser Antilles, which was duly granted in 1628, a rival settlement was established in the south west of the island, on what was to be named Carlisle Bay and later became the principal settlement of Bridgetown.

Accusations, machinations and a pending armed confrontation that was stopped only by clerical intervention saw the triumph of Carlisle's forces, led by his governor, Charles Wolverstone. Carlisle, after all held a royal charter which the Courteens did not.

The proprietary patent of Carlisle ended with the Restoration in 1660, but in the interim, social, economic and demographic patterns were laid which still reverberate in today's Barbados.

The island developed with astonishing rapidity, becoming the most prosperous 17th Century insular colony on the globe. The initial basis for capital accumulation was the growing and export of tobacco, which in the very short run proved immensely profitable and laid the foundation on which subsequent economic activity was to build.

With the consequent increase in tobacco production from other regions, all attracted by high prices for tobacco in Europe, over-production ensued and, by 1635, tobacco prices were so low that Barbadian planters turned to cotton, ginger and indigo (for use as a dye).

Labour during this period continued to be almost entirely European, as young English, propelled by economic depression and increasing political unrest at home, sought their fortune overseas. Many of these came to Barbados. By 1639, just 12 years after settlement, the white adult population of Barbados stood at an estimated 8,700.

Forest clearance had proceeded apace, and over 50 percent of the land had been deforested, largely through burning. Sir Henry Colt, who visited the island in 1631, gives us an idea of the appearance of this frontier landscape: *"your ground and plantations lye like ye ruines of some*

TOP: *Forest clearance of Barbados was mainly done by burning*

RIGHT: *The timber resources of the islands rich forests all but disappeared within the first 30 years of settlement*

FAR RIGHT: *Few hardwood trees survived the land clearance race*

OVERLEAF: *After 1640, the production of sugar, and its by-products, rum and molasses, would become the country's principal economic activity for the next 320 years*

village lately burned all ye earth covered blac with cenders."

Settlement patterns showed a heavy coastal concentration, providing easy access to maritime transport for produce. The interior of the island continued to be heavily forested.

During this period as well, the island's institutions were shaped. In 1639, limited democracy made its appearance with the creation of a House of Assembly, with two elected representatives from each parish. Voting was restricted to free white property-owning Christian males. Legislation originated from this body, as did money bills. These were then passed to the council, made up of 12 senior nominated individuals chosen from among the island's richest planters. They in turn passed them on to the governor, who was the crown's resident representative. He would vet the respective pending legislation and forward it to London for royal assent. This system worked relatively well despite its limitations and gave the island considerable autonomy.

By 1641, all 11 parishes had been delineated. Local government rested in the hands of the parish vestries, who were responsible for areas such as the maintenance of parish roads, poor relief, education, emergency relief and security. The vestry, made up of 16 elected property holders of that parish was also empowered to collect parish taxes and rents.

The Church of England or Anglican (Episcopalian) Church was from the very beginning of settlement, the dominant religion of the island and an influential arm of the establishment. The dominant feature of each parish landscape was the church, which played a social and political role in Barbadian society besides ministering to their mostly white congregations no concerted effort was made during slavery to Christianize Africans and their descendants, this only occurred after Emancipation in 1834.

Another body which rooted itself in this early period was the militia. Designed to be responsive to local conditions, the militia provided both internal security and a measure of protection against invasion. All free males between the ages of 16 and 60 were required to enrol in the regiment of their parish of residence.

In 1640, the island began the shift to sugar cane cultivation. The production of sugar and its by-products, rum and molasses, would become the island's principal economic activity for the next 320 years, and bring about changes so profound and lasting that it would be termed the Sugar Revolution.

Barbados had a head start on the other Caribbean islands in this

process for a number of reasons. The island was politically stable, had a substantial white population which protected it from other European intruders, had no native population to subdue, and had an accumulated capital base from tobacco profits to pay for the expensive infrastructure required for successful sugar production. Soil types and rainfall amounts were also conducive to the growing of sugar cane. International events and linkages also contributed to the early economic success enjoyed by the island, for at a point in time when the young settlement in Barbados seemed on the point of bankruptcy with plummeting tobacco, cotton and indigo prices, the Portuguese in Brazil were engaged in a struggle with the Dutch who had occupied the sugar-producing regions of Pernambucco and Bahia.

Warfare disrupted sugar production in Brazil and created an opportunity for the Caribbean which Barbadian planters were quick to seize. There was an almost complete transfer of sugar-making technology from Brazil to Barbados. Dutch expertise, finance and marketing strategies were made available to the Barbadians.

Another group who were instrumental in ensuring the early success of the sugar industry in Barbados were the Sephardic Jews. Inhabitants of the Iberian Peninsula for centuries, they, like the Moors, were on the losing side with the triumph of the Christian Reconquista. They were expelled from Spain and subsequently Portugal by edicts of Ferdinand and Isabella. They sought and found refuge in the cities of Amsterdam and Rotterdam which, as part of the Low Countries were engaged in a struggle for independence from Spain.

It was natural for cadets of Sephardic families to move to North Eastern Brazil when the Dutch invaded. A network of commerce and finance linked Rotterdam, Amsterdam, London and Recife and Pernambuco. Dutch and Jewish mercantile houses provided the Barbadian neophyte planters with technical know-how, milling equipment, shipping and markets in Europe for their sugar. There was also a more sordid side to the assistance they rendered, for sugar growing needed a constant supply of labour and English indentured labour was becoming both scarcer and more expensive. With a working knowledge of West African slave entrepots, the Dutch and Sephardic merchants were instrumental in initiating a steady supply of cheap African labour to the sugar plantations through the slave trade.

Only a few Dutch actually set up residence in Barbados, but with the military victory of the Portuguese in North Eastern Brazil and the

Warfare disrupted sugar production in Brazil and created an opportunity for the Caribbean which Barbadian planters were quick to seize

OPPOSITE: In this painting, c. 1771, the artist Agostino Brunias has poignantly captured the nuances of Westindian, three tiered society. Using costume and body language to convey the real and psychological distinctions between white, brown and black; free and unfree. A veritable triangle of dominance, insecurity and inferiority, which shifts between the women depicted here - with sexual relationships being the principal catalyst.

Copyright: Barbados Museum and Historical Society

resurgence of Roman Catholicism, the Jews were forced to become Christian converts or flee Brazil. Many chose the latter option and several Jewish families sought and obtained permission in the late 1640s and 1650s to move to Barbados, where what is believed to be the first synagogue to be built in the Caribbean, 'Kaal Kadosh Nidhe Israel' (The Holy Scattered Congregation of Israel) was constructed circa 1660. A walk through the ancient cemetery of the synagogue in Bridgetown evokes those turbulent times. Lists of the congregation are to be found among the surviving synagogue records of Recife and so it is easy to trace families like the De Mercados, Paz, Pinheiros and others, whose trajectory in life took them from the Iberian Peninsula, to Holland, on to Brazil and finally to Barbados, where they now lie buried. The Sephardic community of Barbados dwindled and disappeared in the first decades of the 20th Century as families died out, migrated to places like London, New York or Jamaica or converted to Christianity. Yet for two hundred and fifty years, they played an important role in the economic life of the island, an aspect of Barbados' history which has never been adequately explored. A new Askenazim community, fleeing the horrors of war in Europe, has taken their place and, thanks to their efforts, the old synagogue has been restored and is once again used for worship.

As noted, the Sugar Revolution brought many changes with it. Patterns of land holding - changed and society was reshaped by the plantation complex which rapidly sprang up. The institution of slavery dominated every aspect of life on the island.

The high profitability of sugar saw land values soar. Although Barbados in comparison with Jamaica did not have very large plantations, the norm in Barbados being between sixty to one-hundred acre plantations, the small size of the island put land at a premium and, in the competition for space which ensued, small, poorer landholders suffered, as they were bought out by wealthier individuals. Often, between twenty to thirty landholders were disposed so that viable sugar plantation could emerge.

By 1680, the island was completely deforested and the entire space of Barbados was in private hands. Over ninety percent of the approximately 106,000 acres of land on the island was cultivated. Contrary to popular belief however, all the land was not planted in sugar cane. By 1660, what was termed the 'Barbados custom' had evolved. This saw the land on sugar plantations being divided into three portions. One was used for growing canes. The second was planted in millet, corn, root crops such as

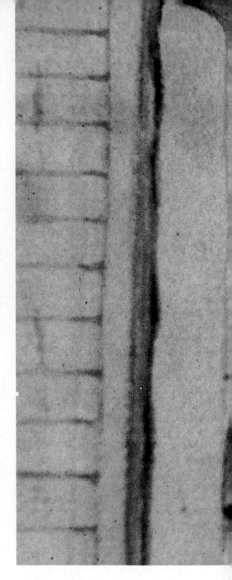

ABOVE: A slave girl being taught sewing skills
TOP RIGHT: A slave woman selling water to earn an independent income
RIGHT:The gravestone of the De Mercado family at the Synagogue in Bridgetown, c. 1685
Photos courtesy: Karl Watson

SEPULTURA DO BEMAUENTURADO
DE DAUID RAPHAEL DE MERCADO
QUE FALECEO EM 24 DE MENAHEM
AN⁰ 5445 SUA ALMA GOZE DA GLORIA

HERE LYETH Y BODY O
DAVID RAPHAEL DE MERCADO
MERCHANT WHO DEPARTED
THIS WORLD Y 14 OF AUGU
1685

yams, potatoes and vegetables. The third was used for growing grasses and legumes to feed the plantation animals or parts were fenced where animals could be confined so as to create a source of fertilizer from their dung, as soil depletion was a constant worry for planters.

A thorough census was ordered by Governor Atkins in 1680 which gives us a clear profile of the Barbadian population. It had grown considerably since the tobacco period. The high profits to be made from sugar encouraged continued migration from the British Isles of three types, voluntary, indentured and exiled prisoners of war or criminals.

However, the large-scale labour needs of the sugar industry changed the racial composition of the population, as thousands of Africans were transported to the island yearly to be sold as slaves. The census counted 23,000 whites and 40,000 black people.

The major point of origin of the Barbadian slave population was the Senegambia region of West Africa, although parts of Nigeria, particularly the Ibo-speaking region along the Bight of Benin, were also tapped for slaves. The Africans who came to Barbados tended to share certain broad-based cultural beliefs. Their religious system was based on polytheism with a strong emphasis on animism and sympathetic magic. This was partially transferred to Barbados with the practise of obeah. Poole's account of the island of 1753 notes *"among the Blacks in this country are some that are called Obeah Negroes, which are supposed by the others to have the power of inflicting Injury or Punishment upon such as attempt to rob their Plantation or Provision Ground."* He gives an interesting example of a *"young Negro Woman, that in going along near the Provision Ground of one of these Obeah Men, and stepping in a Puddle of Water there, was taken with a sudden Disorder, in a Manner she could not describe, but saying that immediately upon stepping into the Water, she felt as tho' her Soul was going from her ... All possible Care was taken of her, but to no Purpose, for tho' healthy and strong before, yet she wasted away extremely fast and died."*

Africans viewed the spirit world as being linked in manifest ways to this physical world and regularly practised ancestral consultation to tap into the body of accumulated knowledge of the deceased, who could be helpful in the right circumstances but who could also be equally capricious and malicious if the correct rituals were not observed.

The Senegalese proverb *"The dead are not dead, they are all around us"* encapsulated this broadly-held West African belief, echoes of which may be seen in a still surviving practise of many Barbadians of letting a few drops of rum fall to the ground from a newly opened bottle for the

ABOVE: A contemporary artist's portrait of an Obeah woman
Copyright: Institute of Jamaica

OPPOSITE RIGHT: Large scale labour needs changed the racial composition of Barbados and the rest of the Caribbean. Estimates range from 20 to 40 million African people sold into slavery
Courtesy: *History of Slavery*, 1978, by Susanne Everett

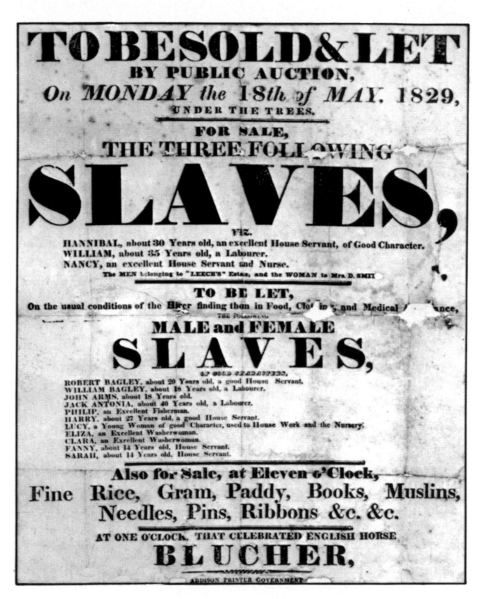

duppies (spirits) - a half-remembered form of libation torn from its traditional ancestral foundation.

More importantly, from an economic perspective, the Africans who came were agriculturalists well versed in aspects of tropical agriculture which would prove invaluable for Barbados' outstanding economic growth in the 17th Century. Nor was it only as agricultural labourers that they contributed but, as this observer noted in 1750, *"Negroes here are the most common Musicians who also are taught every Kind of Artifice: Hence they are principally employ'd in Building, as Carpenters, Masons, Bricklayers."*

The planter class consolidated its political and socio-economic control over the island during the 17th Century. Certainly the principal political development during this period was the involvement of the island in the mid-century political trauma better known as the English Civil War. As members of royalist families took up residence on Barbados during the 1640s, fleeing civil strife in England and attracted to Barbados by the potential of the sugar industry, a political split occurred between the supporters of Cromwell and parliament and those of Charles I. Not merely an extension of English political struggles, the situation in

SLAVERY

by Anthony Philips

It was in 1642 that sugar took root in Barbados, which had previously grown mainly tobacco and cotton and had supported a population of 18,000 white males. By the end of the 17th Century the exports of Barbados to Britain, which comprised almost entirely of sugar, were worth more than the exports of all the rest of the British American colonies put together.

Meanwhile the population had entirely changed. It was the day of the takeover bid. The many small plantation owners had given way to a few extremely wealthy planters and the number of slaves had increased tremendously.

Where Barbados led the other Caribbean islands followed.

The total number of slaves carried by the Atlantic slave trade from its beginning until its end has been variously estimated. As, at least, fifteen million men and women.

First sporadically occupied by visiting bands of Arawaks, Barbados was permanently settled from 1627 when a shipload of Englishmen with a number of captured Africans arrived. By 1680 Barbados was at the height of its wealth and influence based on sugar and slavery. But the white planters hated and feared the hordes of restive black captives with whom they had surrounded themselves. So, in Dunn's summation, *"sunny Barbados was a land of paradox in 1680, both parvenu and traditional, both complacent and insecure, the richest and yet in human terms the least successful colony in English America."*

For two hundred years the system of slavery prevailed in Barbados. Its end had been brought about largely through external pressures. The oppressors and the oppressed and their descendants had slowly to fashion a new society. The emancipation of the slaves in 1838 had left the structure of ownership unchanged and significant changes came very slowly. The land, trade and commerce, the professions and the civil service were in the hands of the wealthy white minority. The new economic relationship was one of white capital and black labour. The heritage of slavery was a racist and class-conscious society, a dependent economy and the lack of even rudimentary social services.

The vast majority of the slaves came from West Africa; Calabar and Lagos in Nigeria were the chief slave centres. The British, Dutch, French, Danes, Portuguese, Brandenburgers and Swedes had between them nearly 50 forts along the West African coast.

Liverpool, Bristol and London, all in Britain, had the lion's share of the slave trade. By 1770 half the total slave trade of the Atlantic was carried by nearly two-hundred British ships with cargo space for nearly 50,000 slaves. The French had capacity for 30,000 and the Portuguese for 10,000.

Some of the slaves were carried by companies and others by individual traders. Triangular trade existed where cloth, hardware, spirits and beads were traded for slaves, gold and ivory which were then traded for sugar, cotton and tobacco. The round trip usually took about six months.

On the slave plantation, the slave was controlled by custom rather than by law. Similarly, habit played a great part, so that one slave driver looked after a gang of about fifty slaves.

Normally, the slaves proffered mainly passive resistance: malingering, bad workmanship, carelessness or malice, as in the destruction of property such as the burning of canefields, damaging tools, or cruelty to animals. Running away was another instance of passive resistance. But there was always a threat of force and there were few places to hide.

The work-day of the slave was from dawn to dusk, with a break of half-an-hour for breakfast and two hours in the middle of the day.

But extra hours had to be worked at crop-time and there was in fact no legal limitation of working hours. A seasonal slack period was avoided by having cane planting follow hard on the end of each crop. The slaves were also used in building roads, aqueducts, mills, and Great Houses.

Agriculture was performed by three gangs: the third gang was comprised of children and undertook light tasks, such as picking grass and weeding. The second gang comprised of teenagers and fragile women and they undertook all but the heaviest tasks. These were preformed by the first gang who cleared the ground, dug caneholes, planted the canes and put out the manure.

The system of slave labour allowed for an extensive use of labour, most inefficiently and unimaginatively. There was little use made of machinery such as the plough or harrow. Slaves were easily replaceable and the greed of the masters constantly led to overworking them.

Among the privileged group of slaves were the artisans - sugar boilers, distillers, carpenters, coopers and masons - who were treated much better than the field slaves because they were more valuable and less dispensable. Their skills were of the greatest importance to the successful operation of the plantation. There was a habit of rewarding them for good work rather than punishment for bad work. This helped to provide incentive.

Large numbers of domestic slaves - butlers, housekeepers, cooks, laundresses, maids, grooms, coachmen, gardeners - were drafted in to allow the masters and their families to live the good life.

Jobbing slaves were in many cases owned by non-plantation whites, who hired them out as laundresses,

maids or coachmen to the wealthy. Others operated as porters and boatmen in the towns and harbours. Many worked as dispensers and attendants in retail shops - their owners picking up their wages. Such jobbing slaves in town had to be licensed and their movements were closely regulated and circumscribed.

In Barbados and the other British colonies the slave was regarded as a person with potential criminal intent. The slave as merchandise became an item of private property. In legal terms the slave was both real estate and chattel.

There was compensation for a slave hanged by the state. Crimes of trespass and robbery could be committed against slaves. The status of the slave as property did provide some protection against injury as the master had the right to sue for damages. Laws against social and economic mobility controlled the activities in which slaves might participate. Slaves were not permitted to own horses or livestock, nor to grow staple crops such as coffee, indigo and sugar. They were not to be buried in coffins similar to those of the whites.

Even the free people of colour were prevented from owning more than eight acres of land since the ownership of ten acres qualified one for the vote.

Severe punishments were laid down for running away and conspiracy. The penalty for striking a white person was death or mutilation - losing a leg, hand or ears. By contrast, in Barbados, the penalty for the deliberate killing of one's own slave or another person's slave was a mere fine of £15 and £25.

Slaves could not be called as witnesses in the ordinary law courts.

The Slave Laws were slightly improved in the latter part of the 18th Century. The master's duty towards his slaves was outlined with reference to allowances of clothing, food, medicine and holidays: there was a general codification of custom.

Further, there were also attempts to prevent mutilation and barbarous punishments and to limit the number of lashes on any occasion to thirty-nine.

Slaves were now also exposed to religious instruction from Baptist, Moravian, Methodist, Anglican and Roman Catholic missionaries. The splitting up of families was ended; slaves were admitted as witnesses in courts and were secured in their property. Manumission was to be allowed if the slave could afford it.

The free coloured group would have been glad to detach themselves from their relation to the slaves and to identify themselves with the dominant class of whites. But there was no welcome for them in the white world. Their descent from slave stock caused them to be viewed almost universally as social and political outcasts among the free inhabitants.

Even their economic activities seemed unnecessary to the whites, who had come to accept that the business of management should be done by whites, while the work of nearly all laborious occupations could be performed by slaves. Like the many poor whites who had been driven from the islands by the pressure of slave labour, the free coloured people found their economic opportunities severely limited by the ever-increasing spread of the slave system. But, unlike the poor whites who emigrated, the free coloured could not leave the islands since there was nowhere else for them to go.

Karl Watson

They had therefore to compete with the slaves for employment or attempt to penetrate occupations in which the whites had established themselves.

In their efforts to find a place in the economic life of the island, the free coloured faced even greater disadvantages than the poor whites, since they were hindered rather than helped by the white group which effectively controlled most economic activities.

They were referred to as the *"Unappropriated People,"* a term used by Jerome Handler as the title of his book about the free coloured and free black groups in Barbados.

Social structure was clearly reflected in the forms of political organisation. Population was heterogeneous in ethnic origin and status, but the ruling class was homogeneous in character.

Only the whites were allowed an active part in political life. The free coloured, whether born free or manumitted, were customarily held to be without political rights. In Jamaica the Legislature sometimes granted some of the rights of white subjects to free persons of colour by private acts covering individual cases.

Also, they were held to be ineligible for any public or parochial office or for militia commissions and they were not allowed to serve as jurors.

Slavery in some societies had been the basis on which a high culture had been developed. For example, in Athens the citizens, freed from the concern of humdrum daily toil, had used their leisure in the creation of a civilization which had attained the highest standards of excellence in politics and political thought in sculpture, in comedy and tragedy, in poetry and philosophy.

In the Caribbean, however, the level of formal culture seems to have been inverse in ratio to the number of slaves and their masters.

It would be much later that the two cultures, European and African, combined to create a creole culture containing elements of both.

Barbados reflected the dynamics of an internal struggle for political dominance among emerging groups on the island.

By 1649, the royalist planters emerged dominant and exiled many of their opponents. With the execution of Charles I, sentiment on the island rose so high that the royalist-dominated House of Assembly declared the island free of the control of Cromwell and parliament in 1650. This early unilateral declaration of independence was accompanied by a stirring manifesto which ends with the lines *"we cannot think that there are any amongst us, who are so simple and so unworthily minded, that they would not rather chuse a noble death, than forsake their ould liberties and privileges."*

Parliament responded by sending out a fleet to Barbados under the command of Sir George Ayscue in 1651 to defeat the royalist sympathizers. Recognizing the strength of the Barbadian land forces, Sir George was happy to control the seas, make occasional raids and encourage a split in the ranks of the Barbadians. This achieved, he felt confident enough to land troops near to Speightstown on 17 December 1651. An indecisive land battle ensued with casualties on both sides but with no clear cut victory. But the end was in sight, for a prominent planter, Colonel Modyford, with over 1,000 men under his command, deserted Lord Willoughby and his royalist supporters. The balance of power now shifted in favour of Sir George Ayscue and with an army of over 4,000 foot soldiers and cavalry, he pursued Lord Willoughby and his 3,000 men to an area above Oistins. Before an engagement of forces took place, however, Willoughby surrendered and pleaded for peace. This was accepted and Articles were signed at Ye Mermaid's Inn, Oistins on 17 January 1652 which confirmed the island's capitulation to the authority of the Commonwealth, but which also confirmed the parliamentary privileges of the local House of Assembly, including the right to enact laws. Barbados, therefore, although technically a colony, enjoyed relative constitutional autonomy, a situation which persisted into the late 19th Century, when, in its reorganization of Empire, Britain greatly reduced the internal semi-self-governing powers of her colonies under the new dispensation of Crown Colony government, a fate which Barbados escaped because the islanders resented and fought against any attempt to annul their institutions.

By the late 17th Century Barbados had become a completely settled, mature sugar exporting country. The 1680 map by Ford shows this transition clearly. All arable land was cleared, subdivided into some 700 plantations and over 2,000 small holdings and put under intensive

Sir George Ayscue
Courtesy: Barbados Our Island Home, 1960, by F A Hoyos

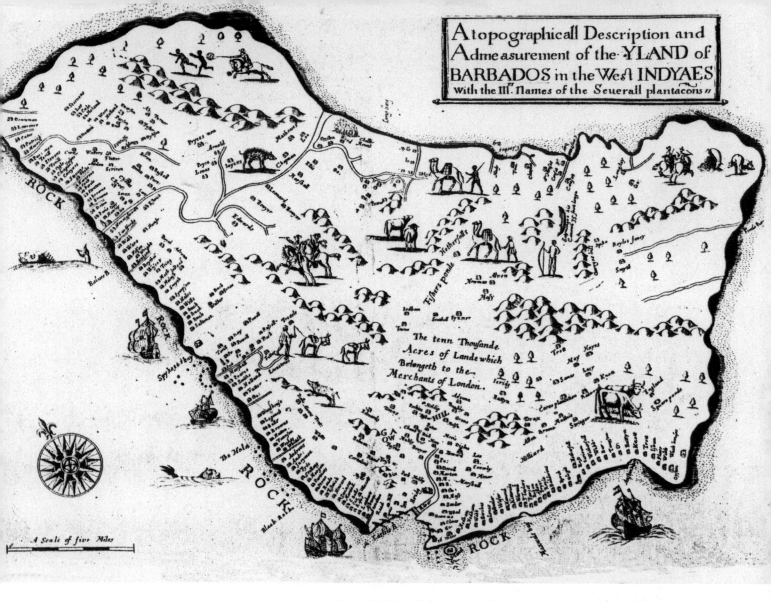

ABOVE: Ligon's Map made by John Swan c. 1640. Camels were tried as 'beasts of burden' but were no match for the torturous tracks

Courtesy: Barbados Museum and Historical Society

RIGHT: The planter class consolidated its political and socio-economic control over Barbados during the 17th Century

Photo courtesy; Karl Watson

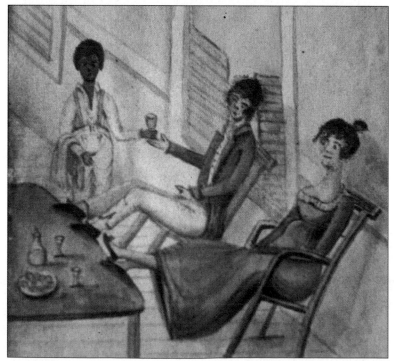

57

cultivation. A network of roads had been created, linking all parishes, and the 36 forts which lined the west and south coasts protecting the island from invasion.

Internally, society had become stratified along lines of class and colour and was generally made up of rich and poor whites and black slaves with severe distinctions between the free and the unfree. Although, it must be pointed out that the treatment meted out to poor whites was often little different from that given to black slaves, as this deposition made in 1705 by Margaret Fisher clearly shows, *"that she has been used by her master George Lillington with great cruelty and severity, that she has no necessary apparel, that her feet are so swelled by going barefoot that she is not able to go about her business, that her master ordered her to be beaten upon her bare body with a cowskin, that the stripes do still appear upon her body and arms, only for taking three oranges, when she had not eaten anything for 24 hours before."*

Several laws were passed by the local assembly, whose prime objective was to maintain social control and stability and to keep the slave population in check.

Insubordinate or threatening behaviour, sabotage, running away or any efforts at physical resistance on the part of the slaves was met with severe and often brutal reprisal and frequently by death. Yet, since society cannot exist in a heightened state of tension indefinitely, daily life was one of compromise and adjustment. Provided the laws controlling master/slave relationships were not too obviously broken, they could be, and often were bent, in an effort by the slaves to make life more bearable.

The theoretical ideal situation may have been absolute control by the planters, but reality was different. A few examples will suffice. The myth is often repeated that planters deliberately set out to eradicate any vestige of African culture retained by their slaves in order to better dominate and control them. This is not true. In fact, quite the opposite occurred, and planters encouraged social and cultural interaction among slaves in which West African forms of dancing and drumming were the norm. The laws theoretically controlled movement, yet slaves moved about freely during both day and night. A proclamation from the governor in 1748 noted, that *"it is Notorious that Negroes frequently do, in the most insolent and tumultuary manner assembled meet together in all parts of the Island and move especially in and about the Bridgetown."* Failure to control these 'midnight Cabals', it was felt, was due to *"remissness and supineness of the white inhabitants, magistrates and JP's, who were lax in their duties and did not enforce the laws."*

OPPOSITE: Insubordinate or threatening behaviour, sabotage, running-away or any efforts at physical resistance on the part of the slaves was met with severe and often brutal reprisal and frequently by death
Photo courtesy: Karl Watson

The laws forbade slaves to carry weapons or to dress well, yet pictorial and archaeological evidence shows that slaves ignored these regulations whenever possible. A slave was first and foremost seen as an economic investment without whose labour and productivity the sugar industry would collapse. Many planters openly argued that it was far better to allow recreational and cultural activities to the slaves on the grounds that *a cheerful slave would work harder.*" So the system therefore incorporated rewards for slaves who cooperated. Slaves themselves were not completely powerless, and often manipulated masters if the opportunity presented itself. One such area was the internal marketing system, in which slaves participated, producing, buying and selling. Despite a series of laws passed to prevent these activities, they provided such an essential service that, in 1784 the authorities bowed to the inevitable and established a slave market in Bridgetown. Though bereft of the legal status of free men and women, slaves on Barbados enjoyed one powerful psychological advantage - they were in the majority, and in many areas of human activity and behaviour, often paradoxically so, were so indispensable to their masters that a reverse dependent relationship arose, leaving one to wonder who was the master and who was the slave.

This relationship was observed by visitors and wonderfully caricatured in the late 18th Century cartoon which depicts a white creole woman looking out of her upstairs bedroom window and calling to one of her female slaves below, *"Phibbbah, I'm tired, come and take my head out of the window."* A gross exaggeration but focusing on the abnormality of relationships fostered by the institution of slavery.

Attempts at outright revolt were quickly suppressed. Slave plots were revealed on several occasions in the 17th Century, but each time the ringleaders were identified and executed. After the 1694 plot, there were no further attempts at self liberation by the slaves until 1816, when the largest and best organized slave revolt took place. The revolt was conceptualized by three free coloured men, Washington Franklin, Cain Davis and John Richard Sargeant, and its subsequent leadership included a slave named Bussa, whom oral tradition remembers as a brave slave and capable fighter. Three days of burning, pillaging and pitched battles took place. This attempt also ended in defeat for the slaves who were unable to match the fire power of the combined forces of the local militia and the British regiments stationed on the island.

The 18th Century was one of consolidation for the island. With the frontier days of the 17th Century behind and the heady financial and land

ABOVE: The laws forbade slaves to carry weapons or to dress well, yet pictorial and archaeological evidence shows that slaves ignored these regulations whenever possible

OPPOSITE: Slaves were not completely powerless and often manipulated their masters by participating in internal marketing - producing, buying an selling - despite laws to prevent these activities

OVERLEAF: A high standard of dress existed - even though laws and regulations forbid slaves doing so

Photos courtesy: Karl Watson

speculations caused by the sugar boom now over, the island settled down to the serious business of competing with the other sugar-producing islands of the Westindies. Several technological innovations were introduced which helped, but a finite land space and near exhausted soil made it difficult to maintain production levels.

One solution was to import additional African labour so that, by 1750, the slave population had risen to some 65,000 individuals, whereas the white population had declined by some 40 percent from its maximum 17th Century total of 30,000 to some 18,000 souls. After 1750, some demographic changes took place which differentiate Barbados from other Westindian colonies of the time. Very slowly, the slave population moved to a point of natural growth as opposed to the other islands which continued to experience a situation where deaths exceeded births, thus making it necessary to rely on the slave trade to maintain population levels. Many factors caused the Barbadian slave population to behave differently. Among them, one must point out that there were more women than men. There was a very high percentage of native born or Barbadians among the slave population which meant that women were younger and more psychologically disposed to bear children. The island was generally healthier, food was more readily available and the low master/slave ratio resulted in a better quality of life for the slaves (relative to what slaves experienced in the other islands). The white population failed to grow because natural increases were constantly siphoned off through migration, primarily to north America.

During the 18th Century, the process of creolization contributed to the emergence of an identifiable Barbadian character. The plural attributes of West African and west European culture merged to form a more homogeneous body, a process facilitated by the fact that culture is not transmitted through genes but through a learning and socialization process. In the confines of a small tropical island, with a flat enough surface to facilitate easy communication, African and European consciously and unconsciously borrowed and adapted each other's cultural patterns and in so doing wove something new, different and shared. This was the crucible from which the 'Bajan' emerged.

One example, that of language, will suffice. English, not Twi or Efik or Gaelic became the sole language on the island, but it was a creolized variety, different from the mother tongue. As early as 1732, Barbadian white women were accused of *"several great foibles, such as valuing yourselves too much on your Negroes, lisping their language, as slaves, using*

OPPOSITE: There were a very high proportion of native born or Barbadians among the slave population which meant that women were younger and more psychologically disposed to bear children
Photo courtesy: Karl Watson

64

them too familiarly." George Washington, who resided in the island in 1750, also observed that *"the Ladys generally are very agreeable but by ill custom ... affect the Negro style."* Dr R Poole, who visited the island in 1753, agreed with Washington's observation, pointing that Barbadian whites *"run too much into the Negro Brogue in their Language."* Dr Pinckard, an astute observer who wrote a fascinating account of the island at the end of the 18th Century, regarded linguistic changes as one of the *"most prominent characteristics"* of the island he wrote to a friend saying, *"to convey to you, by the pen, any idea of their manner of speaking is utterly impossible: to be comprehended, it must be heard ... nor is this wearisome pronunciation confined to the people of colour, it occurs likewise among the whites."*

Coupled with the emergence of a social and cultural awareness of a Barbadian self came political consciousness. Because of racial, gender and class disqualifications, few participated directly in the political process. This does not mean there was no political awareness on the part of the majority of the population, but rather a realization that they were deliberately barred from participation in the political process which ultimately affected everyone.

Full adult suffrage was only achieved in 1950. Until then, internal politics were dominated by the local assembly made up of planters and lawyers. The 18th Century was marked by a constant struggle between the governor, representing the crown's interests, and the assembly, representing local interests. Time and time again, the local assembly resisted efforts to reduce their rights and seized every opportunity to expand their autonomy. In 1694, the assembly sent a not too polite message to the then Governor Russell, asserting that *"it is their privilege to make their own Rules, as the Parliament of England proceeds to make their Rules."*

The American Revolution of 1775 provided the local assembly with the opportunity to press their demands for increased parliamentary privileges, such as freedom of speech and exemption from arrest. The Stamp Duty Act affected all of Britain's colonies but, for areas of the Empire such as the Westindian colonies, their status as islands made them vulnerable to the British Navy, and the large slave populations presented problems of internal security. For these reasons, the islands did not rebel against the crown, although there was considerable pro-American sentiment. The Americans in particular accused the Barbadians of cowardice, but the planter leader of the House of Assembly, Sir John

OPPOSITE TOP: A cut-away artist's impression of a slave's house containing the barest essentials for survival
Copyright: Barbados Museum and Historical Society

OPPOSITE BOTTOM:
In total contrast, George Washington's home when in Barbados lacked nothing in comfort and space - even the black cab-driver was dressed in a top hat

66

Gay Alleyne, refuted these allegations, even though he himself was the leader of the local pro-American faction and regarded by the governor as a 'dangerous subversive'.

One of the effects of the American Revolution was to disrupt trade between north America and the Westindies. Since food imports from the northern colonies formed a large part of this trade, severe hardships and malnutrition resulted in many of the islands. Barbados also passed through a lean period, but survived better than most, because, as previously indicated, traditional agricultural practises on the island had always allocated at least one third of the island's arable acreage to food production. The island, however, was not exempt from the vagaries of nature, and in 1780 was hit by a powerful and destructive hurricane which killed 4,326 people. An eyewitness account says *"nothing has ever happened that has caused such universal desolation. Very few buildings are left standing on the estates. It is as yet impossible to make any accurate calculation of the number of souls who have perished in this dreadful calamity. Whites and blacks together, it is imagined to exceed some thousands, but fortunately few people of consequence are among the number. Many are buried in the ruins of the houses and buildings; many fell victims to the violence of the storm and inclemency of the weather; and great numbers were driven into the sea and there perished.... The loss to this country is immense; many years will be required to retrieve it."*

Other considerations however were looming. From the last quarter of the 18th Century onwards, sentiment in Britain started to turn against the slave trade in the first instance and secondly, against the institution of slavery itself. As for the first, the Barbados House of Assembly distinguished itself by being the only one of the Westindian representative bodies not to oppose the Act which abolished the slave trade in 1805. This was done for the wrong reasons however. Barbados had a slave population which was capable of reproducing itself, unlike the other islands which needed to continuously import Africans to maintain their population levels. By denying labour to their competitors, the Barbadian planters stood to gain economically.

The issue of Emancipation was fought bitterly since, like other Westindian planters, the Barbadians were wedded to the system of slavery and forecast the ruin of the sugar industry should Emancipation come about.

By the end of the 18th Century, a variety of factors, both internal and external, combined to bring unrelenting pressure to bear on local slave-owners.

Sir John Gay Alleyne refuted allegations that Barbadians were cowards because they vowed not to rebel against the crown during the American Revolution

Emancipation
A term in the Caribbean solely associated with the abolition of slavery. As one of the most significant events in Westindian history, it involved the passing of Acts in six European parliaments over a period of more than 40 years before it was completed. The abolition of slavery began in the British Westindies in 1834 and ended in Cuba in 1878.

68

Gun Hill Signal Station was the largest and most important military outpost in a chain-link of signal stations established in 1818-19 after the revolt of 1816

Apprenticeship

The term used in the British Westindies to describe the four years immediately following the abolition of slavery in 1834, during which all ex-slaves over the age of six were obliged to work, without pay, for their former owners for three-quarters of each working week.

A contemporary medal struck in England to commemorate Emancipation

During the 18th Century, a third group had emerged in the Barbadian population. These were the free coloureds who, by 1800, numbered some 2,200 and had achieved a degree of socio-economic stability as tradesmen, shop owners, tavern and hotel keepers. Of course, levels of wealth varied enormously among this group, but a sufficient number of them were wealthy and articulate enough to petition the assembly constantly for civil rights. Their opportunity came in the 1816 slave revolt.

The slaves, aware of the success of the Haitian Revolution, conscious and informed of the political pressures being exerted by the Humanitarian Movement in Britain and believing that the time was right for a self liberation thrust, rebelled. As noted, they were defeated, and playing a part in their defeat were many free coloureds who had special units in the local militia and were the first to mobilize in support of the whites. A subsequent Act of 7 January 1817, as a reward for the "*greatest attachment and fidelity to the white inhabitants during the late insurrection gave free Negroes and people of colour the right to give evidence on any trial or suit of any nature or kind.*"

Following the 1816 revolt, the British government enforced an amelioration period, during which treatment of slaves was improved. But shifting economic forces in the British Empire, focusing more on India, in addition to a concerted anti-slavery effort by the Humanitarian Movement and continued pressure from below by the slave population throughout the Westindies culminated in the passage of the Act abolishing slavery in 1834.

Outright freedom did not come until 1838, for a transition period had been envisaged, during which master and ex-slave would adjust to the changed legal realities of abolition. This was known as the Apprenticeship Period. It was widely felt that ex-slaves would not freely work unless some degree of coercion was brought to bear upon them. This state of affairs turned out to be unsatisfactory to both parties, and as planters recognized that their fears of ruination were unfounded, full, outright Emancipation was enacted in 1838.

From this time forward, there was only one legal status for everyone in society, that of free man and free woman. Social and economic equality however did not come for the newly freed people, and feelings of racial and class differences remained strongly entrenched for over 100 years, so that it is possible to say that Barbados experienced a form of social 'as opposed to legal' apartheid during this period. The Barbadian historian,

Bruce Hamilton, writing in 1956, says *"The Barbadian ruling class, in its attitude towards the negroes, remained in general unwilling to accept the implications of Emancipation."*

Yet paradoxically, the one group in society which suffered most from Emancipation were the poor whites. Their role as militia tenants on the plantation ended with slavery and they were thrown off their small plots of land and left to their own devices. Many of their elderly and children died of malnutrition, and schemes were organized to assist them in migrating to St Vincent, Bequia, Grenada, Trinidad and the US, where opportunities for survival presented themselves.

The newly freed black population had their labour to sell and the sugar industry continued to require labour. Thus an uneasy status quo existed between white plantation owner and black labourer. Barbados enjoyed a surplus of labour, unlike many other territories such as Trinidad or Demerara, Berbice and Essequibo (subsequently Guyana) who felt constrained to import indentured labour from a number of geographic zones, but most heavily from the Indian subcontinent.

Nevertheless, in order to control Barbadian labour, a number of laws were enacted, which were coercive in principle and which confirmed and maintained the upper hand of the planter class. Acts such as the Masters and Servants Act, the Located Labourers' Act, and the Vagrancy Act were designed to restrict labourers' freedom of movement and choice of job. Even though wages were higher in neighbouring territories, especially Trinidad, emigration was discouraged as the planters wanted a secure source of labour at low wages. Since all land was privately owned, the ex-slaves had no choice but to sell their labour to the sugar industry. Although one should note that in the second half of the 19th Century, there was large scale migration to Trinidad and British Guiana and subsequently to Panama, where construction of the canal had started.

The spatial organization of the plantation which existed during slavery was changed once freedom was achieved. No longer was it necessary for labourer and plantation owners to live side by side. Security concerns and the need for vigilance, control and management, which made it essential for the slave quarters to be located next to the Great House, no longer existed. New living space was allocated, usually on the perimeter of the plantation or on rocky, non-arable land. This was the genesis of the tenantry system and labourers who sold their labour to specific plantations were either given house spots or rented houses at low rates.

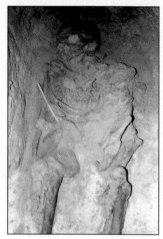

Late 17th Century burial, possibly of an indentured servant, recently excavated. Note the clay pipe with which the body was interred
Photo: Frederick Smith

OPPOSITE: The Emancipation monument - a larger-than-life statue by local artist and teacher Karl Broodhagan. It was erected at the St Barnabas Roundabout (ABC Highway) to commemorate the 150th Anniversary of Emancipation. The figure's arms are outstretched - symbolically breaking the chains of slavery. The sculptor's name for the statue was 'Slave in Revolt', however, some people prefer to think of it as the 'Bussa Statue'. Bussa was one of the leaders of the 1816 revolt who was killed in the fighting

70

THIS STATUE WAS ERECTED BY
THE GOVERNMENT AND PEOPLE
OF BARBADOS TO COMMEMORATE
THE 150TH ANNIVERSARY OF
THE ABOLITION OF SLAVERY
AND THE EMANCIPATION OF
BARBADIANS FROM THE INSTI-
TUTION OF SLAVERY.

THIS STATUE WAS UNVEILED BY

THE PRIME MINISTER

"DE TING COME FROM ENGLAND
TO SET WE FREE NOW LICK
AND LOCK-UP DONE WID
HURRAH FUH JIN-JIN..."

—A BARBADIAN FOLK SONG

RACHEL PRINGLE POLGREEN

by Warren Alleyne

Born around 1753, Rachel Pringle Polgreen was reputedly the daughter of an African slave woman and her master, William Lauder.

Lauder, a Scottish schoolmaster, had arrived in Barbados in 1750 or 1751. He had left England in disgrace as a result of his published attacks on the reputation of the celebrated poet, John Milton.

With the assistance of Rachel's mother, he established a small retail business called a 'huckster shop' in Roebuck Street. It was apparently in this neighbourhood that Rachel was born.

In August 1754 Lauder secured an appointment as Latin Master at Harrison's Free Grammar School, since developed into the present-day Harrison's College in Spry Street. He was, however, discharged in December 1762 when the Trustees discovered that during the entire period of eight years in which he was employed he had not instructed even a single scholar.

It is claimed that after Rachel reached maturity, her youthful charms aroused the unnatural interest of her father. His incestuous advances having been repelled, the dissolute Lauder handed Rachel over to the whipper whose function was to administer corporal punishment to unruly slaves.

The legend has it that she was saved by the timely intervention of a Captain Thomas Pringle of His Majesty's Ship *Centaur*, who happened to come upon the scene. The gallant captain took her away and installed her in a house in lower Bridgetown. She was probably not yet 18.

As Rachel was legally his slave, Lauder is said to have instituted legal proceedings to recover her but the matter was settled out of court when Pringle agreed to purchase her for an extortionate sum.

However, the death of William Lauder, and his recorded burial on 30 August 1771, reveals an element of fiction in the legend. Although Thomas Pringle is no imaginary figure, he did not achieve the rank of captain until 20 November 1776. He had been commissioned lieutenant on 30 November 1760 and, if he was serving on HMS *Centaur* at the time in question, it must have been as a lieutenant, not as captain.

At any rate, Rachel dropped her own surname of Lauder and adopted that of her new-found protector.

The relationship between the couple is said to have ended when Rachel resorted to a low subterfuge in order to strengthen her hold on his affections. On his return from a cruise she allegedly presented Pringle with an infant she had borrowed, representing it to be his son and heir. When the child's real mother turned up and demanded its return, Pringle left the scheming Rachel in disgust.

She however soon found another protector named Polgreen, and presently was letting it be known that her name was Rachel Pringle Polgreen.

The records of the vestry of St. Michael show that around 1780, Rachel was living in Back Church Street (now Suttle Street - St. Mary's Row). Her house carried a tax assessment of £6 per annum. In March 1781, however, her name was listed additionally for the first time among the names of persons owning property in Canary Street (the present St. George Street). She was stated to be the owner of a large house assessed at £50.

Sometime within the previous 12 months Rachel had acquired this property and established the country's first hotel.

At this time, the American Revolutionary War was in full swing with considerable naval activity in the Caribbean. Visiting officers of the Royal Navy welcomed the existence of this facility ashore where they could rest and relax after a spell at sea; consequently Rachel's hotel became quite popular.

In 1786, and again in 1789, HRH Prince William Henry, later King William IV, visited Barbados while serving as a naval captain on the Leeward Islands' Station. In the course of one of these visits the Prince took rooms at Rachel's hotel; and it is said that after wining and dining convivially one night, the Prince and his drunken companions proceeded to wreck the establishment. Rachel sat calmly at the doorway in an armchair while the crash of broken glassware, crockery and furniture resounded within the building, and a cloud of feathers floated downstairs from torn pillows and mattresses. When the revellers had completed their work of destruction and were leaving the premises, the Prince happened to notice Rachel sitting by the doorway, whereupon he capsized her chair, depositing her corpulent figure on the ground much to the amusement of the crowd which had gathered.

She accepted this indignity with no more than a mild protest, then arose and proceeded to take a careful inventory of the damage. The next morning, on hearing that the Prince's ship was preparing to sail, she sent him an itemised bill for £700. Without question he gave orders for it to be paid.

Rachel used the money to refurnish her hotel in a more sumptuous style and renamed it the Royal Naval Hotel in honour of her royal guest.

Rachel prospered, eventually becoming the owner of no fewer than ten properties in Canary Street, as well as her hotel.

She died on 23 July 1791. In her will dated 21 July and boldly signed RPP, she did not forget her former friend and protector, Thomas Pringle. She directed that her houses and lands were to be sold and, after her debts and funeral expenses had been paid, Captain Pringle was to be given one third of the residue of her estate.

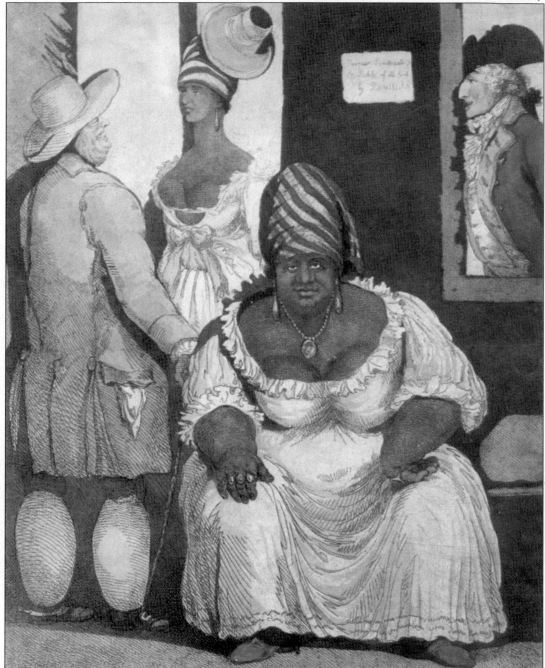

This caricature, executed in 1796 by the renowned Thomas Rowlandson (1756 - 1827), presents a complete picture of the life of his subject. Rachel is twice represented. Dominating the scene is the obese Rachel of middle life. At the peak of prosperity, she sits turbaned and bejewelled on a divan beside her doorway, gazing into the distance. The wall behind her carries a poster advertising the sidelines offered by the establishment:

Pawpaw Sweetmeats
and Pickles of all Sorts
By Rachel P.P.

In the background, symbolising the past, Rachel is seen again, this time as an attractive young woman in a white dress between the two figures who had the greatest influence on her early life. The coarse double-chinned man with whom she converses is her father, William Lauder. Obviously fallen on hard times, his coat is shabby and torn and, additionally, he is severely afflicted with elephantiasis - the dreaded Barbados Leg - quite common in those times. The officer looking on from the window, is of course, Thomas Pringle, the naval officer who changed the whole course of her life.

Yet this arrangement continued only so long as the plantation received that individual's labour. If a neighbouring plantation offered marginally better wages or benefits or a better working atmosphere, then employment at that plantation almost automatically required the worker to abandon the house spot and physically relocate. Unless there was an exceedingly good relationship between plantation owner and worker, it was a case not only of '*take up your bag and walk*', but your house as well, which is the reason why Barbadian chattel houses of the working class were constructed of wooden sides which could be easily removed from their loose stone foundations and reassembled elsewhere.

Tenantries still exist in modern Barbados although much altered from their 19th Century beginnings and during the administration of Prime Minister Tom Adams, legislation was enacted which gave the occupiers of land in tenantries the option of purchasing in lieu of paying rent.

An echo of the time of slavery may still be heard on many of the island's plantations for frequently, the field next to the Great House is named 'Negro Field' or 'Negro Yard Field'. This place-name confirms that this area was once the location of slave houses and archaeological evidence of this is clearly seen after the sugar cane has been harvested, for if one walks through any 'Negro Field', paying close attention to the debris on the ground, bits and pieces of material culture from the past can be collected from the surface - remnants of the meagre possessions of the slaves who once lived on these spots some 200 years ago - bits of locally-made earthenware or imported china, pieces of clay pipes, buttons, coins and other artefacts.

The three decades leading up to Emancipation and the final abolition of slavery brought religious and educational changes. In response to proselytizing activities carried out by denominations such as the Moravians and the Methodists, the Anglican Church became more active in preaching the gospel - after 1800, the baptism registers of the Anglican Church show a marked rise in the number of slaves converted to Christianity.

The elevation of Barbados in 1825 as an independent see in the Church, under the leadership of the first bishop of Barbados, William Hart Coleridge, brought welcome changes, for the new bishop not only began an extensive church building programme throughout the island, but for the first time he spearheaded an effort to extend primary education to the children of poor free coloureds, slaves and poor white children. The extension of educational benefits to slave children was of particular

Redlegs

THE 'Redlegs' of Barbados, so named because they wore kilts when working in the sugar cane fields and their legs became sun burned and red, were poor, white Scottish people who had been either encouraged or coerced into leaving Britain for a new tropical destination. In Scotland, many had been thrown off the land, most of them were destitute and many had turned to crime as a means of survival. They were promised work and a new life. Some were even promised land. Little did they know of the harsh existence that awaited them. Their services were to be utilised in the sugar cane fields, often beside African slaves.

The 'Redlegs' also known as 'Poor Whites' and 'Poor Backra' have been in Barbados for more than 300 years and have remained the poorest community in society. The white indentured servants came to Barbados without a fixed contract with a particular planter, as a result, they were sold like cattle in the open market by merchants. In 1682 legislation intervened to regulate the price of servants. They were treated as commodities and their lives governed by the plantocracy.

As they were becoming a more established fixture of the plantation society, the poor whites began to grow and sell their own vegetables from their gardens. The sale of produce was affected by slave marketing strategies. Huckstering became an aggressive and questionable form of selling amongst black slaves and white servants.

"*In Barbados many whites, of both sexes, till the ground without any assistance from Negroes, and poor white women often walk many miles loaded with the produce of their little spots, which they*

exchange in the towns for such European goods as they can afford to purchase."

Not unlike the Africans, the white servants carried their produce to market on their heads and their babies swaddled to their hips. Cross-cultural habits were not common but they did exist as the Africans and Scottish shared common experiences.

Some servants were allocated land which was often located in rocky, sandy or wet locations. The best land was always kept for growing sugar cane. The poor whites were total outcasts from the white plantocracy. The only thing they had in common was the colour of their skin.

Beckles, Natural Rebels, 1989

William Hart Coleridge

OVERLEAF: A sugar plantation, c. 1885. The slave houses are located on the hills in the distance, on ground where little will grow. The sugar mill is surrounded by vegetable patches and the Great House rests in the shade. The rest of the plantation has been stripped of all trees and shrubs

importance, for this was the foundation on which the island's subsequent famed educational achievements would rest

Not all slaves, one should note, were illiterate. Documentary sources testify to this. In fact, in the second half of the 18th Century, one of the better known teachers of children of the mercantile elite of Bridgetown was an African slave. The learning process was helped by a few rectors like Reverend Duke of St Thomas who sponsored young slave children at private schools in his parish, and by small groups of white women, who held informal classes at a few plantations on the island. In 1818, the Colonial Charity School was created under the patronage of the then Governor, Lord Combermere, to give free education to children of poor, free coloured and of slaves. In its first year of operation, 32 slave children were admitted. However, in general, prevailing elite opinion in the 18th and early 19th Centuries was that education for the masses of any complexion was potentially destructive to the existing system since it was felt that an educated underclass would become unruly and possibly revolutionary.

Therefore Coleridge's move was a bold one and in this he was supported by visionaries like Samuel Jackman Prescod, the first non-white elected member of the House of Assembly (he was elected to represent Bridgetown in 1843) and London Bourne, born a slave of black slave parents in 1793 who, after self-manumission' rose to become Barbados' most successful black businessman, civic personality, black nationalist and campaigner for civil rights for coloured and black people. (It is tragic that his surviving residence and place of business was demolished in 1994 to make way for a car park).

Barbados soon had almost as many schools as the rest of the other British colonies of the Eastern Caribbean combined. By 1834, there were 155 charity schools on the island, as compared to eight in 1825. In the 15 other islands (Jamaica excepted), there were 213 schools. This was a promising beginning, although seen from today's perspective, where access to education is regarded as an absolute right of children, it left much work to be done, for Schomburgk, a contemporary historian calculated in 1845 only 34 percent of Barbadian children attended school. But the situation was constantly improved by the self help ethos of the freed population which came into play immediately after Emancipation. In an 1859 speech Governor Hincks declared, *"I know no country in which the labouring classes have done so much for education as they have done in Barbados."* In the 1850s the Wesleyan Mission built five school houses,

75

EMIGRATION FROM BARBADOS

by Velma Newton

Writing in the late 1940s, Malcolm Proudfoot asserted that overpopulation in Barbados has been such that the only solution envisaged was emigration. Consequently, Barbadians have been among the great emigrants from the Caribbean.[1] However, Barbadians did not emigrate on a large scale until after British slave Emancipation in 1834 as a result of which ex-slaves were free to leave the island. By this time, most of the island's arable land was already owned by a sugar cultivating plantocracy, and free Barbadians could choose to:

• stay in Barbados and continue to work under the Tenantry System arrangement whereby they agreed to work a certain number of hours on a plantation, live in a hut owned by their employer, continue to be in danger of being evicted at short notice and have their wages subjected to fines and deductions for petty offences and failure to work the stipulated number of hours;
• migrate to Bridgetown and hope to find work, or
• emigrate.

Many chose to emigrate and, from 1835, hundreds left Barbados for the Windward Islands, British Guiana and Trinidad where wages were higher and land was available for small farming activity. Barbadians continued to emigrate to those places during the rest of the 19th Century, as wages at home, already low when compared to other islands, were occasionally slashed in response to decreases in the price being paid to Westindian sugar farmers by Britain, and as further economic hardship was caused by the occasional occurrence of droughts, hurricanes and outbreaks of typhoid and dysentery.[2]

Suffering after a year long drought in 1863 was so severe that the government officially sanctioned emigration for the first time and about 2,500 persons were allowed to leave for Antigua and St. Croix.[3] From this decade and continuing until well into the 20th Century they also emigrated to the United States, Honduras, Suriname, Peru, Brazil and other South American countries where railroad construction and banana cultivation provided employment. However, while several thousand may have emigrated to all these countries during the mid to latter part of the 19th Century and first two decades of the 20th Century, by far the greatest outward movement between 1880 and 1914 was to Panama where two French canal companies (during the 1880s) and from 1904 the United States government, undertook construction of the Panama Canal and relocation of the Panama Railroad. It has been conservatively estimated that the net population loss to Barbados caused by emigration to Panama between 1904 and 1914 was about 42,000.[4]

Largely due to emigration, after 1851 Barbados never recorded a population growth rate of higher than one percent, and between 1891 and 1921 the Panama movement would have been the main reason for a population decrease from 182,900 to 172,337 in 1911.[5] Other important consequences of the Panama movement were labour shortages, an increase in the female/male ratio and the enrichment of a number of Barbadians who, as recipients of 'Panama Money' from relatives, or as returning emigrants had the means to purchase land, set up shops and improve their economic welfare.[6]

As the demand for labour on the Panama Canal project decreased, there was a corresponding increase in emigration to Cuba to work on sugar estates, which accelerated during the First World War but came to an end during the early 1920s. Emigration to the United States also increased after 1900 and as no passports or even work permits were needed, Barbadians and other Westindians went there in large numbers to find work in the industrial cities of the north-east. The mid-1920s saw bans on emigration from the Caribbean islands being put in place in Cuba, the United States (in 1925) and in Venezuela (in 1929). Immediately after restrictions were instituted, large numbers of Barbadians and other Westindians were repatriated and this caused a considerable amount of suffering to families who depended on their remittances.[7]

The mid 1920s to the early 1950s were conspicuous for lack of large-scale emigration. However, a movement to the United Kingdom which commenced as a trickle at the end of the Second World War when reconstruction efforts were put in place and labour was needed, increased dramatically from about 1955 and continued apace until 1962. Then, the Immigration Act followed, in 1965, by the drastic recommendations in the White Paper on Immigration, resulted in restrictions being placed on emigration from the Commonwealth. After these developments, numbers emigrating to the United Kingdom from Barbados and the rest of the region were drastically reduced.

Altogether, about 300,000 Westindians were reported to have emigrated to the United Kingdom, most of whom were Jamaicans. Barbadians may have been about the second or third largest group, but all immigrants who were non-Jamaican were lumped together and as a result no statistics for Barbadians only were seen.[8]

During the mid 1960s the United States introduced a preference system of immigration based on family relationship to US residents, and Canadian policy shifted from emphasising race to education, training and skills as the main conditions of immigration. Both these developments were favourable to emigration from Barbados and the other Caribbean islands. For the period

1965 to 1974 the numbers emigrating to Canada and the United States were more or less the same, but as Canada began to experience economic problems, and passed the 1976 Immigration Act, the emigration to there declined.[9] By the early 1980s emigration to the United States accounted for 88 percent of the flow. Available data suggests that total emigration from Barbados during the 1970s could have been about 34,000, and when returnees are taken into account, net population loss could have been about 15,000.[10]

These movements to Canada and the United States, which, incidentally, included a large number of female nurses and educated persons contracting to work as domestics for short periods after which they would apply for landed emigrant status, have also now been reduced to a trickle as more restrictive immigration policies have been put in place in the host countries. There have therefore been no large-scale outward movements during the 1990s. The establishment of a campus of the University of the West Indies in Barbados in 1963 has increased the possibility of obtaining tertiary level education at home, at very little cost, and a number of Barbadian graduates have been able to obtain jobs for which the remuneration allows them to live comfortably at home. Yet, for most of the less fortunate, including the many jobless, emigration is still seen as the best avenue for economic self improvement. They wait for yet another avenue to open.

Notes
1. Malcolm Proudfoot. Population Movement in The Caribbean - New York: Negro University Press, 1970, p. 20.
2. Velma Newton. The Silver Men: British West Indian Emigration to Panama, 1850-1914 - Kingston: I.S.E.R., 1984, pp. 7-20.
3. G.W. Roberts. 'Emigration from Barbados' Social and Economic Studies, No. 3 September 1955, pp. 245-88.
4. Newton, p. 96.
5. Ibid., p. 101.
6. Ibid., pp. 101-108.
7. Proudfoot, pp. 20-21
8. See B.B. Levine. The Caribbean Exodus. - New York: Praeger, 1987.
9. Ibid.
10. Ibid. and Dawn Marshall. 'Migration as Circulation' Unpublished Paper. U.W.I., Cave Hill, Barbados, n.d., pp. 7-8.

80 percent of the costs of which were met by poor agricultural labourers, who recognized that education for their children provided economic and social mobility.

Coleridge also worked to bring about a first for Barbados. In 1711, Christopher Codrington bequeathed his sugar plantations in the parish of St John to the Society for the Propagation of the Gospel in Foreign Parts. He had envisaged the creation of a tertiary institution along the lines of Yale or Harvard, but squabbling and inertia made a mockery of his wishes. However, inspired by Bishop Coleridge's energy, the Committee of the Society set plans in motion which culminated in 1830 with the opening of Codrington College as a degree, granting institution, later affiliated to the University of Durham. It was the only place in the British West Indies where young Westindians in the region and could read for an academic degree until the creation of the University of the Westindies in Jamaica in 1948. Students came from leading grammar schools in Barbados, such as Harrison College and The Lodge School and from neighbouring islands.

The population of Barbados continued to grow. By 1871, the census counted 105,904 blacks, 39,578 coloureds and 16,560 whites. All categories had increased, despite the terrific mortality caused by the cholera epidemic of 1885 when over 20,000 people died in less than three months and the migration of thousands of workers. An observation on the size of the white population is in order, because it is linked to and sheds light on Barbados' economic performance after Emancipation. Unlike the other islands of the British Westindies, whose white populations fell dramatically after 1835, Barbados' white population grew, Jamaica for example losing almost 50 percent of its white population. This indicates a commitment to the island, a feeling of security and stability, and faith in the performance of the sugar industry which despite the challenges of *laissez-faire* economics and European beet sugar, continued to survive with production expanding.

British officials on the island held negative views about Barbadian whites. John Mitchinson, Bishop of Barbados in 1876, complained about their "*odious self complacency and narrow prejudice*" and said that they "*flattered themselves that the world consisted of white snails and that they were the world.*" Not so devastating but carping nevertheless was Governor Freeling's view, expressed in 1875, that "*the well-known characteristic of Barbadians is, also, to consider that they and their institutions are perfect, and to be indignant at criticisms from strangers.*"

Samuel Jackman Prescod

by Anthony Philips

FROM his youth, Samuel Jackman Prescod took the lead in pressing for the end to discrimination against the free coloured people. His radicalism alarmed older members of his group but the agitation and the support of the Colonial Office led to the passing of the Brown Privilege Bill in 1832.

Prescod also joined the campaign to end slavery. During the period of Apprenticeship, 1834-1838, he strove to prevent the planters from continuing their coercion of the labourers. In his newspaper, *The Liberal*, he showed himself to be the champion of fair play within the society.

After the onset of full freedom, from 1 August 1838, he launched into a campaign for the extension of the franchise. He believed that the people would only have a paper freedom if they could not participate in the political decision-making process. He formed a Liberal Party, a regional Colonial Union of The Coloured Classes, and a Barbados Auxil-

iary Branch of the British Anti-Slavery Society.

Little progress was made on the question of franchise extension, but Bridgetown was made into a constituency separate from St Michael. Prescod was elected to the House of Assembly at the first Bridgetown election of 1843 by what has come to be called a 'rainbow coalition' of white, brown and black people.

For some 20 years Prescod was re-elected annually to the House of Assembly. He strove for social justice and his integrity earned him the respect of all.

In 1862 he was appointed a judge of the Assistant Court of Appeal. This body sought to protect the people from unjust decisions of the magistrates' courts. In this sphere too, Prescod earned the gratitude of the people.

John Pope Hennessy

OVERLEAF: Aerial view of Codrington College

Relations between Barbados and Britain became strained over the issue of confederation. Britain was convinced that a union of the Windward Islands would be to the benefit of all. A sensible proposition, but underestimating the strong insular, almost xenophobic feelings of individual islands, which trade, immigration and CariCom officials still confront on a daily basis. In 1844, Sir Charles Grey, Governor of Barbados, in a speech at the opening of the House of Assembly, suggested that, united, the islands of the Eastern Caribbean would be stronger and more prosperous. This proposition was quite unattractive to the House of Assembly, as their reply shows, for they politely told the governor that *"at present, they entertain no larger hope for Barbados than that she may continue to move in her present orbit, with her light undimmed, and her usefulness and importance undiminished."*

Some 32 years later, a political crisis in Barbados was precipitated by attempts made by the Colonial Office to bring about a political union of Barbados and the Windward Islands. This poisoned political atmosphere was exacerbated by bad labour relations on many plantations and the harshness with which the Masters and Servants Act operated.

The governor of the time, John Pope Hennessy, who tried to implement the Colonial Office's instructions, was vilified and accused of seeking to destroy Barbados' political institutions and to replace them with Crown Colony government as had been done on the other islands. This latter accusation was certainly a correct one, as this was the plan of the Colonial Office in their scheme for imperial reorganization and the tightening of British control in the Westindies, in order to ennact various adjustments in the social arena, which it was felt the local planter class would not do, while at the same time guaranteeing the survival of the planter class and the sugar industry.

It was a balancing act which the Barbadian planter class thought would be detrimental to their interests, and so they formed a Defence Association for local protection, while carrying the protocolary and diplomatic fight to the Colonial Office. In this they were greatly helped by a man who was adjudged *"the most remarkable man of his place and period."* This was William Conrad Reeves, born in 1821, the son of a white doctor, Thomas Reeves, and a black slave, Peggy Phyllis. Reeves was a lawyer, who represented the parish of St Joseph in the House of Assembly and had been appointed Solicitor-General in 1875. A remarkable series of achievements for a non-white man in the Barbados

of that era. More accolades were to come his way for Reeves, with his cool intellect and understanding of constitutional principles, was able to strengthen Barbadian resolve to resist British efforts to, as he put it, *"undermine the constitution and lead to Crown Colony government."*

Eventually, a compromise was reached which enabled Barbados to retain its elected House of Assembly while at the same time agreeing to the formation of an Executive Committee *"for the transaction of public financial business,"* thus removing one of *"the most sacred rights of the people, that of initiating Money Bills in the House."* The Colonial Office felt that an intransigent attitude had changed to a more forward thinking one and that reforms would be forthcoming. In this view, they were not mistaken, although considered gradualism rather than radicalism was the order of the day. In 1884, a Franchise Bill was introduced and passed which extended the franchise. This was an important first step towards the eventual political empowerment of black people. In 1891, the hated Masters and Servants Act was repealed. On the other side, British officials abandoned their ideas of a confederation of the islands.

William Conrad Reeves

Reeves was appointed Attorney General and in, 1884, he became the first black Chief Justice of Barbados. Five years later, Queen Victoria made him a Knight of the Realm. Sir Conrad died in 1902, and has been relegated to a minor role in recent Barbadian historiography because of what many perceive to be his conservative character and unsympathetic attitude to his fellow black Barbadians.

The 20th Century therefore began with some socio-economic change, however slow and limited it might have been. Nevertheless, the structure of society remained essentially the same as it had been in the early 19th Century, since the island's economy continued to depend on the cultivation of sugar cane and the export of its by-products, sugar, rum and molasses, to markets in Britain and Canada. Concerned by the continuing economic decline in the Westindies as a whole, the Royal Commission of 1897 made a series of recommendations, many of which were put in place, including the prohibition of imported bounty fed beet sugar into Britain, the creation of an Imperial Department of Agriculture (initially located in Barbados and subsequently moved to Trinidad), subsidized sea transport and the provisions of loans to various islands. Canada for her, part, gave a 25 percent preference to Westindian sugar in 1897. With this assistance, the sugar industry on Barbados survived.

Plantations therefore, and the particular mentality of dominance and

CONTRASTS

by Anthony Philips

Racial classifications for 1891 and 1911

WHITE	Male	Female	Total whites
1891	7,339	8,274	15,613
1911	5,199	6,864	12,063

BLACKS	Male	Female	Total blacks
1891	73,766	92,927	166,693
1911	65,041	94,879	159,920

The extreme disproportion between the black majority and the dominant white minority - declining from about 8.5 percent of the population in 1891 to 7 percent in 1911 - had a range of repercussions in the political and general life of the community.

Barbados was primarily dependent upon the sugar industry which provided between 90 percent and 95 percent of exports. The plantation system which emerged from the slavery period was ill prepared for a wage labour system, despite the compensation money paid by the British Government to the plantation owners.

In Barbados, however, since all the land was occupied, black people had no alternative but to continue to work on the sugar plantations on the terms which the planters were willing to offer. The malaise of the sugar industry was of long standing. This industry was indeed a peculiarly vulnerable operation. The efficient growing of sugar cane required the application of scientific agricultural techniques which the planters were slow to adopt.

It is further subject to natural calamities such as drought, hurricanes and plant diseases. The manufacture of sugar (a separate operation usually also undertaken by the planter) again required the utilisation of advancing science and technology.

Marketing too was a considerable problem owing to price fluctuations, and in the late 19th Century, the European policy of granting bounties on the export of beet sugar.

Sugar was the basis of the country's economy and its social structure reflected the heritage of the slave society. The tiny number of upper class planters, merchants, professional and high officials were almost exclusively white. The middle class included whites of lesser social standing, such as plantation managers, small businessmen, clerks and civil servants, along with brown and black people of similar occupations and incomes. The great majority of the people, however, were working class and overwhelmingly black. The poor whites were notable and highly visible exceptions. There was a stark contrast between the lives of the rich and those of the poor.

The mansions and the shanties are part of the contrast. Farley Hill, the most magnificent of the mansions, has been described many times, but perhaps never better than by Froude following his visit in 1887:

"Passing through a hall, among a litter of Carib curiosities, we entered the drawing-room, a magnificent saloon extending with various compartments over the greater part of the ground-floor storey. It was filled with rare and curious things, gathered in the days when sugar was a horn of plenty, and selected with the finest taste; pictures, engravings, gems, antiquarian relics, books, maps, and manuscripts... the English settlers... had the tastes of a grand race... It was a palace with which Aladdin himself might have been satisfied, one of those which had stirred the envying admiration of foreign travellers in the last century, one of many then, now probably the last surviving representative of Anglo-West Indian civilisation."

By contrast, areas such as Church Village, Racoon Quarters and Forty-Leg Alley were cluttered with little huts in an overcrowded condition which rendered them liable to outbreaks of epidemic diseases. In some of the localities one found 'houses packed so closely to each other that the windows could not be opened.' The urban tenantries had developed without any regard to roads, drainage or ventilation. Traves noted that, on the outskirts of the town and indeed all over the island, were to be found *"in rows, in clumps, in halting lines, or in infrequent dots"* the mean dwellings of the black people. He described them as:

"Tiny huts of pewter-grey wood, raised from the ground on a few rough stones and covered by a roof of dark shingles. They are as simple as the houses a child draws on a slate a thing of two rooms, with two windows and one door. The windows have sun shutters in the space for glass."

He added: *"It makes one gasp to think how many human beings crowd into these tiny rooms after sundown."*

Many of the houses had earthen floors, on which sand was sprinkled from time to time. Aspinal was sufficiently insensitive to state that the black people were *"content to pass their lives"* in wooden huts which were so light and flimsy that they fell an easy prey to hurricanes.

It is necessary to bear in mind that everyone in Barbados fell within the money economy. There was no traditional or subsistence sector, no barter system. Some food crops were grown on plantations and small holdings - sweet potatoes, yams, other vegetables and fruit - some livestock gave a partial supply of milk and fresh meat, and there was a fishing industry. But all of these together provided only a fraction of the food needs of the people. Therefore, foodstuffs had to be imported as well as building materials, cloth and clothing, and a wide range of necessities and luxuries. Everyone needed a money income.

subservience they generated, continued to dominate the physical and psychological landscape of Barbados.

Production totals of sugar had increased steadily, as acreage previously utilized for growing food crops and fodder were converted to sugar cane fields. The old pre-Emancipation pattern of land usage, which saw only one-third of arable plantation land used for sugar cultivation, was abandoned. A shift began to increased centralization of factories. Previously every estate however small, erected its own windmill and boiling-house and milled and produced its own sugar for export. Loans from Britain and the creation of the Sugar Industry Agricultural Bank helped to speed the transition from many wind-driven mills to fewer steam operated factories. From a total of 500 mills in 1840, the number dropped to 52 in 1946 and the last windmill ceased operation in 1947. Today sugar is produced by three factories: Andrews, Bulkeley and Portvale. Other technological innovations were put in place, including the increased use of fertilizers and the constant upgrading of new varieties of sugar cane that were both disease-resistant and contained higher amounts of sucrose.

Barbados was fortunate in this respect, because a solid foundation for sugar cane research had been laid in the last decades of the 19th Century with the work of J R Bovell on the propagation of new, improved varieties of sugar cane based on the discovery of sugar cane seedlings in 1858 by an overseer I Harper, on Highland Plantation, then owned by James W Parris.

Bovell's work was utilized throughout the sugar industry worldwide, but was of special importance in the Caribbean, particularly in the growth of the industry in the Spanish speaking islands of Cuba, Puerto Rico and the Dominican Republic. His lasting contribution can be seen today in the advances made by the Westindies Central Sugar Cane Breeding Station at Groves, St George.

Sugar continued to dominate the island's economy until the 1970s. Despite the effects of the Great Depression which brought on a virtual collapse of the prices of agricultural products throughout the world, no viable alternative presented itself to the owners of land and capital in Barbados. Sugar cane is without a doubt ideally suited to the soil and rainfall conditions of the island, and harvesting of green cane as opposed to burning has helped to control erosion and build up the thin soil layer which covers the coral cap of Barbados.

In 1946, sugar provided jobs for one third of the working population

THE WEST INDIA REGIMENT

by Brian Dyde

The West India Regiment came into being in 1888, but before that date each of its two battalions has enjoyed an unbroken, independent existence as one of the British Army's numbered West India regiments for nearly 100 years. At one time during the long wars with France between 1793 and 1815 there has been no less than 12 such units, with a combined strength of perhaps 10,000 men.

For 12 years after 1795, when the first of these regiments was authorised, the vast majority of the troops were slaves, either purchased by the Army authorities in the Westindies or brought direct from Africa. Their manumission in 1807 represented the freeing of the largest number of slaves at any one time anywhere in the Americas prior to the general abolition of slavery in the British Westindies in 1834. But even as free men they could hold no rank higher than that of sergeant, and this continued throughout the entire history of the regiments. Right up until the last remaining battalion was disbanded in 1927 all the officers and senior NCOs were white.

During the 19th Century the First and Second West India Regiments, sometimes aided by briefly re-raised Third and Fourth regiments, provided garrisons throughout the Caribbean and, from 1819 onwards, in all the British West African colonies. The garrison in Barbados was not withdrawn until 1905. Westindian soldiers assisted in the early stages of the creation of Nigeria, took part in several of the seven Asante wars which helped produce the present boundaries of Ghana, and played a decisive role in the history of both Gambia and Sierra Leone.

Punitive expeditions against hostile tribesmen in the Gambia produced two recipients of the Victoria Cross, Britain's highest award for gallantry. In 1866 Private Samuel Hodge from Tortola in the British Virgin Islands, while serving in the Fourth West India Regiment displayed outstanding bravery during an attack on the fortified village of Tubab Kolan, and became only the second man of African descent to win the award. Twenty-six years later, a Jamaican Lance-Corporal, William Gordon of the First West India Regiment, was seriously wounded in saving the life of his commanding officer in an attack on Toniataba, and he also earned the VC.

From 1858 onwards the full ceremonial dress of the soldiers was the colourful Zouave uniform of scarlet, white and blue, worn with a red fez wound round with a white turban. This uniform is still seen today, worn by the band of the Barbados Defence Force and also the Jamaican Military Band. Although uniformed in this way the regiments were and always had been integral parts of the British Army, and were never classified with colonial units such as the King's African Rifles or the West African Frontier Force. Unfortunately none of their exploits in the Caribbean or Africa ever succeeded in raising their status in the eyes of the rest of the army or the British political establishment. After the First World War, during which the two battalions of the West India Regiment were given only supporting roles in out-of-the-way places, recruiting slowed to a trickle and the regiment was disbanded in 1927. It was re-raised, briefly soon after the Federation of the West Indies came into being in 1958, but then disappeared into history four years later along with the Federation itself.

Below: A band of the West India Regiment wearing the Zouave uniform

and accounted for almost 40 percent of Barbados' gross domestic output and almost all visible foreign exchange earnings.

The Commonwealth Sugar Agreement put in place in 1951 and its subsequent replacement, the Lome Convention agreed between the EEC (now European Union) and the ACP (African, Caribbean and Pacific countries) provided guaranteed prices for sugar, thus providing some long term stability for a commodity often adversely affected by fluctuation in world prices.

Notwithstanding this support, sugar production has declined steadily in Barbados to a point where it earns less than ten percent of foreign exchange and provides employment to an ageing and dwindling labour force (most of them over the age of 50).

Several factors have contributed to this state of affairs, including high production costs, injudicious borrowing by estate owners, the fragmentation of sugar cane lands for real estate speculation, government ambivalence, and the general overall negative attitudes held by many Barbadians to an industry hampered by its bitter association with slavery, oppression and entrenched socio-economic inequalities. This was exemplified in the period 1968 to 1973, when deliberate arson and sabotage discouraged many planters.

The nadir came in 1995, when sugar production totalled only 38,000 tons, the lowest of the century, down from a peak of 208,000 tons in 1957. This present government, recognizing a diminished, but still important industry which has many linkages throughout the economy, has put in place additional measures in an attempt to save it. A management/consultancy programme using personnel from Tate and Lyle is in operation, the Barbados Workers Union has agreed to the increased use of mechanical harvesters and all relevant technologies are being implemented in order to improve efficiency and production in the industry. There is guarded optimism about its survival.

Following the Depression of 1929, the decade of the 1930s was one of economic distress. It was this decade which provided the impetus for the formation of trade unions and political parties throughout the Westindies.

Political participation by non-whites in local institutions was on the rise, although minority whites were still firmly in control. By 1910 out of a total of 24 members of the House of Assembly, only eight were non-white, (seven coloured and one black person). Black people were conscious of this situation and started to articulate their resentment

OPPOSITE: The Morgan Lewis Windmill ceased operation in 1947

89

through the popular 'Joe and Lizzy' cartoons which appeared in the local press.

World War I had stripped Europeans of much of their mystique and returning black servicemen acted as a conduit for the dissemination of an early black nationalist position which was to receive its fullest expression through the Jamaican Marcus Garvey, whose message of upliftment and psychological healing to the black masses was well received by many Barbadians.

Slowly changing social and economic forces also contributed to the growth of this muted and considered challenge to the white oligarchy. Some 20,000 Barbadians had contributed to the building of the Panama Canal and their remittances were used to buy land, build houses and improve the standard of living of their families. Increasing numbers of black people entered the electoral rolls.

In 1924, Dr Charles Duncan O'Neale, a black doctor, with the help of other middle-class professionals, founded the Democratic League and through their work, black representation in the House of Assembly increased. In 1925, the Workingmen's Association, a prototype trade union was launched, designed to foster and protect the interests of the working class.

Outbreaks of strikes and rioting took place throughout the Caribbean in response to bad socio-economic conditions, exacerbated by the depression. Rioting began in Barbados on 26 July 1937 fueled by the anger of a crowd protesting the deportation of Clement Payne. He was a charismatic young Trinidadian of Barbadian ancestry who had galvanized the people of Bridgetown by his public addresses highlighting social inequalities and worker oppression.

Wages were low, a situation which affected whites as well as black people, for the majority of whites of the island were working class. However, they removed themselves from the struggle, finding it impossible to bridge the centuries of distrust that had pitted free against non-free; white against black. The psychological burden of their minority status and the fears this generated, especially the fear of marginalization and absorption, militated against their finding common cause with their black co-workers. It is highly ironic that the only white Barbadian to rise to leadership status in this time of crisis was TT Lewis, when he was dismissed by his employers for his political activities, was supported by a show of solidarity by the black workers of Bridgetown. They paralysed the city with a march with TT Lewis at their head, while white employ-

Charles Duncan O'Neale

Clement Payne

OPPOSITE: The West India & Panama Telegraph Company was established to transfer 'Panama Canal' monies to Barbados

CLEMENT PAYNE AND THE RIOTS OF 1937

Clement Payne was a man who sought justice and equality. He denounced the working conditions and low wages inflicted upon workers and called for working class organisation. His views conflicted with the British interests.

Clement Payne (1904-1941) was born in Trinidad of Barbadian parents. He arrived in Barbados aged four and returned to Trinidad as a young man. He joined a number of radical groups which were seeking political and social change in the Westindies.

In 1937 Payne returned to Barbados and held public meetings denouncing working conditions for ordinary Barbadians. He called on people to form working class organisation but warned against violence.

His speeches struck a chord with the people but alarmed the authorities who, on the 22 July 1937 charged him with having made a false declaration on entering Barbados. Payne had declared that he was born in Barbados.

After being convicted and fined Payne rallied his supporters at a public meeting. The next day Payne and the protesters marched to Government House to protest about the conviction. When they refused to leave, the police arrested Payne and some of his followers - who were later released on bail. Payne was kept in prison and served with a deportation order.

Payne's supporters held public meetings in Bridgetown on three consecutive nights to protest about the deportation order. Grantley Adams, who was a barrister, at first refused to appear on Payne's behalf, but won an appeal against Payne's conviction and had the deportation order rescinded on the afternoon of 26 July - however, the authority had Payne put on a ship bound for Trinidad.

On learning that the authorities had already deported Payne that same afternoon the public meetings turned into the 26 July riots, in which 14 people died, 47 were wounded and over 400 arrested.

The riots and unrest which swept Barbados and the Caribbean, forced the British government to pay some real attention to its neglected responsibilities in the Westindies. Trade unions were legalised and a minimum wage introduced.

In March 1938 the Barbados Labour Party was formed and in July 1939 Grantley Adams was elected leader. In 1941 the Barbados Worker's Union was formed. It would take another 14 years for universal suffrage (1951) to come into effect and 29 years before independence (1966).

Payne continued to be active in the labour movement in Trinidad until his death in 1941. The Barbados Worker's Union have honoured those who took part in the Riots of 1937 with a marble plaque at the union's headquarters.

ees who themselves earned pittances, stood in doorways watching on, silent and inactive. Later, many of them would say - *"our hearts were with Lewis, but we were desperately afraid of being singled out because of our high visibility and victimized."*

Yet the aftermath of the riots, with improved wages and conditions, benefited whites just as much as black people. With economic changes, Barbados' middle class grew, but the unfortunate development was that two parallel middle classes emerged, one black and one white. They communicated in public but lived in separate and distinct social and private spheres.

Only within the last decade can one say that there are signs of amalgamation of these two branches of the middle class, which, when it does take place, will be of considerable benefit to the island in all avenues of life.

ABOVE: Donkey-drawn wagons operated for over 100 years as the cheapest method of transport for cane and other goods
Photo: National Heritage Trust

Out of the crucible of 1937, one man emerged dominant and undisputed leader. This was Grantley Adams, a British trained lawyer, familiar with and sympathetic to the ideals of Fabian socialism. He was also a pragmatist who mobilized the masses without radicalizing them, working for and achieving remarkable political and socio-economic change in an ordered, controlled fashion.

Revolution through the ballot, not the bullet was his aim. Through the formation in 1938 of the Barbados Progressive League, which became the Barbados Labour Party and the Barbados Workers Union in 1941, Adams and his colleagues in the House of Assembly were able to pass a Minimum Wage Act and other legislation protecting workers. A major victory was secured by him, with the passage in 1942 of a Bill reducing the income qualification for voters to £20 and giving women who

qualified the right to vote and seek office as parliamentary representatives. The full franchise would not come until 1950.

Further political adjustments led to the reduction of power of the Upper House, the Legislative Council, which was still planter-dominated. Ministerial government was introduced and a fully-fledged cabinet government was introduced in 1958, with Grantley Adams becoming Premier of Barbados. At this stage the island had achieved virtual autonomy in government, making eventual independence the formal recognition of a process which had started as long ago as 1639 with the formation of the House of Assembly.

It was during this period as well, that steps were taken to begin the diversification of Barbados' economy with the passage of the Pioneer Industries (Encouragement) Act in 1951, the Hotel Aids Act in 1956, and the establishment of the Barbados Tourist Board in 1958.

Dr Hugo Cummins. 1891 - 1970. Became the second Premier 1958 - 1961 when Sir Grantley Adams took over the Prime Ministership of the Federation of the West Indies

Grantley Adams was a man whose vision went beyond the shores of Barbados. Along with other Caribbean leaders he recognized that a union among the English speaking islands was the only sensible solution to grinding individual poverty and unnecessary duplication of services. Political sentiment in Britain also favoured this seeming solution to the problems faced by the region.

Agreement was reached for Westindian Federation at the London conference of 1956. Almost immediately, however, insular jealousies started to appear. The choice of a site for the capital was acrimonious. Barbados was the logical site and was so recommended by the Site Commission. After several unconvincing and emotional arguments, Barbados was rejected and Trinidad chosen instead, with Grantley Adams as Prime Minister. Dr Hugo Cummins, former Minister of Social Services and Speaker of the House, then took over the Premiership of Barbados in 1958. For a variety of reasons, including Jamaica's withdrawal, the Federation collapsed in 1962.

Sir Grantley Adams. 1898 - 1971. First Premier of Barbados 1954 - 1958, and first Prime Minister of the Federation of the West Indies 1958 - 1962

During Adams' absence from Barbados, a young World War II Air Force veteran and lawyer, Errol Walton Barrow, broke with the Barbados Labour Party and formed the opposing Democratic Labour Party which came to power in 1961. It was he who would lead Barbados to Independence on 30 November 1966.

Prime Minister Barrow led the nation for ten years after Independence, and again in 1985 until his death of a heart attack in 1987. During his first administration, his development policies emphasized a shift from sugar production to manufacturing and tourism. The latter grew swiftly, rising from some 17,800 arrivals in 1956 to some 210,000 by 1976.

Tourism has had vitally important spin-offs for the island's population. It has given Barbadians, directly and indirectly, a much higher standard of living, with per capita income rising from US$188 in 1946 to US$290 in 1980 to US$6,000 in 1995.

The quality of Barbados' infrastructure and the variety of services provided must also be linked to tourism. There are multiple linkages of many other types as well, which enhance the quality of life for all.

In 1976, the Barbados Labour Party won the elections, led by the son of

Errol Barrow. 1920 - 1987. Third Premier and first Prime Minister of Barbados. In office 1961 - 1976 and 1985 - 1987

"Tom" J M G M Adams. 1931 - 1985. Second Prime Minister of Barbados from 1976 - 1985

Bernard St John. Third Prime Minister of Barbados for three months in 1985

Lloyd Erskine Sandiford. Fourth Prime Minister of Barbados from 1987 - 1994

Owen Arthur. Fifth Prime Minister of Barbados 1994 -

OVERLEAF: The Barbados Hilton Hotel was opened by Prime Minister Errol Barrow on 27th November, 1966 - two days before Independence - a boost to the government policy of diversifying from the sugar industry to tourism

Sir Grantley Adams, "Tom" J M G M Adams. Under him, Barbados continued to progress. Prime Minister Tom Adams, who died unexpectedly of a heart attack in 1985 at the age of 53, had a clear vision of Barbados entering the 21st Century as a fully developed island/city state. Under his administration, Barbados expanded its economy into the services sector, with an emphasis on offshore banking, captive insurance and the informatics industry.

After Tom Adams' sudden death, he was replaced by Mr Bernard St John as Prime Minister. After three months in office, Mr St John decided to seek his own mandate and was defeated at the polls, thus ushering in the return of Errol Barrow and the Democratic Labour Party.

When Mr Barrow died in office, he was replaced as Prime Minister by Lloyd Erskine Sandiford, whose administration was seriously hampered by external and internal economic problems. Although devaluation was staved off, the structural adjustment programme put in place to secure International Monetary Fund balance of payments support was so unpopular that this contributed greatly to the defeat of the Democratic Labour Party in the 1994 elections and the assumption of political leadership by the Barbados Labour Party under the leadership of Prime Minister Owen Arthur. These events are now so current and unfolding, that they await the analysis and judgement of future historians.

Since Barbados' independence, has undergone many changes. Several of these are reflected in the physical landscape of the country. The spatial distribution of housing and related human activities is now such that it is no longer feasible to talk about a separation of town and country. Barbados has become a city, the socio-cultural implications of which are still working themselves out.

In material terms, life has vastly improved in all areas. When one considers all the indices, it is clear that Barbados has made outstanding strides forward in areas such as health, education, communications and the general physical infrastructure of the country. Barbadians are proud of these achievements and this undoubtedly contributes to the charge of 'smugness' levelled against us by many of our island neighbours. Yet one cannot deny that, with limited resources, Barbados has performed creditably, and today reverberates with a cultural vibrancy and self-assuredness.

There are difficulties of course. Critics of past administrations charge that politicians have not done enough to empower black people economically. The truth or not of this allegation has yet to be

95

demonstrated statistically. It is evident that inherited historical imbalances in all the islands of the Caribbean have seen the retention of economic power in the hands of a few, largely white families. It is also true that Barbados has gone further than its neighbours in ensuring a fair distribution of income for its people. This is the result of the high quality of political leadership which Barbados has enjoyed since independence, the pro-worker activity of the island's trade unions and recognition by the private sector that social stability could not be achieved if workers continued to be exploited.

Out of these changes, the island's black middle class has expanded considerably, so much so that it is on the verge of becoming the single largest socio-economic group. It is too young and too unsure of itself yet to articulate strong positions of leadership and has not yet shaken off the emotional scars of the past. This is the reason why discourse on social, economic and political issues still centres around the syndrome of the 'small man' and why, for example, the plantation icon is still the psychological point of reference, even though most plantations are bankrupt and that mode of life has disappeared.

The 21st Century beckons and Barbados is well poised to make a successful entry, provided residual issues of race and class are resolved, the problem of drugs is seriously addressed and the emerging underclass of some ten percent of the population is rehabilitated and brought back into the mainstream and provided that potential environmental flash points such as pollution, heavy pesticide use and dumping are controlled.

These suppositions take us into the realm of the future - outside of the scope of the historian one may say, yet one of the goals and purposes of history is to give us an insight or fore-warning of future probabilities through careful use of the scrying mirror of the historical past.

Statue of Sir Grantley Adams, outside the Government Headquarters

Barbados is Bajan

by John Wickham

Statue erected in gratitude to Horatio Nelson who saved Barbados from a French invasion in 1805

Where in today's modern world would you hear a pharmacy called a 'doctor shop' or a man's under-vest a 'merino'? These words, now out of fashion in Barbados, survived in the vocabulary of a 93-year old woman, Violetta, born Violet in St Joseph, Barbados, who took them with her when she went to Brazil in 1910. Violetta lived among her children, grandchildren and great grandchildren in the town of Porto Velho, the capital of Rondonia, the newest state of Brazil.

Yet how did a community of Barbadians come to be living happily in a remote corner of Brazil, settled on the bank of a tributary of the giant Amazon River, out of touch with their native island but still carrying the accent and language of their mother country? The answer to that conundrum lies in the history and culture of a small island lying so flat in the Atlantic that Columbus never saw it, although his claim to discovery of nearly all of its neighbours is a matter of recorded history.

The existence of Barbadian dialect and vestiges of its culture in Brazil is only one illustration of the common boast that you can find a Bajan (not to be confused with the same word used to describe first-year students at some Scottish universities) anywhere in the world. The intense cultivation of sugar which made the island one of the richest possessions of the British Empire in the 17th Century depended on large numbers of slaves and so, early in its life, Barbados was heavily populated. Emigration has long been a means of population control and economic management and Barbadians have left the island in their thousands for other islands in the Caribbean, the United States, Canada, Panama, Cuba, Brazil and later, at the end of World War II for Britain itself. It is said that there are more Barbadian descendants in Brooklyn and Queens than there are in Barbados itself.

Barbados has been called by several names: the singular island, because of its separation, one hundred-miles to the east of the chain, which was enough in the days of sail to provide a defence against the enemy fleets, making it difficult to tack against the prevailing easterly winds. It has also been called Little England, sometimes affectionately 'Bimshire' a recognition of its long and uninterrupted connection with the other England reflected in many place names in the island - Trafalgar Square, Nelson Statue, Worthing, Hastings and Cheapside.

And no wonder, for when the first English settlers landed in 1627, the only welcome they received was from a multitude of wild hogs, whose ancestors had been left on the island more than a hundred years before

by the crew of a Portuguese ship which had called in for fresh water. While all the other islands which eventually fell under British rule experienced their share of French or Spanish dominion, Barbados remained resolutely British until 1966 when it became an independent state within the British Commonwealth.

Barbadians have a reputation wherever they go, especially among other English-speaking Caribbeans, for being know-all, opinionated and they have been referred to as the Scotsmen of the Westindies because of their frugality and thriftiness. No wonder again, for the realities of life on a small crowded island earning its living from a single crop - sugar - bred a hardy, no-nonsense attitude and a sense of order which was not in such stringent demand in less populous and more generous landscapes. But it is true that Barbadians are not slow to trumpet their own virtues: they tend to believe, in the words of a piece of doggerel of 50 years ago that *"when the great trump shall blow, all other nations will please stan' back and Buhbadians march up first."*

For the discerning visitor, however, who is not content with the tourist image of sun and sea and the touted jollification of a tropical merry-go-round, Barbados is the perfect human laboratory for the observation of how men and women are shaped in their characters and behaviour by the elements of geography, history and landscape. The laboratory is of a convenient size and the observations it permits are valuable. If the new architecture is an imitation of the overseas metropolitan, there is still visible the chattel house, product of the plantation system and a beautiful example of the vernacular. If the game of cricket confuses the stranger, it is yet a reminder of the island's earliest connections with England and if the monument of the hero of Trafalgar at the head of Broad Street seems amusing, it will be as well to remember that it was erected before Nelson's Column in London.

Many visitors have written about Barbados from its first historian, Edward Ligon, who described two typical feasts of the sugar lords of the time in glorious terms, to John Hearne, the Jamaican novelist, who when writing in 1966 thought the island puzzling. Nearly all of them have found the character of Barbados elusive, sometimes frustratingly so.

One writer, Bruce Hamilton, says that Barbadians *"display in their attitude towards and relations with sister colonies a national pride (or complacent insularity), which, however galling to their neighbours and faintly ridiculous to the detached observer, is undoubtedly deep-seated and unaffected."*

A careful look at what Barbadians do and the things they place weight

ABOVE: Mounted police in Bridgetown

on will explain. In the other islands, whose antecedence includes French and/or Spanish cultural influence, Barbadians have a reputation of stodginess, a lack of imagination and a down-to-earthiness which is said to discourage flights of fancy and lighthearted gaiety. But consider the type and character of the Barbadian who has settled in and contributed to the development of the other islands. The fact that Barbados has supplied policemen, teachers and preachers to many of its neighbours is not only an indication of what kind of people were in demand in the other colonies but also of the qualities which were bred by the Barbadian environment. In the small, crowded space, order and discipline were essential requirements.

The theory that the characters of any group of human beings comes eventually to be a reflection of the landscape they inhabit is amply

101

confirmed in the case of Barbados. Father Biet, a Jesuit priest who visited the island around 1654, remarked on the flatness of the landscape, pointing out that the hills were so modest that the land could be cultivated almost to the tops. This intense cultivation was necessary of course because the husbandry this shortage imposed made a virtue out of necessity.

The modesty of the Barbadian landscape, flat, tidy fields marked by their separating hedgerows and stretching out to the encircling sea, has had its effect also on the character of Barbadian painting. Whereas the hills and mountains of Trinidad and the Windward Islands offer a dramatic picture of lush, green forest, bright colours of birds and flowers that catch the eye, the Barbados offering is a palette of gentle greens and mild browns, infinitely less splendid and, for that reason, more difficult to capture on canvas. For that same reason, perhaps, when caught in the heart and spirit, the landscape makes more demands on the loyalty and affection of its lovers. That is why the accent of home is so durable among Barbadians.

The passion of Barbadians for that most English of games, cricket, is a continuing wonder to visitors, especially north Americans, but it seems to come so naturally to Barbadians that they have no need to explain it. The most likely answer is that the formality of the game, its order and mystique, speak to the Barbadian nature. Moreover, it offers within the rigid discipline of its rules, team spirit and room for individual performance and the display of individual skills.

It is often said as a kind of joke that cricket is a religion in Barbados. But the jokers speak truer than they know. Consider the setting and the order of the game as formal as that of a Mass. It is not fanciful to conceive of the cricket field as a vast church and the spectators as a congregation, the two wickets as a pair of altars, the two white-coated umpires as joint celebrants of the Mass and the players, each in his special role and place,

The modesty of the Barbadian landscape has had its effect on the Barbadian character

as the attendant acolytes. Talking about cricket as a religion, the enquiring visitor may wish to ponder the interrelation of the two pursuits and the significance of the multiplicity of religions and church organisations in Barbados. A recent count shows a total of nearly 200 cricket teams in the island and there cannot be fewer than a 100 or more denominations of various religious sects scattered over the countryside. Barbados is nothing if not a church-going community.

An assessment of the character of Barbados and Barbadians cannot be complete without some attention to their contribution to the spirit of Caribbean regional cooperation. The choice of the island as the headquarters of a number of regional institutions is not without significance. Small as the island is, it meets the requirements of such organisations as the Caribbean Development Bank, the Caribbean Examination Council and the Caribbean News Agency, while a number of foreign embassies located in the island service the needs of the neighbouring islands of the Eastern Caribbean.

In the cultural field, the foremost literary journal of the English-speaking Caribbean, BIM Magazine, achieved international status for its contribution to the literary development of the area. The magazine started in 1942 and attracted the work of several of the most reputable and most promising writers in the region and beyond, a remarkable achievement, considering the size of the island and its geographical insignificance. Sadly BIM no longer exists.

It is often said, as a kind of joke, that cricket is a religion in Barbados

Barbados is a text book example of 'small is beautiful' in more ways than one, where, in the words of one of its poets, *"the sugar cane impersonates wheat and Sedgemore sleeps beside the Guinea coast, a land of pastel tints and compromise."* It is a lovable place but its qualities are not blatant. It takes a deal of perception and time to know it but the reward of its affection is genuine and unmistakable. Barbados is a singular island and Bajans know it.

Not 'Sundays Only' Religion

by John Gilmore

The Mosque is located in Bridgetown

One of our earliest histories records how the first Englishmen to land in Barbados set up a cross on the shore - somewhere in the vicinity of what is now Holetown - with the inscription 'James K of E and of this Island'. In many ways this is an apt symbol of the religious history of Barbados.

In some parts of the Caribbean, later events brought major religious influences from other traditions, particularly Hinduism and Islam. In Barbados, however, while there is now a significant Muslim community and other religions (such as Judaism, Hinduism and the Bah'ai faith) have their followers, most people see their country as a Christian one. There are indeed many, especially young adults, who are seldom or never seen in a place of worship of any kind except for a wedding or funeral, but these are greatly outnumbered by those for whom religious observance is a regular and important aspect of their lives.

In villages and urban areas throughout the island, Sundays are characterised by the ringing of church bells and the sound of hymns sung by large and enthusiastic congregations. The transport board provides 'Sundays Only' bus-stops near major churches for the convenience of worshippers, but for many people, services during the week are also popular.

Religious broadcasts are common, and it is not unusual for a secular call-in programme on the radio to turn to a sometimes heated discussion on points of doctrine. Many complain that rampant commercialisation has robbed Christmas of its significance, but Christmas Eve and Christmas morning will still see churches packed to the doors from Whitepark Wesleyan Holiness in Bridgetown to Shrewsbury Methodist in St Philip, from St Swithin's Anglican in St Lucy to St Dominic's Catholic in Maxwell, Christ Church.

Some things have changed - Sunday cricket, once unthinkable, is now taken for granted - but it is a rare Bajan who will break an ancient taboo by venturing into the sea on Good Friday, even though it is an official holiday.

Few public occasions, from the opening of the Assizes to the celebration of Nurses' Week, are considered complete without a church service.

Much of this is similar to what can be seen in other parts of the Caribbean, but there are ways in which religion in Barbados presents a distinctive picture. In the region as a whole, Christianity usually means

the Roman Catholic Church, which continues to play a major role in the Hispanic and Francophone territories and, indeed, in some former British colonies.

In Barbados, however, for some three centuries it generally meant the Anglican Church, that Church of England whose intimate connection with the temporal power was symbolised by the fact that King James I was recognised as its Supreme Governor and Defender of the Faith - titles held by his heirs and successors to the present day.

In other former British colonies in the Caribbean, the Anglican Church was likewise the 'established Church' for longer or shorter periods of their history, but Barbados was different. For one thing, the Anglican Church remained established in Barbados until 1969 - or almost a century after it had ceased to enjoy or endure this status everywhere else in the Caribbean, or, for that matter anywhere else in the world outside the British Isles. And establishment meant much more than the honorific official recognition which is virtually all it means in England today, for in Barbados the Anglican clergy were paid directly out of taxes of the general public. Elsewhere in the Caribbean, Anglicanism remains what it always was in most of the region, the religion of a minority, but Barbados has more practising Anglicans in proportion to its total population than perhaps any other country, certainly more than has long been the case in England.

In 1627 the English found Barbados uninhabited though a few Amerindians were brought from South America in the 17th Century. The first Africans arrived on the same ship as the first English settlers, but for some years Barbados was largely a colony of English smallholders, with much of the labour performed not by African slaves, but by white indentured servants. Many of these were Irish and Scots, rather than English, and many were Catholics.

The 'Sugar Revolution' of the mid-17th Century transformed the colony into one in which the sugar plantation was the major form of agriculture. At the same time, it became cheaper for the planters to supply the necessary labour by the import of slaves from Africa rather than of European servants, and by about 1680 black people outnumbered whites in Barbados by about four to one.

St Patrick's Roman Catholic Cathedral, Bridgetown

BELOW: Pentecostal worshippers

The first minister of religion known to have been in Barbados was an Anglican, in 1628, and by 1637 there were six Anglican parish churches on the island. There was a Jewish community from 1654, which played a significant part in the island's commercial life, and they were allowed to practise their religion freely, although they suffered from a number of civil disabilities until 1831, by which time they were already declining in numbers.

In Barbados as in England, the Catholic Church was for a long time actively discriminated against and there was no resident Catholic priest until 1839. In the late 17th Century, the Quakers (or Society of Friends) gained a following in Barbados, though they were persecuted by the authorities partly because they were pacifists who refused to serve in the island's militia and partly because they sought to convert slaves.

By the early 18th Century, most of the white Barbadians were Anglicans, at least in the sense that they were baptised, married and buried in Anglican churches. Both the Anglican clergy and other observers repeatedly complained that their religion meant little more than that to the majority of them, one visitor saying they *"hardly think of God but in their curses and blasphemies"*.

A few black Barbadians, both slave and free, were baptised in the 17th and 18th Centuries, but it was generally the case that, as a visiting French priest put it, *"The masters never think of their slaves' souls."* While some Anglican clergy in England repeatedly called for the conversion of slaves in the Westindies from the early 18th Century, they got little response. In 1750 the rector of St Lucy, Barbados, claimed that, while converting slaves was a good idea in theory, *"the difficulties attending it are, and I am afraid ever will be, unsurmountable"*.

The enslaved population was thus largely left to choose its own path in religion. Ancestral faiths unquestionably survived the middle passage, but the vague references of white writers to *"the rites ceremonies, and superstitions"* of the black people, and the very limited archaeological evidence available makes it difficult to say how these faiths developed, changed and ultimately disappeared in Barbados. There is nothing in Barbados comparable to the survival of the Orisha religion in Trinidad or the growth of Voodoo in Haiti as a Caribbean religion created largely of African elements. However the survival in present day Barbados of lingering traces of belief in obeah, a magico-religious system of African origin, is a tribute to the strength of resistance to the imposition of European cultural norms.

St John's Church in the parish of St John

108

In 1765 the first Moravian missionaries arrived in Barbados. Their express purpose was the Christianisation of the slave population. They made few converts at first but they avoided all controversy about the legitimacy of slavery as an institution and were generally left alone by the planters and the authorities. Their example perhaps stimulated others into activity, for by the 1780s a few Anglican clergy were working along the same lines, even before the arrival of the first Methodist missionary in 1788.

St Lucy's Church

Many white Barbadians continued to be openly hostile to the Christianisation of slaves, the best known examples being the demolition of the Methodist chapel in Bridgetown by a mob of white rioters in 1823, and the prosecution in 1827 of the Reverend William Harte, an Anglican rector, as a result of his allegedly *"endeavouring to alienate slaves from a sense of their duty by inculcating doctrines of equality inconsistent with their obedience to their masters and the policy of this island."*

However, from 1823 the British government actively supported conversion and its opponents in the Caribbean were forced to give way. The first Anglican bishop of Barbados arrived on the island in 1825 and was able to use the generous financial support of the British government to produce a considerable increase in the number of Anglican clergy, places of worship and schools. By the 1840s, a few years after Emancipation in 1834, most of the population had been baptised.

Unlike other parts of the Caribbean, where they faced strong competition from the Catholics or from other Protestant denominations, the Anglicans in Barbados greatly outnumbered their rivals in terms of clergy and church buildings. In most parishes of the island, anyone who wanted to go to church had little choice except to go to an Anglican church. The official census of 1881 showed that nearly 90 percent of the population were Anglicans.

There were those who questioned how deeply the process of Christianisation went, particularly since long afterwards, the bulk of the population received only the most rudimentary education. There was also the point that the social attitudes of the Anglican Church were

generally extremely conservative - as they were in England - and that the Church generally encouraged acceptance of the repressive oligarchy which characterised Barbadian society until comparatively recently. Such things as pew rents maintained segregated seating in churches long after it had been abandoned in theory, and there are those still living who can remember how some Anglican clergy managed to hold services for white and black members of their congregations at different times. Although only a small percentage of nominal Anglicans attended church regularly, it was often the case that getting on in life required the support of an Anglican clergyman or an Anglican schoolmaster.

Some criticism of this came from within the Church. John Mitchinson, the Anglican bishop from 1873 to 1881, once suggested that the Barbadian society of his day was a *"whited sepulchre, which indeed, appears beautiful outwardly, but within is full of dead men's bones and of all uncleanness."* However, in religious matters as in other aspects of Barbadian life, real change began in the early 20th Century with the building of the Panama Canal. Many thousands of Barbadians went to work on the canal, and many of those who survived the harsh conditions were able to bring home or send home money which enabled them or their relatives to enjoy comparative independence. Many more Barbadians were for the first time able to choose not to work for the plantation system - and were also better able to choose which church they would attend. The canal builders and those who returned from working in other parts of the Caribbean and in north America also brought back with them knowledge of a much wider variety of faiths.

In the early 1920s there were perhaps no more than a dozen denominations of any size in Barbados. Now there are well over a 100. Since the 1950s, the general acceptance of the idea that the government, rather than the churches, is responsible for providing education for the entire population, has also helped to make freedom of choice in religion a reality. While Anglicanism is still by far the largest single denomination, it no longer has an absolute majority. One effect of these changes in the 20th Century has almost certainly been the growth of a more profound and sincere commitment on the part of members of all denominations.

The occasional visiting minister or overseas missionary is still to be found, but nearly all the clergy of all denominations are now Barbadians. Even in the late 18th Century a high proportion of the Anglican clergy were Barbadians by birth, but until well into the 20th Century this meant

110

mainly white Barbadians, now the Anglican clergy are almost without exception black Barbadians.

The religious scene has changed in other ways as well. The Spiritual Baptists, a church which seeks to emphasise its African heritage, was ridiculed when it first came to Barbados from Trinidad some 30 years ago, it now enjoys a large and growing following and a generally respected position in society.

"The Resurrection" by American artist Benjamin West (1776) hangs above the altar in St George's Church. It is said that while the painting was in storage in an outhouse, the eye of the centurion was punched out by a thief who thought he was being watched. The painting was taken to England for repair - but received only a black patch over the damaged eye

Other churches, including the Anglican Church, are actively seeking ways in which they can make their institutions and worship more reflective of the cultural heritage of Barbados and the Caribbean as a whole, though this can still be a controversial issue for some congregations. There is a much wider acceptance of female leadership in churches. The first women priests in the Anglican Diocese of Barbados were ordained in May 1996, and this seems to have caused much less controversy than it has in some other parts of the Anglican communion.

Clergy and laity of different denominations are much more willing to cooperate publicly with each other than was the case even 20 years ago. This, at least in part, reflects the fact that for a very long time many Barbadians have been in the habit of regularly attending the services of more than one denomination.

Some clergy occasionally speak their minds in forthright terms on what many would consider to be issues of party politics. The presence of a minister of religion on a government board or in the Senate is more or less usual and, in a broader sense, churches are actively involved in public issues. For many Bajans, this is as it should be. For many, perhaps a large majority, religion is not a 'Sundays Only' affair, but something which is part of their entire lives.

RASTAFARIANISM IN BARBADOS

by John Gilmore

There is nothing strange these days about walking down the street in an English city - or indeed almost anywhere in the world - and meeting someone in a Tee-shirt with a design in red, green and gold, perhaps showing a stylised locksman beating a drum and dancing. The global triumph of reggae music has ensured that the image of the Rastaman is universally known, even though most of those to whom it is familiar have little knowledge of the faith it symbolises. That Tee-shirt could be the souvenir of a holiday, not to Jamaica, but to almost anywhere, so widely have the superficial trappings of Rastafari been absorbed into the international consumer culture.

In view of the origins of Rasta, this is ironic. The faith is not only specifically Caribbean, but rooted in the grinding poverty which was the lot of most Jamaicans in the period between the two World Wars, and in a Jamaican tradition of prophetic leaders whose messianic interpretations of scripture challenged the establishment in Church and State. This tradition goes back to the days of slavery, but perhaps its greatest flowering was in the teaching of Marcus Garvey, whose call of *'Africa for the Africans, at home and abroad,'* and *'One God, One Aim, One Destiny,'* has struck a chord in the hearts of millions of black people in the Caribbean and around the world from the early years of the 20th Century to the present.

One statement attributed to Garvey was that his hearers should *"Look to Africa, when a black king shall be crowned, for the day of deliverance is near."* When Haile Selassie I was crowned as Emperor of Ethiopia in 1930, a number of Jamaicans (apparently independently of each other) came to see this as the fulfilment of Garvey's prophecy. Leaders such as Leonard Howell, Joseph Nathaniel Hibbert and Archibald Dunkley began to gather followers for their belief that the Emperor was the Messiah, and that redemption for black people was to be found in a return to Ethiopia. The Emperor's title and name before his coronation - Ras [Prince] Tafari - came to be applied to the movement. The Italian invasion of Ethiopia and the acquiescence in this of the other colonial powers made the exiled Emperor into a powerful symbol of conflict between black and white, and helped rather than hindered the growth of the movement. Haile Selassie's return to power after the Allied defeat of Italy in the Second World War provided a further boost.

The apocalyptic visions of some of the early Rasta leaders were often expressed in violent terms. Together with their advocacy of the sacramental use of ganja (marijuana), this led to frequent clashes with the police. However, in 1960 an influential report to the Jamaican government by three academics of the University College of the West Indies (now UWI) drew attention to the fact that the movement's large following was the result of a rejection of the social and political system - characterised as 'Babylon' - which had failed the poor. The report recommended both practical measures to improve social conditions and a greater acceptance of Rastafarianism. To some extent the report did lead to a change in official attitudes. A visit by Haile Selassie to the Caribbean (including Jamaica) in 1966 certainly helped the movement, in spite of reports that the Emperor was a devout Christian who was not particularly pleased to have the role of God thrust upon him. The conversion of popular musicians such as Bob Marley to Rastafarianism and a growing interest among students at the Mona Campus of the UWI from the 1970s helped to spread the movement beyond the Kingston poor. Some middle-class Jamaicans began to adopt the faith, and it also spread to other parts of the Caribbean.

The very existence of Rastafarianism was virtually unknown in Barbados before the 1970s.

> *"The very existence of Rastafarianism was virtually unknown in Barbados before the 1970s. Since then, however, it has acquired a small but significant following."*

Since then, however, it has acquired a small but significant following, and a wider group of sympathisers with at least some aspects of its philosophy. It attracts both those who feel that 'Babylon' has failed them and those who are drawn to it for cultural reasons. In Barbados, as in many other Caribbean societies, the dominant culture is heavily 'westernised,' and acceptance of European and, increasingly, north American standards is often taken for granted. By contrast, Rastafari emphasises the claim that the black race is God's chosen people, and insists upon the Africanness of Caribbean black people. Conventional churches are rejected, and the Bible is interpreted in ways which can seem highly idiosyncratic to outsiders.

As is the case elsewhere, Rastafari in Barbados means different things to different people - there is no one Rastafari organisation or leader. Some believers refuse to accept that Haile Selassie did in fact die in 1975 following his deposition by a revolution in Ethiopia and see him still as a living God in a literal sense. Others interpret his continuing divinity in a more metaphysical way. The importance of the return of black people to Africa is widely accepted by Rastafarians, but this can be interpreted in a purely spiritual sense. Some Rastas insist the sacramental use of ganja is essential - a belief that brings them into conflict with the law - while others disagree. Attitudes to alcohol, tobacco and the importance of 'ital' (vegetarian foods), vary greatly. Even the importance of wearing the hair in dreadlocks, regarded by outsiders as the distinguishing characteristic of Rastafari, can be a matter of personal interpretation. There are some who wear locks but whose conduct leads others to regard them as not being 'true' Rasta, while in contrast there are 'bald-head' Rastas who accept what they see as Rasta spirituality, but who do not grow their hair, at least in part because of social pressure.

Rastafari is nothing like as widespread in Barbados as it is in Jamaica, and while there is wider acceptance now, Bajan Rastas still face some popular prejudice. You can now see Rasta schoolchildren wearing their locks in a tam hat knitted in the colours of their uniform, whereas a few years ago they would have been pressured to cut their hair. While there is a more relaxed attitude in areas such as the media and entertainment, it would still be a bold employee in a more conventional business who decided to grow his or her hair in locks. However, some Rastas have achieved prominence in Barbadian society, particularly in the arts. They include the poet and actor Winston Farrell, journalist and calypsonian Adonijah, and artists Ras Akyem and Ras Ishi.

Tony Henderson - the coconut man - specialises in Asian and African arts & crafts using coconut shells and sugar cane. He operates outside Dover Beach Hotel. Tony was born in Bridgetown and is a self-taught artist

113

Harrison's Cave

A south coast beach

Pomp and pageant of the West India Regiment in Zouave uniform

A typical chattel house

The Story of the Press in Barbados

by John Wickham

When Sir Robert Schomburgk, whose *History of Barbados*, 1848, is so reliable a standard commentary on the island's early life, turned his attention to the subject of the state of literature and the public press in the island, even he could not avoid a trace of condescension. In his chapter on the civil and social state he wrote:

> *"Native periodical literature (with the exception of a few newspapers) meets with no support as yet in the West Indies. Attempts have been made from time to time in Jamaica, Demerara*, Antigua and Grenada to keep up a monthly magazine devoted to literature and science, but all have failed; and the only periodicals at present maintained, exclusive of the newspapers, are the annual almanacs, in some of which literature finds a nook."*

* Demerara was to become part of British Guiana (now Guyana) in 1814

In the event, however, over the years Barbados has been well served by its newspapers. For one thing, together with the authorised version of the Bible, the newspaper has been a major instrument in the education of the masses. One had only to hear the lilt and cadence of the speech patterns and the vocabulary of the older generation of Barbadians to recognise the substantial influence of the Old Testament texts and the parables of the New Testament. The high rate of literacy with which Barbadians have traditionally been credited owes a great deal to these two sources.

So far as the newspaper is concerned, it has very often proved a more accurate and trustworthy indicator of moods and trends than the mere studies and artificial compositions of the poets. For one thing, it is closer to the events it chronicles; for another, it is bound, by definition, to be more literal and less metaphorical in the presentation of its material.

Schomburgk reports that printing was introduced into the island about 1730 and a newspaper first appeared in 1731 which is quoted in the first volume of the *Gentleman's Magazine* published in that year. There was no other press in the Caribbean islands for several years subsequent to that period. During the period between 1800 and 1880 at least 18 newspapers made their appearance. True, some of them lasted only a few months, but the frequency of their appearance suggests that they met a perceived need in the community. According to Schomburgk, the *Barbados Gazette* was the first newspaper known to have been published twice a week for any considerable time in any part of America. It was published by Samuel Keiner, originally of Philadelphia, and became a weekly journal.

In its very first issue on 25 November 1973, the *Nation* newspaper published a list of its predecessors which included some of the following

names, with the dates of their first appearance and the names of their editors or publishers.

> *The Barbados Gazette* (1731) becoming the *Barbados Gazette* or *General Intelligencer* (1783); *The Barbados Mercury* (1762), George Esmand; *The Barbados Chronicle* (1807); *The Barbados Globe* and *Colonial Advocate* (1819), Andre G Drinan, solicitor and printer to the House of Assembly; *The Barbadian* (1822), Abel Clinkett; *The Barbados Times* (c1814); *The West Indian* (1833), R King and Co., first editor Samuel Hyde; *The New Times* (1836), Nathaniel Roach and James Ford Reed; *The Liberal,* edited by Samuel Jackman Prescod for more than 25 years; *The Sun* (1840), James Ford Reed and Daniel Donovan; *The Morning News* (c1840); *The Agriculture Reporter* (c1838); *The Standard* (1844), H W Sukins; *The Barbados Herald* (1878); *The Barbados Advocate* (1895-), Valence Gale; *The Weekly Recorder* (1905); *Sparklet* (1909); *Midweek Democrat* (1913); *The Illustrated*; *The Observer*, W A Crawford; *The Torch*, D F Blackett; *The Daily News* (1960), E L Cozier; *The Nation* (1973-), edited by Carl Moore.

The Barbadian newspaper laid the foundation of the eruption of the social unrest in the 1930s which represented the first of the national consciousness which expressed itself in the post World War II articulation of Barbadian culture. It was against a background of passionate and muscular prose which did not sacrifice elegance for relevance.

It was against this background and the recognition of the power of the word that the fiction writers emerged after 1937, the year of the riots. Tradition is not lightly put aside.

The Newspapers

by Karin Dear

"The basis of our governments being the opinion of the people, the very first object should be to keep that right; and were it left to me to decide whether we should have a government without newspapers, or newspapers without a government, I should not hesitate a moment to prefer the latter."

Thomas Jefferson

As Barbados heads into the 21st Century, it does so armed with a press determined to preserve its nation's democracy and a government committed to accountability to its 264,000 inhabitants. While the press may not determine what the public thinks, it certainly does influence what it thinks about. And it is a well-established fact that the press is frequently used by policymakers to assess and create public attitudes. It is no understatement that the press play a critical role in keeping the public informed while at the same time guarding against the nation's recalcitrants. It is a long-established fact that all over the world there are reports of governments striving to either muzzle or intimidate media with a view to enhancing their image and subsequent survival, through an adoring and unsuspecting public. Westindian countries are no exception and reinforced by global support from colleagues, the media in this latter part of the decade and on the threshold of a new millennium, collectively is venturing out into the more politically controversial corridors, striving simultaneously to raise the consciousness of its readers and political leaders in order to ensure a free and fair future for all individuals. It therefore bears repeating that freedom of the press is one of the most important cornerstones of democracy, one which must be guarded at all times.

In recent years, a new courage has blossomed in reporting the wrongs and shortcomings within this somewhat parochial society, encouraged to a large extent by the investigative prowess of its oldest daily newspaper *The Barbados Advocate*. In a message from Senator Glyne Murray, Minister of State responsible for information, on the occasion of that publication's 100th anniversary, he stated:

"I make bold to say that the Barbados we know and love today would be all the worse had *The Barbados Advocate*, over the last 100 years, not taken its role seriously and worked assiduously to fulfil its social and moral contract with the public it has served with distinction."

It is no exaggeration to state that with the 6 September 1994 election of the Barbados Labour Party headed by Prime Minister Owen Arthur, the media in Barbados has enjoyed more press freedom than at any other time in its

OPPOSITE: Pro-Independence marches on their way to a political meeting in Bridgetown, December, 1965

ABOVE: Thousands of enthusiastic supporters of Independence gather at Seawell Airport (now Sir Grantley Adams International Airport) to greet Premier Errol Barrow on his return from England, 18 July, 1966

history and perhaps more than any other country within the CariCom region.

Nor is it unusual for government members be they cabinet ministers, backbenchers, senators, or the prime minister himself, to take to the airwaves and address issues through talk shows or phone-in programmes through which public views can be exchanged freely. Barbados is blessed with two daily tabloids. *The Advocate*, whose banner-head slogan *"For the cause that lacks assistance: 'Gainst the wrongs that need resistance: For the future in the distance and the good that I can do"*, is celebrating its 100th anniversary this year and is affectionately dubbed 'The Old Lady of Fonatabelle' where it resides next door to its more fledging competitor of 22 years, *The Nation*.

The Advocate was launched in 1895 by Valence Gale, who at the age of four lost both parents during the 1854 cholera epidemic that swept this tiny country killing almost one-eighth of its population. As Gale grew up, his passion for newspaper reporting flared and for more than two decades he wrote leading articles that attracted widespread attention. It wasn't long before he was hailed as the best reporter of the day. When he died in 1908, his brother-in-law, Charles Lynch Chenery took over as editor and soon established his place in journalism weaving his way through the intricacies of governments and demonstrating a deep and keen knowledge of every aspect of the community's affairs. For 30 years he wrote the newspaper's daily editorials, a record that still remains to be equalled since his death in 1925.

On 23 November 1973, Barbados' second daily tabloid, *The Nation* was born, challenging its matriarch, *The Advocate*, in breaking news and addressing issues. Enshrined in its front-page objectives on that historic September day,

was a fierce determination to raise the standards of journalism which 25 years ago had plunged significantly in both quality and scope.

"We've come to the scene because we share the view that an uninformed public is an enslaved public," intoned the newspaper. As an independent publication, *The Nation*, under the leadership of President and Editor-in-Chief, Harold Hoyte, grew rapidly in popularity strongly supported by chairman of the Nation Corporation Fred Gollop, who resigned his post following the 1994 general elections and his subsequent appointment as President of the Senate.

Like *The Advocate*, *The Nation* is committed to securing the future of Barbados by doing all in its power to ensure the survival of democracy and the rule of law.

Equally importantly, both newspapers have succeeded in encouraging readers to express their fundamental right to state their views regardless of the issues at stake.

In its 20th anniversary address to its readers, the possibility of cross-ownership to ensure its growth, was raised.

The publisher suggested that collective capability *"should serve to strengthen press freedom in our country and make Barbados relevant in the skies where the cross-national value of electronic news output by satellite will shortly be as competitive as international trade."*

Five years ago, Barbadians were introduced to yet another publication, *The Broad Street Journal*, the country's only weekly business and financial newspaper which is rapidly blazing a trail in business publishing.

Add to this the Caribbean News Agency (CANA), plus some ten radio stations, ranging from rock to religion, and it soon becomes apparent that

Barbados is one of the most informed country's in the Caribbean, benefiting from a more liberated freedom-preserving news media, enhanced by several national award-winning investigative journalists.

In the past five years, *The Broad Street Journal*, which has the exclusive publishing rights in Barbados for The New York Times News Service, has also made tremendous strides in Barbados and throughout the wider Caribbean.

Since its inception in November 1993, this financial newspaper has carved a special niche for itself in a highly competitive local media environment, through its timely and accurate reporting on local and regional business and insightful analysis and commentary on business and financial matters.

More importantly, however, *The Journal*, whose readership includes about 5,000 business people, while refusing to be sensational, addresses in no uncertain terms political issues of the day and in particular decisions which will impact strongly or perhaps in its opinion, negatively, on the future development of Barbados.

To this end, it is not unusual to hear editor and publisher Patrick R. Hoyos relentlessly grill government, and in particular, the prime minister on decisions regarding everything from the development of the sugar industry to the establishment of a multi-million dollar marina in the historic village of Speightstown. *The Journal* also plays a critical role in that it features in-depth analyses of policy issues facing government as well as the private sector.

Embodying a more regional thrust is yet another tabloid, *Caribbean Week*, launched on 4 October 1989 and celebrating its seventh anniversary of publishing committed to a unified Caribbean.

"Our vision of a unified Caribbean is finally coming into focus," writes *Caribbean Week's* President, Tim Forsythe.

On 14 October 1995, the front page of *Caribbean Week* went on the World Wide Web in a bid to reach an even wider reading audience. In fact, *Caribbean Week* is the only English-language publication with distribution throughout the entire Caribbean Basin which includes 26 island nations. It is also distributed in selected major cities in the United States, Canada and Europe. As a high-quality full colour newspaper, it addresses political issues, press freedoms and is the only newspaper in the Caribbean to publish all three Caribbean exchange listings.

Caribbean banking began in Barbados

Barclays Bank Plc is the oldest banking institution in the Commonwealth Caribbean, having provided unbroken service since May 1837 when branches of the Colonial Bank first opened their doors to the public in the British Westindies. This long period encompasses the history of the islands from Emancipation to Independence and after. Just as conditions have changed in countries and territories, the bank's services have changed and the bank has evolved.

The bank was the product of favourable circumstances in the economies of Britain and the Westindian colonies. In England, the early decades of the 19th Century saw the establishment of the first joint stock banking companies with their ability to mobilise greater resources and provide greater security for shareholders and customers alike. The mid-1830s were prosperous years in the United Kingdom, encouraging people to invest their money, and in the Westindies, the 'Great Experiment' of Emancipation was under way, creating new economic circumstances and new opportunities for businessmen.

Not only did planters have their compensation monies to dispose of, but in recent years the old system of merchant-financing of the sugar industry had come under growing strains from heavier demands for funds, which the greater resources of a bank could meet. Finally, with the former slaves now being paid a money wage, the use of cash in the islands was expected to increase.

In these circumstances, a group of merchants and bankers in London decided to establish a bank to operate in the Westindies, with a head office in London. At the first meeting of directors at the end of March 1836, they decided to engage James McQueen to visit the islands to make the necessary arrangements, and in April, they inserted advertisements in newspapers at home and in the Westindies, outlining their purpose. It was a popular project. Capital was £2,000,000 in 20,000 shares of £100 each, 3,000 of which were reserved for residents of the colonies. Applications worth nearly £7,000,000 were received, allowing the directors to refuse those who they supposed sought shares 'merely for the object of speculation and immediate sale to make gain' without fear of missing their target. A Royal Charter establishing the bank with the name The Colonial Bank was granted by William IV on 1 June 1836.

The enthusiasm that greeted the project in England was shared in the Westindies. *The Barbadian* described its charter as *"one of the most important documents that ever found its way from Europe to the Western Tropical World..."* and explained why:

"Without such an institution, conducted by men of substance, intellect, and commercial experience, we are led to understand that the agricultural proprietors will not be able to stand the shock of the year 1840" (1840 was the year originally chosen for the termination of Apprenticeship, which actually occurred in 1838). Under its charter the bank was to engage in all the normal activities of metropolitan banks: dealing in bullion, money, and bills of exchange, and lending money on commercial paper and government securities. It could issue its own bank notes in dollars, without limitations, and the charter did not require the issue to be secured in any way. The only qualification was that dollar notes be redeemed in dollars, which were sometimes in short supply. A supplementary charter, dated 30 October 1838 removed this requirement, so ensuring that the bank had the flexibility that the currency situation required. Against this rather remarkable freedom, the bank was prohibited from lending money on the security of fixed property (a prohibition that was modified in 1856 and 1898, before being withdrawn in this century). And, of course, it was a deposit taking institution: when it opened, it offered for example, current deposits for merchants who *"shall always keep a respectable balance in the bank, or if preferred, those accounts will be kept without a deposit balance at moderate percentage."*

Obviously, the services the bank offered were of use largely to those who already had money and property, which in the Westindies in 1837 meant principally the planters and the merchants. However, at the start the bank hoped to tap the savings of the labouring classes, the former slaves, who were now to be paid wages.

Accordingly, it was organised after the 'Scottish' system. In that country, depositors

PREVIOUS PAGE and BELOW:
Barclays Park, located on the scenic east coast, was an independence gift from Barclays Bank to the government and the people of Barbados. This is a popular picnic spot and is adjacent to the venue (dubbed Calypso Bowl) now used for the Pic 'o' de Crop semi finals, a significant event on the Crop Over calendar

Barclays today

One of the first branches to begin operations in the Caribbean was Barclays Bank in Bridgetown, Barbados, which commenced business on 15 May 1837. The main business of the bank at first was financing agriculture and trade. In some instances the bank also served as the government's banker, though the government had no power over the bank.

The bank employed only men prior to World War I when, as a result of their departure to join the armed services, women began to join the bank's staff in considerable numbers, and were called lady clerks. The first lady clerk joined Barclays Bank in Barbados in 1920.

Today women represent the majority of the bank's staff in Barbados and successfully fill junior and senior management positions.

Barclays Bank Plc is now represented by nine service outlets, six branches offering a full range of commercial services, located in the north, west, south and central parishes of Barbados.

Barclays' Caribbean Regional Office

Barclays Bank, Broad Street is a complete financial centre, encompassing a full range of banking services. In addition the bank also provides offshore banking services, foreign exchange services and trustee and investment services. Barclays Finance Corporation provides mortgages, fixed deposits and insurance broking services. The Lower Broad Street branch which opened in 1972, is the main centre for personal lendings.

The Caribbean Regional Office is also based in Barbados and administers the operations in the Caribbean stretching from Bahamas in the north to Grenada in the south.

A community-minded organisation, Barclay's contribution to health, sports, youth, education and culture has been significant over the years.

were paid annual interest on deposits up to a limit of £200. In the Westindies, it was hoped that the system would be *"most extensively followed by the peasantry and labouring population of the British Colonies, in whose hand it is well known that there are very large sums of money locked up useless to themselves and the community. Scarcely anything can tend more than this system adopted to secure and perpetuate their industry ...."*

In practice, either these very large sums were imaginary, or their owners found the bank's terms unattractive, and small savings deposits remained a minor and apparently unsought after part of the business. (In Barbados, the government established a savings bank in 1852, and the Colonial Bank became its banker, and so indirectly a beneficiary of the small man's thrift).

Throughout the Caribbean, the bank opened its offices, beginning on 15 May 1837 in Barbados, Trinidad and British Guiana. A little later in the same year it opened in other territories, St Lucia, Grenada, Antigua, Dominica, St Kitts, St Vincent and the Danish Virgins, and it had short lived sub-branches in Caracas and San Juan, Puerto Rico.

To the west, it opened in Kingston, Jamaica. Usually it had a monopoly, a circumstance that led a few to regard it with the deepest suspicion. In 1838, when the bank was scarcely a year old, The Hon J Bovell told the Barbados Assembly:

"I look upon that leviathan establishment (the bank) as the greatest evil with which the West Indies were ever visited ... for there is nothing, Sir, too low for its cupidity, or too high for its avarice. Indifferent as to what comes within the verge of its rapacious appetite, it takes all with one fell swoop, and like the daughter of the horse leech, still cries 'give, give, give'."

However, Bovell was not against banks as such, only the Colonial Bank, and became one of the founders of the West India Bank, which established branches in other colonies.

The West India Bank was the only significant competition the Colonial Bank faced until Canadian banks made their appearance towards the end of the century. Originating in Barbados, and drawing capital from the Westindies and merchants in Britain, it provided spirited competition for most of the 1840s, so much so that the Colonial Bank's business in Barbados made a loss for some years, though by 1847/48, when the West India Bank failed, the branch was profitable.

Extract from a 1987 report on Barclays 150 Years in the Caribbean, courtesy of Barclays Bank, Barbados.

131

Lest we forget

Barbados' role in the World Wars

by Sarah Venable

During the first and second world wars, the Caribbean once more became an arena of conflict between world powers, with submarines and warships plying its lovely waters. In the first World War, the Barbados Cable Office and Wireless Station were targets of the German cruiser *Carlsrhue*, which exploded en route to attack.

During World War II, the shores were posted with machine guns. It was to Barbados that the tanker *San Eliseo* limped for repairs. Submarines were spotted off Needham's Point and Hastings, and the German U-boat *162* was sunk by the British 40 miles southwest of South Point Lighthouse. The harbour was the scene of an intense battle between the German *U514* submarine and the Canadian ships *Cornwallis* and *Betancuria*. (The Barbados Museum later acquired the engine propeller which powered the striking torpedo).

During this time, Barbados also used its Cable and Wireless stations to monitor intelligence that passed along a communications cable that stretched from Recife, Brazil to Miami, Florida. Many maps showed this as an American Western Union cable, although not all revealed that it passed through Barbados. Through this route German Embassies in South America sent all their important messages to and from the continent. Meanwhile, a corps of 'mystery men' from Barbados and the UK worked round the clock to intercept these telegrams. One result was the historic battle of the River Plate (Rio de la Plata) in December, 1941. Patrick Roach, a son of St Lucy soil, was on duty in Barbados when information indicating the presence of a powerful German ship which turned out to be the *Graf Spee* was intercepted. His 'earwitness' report in *The Bridge Barbados* makes fascinating reading for history buffs. In short, it was Bajan intelligence that led to the *Graf Spee's* scuttling in Montevideo harbour and the ensuing suicide of her captain.

ABOVE & BELOW: Graves and memorial headstones at the Military Cemetary, near Fort Charles, Bridgetown

IN MEMORY OF
ERIC FRED SPIERS PULLEN
CORPORAL
ROYAL AIR FORCE. WW2
10 JUNE 1994
AGE 74
REST IN PEACE

IN MEMORY OF
NEVILLE WILFRED BOXILL
LEADING SEAMAN
TRINIDAD ROYAL NAVY VOLUNTEER
RESERVE. WW2
12 FEBRUARY 1994   AGE 74
LOVING WIFE AND CHILDREN

The Barbados Volunteer Force

by Major Mike Hartland

Memorial headstone for a member of the Barbados Regiment, Military Cemetary, Bridgetown

The Barbados Volunteer Force (BVF) was formed on 31 December, 1901, when the legislature voted the great sum of £175 for the formation of the force. That was a lot of money in those days.

Promptly on 2 January 1902, the then governor, Sir Frederic Hedgoon KCMC VD, summoned a meeting of those interested at the Assembly Rooms. His Excellency presided over the meeting.

Addressing the gathering, Sir Frederic told those present that the object of the meeting was to form the Volunteer Force. He said that 30 drill instructions would have to be taken by each member of the force during his first year, and that, after leaving the recruit class they would be required to do ten drills.

Members had to enrol for three years. Drill instruction would be in the evenings in the drill yard of the central police station and fines would be imposed for irregular attendance. Dress would be khaki with blue cuffs and collars and a cap.

Armaments for infantry would be the Lee-Enfield rifle; for the Artillery the Carbine, the Maxim and two-nine pounders. For the Cyclist Corps, the Martini-Henry Carbine.

His Excellency would command the Volunteer Force himself and would appoint officers to various sub-units. In response 37 persons enrolled their names. This number was to increase dramatically as the years went by.

In World War I many members served with the British West Indies Regiment in Europe and the Middle East. In World War II the Volunteer Force was embodied to form the Barbados Battalion of the South Caribbean Forces. In 1947 the name the Barbados Volunteer Force was changed to the Barbados Regiment which enabled it to receive its first colours in 1953. The Regiment is still in existence today as the reserve element of the Barbados Defence Force.

A detachment of the Barbados Volunteer Force, from a postcard published about the time of the first World War

The Barbados Volunteer Force was just one in a long line of locally raised militias, stretching back to 1640 when the first militia was formed.

The National Cannon Collection

Cannon on display at the Garrison Savannah

The Barbados National Cannon Collection of mainly 17th Century English Iron Guns is now recognised internationally as of great importance. It includes a Commonwealth Gun of circa 1650 with Cromwell's Republican Arms on it, one of only two known to exist. An Elizabethan Gun of circa 1600 has recently been unearthed in excellent condition and could be the only one of its kind still remaining. Other very rare guns are displayed in the National Armoury in St Ann's Fort and on the Garrison Savannah.

Barbados was always very important to the British, not only because of its sugar production but because of its strategic position in relation to the other Caribbean islands. During the Napoleonic Wars it was the launch pad for the recovery of those islands overrun by the French. Located 100 miles into the Atlantic, the prevailing winds and currents enabled the British Fleet to land troops at will and achieve complete surprise. It was therefore essential to the British that Barbados remained intact and to this end it was heavily defended. Records show that in 1780 there were 41 forts and batteries with a total of 442 cannons. All these were sited in a space of 35 miles along the south and west coast, the east coast being protected by the rolling Atlantic waves and the coastal reefs.

Until recently these cannons were lying abandoned on their original sites but with the help of the Barbados Defence Force many have been recovered and now form the basis of the National Collection.

Sam Lord's Castle

For more than 150 years, Sam Lord's Castle in St Philip has dominated the south-east coast of Barbados. The home of Samuel Hall Lord, born in 1778 into Barbados gentry, was built with slave labour in 1820 for £30,000.

Rumours claim Sam Lord acquired his vast wealth from 22 ships that were wrecked on Cobblers Reef in front of Castle beach. The existence of a tunnel leading from the beach to the castle, filled with treasure, has never been proved. It was rumoured that Lord was a pirate but this claim has never been proven, however, it was also said, that to deceive ship's captains into thinking they were at the mouth of the harbour in Bridgetown, Lord instructed his slaves to tie lanterns on palm trees. Ships turning towards the distant lights, crashed onto the reefs becoming easy prey for Lord and his pirate band.

Sam Lord remains as much a mystery today as he did in his own time. A handsome, dashing young rogue who, aged 26, charmed societies in London and Bath in 1804. He married an heiress, Lucy Wightwich against her family's wishes and the couple sailed for Barbados in 1809.

Lord was not a model husband and Lucy left him three-years later. His treatment of his immediate family was equally startling. His nephew John, part-owner of the Lord estate, died mysteriously from 'natural causes' in 1821. Then his niece, Eliza, who had acquired an interest in the castle from John, also died under strange circumstances. The last remaining heir, Frances Lord Trollope, eventually agreed to relinquish her share to her uncle for a yearly allowance which was never paid .

After life long brushes with the law, a warrant was issued in 1817 on charges of forgery and perjury which were later dropped. Sam left for England in 1844 at the age of 65, where he died later that year on 5 November and was buried in Kensal Green Cemetery, London. His coachman, Rolestone, reported that he last saw his master enter an unidentified house, rumoured to be the home of a surviving ship-wrecked captain. When he did not come out, Rolestone questioned the hall porter, who allegedly replied, *"I would never wish you to be as your master is now; you will never see him again."*

Sam Lord's Castle

Named a National Trust House, Sam Lord's Castle and its legends are testament to the Bajan pirate who, it is rumoured, plundered ships off Cobblers Reef in Barbados and amassed great wealth. It is known that he died a sudden mysterious death in London in 1844. After the death of Sam Lord the castle finally passed to Frances Lord Trollope. Over the years it has had several owners who rented it for the summer much like any other bay-house in Barbados. In 1940, George Stewart, an English insurance magnate, purchased the property and spent close to BD$1 million on restoration before it was acquired by Marriott Hotels.

The castle has been remodelled into hotel suites and is surrounded by lush, tropical vegetation, including pink and apple blossom casia, flame trees, frangipani and a variety of palms.

Marriott Hotels, owners and operators of the Castle Resort

since 1972, have meticulously preserved the mansion's 19th Century grandeur. Hotel guests can still occupy one of the castle's nine bedrooms, including Sam Lord's own suite with his magnificent four-poster bed with its three-tiered stepping stool and massive cedar wardrobe six-feet high and eight-feet wide. Sam Lord's Castle is a two-story mansion with verandas of white marble, plasterwork ceilings fashioned by Windsor Castle craftsmen, fluted mahogany columns, paintings and antiques worth more than US$1 million.

Inside the castle, guests may view some of the finest furnishings and art of the time. Massive regency mirrors, gilt-framed and tarnished by sea spray, hang from the walls. Lords' sofa with brass legs carved into lion's paws sits at the bottom of the mansion's staircase. Pieces of Lord's English dinner service are on display in a period sideboard.

One of the hotel's restaurants, the *Wanderer* is named after a ship wrecked in 1833. Rumour has it the captain of the *Wanderer* survived and killed Sam Lord in England 11 years later.

The castle's dungeon is now the management offices. Sam Lord is said to have imprisoned his English wife Lucy there. Eventually, she escaped back home to England by bribing the slave jailer with jewels.

Other reminders of Lord include his castle shaped bathhouse. A short walk from the main house towards North Beach are wells where he kept turtles fresh for the castle table.

Fanciful stories of Lord's exploits still thrill Bajan children more than 150 years after his death. The castle continues to intrigue visitors.

Today, Marriott's Sam Lord's Resort, located just 20 minutes from the Grantley Adams International Airport, and 30 minutes from Bridgetown, features luxurious accommodation, beautiful sandy beaches, spectacular views as well as meeting and conference facilities.

Joshua Steele: The great innovator

by Colin Hudson

Joshua Steele was born in Ireland in the 18th Century, possibly as early as 1700. Nothing is known about him until he married a rich widow in 1750. Part of her riches came from her inheritance of one of the largest Barbados estate groups - Kendal, Guinea and Hallets - amounting to over 1,000 acres. Although much younger than him, she died seven years later, leaving him a rich widower.

He joined the Society of Arts, Manufacturing and Commerce in 1756, becoming vice president in 1779 as well as chairing a number of committees. Being most innovative his work on linguistics included devising a speech notation similar to musical notation. He was also involved in the early development of steam engines - then called fire engines - when in 1768 he offered to carry out an experiment with a steam engine for grinding cane on the estates he had yet to visit. That was 72 years before the first steam plant was actually installed in Barbados.

Steele's closest friends included the famous botanist Sir Joseph Banks, and the innovator, Dr Benjamin Franklin. He maintained correspondence with both men over many decades, including with the latter even in the midst of the traumas of the War of American Independence.

Steele had been noting for some time a decrease in his income from Barbados and, in February 1780, he decided to investigate personally; quite a decision for a man in his 80th year.

Within a few weeks of arriving in Barbados he had come to two conclusions. The first was that his attorneys, managers and overseers had not only robbed him beyond belief but were not even managing his estates efficiently in their own interests. His second conclusion was that the social life of the upper classes disgusted him, as so much of it centred around gambling and drinking. He was deeply disturbed by the illiberal and backward nature of society. What distressed him most of all was that for the first time here he had to face the inhuman realities of being the owner of slaves.

Instead of returning to England after putting the plantation in order, he set himself some very difficult tasks: the manumission of his slaves, the betterment of the poor white community, the reform of Barbadian Law (particularly as it affected slaves) and the reduction of dependency on sugar for the island's export trade.

However, before Steele could set any of his schemes and projects in motion, Barbados was struck by a terrible hurricane on 10 October 1780.

Steele suffered huge losses with the destruction of his windmills, boiling houses and various buildings. But he realised that this destruction provided the opportunity for updating and adopting the latest technology during the reconstruction period.

As a matter of urgency Steele started a Barbados version of the London Society of Arts, which was called the 'Society for the Encouragement of Arts, Manufacture and Commerce'.

The Society managed to attract only 19 members in the first year. This grew to 56 three years later partly because the new governor, David Parry, became an enthusiastic member (and later its president) and because Steele was to invite ladies to join - eight did. They also admitted non-resident members, which included a general, an admiral and incredibly, the Prime Minister, Lord Shelburne, as well as two Baronets. There were also clergymen, doc-tors, lawyers and perhaps 30 progressive planters.

The Society carried out a large number of experimental projects and was in constant communication with the London and Dublin Societies and occasionally with their lordships in White-hall for advice, materials or support. For example, the Lords Commissioners of Trade and Plantations were asked to approve the export from England of *"such instruments as appertain to hackling, spinning, reeling, weaving and frame knitting"* for Steele's workhouses; their lordships were also asked whether the seeds and plants of nutmeg, clove, cinnamon and pepper could be transported from Asia to Barbados. Cotton material produced in Barbados can still be seen in the archives of the Royal Society of Arts. Thus the spinning, weaving and even dyeing of cloth was accomplished in Barbados more than 200 years ago.

The Society gave not only advice, aids for products and rewards for them, but also people - notably a Lancashire weaver and his wife, who were sent out to Barbados to give public demonstrations of a *"newly invented engine for spinning on 20 spindles"*. The area of experimentation and interest in Barbados seemed limitless: growing cotton, coffee, cocoa, ground nuts, experiments in dyed stuffs, medicines, leather tanning, the use of the plough, cultivation of vines, the milling of flour, silk kersimer, the breeding of colts, the erection of a salt works and the production of tomato ketchup.

Perhaps of even more interest was that Steele saw Barbados as having great tourist and sanatorium opportunities and he wrote to friends, like Sir Joseph Banks, urging this idea, thus foreseeing a Barbados tourist industry.

And what about this item? *"Coffee and chocolate both grow on my estate .... we have at least 40,000 people, black and white, who use chocolate or coffee, morning or night, or both, as a principle part of their diet. The value of this at their lowest rate must amount to £50,000 currency, of which £30,000 worth is imported and for the most part smuggled. We might easily raise enough to supply ourselves and export much more to Europe, by planting these trees in our gullies, which are the most proper places, as both require shelter from the wind."*

But the greatest innovation of all concerned his fight against slavery. Not only was this by his writings and speeches, but by the practical steps he took on his own properties, which included: abolition of the whip and all arbitrary punishments, the introduction of a jury composed by the slaves themselves for punishing delinquents and the introduction of wages (based on task work). One result of this revolutionary action was that the labour productivity increased and his profits tripled!

In spite of Steele's achievements and those of the Society, the best indication of his relative unpopularity was the fact that the Society remained so small and petered out as Steele aged.

However, the island did benefit from a wider crop base as a result of Steele's influence.

Steele had an asset which is denied to most innovators - he had wealth and the power which went with it. He was a particularly fascinating example of what can be achieved when competence and power are connected, even in a pretty awful environment of indolence, infelicity and devastating hurricanes.

Sixteen years after setting foot on Barbados, Steele died in 1796 and was buried at St Philips Parish Church.

Early forms of transport

Beginning with the first vehicle in July 1847, the horse-drawn omnibuses in Barbados plied almost exclusively between Bridgetown and Speightstown. In 1900 the fare was statutorily fixed at four cents per person for each mile or part of a mile. The introduction of a motor omnibus service on the Leeward route in 1907 finally signalled the end for the horse-drawn vehicles and the last two disappeared around 1910.

The horse-drawn cab stand in the 'The Green', Trafalgar Square, centred on a large spreading tree and came into existence around 1870. A statute of 1891 prescribed two different rates of cab fares based respectively on distance and on time and every cab-driver was obliged to display a table of these rates conspicuously under penalty of a fine of $9.60. The arrival of motor services inevitably doomed the cabs to extinction and the last survivor finally vanished around 1940.

The Barbados Tramway Company commenced operations in March 1884 and eventually operated on some six routes altogether. Travelling on rails, the trams could not be turned around; the mules were simply transferred to the opposite end for the return journey. Unable to compete with the newly-established motor omnibus services, the tramway ceased operations on 31 July 1925.

The Barbados Railway, which operated from 1881 until 1937, ran 24 miles from Bridgetown to Belleplaine, St Andrew and the main station on Fairchild Street stood on reclaimed marshland leased by the company for 500 years at a peppercorn rent.

The station at Bathsheba, some 20 miles from Bridgetown, was built in 1883 to serve that picturesque seaside resort.

Following the closure of the railway, the main station buildings were relegated to other purposes and the rural stations were demolished.

Early Marine transport

The Lighter. These sturdy boats were built of extremely thick planks and were of two sizes, some of 20 and others of 30 tons laden, and were utilised to transport cargo to and from the ships anchored in Carlisle Bay.

Row Boats (also known as Shore Boats). These boats were about 20 feet in length and four feet wide, with cross seats towards the bow to carry either two or four oars-men, while towards the stern there were seats for the individual steering.

Speightstown Schooners. These small schooners were really droghers of about 50 tons cargo capacity, that plied between Bridgetown and Speightstown carrying both human, animal and all sorts of cargo. They mainly transported sugar and molasses between the two towns.

Inter-Colonial Schooners. These vessels plied throughout the Caribbean transporting passengers as well as cargo.

TOP: Bum boat in Carlisle Bay. Courtesy of Barbados Museum and Historical Society. MIDDLE: Horse-drawn funeral service. BOTTOM: Barbados Tramway Company

The Egyptian-Barbadian connection

An early morning shower off South Point is enough to dissuade most from a 3,200 mile Atlantic crossing - by any means

Barbados receives visitors from many points of the globe but it is the rare traveller who crosses the Atlantic on an ancient Egyptian- style papyrus boat to get here. Barbados captured world attention in July 1970 as the landfall of Thor Heyerdahl's tiny sailing craft, *Ra II*, which had set sail in May from Safi, Morocco bearing a crew of eight men from eight nations. It was Heyerdahl's second attempt to prove his theory that Egyptians of the pharaonic era could have reached the new world in vessels like this. This link is suggested by the presence of pyramids and other geometrical forms in both Egypt and Central and South America, and by the development of advanced astronomical knowledge in the early civilizations of both regions.

The Norwegian explorer attained international fame in 1947 when he and a small crew travelled 4,700 miles in 101 days on the raft *Kon Tiki*. That voyage spanned the Pacific from Peru to Polynesia and suggested a South American Indian derivation of the original people of those islands.

Built by Bolivian Indians, *Ra II* was made of the Egyptian bulrushes known as papyrus, which will not sink when saturated with water. The craft had a single, trapezoidal sail bearing an orange disk to represent the ancient Sun God for which the vessel was named. Aside from her sextant and hand-crank shortwave radio, the *Ra II's* equipment and provisions were copies of those used by Egyptian sailors of pharaonic times.

During the dramatic 3,200 mile, 59-day Atlantic crossing, the *Ra II* encountered becalmed seas, a storm with 40 foot waves that broke the steering rod, and pods of oil pollution so disgusting that on some days none of the men dared bathe. In the final days of *Ra II's* approach to Barbados, both the seas and the tension mounted; she was pushed off course by opposing currents, lost radio contact, and even her flares were invisible to a would-be meeting craft in the poor weather.

When the *Ra II* arrived, her sodden deck was barely above water. She was described variously in the press as a *"floating haystack"* and *"looking like stacked driftwood"*. Still, she sailed serenely into the Careenage while harbour craft bobbed like corks on the billowing water. Heyerdahl and crew's triumphant landing in Bridgetown was greeted by thousands of cheering onlookers, and welcomed by Prime Minister Errol Barrow and other dignitaries. *Ra II's* arrival in Barbados had proved another of Heyerdahl's startling theories of ancient navigational prowess and cultural transmission.

It also confirmed another of his strong beliefs, that people of different backgrounds, races and creeds can work together when they have a common purpose. Given that Barbados to a great degree exemplifies that principal, it was most appropriate that Heyerdahl admitted, *"It was our secret hope that Barbados would be our point of arrival in the New World."*

The story of the Barbados railway

Few visitors to Barbados today are aware that between 1881 and 1937 there was a railway that linked many beautiful, scenic places such as Bath, Martins Bay, Bathsheba, Kingsley and Belleplaine.

In 1845, German born Sir Robert Schomburgh, a chronicler of Barbados, surveyed the island for the plausibility of railway locomotives, and a Mr P L Simmons, editor of the *Colonial Magazine*, agitated for a system of railroads, based on several premises. There was a commercial importance in transporting the sugar cane from the plantations quickly and cheaply as possible. Boats were slow and costly. Whilst the roads were at the mercy of the weather, prone to flooding and often in a poor state of repair.

Due to economic restraints, the vision of linking the island with a railway was not to materialise until 1873 when Joseph A Haynes from Newcastle, England, persuaded fellow financiers to invest in a company to construct a railway line from Bridgetown to St Andrews.

The railway opened on 20 October 1881 from Bridgetown to Carrington. There were two trains daily in each direction, taking 40 minutes for the single journey. However, there were foreboding signs, as the undulating nature of the track derailed a carriage just one week after it came into service.

The company drew up rules, regulations and bye-laws , included instructions for the ascent and descent of the notoriously steep Consetts incline. Staff were exhorted to *"have their trains well under control"*, and to use *"every exertion to stop any runaway vehicles"*.

Despite the treacherous sounding journeys, the railway was initially a great success. By 1890 freight receipts reached an all time high, whilst large numbers of townsfolk availed themselves of pleasure trips into the country and the seaside, revelling in the novelty of the new method of transport.

The company unfortunately failed to make allowances for depreciation of rolling stock or maintainance and extension costs. Heavy rains and landslides often wrought havoc on the lines, causing derailments, falling bridges and line closures. Finances were invested over the years in maintaining the existing lines and as a consequence there were no funds put aside for extending the service.

The railway's financial situation worsened and winding-up petitions were issued, but fortunately two other companies tried to make a go of it: The Bridgetown and St Andrews Railway Ltd and The Barbados Light Railway Ltd.

The last passenger train ran on 20 January 1934, and in 1937

ABOVE: Railway station at Bathsheba
BELOW: Exposed coastline railway track

the line was finally closed. The roads, which had been upgraded and greatly extended over the years, making them more reliable and financially viable than the railway which had failed to reach 20 of the 29 main sugar factories.

However, the railway not only benefited the estates it reached, but made tourism a reality. Visitors fron British Guiana (Guyana) and Trinidad came to Barbados to enjoy the Atlantic breezes. Indeed, tourism was one of the major reasons for keeping the railway in operation.

Music and Culture

The effect of Barbados' history has created a blend of African and European culture which is uniquely Barbadian. This can be seen in the island's cuisine, its architecture, in the indigenous musical art forms such as the 'Tuk band' and, above all, in the heritage of Barbadian folklore and language. The official language of Barbados is English, but the popular speech is often the richly expressive 'Bajan' a Creole which combines an English lexical base with African grammatical forms and items of purely indigenous vocabulary. Many Barbadians are equally at home with standard English and Bajan, a context which has enabled the island to produce distinguished and widely-known writers such as Edward Kamau Brathwaite and George Lamming.

In recent years an upsurge in activity has been evident in all areas of the arts - particularly in painting, dance and music, and Barbados has produced a number of international performers in dance and classical music. Recent years have also seen an impressive development in popular music, especially calypso, which rivals Jamaican reggae, currently enjoying international acclaim.

George Lamming

All artistic forms receive official encouragement from the Government of Barbados and this is channelled through the National Cultural Foundation (NCF), a statutory corporation set up to oversee the cultural development of Barbados.

Steelband

It is rumoured that the steelpan was introduced to Barbados by a St Lucian seaman who had spent some time in Trinidad and Tobago. In the 1950s and early 1960s the instrument was combined with other types of pan and used to create music for the Barbadian community. Steelbands often provided music for dances and house parties and at that time some 40 bands existed. After this early flourish, however, steelbands declined in number in Barbados. Now the National Cultural Foundation is paying some attention to the preservation of this art form and have introduced a **Pan-A-Lang** competition as part of Crop Over festivities.

Instruction in steelband music does not exist universally in the school system and there is no directive to include it in the curriculum. Across Barbados, there is no participation of school-age children in the steelband movement and, as a result, there is no schools' steelband festival.

ABOVE & OPPOSITE: Pic 'o' de Crop festival

Steelbands in Barbados perform primarily in the tourist industry sector, at clubs and hotels. As a result, repertoire ranges from pop through to reggae, calypso, top-40s and some simple classical pieces.

140

During Crop Over festival there is a steelband competition, where the popular calypsoes are played. For the most part, the steelbands perform topical calypsoes which have become favourites during the Crop Over festival. Occasionally band leaders will create original compositions for the competition. This is common to the calypso genre.

Calypso

The 'African' derivation of calypso rhythms dates from the arrival of the first African slaves in 1627. These slaves, plus later arrivals, undoubtedly brought their skills and customs of instrument-making, singing and story-telling which evolved into present day calypso, a fusion of African, European, north American and Caribbean cultures.

Calypso in Barbados became more organised with the advent of the first Crop Over festival in 1974 which was hosted by the Barbados Board of Tourism. With the formation of the National Cultural Foundation (NCF) in 1984, Crop Over became synonymous with calypso. The NCF has, through its organisation, made calypso into a legitimately accepted art form by staging various competitions which culminate in the Crop Over, 'Pic 'o' de Crop' Calypso Finals, held at the National Stadium and attracting over 16,000 spectators. Barbadian calypso is performed with increasing frequency in north America and Europe.

Calypso is not taught in the schools nor included in the overall curriculum design. However, in the music department at Harrison College the art form has been studied as part of the sixth form related arts course.

A Junior Calypso Monarch Competition organised by NCF since 1986, attracts children from age six to 15 years. So popular has this competition become, that it has had sell-out houses since it its inception. On account of age groupings, school teachers and music teachers, as well as some of the calypsonians who are also teachers, have composed and taught the various techniques to the competing children. It was previously held at the National Stadium where it competed with Junior Kadooment Crop Over festivities which were billed on the same programme. In 1989 these two events were separated and the Junior Calypso Monarch competition was established. It has since become the nursery for calypso in Barbados, thus ensuring the continuity of the art form.

Calypso accompaniment varies quite dramatically in Barbados, depending on the availability of players and time frame. During Crop Over, approximately nine calypso tents or groupings perform and the

A typical calypso band combination is:
- one drummer
- one percussionist
- one rhythm guitarist (electric)
- one bass guitarist (electric)
- one keyboardist (electric or synthesist)
- one alto saxophonist
- two trumpeters
- one trombonist

Pic 'o' de Crop festival

142

make-up of the bands vary. The more established tents usually have the better musicians and, consequently, the best bands.

Many of the band members are drawn from the local Police Band and usually these members determine the style of performance.

Chorus singers usually comprise three persons, mostly female, who are heard during the performance singing in unison. Occasionally they venture into harmonisation - two part singing.

The Festival Band is a grouping of 16 of the island's best and most popular musicians,   contracted by the National Cultural Foundation as the official backing band for all the calypsonians appearing at the Pic 'o' de Crop semi-finals and finals during Crop Over festival. The Festival Band is undoubtedly the best of its kind in Barbados.

Reggae

Reggae has developed as an internationally acepted Caribbean music with roots in Jamaica. It is very popular with the youth, as was 'ska' and 'rock-steady'. Today greater interest exists for 'rap' as well as 'dub', 'lovers rock', 'dance hall' and Bob Marley standards. Most popular music performers will use some aspect of reggae in their stage presentation.

No real organisational structure exists in schools. Reggae is performed in Barbados and enjoyed by young adults and the school-age population. The music also forms part of the accepted repertoire of most popular groups on the island.

At Harrison College, in the music department, analysis and playing experience is provided for small groups and the style is fused in ensemble work with the school band, 'The Harrison College Ensemble'. Out of these efforts 'Raw Material', later becoming 'Exodus' became a popular band.

Spouge

Spouge music was the Barbadian sound of the 1960s, nurtured in St Lawrence, Christ Church by the Troubadours, a pop band on the entertainment scene at the time. The late Jackie Opel developed spouge in an attempt to create a Barbadian sound. The Troubadours, the Draytons Two and recently, Richard Stoute have endeavoured to revive spouge by including it in their stage performances. The Troubadours' instruments at the time included bass guitar, electric organ, drum, cowbell, bongos, congas, rhythm and lead guitars and vocals.

Barbados Caribbean Jazz Festival attracts players and enthusiasts from around the world

Church Music

Church Music with Caribbean idioms are experienced in churches all over Barbados. The music of Joseph Niles and the Consolers, Sister Marshall and the Victory Voices and other church stalwarts incorporates English hymns with Caribbean rhythms and African responses.

Jazz

Since the 1980s, jazz has become popular with the introduction by NCF of the Barbados Caribbean Jazz Festival where opportunity exists for players to create around the 'calypso jazz' idiom and include local rhythms for improvisation. Instruments include keyboard, brass, drums, vocalists, bass and electric guitars.

Folk

Folk music has always played a major role in the free expression of Barbadians. Artists such as the Merrymen, Pearson Bellamy of the St John Dramatic and Cultural Group, the work of

Sing Out Barbados, Ellerslie Chorale, the Mighty Gabby and more recently, Richard Layne, are all part of the folk heritage. Many have researched folk music, however, the book *Folk Songs of Barbados*, compiled by Trevor Marshall, Grace Thompson and Peggy McGeary, is a landmark in Barbadian folk music.

Gospel

Gospelfest in May each year brings together local and international artists for a three-day festival. Gospel is very popular in Barbados and the early cornerstones set by Joseph Niles and the Consolers and Sister Marshall and the Victory Voices, were responsible for the wide use of Gospel as the force for meaningful worship among the younger generation.

Classical Music

Classical music is much enjoyed by audiences in Barbados though it is not as popular as calypso. Many professional classical musicians reside in Barbados while others have sought to earn

144

Gospelfest is vigorous, lively and real fun

a living in England and north America. The work of the Barbados Symphonia; the newly formed Caribbean Latin American Society (the brainchild of violinist William Clairmonte), the Cecilian Singers, the Cathedral Choir and the Society for the Promotion of Church Music, among others, provide audiences and listeners with opportunities to hear concerts year round. These are usually supplemented by visiting artists from Europe, north America and Latin America.

Dance

Dance has a close association with all art forms of the Caribbean, and Barbados has been exposed to many of these, including the 'sagating' and the 'marico' dances to the calypsoes of early Trinidadian compositions. Ballroom dancing which was the order of the day with the big bands of Percy Green; the dance of the Bank Holiday Bears and the Donkey Man to accompany the Tuk band; the 'wine and jam' or 'wuk up and wine' to express calypso, and 'shanking' to express reggae and its forms; traditional dances: waltz, quadrille, square dancing, two-step, all exist, as well as ballet, modern dance, jazz and tap-dance classes.

Administrative Arrangements

There is a Ministry of Education, Youth Affairs and Culture. The NCF, a statutory corporation, falls under the above ministry. In the NCF there is a Chief Executive Officer, and assistant staff including cultural officers, in the performing arts, dance and drama. Music education and training at official governmental level comes under the Ministry of Education.

Music education, both oral and formal, exists daily in community life. In primary schools, education is confined to singing and movement classes and few children in the two to four age group learn an instrument. Primary education level involves pupils in singing, recorders and percussion bands. Secondary education has had increased interest in music for students and schools now advertise music departments.

Combermere School's programme has existed for over 50 years, and Harrison College's music department is the only

145

department of its kind in the government school system.

There is no curriculum at the University of the West Indies or Barbados Community College, however, the Extra Mural Department (the School for Continuing Studies) has contributed with violin and theory classes and more recently 'pan' music classes.

The Barbados Association of Piano Teachers hold seminars, conferences and assessment series every year at Easter and courses exist in music theory and music history for adults continuing education

Erdiston College provides initial training for primary teachers in classroom music.

Private Music Schools

Doris Provencal's Singing School and M & M Music Centre are the only institutions of their kind offering tuition for students from four-years to adulthood and covering classical, jazz, Caribbean studies and theory. A research area, based on traditional Barbadian and Caribbean music exists. To date, only seminars, workshops and concerts exist as aids to music education.

146

Private Studios

There are private studios, teaching piano and singing and many give private lessons in the home.

Music Industry

Musicians record in Barbados, regionally, the US, UK, Canada and Europe. There are approximately six studios for recording and a record production pressing plant in Barbados. Three of these studios use hi-tech equipment, others continue to upgrade. Sound engineers are either trained locally, in the US or UK, while others from Trinidad and the region contribute to the development of the industry. NCF holds occasional workshops covering the topic.

This chapter was based on information from NCF with the support and cooperation of the CEO of NCF, Mr Antonio Rudder, Cultural Officer (Music), Mr. Hal Archer, Janice Millington-Robertson, Addinton Forde, Andrea Wells and other members of NCF.

Sticklicking

Sticklicking is an ancient martial art practised very early in Barbados' history by the slaves and, after Emancipation, mainly by working class black people.

It was taught primarily as a means of self-defence, second only as a sport. Though widespread until the first half of this century, it had a social stigma attached to it, mainly because of the many brawls in which it was used. As a result, very few men outside the working class engaged in sticklicking, as did very few women of any class.

The weapon is a straight stick obtained from a variety of hardwood trees, about one metre in length and half an inch (1.3 cm) in diameter. This is prepared with heat to make it tough enough to withstand rigorous strikes.

There are seven progressive strategies, called cuts or positions, each with a number of guards, a term used for the defensive position in which the stick is held.

Contests called seitus were once very popular, held usually on Saturdays, or bank holidays, but seldom on Sundays. They were never held at night, since inadequate artificial lighting at the time would have made it dangerous.

Each village had its champions and, at big seitus, there were preliminary bouts with second-rate players. Bouts usually ended with bloodied heads, although contestants strictly avoided the dangerous punches or strikes to the groin or eyes.

The art had its origins in Africa, with influences from European styles of cudgelling and sword fighting. Although found in other parts of the Caribbean, Barbados' was the most feared style. Even within Barbados there were a number of styles, some of which could match stick-fighting in any part of the world.

Sticklicking declined during the 1940s, when many young men returning from the US after World War II smuggled in illegal firearms, making the art less meaningful as a method of self defence. They also brought in the art of boxing, which was seen as more dignified and replaced the sporting aspect of sticklicking.

There is now a small group of dedicated men who are keeping the sticklicking art alive with demonstrations at various occasions.

TOP: A cudgelling (sticklicking) match in the Westindies, from a lithographic print by Agostino Brunias, c. 1779. Courtesy: Barbados Museum and Historical Society.
ABOVE: A modern sticklicking demonstration. Photo: Addinton Forde

The Landship

The Landship is an institution which is unique to Barbados. It owes its origins to Moses Ward, who founded it between 1863 and 1868.

Ward was a Barbadian who had served in the Royal Navy, and on his retirement he sought to recreate some of the camaraderie and discipline of the navy, along with some of its pomp and splendour.

Landship members dress in naval uniforms and have naval ranks and titles. Female members were inducted after World War I and dress as nurses. They are referred to as stars, a term believed to have come from the Universal Negro Improvement Association founded by Marcus Garvey.

Landship in Trafalgar Square, Bridgetown. Performances usually take place on Saturday mornings

Ships have names such as *Cornwall*, *Vanguard*, *Director*, *Duke* and *Rodney*.

Nautical terms are applied to all activities; the meeting place is known as the dock and at the start of a parade, the ship is said to set sail.

As the name suggests there is no actual vessel, and all manoeuvres take place on land. By the 1870s there were Landships all over Barbados, parading in full regalia on a variety of social occasions.

The authorities viewed them as making a mockery of the navy, and by the early part of the 1900s they were suppressed almost out of existence. However, by 1930 they had resurfaced, with close to 50 Landships. The movement actually had its own magazine, "*The Barbados Landship Review*".

The manoeuvres consist of a combination of marching and dancing to simulated naval conditions, which include rough seas and man overboard. Orders are given by the officer in charge, while the music and rhythm is provided by the ships engine, the Tuk band,

One of their popular dances is plaiting the maypole, where dancers holding long coloured ribbons, dance around the maypole until the ribbons are intertwined; then they reverse the process.

The Landships are also friendly societies where members pay contributions, and when funds permit there is an annual bonus, as well as sickness and death benefits.

The Landship movement, which is an activity of working class people, is today at its lowest numbers, and is finding it difficult to recruit young members.

Nonetheless, the Barbados Landship, a combined crew from several decimated ships, can still be seen sailing in various parts of Barbados on festive occasions.

TRIBUTE TO BARBADOS LANDSHIP

by Winston Farrell

when i die
plait me in de may-pole
dance me 'long
familiar streets
in full regalia

let my children know
how i have manoeuvred
a century and more
of rough-seas
from the hole of my ship
to the deck of my
horse and buggy
from pond-grass and plantations
to a new language of drums borrowed
rhythms that now cash
my own mortgage

with a skip
hop/skip
with a dip
down low
in a wangalo
with a hip
hop/high
with a low
low tongue
with a low
down whisper

when i die
sail me thru
these paved highways

like a napoleon
like a nelson
with my navy
of land lovers
with my pride in my pocket
with my pain in my penny-whistle

let my children know
how half cent stretched
meant a tuppence saved in de susu
and the back house built
from shingle to soft-stone
from shop-counter to mini-mart
with the rough seas rising
with the bo's'n braving
man overboard
and the captain drilling
fire in the engine
and the chief nurse scurrying
to and fro with the smelling-salts
and the quinne to steady the rudder

thru gulley and pasture
thru rum shop and tenantry
the landship sails into dock
and the flock of villagers
weighting with laughter
watching on with the point of a finger
some turning their backs
on the spectacle of tuk drums
others rattling like kettle and base
hiding their face from the culture of the poor

when i die
wrap me in the flag
of the landship
sink me 'longside
De Hood
De Calcutter
De Hamshure
De George Simmons

proclaim my independence
for my children's ear's sake
De Rodney
hailing from Marricks St. Philips
under Commander James Franklyn
De Unconquerable Queen Mary
from Rotten Town
under Uriah Mayers
De Vanguard
Briggs Hill
under Captain Da Costa Eversley
De Cornwall
the toast of Carrington's Village
under the old veteran Commander Marshall
De Iron Duke
from Licorish Village
under Captain Perch
De Director
sailing from Highland St. Thomas
under Captain Watson,
proclaim my independence
rest me in the bosom of history
for my children's sake
when i die.

Winston Farrell

Winston Farrell is a versatile and durable performer. As an actor he has performed in over two dozen plays. In 1989, he received the National Youth Award for outstanding achievement in the field of drama; he gained a writer/artist in residence with the Hudson Valley Writers Guild and the University of Albany NY; first and third prizes in the 1987-88 ESSO Play Writing Competition and in 1993 a British Council Visitorship where he toured and worked with leading theatre companies.

In addition to his first collection of poems *Echoes of Young Blood* Farrell has been published in literary journals such as *Race Today* (London); *Crossing Water* by the Greenfield Press, NY; *Kyk-over-al*, July 1991; *Trinidadian New Voices*, and *Banja*. He has also released recordings of his rhythm poetry, *Lion on the Loose*, 1993; *Earth Spirit*, 1994 and *Busman* and *Minibus Hustle*.

He has travelled extensively and has performed in the Caribbean, Britain, Canada, Moscow and Asia. Farrell also has credits as a stage director.

Landship 'plaiting' the maypole

Marble Cricket & Warri

Marble cricket is a novel way to enjoy all the thrills and spills of normal cricket in a much smaller space. The equipment for the game is a reduced version of big cricket. The pitch is 20 feet long, the stumps are low and usually made from discarded soft pop bottles, sticks or sometimes even stones.

The ball can be either a golfball, a tennis ball or homemade with marbles wrapped in materials, hence the name of the game. Sometimes a piece of tar the size of an egg would be wrapped in rubber bands and also used as a ball. The size of the bat is 24 inches long and six inches wide and is usually made from the branch of a coconut tree.

Marble cricket is very much an individuals game rather than a team sport. Each player from the village would normally come and pit their wits against each other in both batting and bowling. The winner would be the person with the highest individual score at the end of the game.

The bowling takes place from a stationary position with a choice of both underarm and overarm bowling. If the bowler decides to bowl overarm they have to kneel but are allowed to stand if bowling underarm. Most choose to bowl underarm to reduce the bounce of the ball and minimize batting scores.

The person batting has to kneel on one knee, making sure not to block the wicket with the other. Normally right-handed players kneel on the right knee. Runs are scored by the batter running to the opposite side of the pitch and back. They must make sure to ground the bat in the crease after each run, otherwise they risk being stumped. No part of the body must be grounded in the crease.

The wicket-keeper squats safely behind the stumps as the bowling restrictions reduce the pace of the ball. Boundaries are the nearest obstacles at hand such as a ditch or a canefield. The game is rarely seen nowadays and is played in only a few areas of Barbados.

Warri is a pit and pebble game which originated in Egypt over 3,500 years ago. The game is traditionally played on a board approximately 24 inches long by eight inches wide. It has two rows of six, shallow depressions, called "houses", hence the name warri, which still means house in some African territories.

There are two players, each of whom start with 24 pebbles or seeds, four in each of the six houses on his side. The traditional seed used in Barbados is the horsenicker, a corruption of arsenical because it contains arsenic.

A forerunner of chess, warri is a simulated war-game, with the object being to capture as many as possible of your opponent's "men".

Though the game is not seen island-wide, it is still very much alive in some areas, particularly in the Speightstown district.

The decline of warri has been attributed to the rise in popularity of dominoes, introduced to the island by Barbadians returning home from the US during and after World War II.

Warri competition at the Cultural Village during Crop Over festival. Photo: Addinton Forde

It en' de gun dat does kill yuh, it is de shot.
It is small issues, rather than large ones, which give the most problems.

It don' tek a big axe to cut down a big tree.
Size, or lack of it, does not limit capabilities.

Ole stick o' fire don' tek long to ketch back up.
Once two people have been lovers it takes very little for them to become lovers again.

When big man in trouble, lil man trousers can fit 'e.
When a man is in trouble he loses much of his pride, dignity and self-confidence.

Yuh got to christen yuh own child before yuh can len' out de christening clothes.
You must solve your own problem before trying to solve someone else's.

Bad guh, wuss come. (Bad go, worse come.)
In trying to rid yourself of a bad situation, you may very well replace it with a worse one.

Don' limp before yuh lame.
Do not try to gain sympathy by pretending that you have a misfortune.

One hand can' clap.
It requires co-operation to achieve anything worthwhile.

Wha' do in de dark does come out in de light.
It is impossible to hide all of one's actions.

'E ketching 'e tail.
He is having a difficult time of it.

Yuh can' prevent yuh ear from hearing, but yuh can stop yuh mout from talking.
A warning against repeating what one has heard.

stone. A wooden wall is 'siding' or 'partition'.

To say sit on the ground could mean sit on the floor, and to lick down means to strike so hard, the person or object falls.

Intonations change the meaning of words and phrases, as happens in many languages. A 'sweet' (stress on sweet) boy 'is a pleasant child'. A 'sweet' (unstressed) boy 'is a persons who lives the easy life'.

One aspect of Barbadian dialect which is frowned upon by many, is that it is replete with expletives, many of these words used by other English speaking people, but used in different combinations, and at times in different contexts.

Another significant aspect of the dialect, is that its vocabulary, rhythm, and dramatic capability makes it a great conveyer of humour. Many jokes which would leave a Bajan in stitches, would be lost if translated into standard English.

There is much use of onomatopoeia, words whose sound reflect their meaning, like pangalang! the glass broke; splashae! she threw water on him; brugadown! he fell off the bicycle.

Many words and phrases are found no place else; like a 'braba rabba' or 'lick mout' meaning a person who talks too much; 'pow'ful foolish' for a person who is loud and aggressive, but a coward.

The Barbadian dialect is able to communicate any range of emotions, and as proof of its effectiveness, many skills have been passed from one generation to the next, by people with extreme limitations in standard English.

Island Legends

The Mystery of the Chase Vault

The fishing town of Oistins lies ten miles from Bridgetown, in the parish of Christ Church, on the south coast of Barbados. The Treaty of Oistins, said to be the Magna Carta of Barbados, was signed at the Mermaid's Tavern in 1852. Apart from this event, there seems to be nothing else of any great significance that occurred in that part of Barbados - nothing that is, except for the mystery of the Chase Vault.

The vault is in the graveyard of Christ Church Parish Church, an Anglican church situated on a hill half a mile to the north of Oistins. It was originally owned by the Elliot family and had been unused for several years prior to 31 July 1807.

It was on that day that the body of a Mrs Goddard was laid to rest in the vault. Seven months later on 22 February 1808, Mary Anne Maria Chase, the infant daughter of the Honourable Thomas Chase, was interred in the vault. Little Mary was buried in a leaden coffin and placed beside Mrs Goddard, whose coffin lay undisturbed for these seven months.

Almost four and a half years passed before Dorcas Chase, sister of Mary, was laid to rest on 6 July 1812. When the vault was opened to receive her leaden coffin, all inside was as it should be.

One month later, on 9 August 1812, the vault was opened once again, this time to receive the body of the Honourable Thomas Chase. It was of no little surprise to everyone concerned to find that the two leaden coffins were in total disarray. The infant's coffin was standing almost upright, head down, and on the opposite side of the vault from the north-east section where it had previously been laid. It was as if someone had carelessly flung it there.

The coffins, including Thomas Chase's, were all placed in an orderly fashion and the vault sealed once more in cement.

Four years later on 25 September 1816, the vault was re-opened to receive the body of another infant, Samuel Brewster Aimes. Once again the leaden coffins were found in a state of disorder. Again they were replaced in the correct position and the vault sealed in cement. This time, to make absolutely sure that this was not the work of pranksters, the floor of the vault was sprinkled with sand in the hope of capturing any human footprints.

On 17 November of the same year, the vault was opened again to receive the body of Sam Brewster who was murdered in the slave insurrection in which the well known slave Bussa was involved. Again, the leaden coffins were found in disorder, flung against each other as if they were fighting.

What was more astounding was that there were no footprints on the sanded floor and, even if it was possible for someone to enter the vault, it would have taken the combined strength of eight men to shift those leaden coffins, a number much too large to keep such a secret for so long.

For the third time the coffins were laid out in an orderly fashion, the floor freshly sprinkled with sand and the entrance to the vault sealed in cement.

Three years later, on 7 July 1819, when the vault was re-opened for the interment of Thomasina Clarke, those present were met with the same weird sight - leaden coffins on top of each other, as if tossed by some super-powerful hands.

Once again the coffins were put in their places, more sand sprinkled, and the mouth of the vault cemented in front of the rector and other officials. Private marks were made in the mouth of the vault and, on 18 April the next year, it was opened at the request of Lord Combermere, witnessed by him and three other influential men. The coffins had been fighting again!

At the request of the family all the coffins were removed and buried in graves. From that day the vault has been left opened. Until the present time, there has been no explanation for the strange happenings.

The mystery, however, did not end there. Recently, in the 1970s, two British tourists visited the vault and removed a stone each as souvenirs. For the next year after their return home, their lives were sheer hell, as one after the other misfortunes befell them.

At last in desperation, they mailed the two stones back to a local newspaper and begged that someone replace the stones.

Whatever demon or demons possessed the vault are still guarding it jealously.

If De Doctor Say So

The greatest natural disaster ever to strike Barbados in recorded history was the cholera epidemic of 1854, which swept through the Westindies for a period of several years, leaving an estimated 20,000 people dead in Barbados alone.

People died at such a fast rate that the ordinary grave-diggers could not cope with the burials and many healthy men made extra money helping to bury bodies. Many of these were buried in areas not originally intended as cemeteries, since the unusually high death rate exhausted some of the traditional cemeteries.

Such was the fear of this disease that, according to folk stories, many of the seriously ill were buried alive for fear that they would contaminate others, and some who lapsed into deep unconsciousness were unwittingly pronounced dead by careless doctors and suffered the same fate..

One woman had just regained consciousness to find herself in a coffin, along with one of these grave diggers preparing to bury her. Knowing the fate of others before her, she begged to be let out.

Not about to lose his few shillings, the man said "De doctor say yuh dead, ent? Well yuh dead!" and with that he nailed the coffin shut and buried the poor wretch alive.

Arts & Crafts

by Andrea Wells

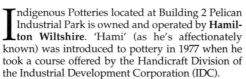

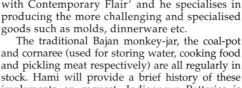

Turned mahogany items by Henderson Harwood

Three Barbadian Craftspersons...

Barbadian craftwork has developed significantly over the last twenty years due to the input of various governmental and other agencies. Now, more than ever, a pleasing diversity of finely crafted objects are available on the island. We take a look at three of Barbados' craft producers.

Diane Bourne-Daniel is well known for her colourful, collectable dolls. This charming lady has made dolls of high quality for nearly thirty years, utilising local materials such as khus khus grass, casuarina berries and pandanus. Cricketers, Tuk-band musicians, Landship members and other everyday Bajan folk are regularly captured in miniature by this artisan. Each one of her dolls has its own story. When you meet her be sure to ask about the significance of the doll's head-ties and aprons.

Mrs Daniel was named "Craftsperson of the Year" in 1990 for her outstanding contribution to the local craft scene. She is a founding member of the Barbados Craft Guild. She may be contacted through the National Cultural Foundation Tel: 424-0909.

Henderson Harwood's fascination with a miniature turned barrel inspired his entry into the profession of woodcarving. He has been pursuing his 'first love' since 1965. He has established himself as one of Barbados' foremost wood-turners having experimented with various techniques and different woods. This self-taught craftsman, although equally skilled in other areas of woodworking states that he gets 'great satisfaction from wood turning'.

Located at 22 Pelican Village, Bridgetown, Mr Harwood presently works in Barbadian mahogany (one of the world's finest woods) because of it's popularity. His shop is always stocked with superbly finished bowls, mortar/pestles, trays and a variety of other household implements, and he is also willing to make special pieces on commission. His work can be found in the collection of Westminster Abbey and Buckingham Palace, as well as in the homes of many discerning locals. His shop is open Monday - Friday 9.30 am - 4.30 pm.

Indigenous Potteries located at Building 2 Pelican Industrial Park is owned and operated by **Hamilton Wiltshire**. 'Hami' (as he's affectionately known) was introduced to pottery in 1977 when he took a course offered by the Handicraft Division of the Industrial Development Corporation (IDC).

Further training followed in Fiesole, Italy in 1985. Since then he has been fully employed in this field, four years of which were spent based at the historical 'home' of Barbadian Pottery - Chalky Mount, in the parish of St Andrew.

His business theme is 'Traditional Pottery with Contemporary Flair' and he specialises in producing the more challenging and specialised goods such as molds, dinnerware etc.

The traditional Bajan monkey-jar, the coal-pot and cornaree (used for storing water, cooking food and pickling meat respectively) are all regularly in stock. Hami will provide a brief history of these implements on request. Indigenous Potteries is open Monday - Friday 7.30 am - 7.00 pm.

A visit to these craft producers will certainly be rewarding. Pelican Village and its environs houses a diversity of craft producers and is a 'must see' for the visitor in search of authentic Barbadian craft.

"Terracotta Urn" by Hamilton Wiltshire

... and Three Painters

The vibrant art community in Barbados has produced some of the finest work in the Caribbean. In recent years top artists have literally 'brought home the gold' from international art biennials thereby raising Barbadian art to a position of prominence regionally and internationally. We take a brief look at three of the island's artists.

Ann Dodson is a painter and art-teacher. Her innate ability for visual expression was evident from childhood. This was further developed by formal study at the Barbados Community College, (where she currently teaches) and Concordia University, Montreal, Canada.

Ann's paintings often reflect her interest in the 'human condition'. She resists labelling herself but notes that she admires (and therefore is probably influenced by) the work of local artists Stanley Greaves and Ras Ishi (gold award winners), and the work of Alison Chapman-Andrews.

Ann Dodson lives and paints at Mullins Bay, St. Peter Tel: 422-2940.

Visitors are welcome by appointment.

Iwin, one of Barbados' younger breed of artists, was encouraged to paint at an early age by his family and school teachers. He has been selling his work at festivals since 1985, when he was only 14 years of age.

A member of the Rastafarian faith, his spiritual beliefs play an important part in his style of visual expression. The bold use of colour is his trademark and much of his work reflects his attachment to the land, as he is also a small farmer.

Iwin counts his exposure to slides of African paintings while at school and his friendship with, and admiration of, Ras Akyem and Ras Ishi as the greatest stylistic influences on his work. The shared Rastafarian faith of these three artists is also a bond.

Iwin is currently working towards his first major exhibition. He may be contacted on Tel: 425-4256 or 424-3724.

'Vendors' by Ann Dodson

''Sweet Hibiscus' by Iwin

Arlette St Hill creates work reflective of her concerns as an African-Caribbean woman. A preference for creating and absorbing visual expressions was noted from early on. Art History classes at school exposed her to the work of various European artists and furthered her determination to pursue art as a career.

Formal training at the Jamaica School of Art greatly impacted on her development. It was in Jamaica, surrounded by various art-forms that she began to examine her spiritual side and consciously began exploring her African heritage.

She taught art at secondary school level for twelve years, and also has designed and produced costumed bands for Barbados' annual Crop Over Festival. She currently holds the post of Audio Visual Aids Officer at the Ministry of Education, Youth Affairs and Culture. All of her paintings are reflective of some aspect of Barbadian culture. She welcomes visitors to her studio by appointment. Tel: 436-8547.

'Mas Party' by Arlette St Hill
Photo: Addinton Forde

156

Architectural Heritage

by Professor Henry Fraser

ABOVE & BELOW:
St Nicholas Abbey

Drax Hall

Barbadian architecture retains a rich assemblage of unique building styles evolved over 300 years. Although Bridgetown lost many buildings to fire over the years, and two hurricanes wreaked havoc in 1780 and 1831, many buildings survive from the 18th and 19th Centuries. There are even a few very ancient ones from the 17th Century, such as the Jacobean plantation Great Houses, St Nicholas Abbey and Drax Hall.

Since Barbados' colonial history was entirely English, it is not surprising that English architecture provided the basic ingredient in the evolution of the Barbadian vernacular style. Buildings must be primarily functional, and in early days could only be built with the materials at hand. The earliest settlers therefore built of wood and thatch, destroying the indigenous forests that once covered the island to build their houses and plant their crops.

By the middle of the 17th Century, production of sugar cane, molasses and rum was making Barbadian planters rich and elegant mansions were soon being built. The earliest record we have of buildings in Barbados is the account of the erudite English traveller, Richard Ligon, whose book A True and Exact History of the Island of Barbados (1657) described the planters' houses in the most scathing terms: *"The planters never consider which way they build their houses, so long as they get them up - which is the cause that many of them are so insufferably hot."* Yet St Nicholas Abbey, believed to have been built a year later, Drax Hall, Codrington, Holborn (the Governor's House in the 17th Century but now demolished), Pilgrim (today's Governors' House) and Warrens were well designed, elegant houses, all built within the following two or three decades. Many other fine houses would have been destroyed by the great hurricanes. Some, like Harmony Hall, now the headquarters of the Barbados Workers Union, were partly destroyed but rebuilt.

Since Barbados was a sugar plantation economy, much of the personal wealth of the planters was spent on their houses. However, there were many other impressive buildings, from the industrial buildings (sugar factories and warehouses) and the civic buildings (the Town Hall, the Parliament buildings), to the commercial buildings (shops and town houses) and the churches. After one of the destructive Bridgetown fires, a law was passed stating that all buildings should be built of stone. Since Barbados is covered with a thick coral limestone cap, good building stone was very easy to quarry. The result was

157

strong, well built, stone buildings which exploited the nature of the material to best advantage. Building styles were also modified by the need to resist hurricanes, to keep cool and to be protected from driving rains.

For all of these reasons the original English style, imposed at the height of economic success, was the Georgian style - a harmonious, simplified version of the fashionable Palladian (Italian) style. To this was added the verandah (imported from India) to provide shaded areas around the main rooms, and a wealth of details, from jalousie windows to wooden hoods that are characteristically Barbadian.

In addition to the beautiful and easy-to-work coral stone, bricks were also useful in building. After the slave trade ended (earlier in Barbados than in most other Caribbean islands), ships came directly from Britain and used bricks as ballast. These were replaced by sugar, molasses and rum on the homeward journey, and the bricks used in building. The entire British Garrison, the finest in the Caribbean, was built of bricks, and the magnificent arcaded barracks, built to house up to 2000 soldiers, must have greatly influenced local builders for many years.

After the last great hurricane in 1831, building styles changed little for nearly 100 years. After emancipation in 1838, the workers evolved their own style of movable (chattel) houses made of imported pine. The whole range of buildings evolved slowly, but not until after the Second World War was there any significant penetration of international styles. A major building impetus began in the 1980s, with modern international styles competing with evocative vernacular recreations by new teams of architects, particularly Selby, Rose and Mapp, Larry Warren and Peter Burke.

Largely as a result of the work of the Barbados National Trust and a few eloquent enthusiasts, the architectural heritage of Barbados is now widely appreciated and much thoughtful restoration has been carried out. Historic buildings play a major role in tourism as restaurants (the Waterfront Cafe), visitor sites (Tyrol Cot Heritage Village and Gun Hill Signal Station, among many), shopping centres (DaCosta Mall and Jamestown Mall) and many other uses. Indeed the government has plans for major restoration of Bridgetown and Speightstown, the 18th Century seaport in the north once known as Little Bristol. The role of heritage buildings is now seen to be an extremely important part of Barbados' attractions.

The Great Houses

Barbadian planters who made good, clearly tried to "live like kings". Many accounts exist of their fine furniture and silver and lavish banquets served to guests. The era of greatest wealth, the late 17th and early18th Centuries, coincided with the great English country homes and every planter must have set his sights on such a palace in the tropics. Some put their owners in the bankruptcy court. Lancaster Great House, occasional site of meetings of the Governor's Council, was reputedly one of these.

Farley Hill ruins

Only a few of the finest survive. Many were destroyed by storm or termite and replaced by more modest structures. One of the most magnificent ruins in Barbados is **Farley Hill**, the home of Sir Graham Briggs, Baronet. Sir Graham was an extraordinary Barbadian of innovative ideas, artistic and horticultural interests and his mansion was described as a veritable palace of treasures. He was also one of the few 19th Century planters of liberal views. He supported the reformist Governor, Sir John Pope-Hennessy, for which he was expelled from the Bridgetown Club (his own brother-in-law, as secretary, wielded the axe), and went into self-imposed exile in Nevis.

The most elegant of the surviving Great Houses is also the most unusual - **Sam Lord's Castle**.

Sam Lord was undoubtedly a highly amoral and greedy character. He almost certainly got rid of relatives to acquire their property, he treated his wife badly, and he was accused of causing the wreck of ships off the cliffs on which his mansion was built. Here legend and fact are inextricably intertwined, and no one knows the truth, but it makes a good story and a good song, sung by the famous Merry Men of Barbados, which claims that:

"He hung those lanterns on the coconut trees,
To lure the ships upon the reefs...."

Sam Lord's Castle

His castle, now the centre piece of Sam Lord's Castle Resort, is without any doubt the finest completely intact survivor of the Westindian plantation Great House era. It is essentially a massively built Georgian house of two floors and a basement, topped with battlements, a romantic concession to the Neo-Gothic style only then appearing in England. Its ceilings were decorated by the Italian plasterwork master, Rutter, who had worked on the ceilings of Windsor Castle, in England. They are probably the finest plaster ceilings in the Western hemisphere.

Other Great Houses which are open to the public include one or more from each century. St Nicholas Abbey is a classic Jacobean 17th Century manor house with curvilinear Dutch gables and corner fireplaces, and the largest domestic chimney breast most people have ever seen! It has cedar wainscotting, a Chinese Chippendale staircase and a fine collection of fascinating antiques.

Sunbury Plantation House, almost certainly begun in the 17th Century but of uncertain date, had become one of the leading heritage sites for visitors in the Caribbean until it was destroyed by fire in 1995. It is now being rebuilt. **Villa Nova**, built in 1833, is perhaps the finest example of a more typical Great House on a smaller scale than Sam Lord's.

Francia, built in 1912, was one of the last of the Great Houses in the grand style - its slightly French flavour derives from its French builder, who fell in love with a Barbadian and made Barbados his home. It boasts a superb set of coral dripstones, for purifying the domestic drinking water. These huge hand-carved stone pots were a major Barbadian export in the 18th Century.

Interior of Sunbury House

Tyrol Cot, built in 1854, is an elegant villa, Palladian in its inspiration, with an interesting history. Built by the leading Barbadian builder of the time, it became the home of a wealthy Danish merchant and, in 1929, the home of Sir Grantley and Lady Adams. Sir Grantley was a brilliant Barbadian lawyer who became the leader in the fight for democracy, the first Premier and the only Prime Minister of the West Indian Federation (1958-1962). His son Tom, Prime Minister from 1976 to 1985, grew up there. The house was acquired, restored and preserved intact by the Barbados National Trust, with all of the artefacts and collections of the Adams family. The rest of the site has been developed as a Heritage Village, a living outdoor museum, with chattel houses featuring traditional crafts and relics of a bygone age.

Francia

But the great wealth of plantation house architecture is in the sheer number which dot the countryside. From the palatial to the modest, such as the old stone cottage 'The Garden' in St Lucy, where Prime Minister Errol Barrow was born, they define the Barbadian landscape, surrounded by ancient trees and plantation buildings, built of stone, on stone, to last, it would seem, forever. Ironically, while sugar no longer brings Barbados much wealth, these houses have changed hands many times and are more likely to be owned by an English or American winter resident or a Barbadian lawyer or businessperson than a farmer or planter.

THE CHATTEL HOUSE

The chattel house is without any doubt one of the major icons of the cultural heritage of Barbados. It is as distinctly Bajan as the accent, as pervasive as cricket or cou-cou. It evolved as a result of historical circumstances and local ingenuity. While the landless poor of most Caribbean countries built the most basic shacks, the Barbadian plantation workers devised a modular, mobile house design that suited the situation while providing a measure of independence.

After Emancipation, the freed slaves were landless but were given the right to build homes on specified lands of each plantation for 'peppercorn rents.' Since the owners reserved the right to evict at short notice and since conditions were hard and management practices a far cry from today, the worker had to be readily mobile. And so houses had to be chattel which means 'movable possession.' They were built of timber and put together in such a way that they could be quickly taken apart in sections, moved to another spot by ox-cart and reassembled in a single day.

Cheap pine was imported from north America in pre-cut lengths, from 12 to 20 feet, all in even numbers, and the dimensions of houses reflect these lengths. Facades are invariably symmetrical, with a front door in the centre of the long side of the house, flanked by a window on each side.

Many houses would begin as a single unit, divided into two rooms. This was a 'one-roof' house, and the roof would be four-sided or 'hip' roof or a steep two-sided 'gable roof'. As prosperity or families grew, a shed would be added at the back, with a flat, sloping roof, the addition being called a 'shed-roof'. Or a complete unit with a hip or gable roof would be added. This would often be wider than the first unit, with two bedrooms, pierced by a corridor. With increasing prosperity porches or verandahs might be added, with three or four units, and, if the land was acquired stone foundations or stone additions were substituted.

Improvement in the size, features and embellishments of the chattel house came with the foreign earnings of the thousands of Barbadians who emigrated to Panama, Brazil, Curacao and New York early in the 20th Century. The apogee of the chattel house perhaps came in the 1920-30s and the most elegant survivors date from that period. The ingenious window designs, jalousies, 'bell pelments' or curved window hoods, pedimented barge porches and fretwork designs on the gable ends all give the Bajan chattel house a unique flavour, distinct from any other Caribbean folk architecture.

With its unfailing symmetry, tidy, harmonious proportions and pedimented porches it resembles a miniature of the Georgian house style imported by the planter. Yet it evolved utilitarian and aesthetic details to suit the life-style of the owner. Two other fascinating features of the chattel house are worth noting: the 45 degree slope of the roof and the ventilation of jalousie windows appear to protect them in hurricanes while more solid structures are destroyed. And it is clear that with increasing affluence the well known, traditional modular design was applied in much larger and more lavish versions to middle class suburban houses, in both wood and stone. It is one of the few examples of folk architecture influencing the styles of the more well do to.

Today, of course, most people's aspirations include a comfortable, modern house. But the chattel house remains a treasure for many older folk; a valuable tourism asset, often adapted as boutique, restaurant or bar. In response to the wide national interest in the chattel house and the need to preserve it for posterity the Barbados National Trust has created a Heritage Village of chattel houses and traditional crafts at Tyrol Cot, the historic home of Sir Grantley Adams, first Premier of Barbados. Here a range of facsimiles of some of the finest chattel houses has been created by architect Bruce Jardine, and they house some of the finest potters, basket weavers and other craftsmen - an outdoor museum of Barbados' finest building skills.

SUNBURY PLANTATION HOUSE

The history of Sunbury Plantation House goes back over 300 years to Matthew Chapman, an Irishman and one of the first settlers in Barbados. The estate was known as Chapman's Plantation and is shown on several early maps. After Matthew's death in 1693, the plantation was sold to Nathaniel Branker and the name changed to Branker's Plantation. It remained in the Branker family for some 60 years until it was sold to James Butler Harris.

After the death of Mr Harris 14 years later, the estate was purchased by two brothers John Henry Barrow and George Barrow, who greatly enlarged the plantation and changed the name of the estate to Sunbury, the name of their home in England.

John Henry's son the Hon John Barrow, inherited the estate from his father. During the 1816 slave rebellion, which started at a nearby plantation and was led at Sunbury by the slave King William, the Hon John Barrow was colonel-in-charge of the militia. Sunbury Plantation sustained almost £4,000 in damages during this uprising.

Thomas Daniel, a shipping merchant and landowner bought Sunbury in 1835 for £33,000. At the time there were 244 slave apprentices working at Sunbury.

Sam Lord was a great friend of Thomas Daniel and he spent many an evening as a guest at Sunbury. It was Thomas' ship that brought the candelabra and chandeliers from England for both Sam Lord's Castle and Sunbury Plantation House.

In 1896, a Scotsman, Alistair Cameron, came to Barbados to work in shipping with Thomas Daniel. After Thomas' death, Alistair purchased the estate and married Thomas' niece. They had five children. Their only son was killed in World War I, and their daughters Helen and Francis remained spinsters and ran the plantation until their deaths in 1980 and 1981 respectively.

In 1981 the house was separated from the sugar plantation and sold to Mr and Mrs Keith Melville, a Barbadian couple.

Sunbury Plantation House was first opened to the public for charity in 1983 and was officially opened as an Heritage House in 1984.

Sunbury House was built of flint and other hard stone originally brought from England as ballast in the holds of English schooners.

A survivor of innumerable hurricanes, Sunbury boasted walls approximately two feet six inches thick. Its sash windows were protected by jalousies on the outside and storm shutters on the inside. In the event of a hurricane, the whole house could be quickly closed up.

Inspired by a firm commitment to preserve the heritage of a gracious past, the new owners exercised impeccable taste in the choice of fixtures and furnishings with the result that Sunbury House once possessed one of the country's superior collections of antiques, china, crystal, glass and silver, as well as an interesting collection of old prints and paintings. The cellar, originally used for storing yams and other root vegetables grown on the plantation, housed a unique collection of antique carriages, the largest collection in the Caribbean, as well as many items used in the domestic life of the plantation. Tragically, much was lost in a recent fire.

In the extensively landscaped grounds are fine authentic examples of old carts and machinery used in the last century to cultivate the land.

Sunbury Plantation House is located in the tranquil St Philip countryside.

Historic Churches of Barbados

St Joseph Anglican Parish Church

Houses of worship have always been of the greatest importance in the lives of Barbadians. They still are, and Barbados boasts not only a large churchgoing population but reputedly over a hundred denominations and a very considerable number of churches. More than 60 of these are over 100 years old and many date back to the 1830s. Most of the early churches were completely demolished by the great hurricane of 1831 and a wave of ambitious rebuilding was undertaken.

The oldest site of worship was the St James Parish Church. It was near here, at 'The Hole' or Jamestown as it was first called, that the good ship *William and John* landed with the first African-European settlement in 1627. The first church must have been a simple wooden building. We know from a letter of the Reverend Thomas Lane, Minister of St Michael to Archbishop Laud, Archbishop of Canterbury, that by 1637 six churches had been built to serve the first six parishes of St James, St Michael, St Peter, St Lucy, St Andrew and Christ Church. The other five parishes were carved out of these first six between 1639 and 1652. It is clear that the catalyst for the division into more parishes was the building of 'chapels of ease', or smaller churches, closer to the distant parts of the original parishes - an attempt to bring the churches to the people, most of whom would have had to travel on foot.

This process continued with almost feverish haste in the decades before and after Emancipation. In the days of slavery, Christianity was not considered relevant to the lives or souls of the slaves, and it was only exceptional slave owners and indeed exceptional priests who encouraged their slaves to accept Christ as their saviour. But while the Anglican Church steadfastly ignored the contradictions of their creed and the society of slavery, two groups, the Moravians and the Methodists, were making brave inroads in Barbados. The Moravians came in 1765, specifically to bring the Gospel to the slaves, and by 1799 they built an ambitious stone church at Sharon in St Thomas. This is of an unusual design, and has recently been handsomely restored.

The Methodists came a little later (1788), but they faced much opposition from the planters. Their first meeting house in James Street was vandalised by an angry mob and the Reverend William Shrewsbury driven out of the island. The community was kept together by a brave free coloured woman, Mrs Sarah Gill, who resisted threats, persecution and prosecution for holding 'illegal meetings' - truly a Barbadian heroine. The church she helped to build, in James Street, was the scene of the State

Funeral for Her Excellency, Dame Nita Barrow, the late, great Governor General of Barbados.

When the work of the Abolitionist Movement made it clear that slavery must be brought to an end in the British Empire, the state of Church affairs in Barbados was at an all time low. The Reverend William Hart Coleridge was appointed to a new Diocese of Barbados and the Leeward Islands with the express task of establishing churches and schools to provide a newly freed population with education and religious instruction. Bishop Coleridge was obviously an inspired choice. Within six years of his arrival six new chapels were completed. All were totally destroyed by the hurricane of 1831. Seven of the 11 parish churches were destroyed, as well as three other chapels of ease.

Undaunted, Bishop Coleridge set about a massive rebuilding programme - all of the demolished churches and chapels plus nine more chapels and chapel-schools. He not only planned and raised money for them but he seems to have had a big hand in designing them. His ten chapels and 11 chapel-schools have been designated by Barbara Hill (author of *Historic Churches of Barbados*, 1984), as the Coleridge Chapels and they constitute a most interesting architectural achievement. They have a unity and charm which remains largely unblemished today, and together they demonstrate a fascinating evolution of the Neo-Gothic style just becoming popular in England into a robust vernacular expression which was to become the benchmark of church design for the next hundred or more years. Chapels like St Mathews and St Paul are as attractive as the larger parish churches. St Michael's Cathedral, by far the largest of the historic churches, has had a dramatic history. Destroyed by the hurricane of 1780, it was rebuilt with the proceeds of a lottery, a fact often invoked by those who would like to introduce casinos into Barbados. It has many interesting details, monumental carvings and tombstones.

All of the parish churches are of interest but by common consent St James and St John are of particular beauty and fascination. The present St James is the result of rebuilding in 1789 and 1874 on the site of the first stone church of 1660. The baptismal font is dated 1684 and there is a magnificent King William III bell of 1696. The church has massive circular columns and unplastered coral stone walls, which emphasise its spirit of antiquity. It is beautifully maintained and has been embellished with several new works of art, including a superb abstract stained glass window by Barbadian artist and potter, Bill Grace.

St John's Church is a sturdy Gothic church with a graceful tower - the

Eagle lectern in St John's Church

Bibliography

Alleyne, Warren. *Historic Bridgetown*, Barbados National Trust, Bridgetown, 1978

Campbell, Peter. *Chapters in Barbados History*, The Barbados Museum and Historical Society, Bridgetown, 1986

Fraser, Henry. *Treasures of Barbados*, Macmillan Caribbean, 1990

Fraser, Henry and Hughes, Ronnie. *Historic Houses of Barbados*, 2nd Edition, Barbados National Trust and Art Heritage Publications, Bridgetown, 1986

Fraser, Henry; Carrington, Sean; Forde, Addy and Gilmore, John. *A-Z of Barbadian Heritage*, Heinemann Caribbean (Publishers) Ltd., Kingston, 1990

Hill, Barbara. *Historic Churches of Barbados*, Ed. Fraser, Henry, Art Heritage Publications, Bridgetown 1984

prototype of the 1830s style, repeated with variations across the country. Its delightful wooden carvings, fluted columns and ornate pulpit built of six different woods (ebony, locust, Barbados mahogany, manchineel and imported oak and pine) are complemented by fascinating memorial tablets, including an exquisite sculpture by Sir Richard Westmacott, sculptor of the statue of Lord Nelson in Trafalgar Square. Built on a prominent part of Hackleton's Cliff, the escarpment that separates the St John and St Joseph uplands from the Scotland District, St John's Church gives the impression of being carved from the cliff itself. It is famous for its magnificent view, from Pico Teneriffe in the north, across the Bathsheba coast to the cliffs of Consett Point and the Ragged Point lighthouse in the east

Ferdinando Paleogus' tomb at St John's cemetary

It is also famous for its ancient tombs and family vaults. The most interesting of these is the tomb of Ferdinando Paleologus. He was the last traced member of the family of Paleologus, ancient Greek Emperors of Constantinople and Princes of the Peloponesus. He claimed descent from Thomas, brother of Constantine XI, last Emperor of Constantinople. His father settled in Britain in the late 16th Century and Ferdinando fought for King Charles I in the Civil War. He fled to Barbados with other Royalists after King Charles' defeat and was a vestryman and churchwarden of the parish of St John.

These 60-odd historic churches provide a rich tapestry of the history of Barbados - church architecture and decoration, the lives of the famous or the unknown, are all recorded here. The human emotions and tragedies of young lives lost, sadness and devotion are elegantly recorded and are especially worth seeing at St George Parish Church. St George is also famous for its magnificent altar piece, the famous painting 'The Resurrection' by Benjamin West

A marble laver, c. 1800, for washing hands, at the Barbados Museum. It was originally in the courtyard of the synagogue

Also of great interest are the Roman Catholic Cathedral of St Patrick's, on Bay Street, and the superbly restored Jewish Synagogue, in the centre of Bridgetown. Believed to have been first built in the 1650s, the Synagogue was destroyed by the hurricane in 1831 and rebuilt on the same foundations in 1833. Sold by the sole surviving member of the old Jewish community in 1929, it was used as offices until 1983 when it was acquired and restored by the new local Jewish community under the chairmanship of Paul Altman, now President of the Barbados National Trust Beautifully restored with perfect replicas of chandeliers and other artefacts, it is both an active place of worship and a proud testament of one of the first major Jewish communities in the Western hemisphere.

165

The History of Bridgetown

by Warren Alleyne

The High Court

The High Court in Coleridge Street, probably Bridgetown's oldest building, stands on the site that was occupied from 1683 to 1728 by the town's magazine.

Originally named The Town Hall, it was erected in 1730 to accommodate the two chambers of the legislator and the courts of law, with certain parts of the building, including the basement, set aside as a prison for both civil and criminal offenders. This rather curious arrangement of having law-breakers sharing the same premises with those who enacted the laws and those who enforced them was for a long time regarded with amusement by visitors to Barbados.

In 1874 the Houses of Legislature moved out into their new chambers in the recently built east wing of the Public Buildings; and when prisoners were finally removed from the premises in late 1876 the law courts were left in sole occupancy.

In 1949 an extension was added at the rear to provide some more courtroom space, and in 1956-1957 a further extension was added at the front linking the building to the Records Offices of the Registration Department.

Following the reorganisation of the Judicature in 1958 the name of the building was statutorily changed from Town Hall to High Court.

St Michael's Cathedral

The first parish church of St Michael was a wooden building, erected about the year 1630 on the ground in lower Bridgetown now occupied by St Mary's Church. In 1660 a wealthy merchant, William Sharpe, offered a more centrally located plot of land in upper Bridgetown as a site for the parish church, and the parish authorities had a more imposing edifice of stone erected there in 1665.

The construction of this building was however faulty, and after repeated remedial work had to be carried out over many years, the building was taken down altogether in 1751-1752 and rebuilt from three feet above the foundation. Finally, in the great hurricane of October 1780, the building crashed to the ground in a heap.

The present edifice, which was completed in 1786 on the original foundation, was lengthened slightly in 1938 by the addition of a Lady Chapel at the eastern end.

St Michael's, which became a cathedral in 1825 when Barbados got it's first bishop, has its original bells and a baptismal font dating from 1680. Some interesting monumental sculpture decorates its interim walls and some ancient tombstones are to be seen on the floor, dating from early times when graves were dug also within the church.

During his episcopate, (1825-1842) the first bishop, William Hart Coleridge, D D, disallowed burials inside churches, but his fourth successor the Right Reverend William P Swaby, D D was interred in the church directly in front of his episcopal throne in 1917 at his own request

Queen's Park

Queen's Park occupies an acreage of land bought in 1782 by General Gabriel Christie, then commanding the British troops stationed in Barbados.

In 1783 he built King's House - renamed Queen's House in Queen Victoria's reign - as a residence for the general officer commanding in this region of the Caribbean, and some time later two other houses called 'The Retreat' and 'The Pavilion' were added as residences for certain senior officers on the general's staff.

In 1906, shortly before the British Garrison was withdrawn from Barbados the government bought the entire Queen's House establishment for £3,000. The house called 'The Retreat' was soon given to Harrison College, and the rest of the property assigned to the St Michael Vestry, the parochial authority, together with a grant of £1,000 for its conversion into a public park for Bridgetown's citizens.

This was done between 1907 and 1909 to plans prepared by the talented American-born wife of Governor Sir Gilbert Carter who also officiated at the opening ceremony on 10 June 1909.

On Christmas morning 1907, when the park's development had barely started, the police band gave a concert in the grounds that has now become a traditional part of the Barbadian Christmas celebrations. For many years the band also used to give a concert in the park in the first Sunday of every month. Altogether, over the years Queen's Park has harboured a wide variety of social activities including seven political meetings. Up to December 1972 it was the home of the annual agricultural and industrial exhibition, the island's most prestigious social event.

During 1973-1974 Queen's Park House, as it was now known, was thoroughly restored under the direction of the late Oliver Messel, the distinguished British theatrical designer, then resident in Barbados. A small theatre in the building, disused for several years, was provided with modern equipment and officially re-

opened on 3 December 1973 as the Queen's Park Theatre. In October 1990 it was renamed the Daphne Joseph-Hackett Theatre in commemoration of a Barbadian well noted in local dramatic art until her passing in 1988. Queen's Park House is, however, now mainly used for art exhibitions.

The 'Steel Shed', another auditorium located in the grounds of the park, was developed in the 1980s out of a large open-sided metal structure that was erected in 1930 as a shelter for livestock being displayed at the annual exhibition.

The plant life in Queen's Park includes a large baobab tree (*Adansonia digitata)* that is one of only two or three known in Barbados. Near the 'Steel Shed' there is also a fine evergreen tree (*Ficus benjamina*) which was planted by HRH Prince Albert, Duke of York (later King George VI) on 10 March 1913 while he was visiting Barbados.

Queen's Park came originally under the authority, first of the St Michael Vestry, and next, in 1959, under the Bridgetown City Council. But with the abolition of local government in 1967 it is now controlled by the National Conservation Commission, a government statutory board.

Nelson's Statue

When in February 1805, during the Napoleonic Wars (1803-1815), powerful French forces arrived in the Caribbean and launched a campaign of intimidation against Dominica and the Leeward Islands, sinking vessels and extorting large sums of money from the people under threat, the people of Barbados became greatly fearful at the news, fearing that they were marked down for a similar fate.

Their apprehensions became greatly intensified when, in May, an even more powerful enemy fleet entered the region. It is therefore not surprising that when Admiral Nelson, in pursuit of the enemy, arrived unexpectedly in Carlisle Bay on 4 June in command of a powerful British fleet, he was hailed as a deliverer from a possible French invasion.

His victory over the combined French and Spanish fleets at Trafalgar on 21 October was greeted with much jubilation when the news reached Barbados on 20 December, but his death in the action was greatly mourned, and a memorial service was held at St Michael's Parish Church.

A subscription list was opened for a memorial to the admiral and the government donated £500. Some people were in favour of a fine building, but finally it was thought that a statue was more fitting and the builders agent in London placed an order with Sir Richard Westmacott, a leading British bronze sculptor.

A small plot of ground in Egginton's Green, close to High Street was purchased as a site, and on 22 March 1813 the Admiral's statue was erected with appropriate ceremony.

In 1891 the government had the statue raised on a higher pedestal, adding some current coins at the same time to the collection found sealed beneath the statue. In November 1990 the statue, which had always faced westward, was shifted some eight feet from its position and turned to face the opposite direction.

When Nelson's statue was removed from its pedestal, a sealed leaden box which had been put under the statue in 1813 was removed and sent to the Barbados Museum, where it was unsealed and the contents examined. It was found to contain 29 coins of which four were gold, 16 of silver and nine of copper. The collection was put on display for some days and then deposited in a bank vault.

The Barbados Nelson monument is actually the third oldest in the world. The first was erected at Montreal, Canada, in August 1809, and the second at Birmingham, England, in October that same year. The London monument was erected only in the 1840s.

The Parliament Buildings

The Barbados Parliament, the third oldest in the British Commonwealth, was constituted in 1639 when the newly formed House of 'Burgesses' the assembly, began meeting jointly with the governor's private council.

Initially, meetings were held at the State House in Bridgetown; but after fire destroyed this building in April 1668, meetings shifted to various taverns until 1701 when a 'Sessions House' was specially erected. In 1704, however, when the government suddenly decided to take over this building for use as the common jail, parliament was obliged to return to taverns or, occasionally, private houses.

In 1730, the building in Coleridge Street, originally called the Town Hall, was at last erected to accommodate parliament together with the law court and also the common jail. But parliament was still often forced to meet elsewhere for one reason or another, and did not finally settle at the Town Hall until 1816.

In 1870, with funds appropriated since the late 1850s the government began erecting the 'public buildings', beginning with the west wing, completed in 1876. Then in 1874 the east wing was completed, with the top floor appointed to accommodate the two parliamentary chambers and their ancillary offices, and with the ground floor reserved for those government offices that couldn't be housed in the west wing.

The parliamentary chambers, and the offices attached contain some fine stained glass. Some 13 windows in the assembly chamber feature the portraits and the coats of arms of British sovereigns, beginning with James the First and including even Oliver Cromwell. The glass in the senate (formerly council) chamber depicts the coats of arms of some former speakers of the House of Assembly and some presidents of council.

The clock, which is the most conspicuous feature of the buildings, was originally located at the east wing in a massive tower that stood over the entrance. This tower had to be taken down in 1884 and replaced with the present porch after it had subsided through lack of a solid foundation. The south tower at the west wing was then reconstructed to accommodate the clock and bells, and the work was completed in 1886.

In May 1889 the public buildings were officially renamed the Parliament Buildings, and Trafalgar Square renamed Parliament Square.

The Synagogue

There is some reason to believe that there were a few Jews, probably of Dutch origin, among the earlier settlers of Barbados; but there was no significant immigration of Jews until 1654, when a number arrived from Brazil seeking asylum from the Inquisition.

In admitting them Barbados gained the distinction of being the first English territory to accept Jews since they were expelled from England in the late 13th Century. In 1681 their community was estimated to number some 260 people.

Exactly when the Bridgetown synagogue was built is uncertain, but it was probably as early as 1655. That first edifice was destroyed by the hurricane of 1831, but in 1833 it was rebuilt and reconsecrated on 29 March.

A fall in sugar prices towards the end of the century led to the emigration of most of the island's Jews and by 1900 only 17 were said to remain. In 1929 when only one was left the synagogue was sold to a private purchaser, who converted it into an office building.

In late 1983 the government compulsorily acquired the property for demolition to make way for a new supreme court, but the present Jewish community, which had its genesis in the 1930s, supported by the Barbados National Trust and the Caribbean Conservation Association, managed to persuade the government to accept plans for the restoration of the synagogue.

With assistance from a number of Jewish organisations overseas, a local committee restored the building during the period 1984-1990.

The cemetary attached to the synagogue is one of the oldest in the Western Hemisphere, having grave-stones dating back to the 17th Century. Inscriptions are to be seen in Hebrew and Portuguese as well as English.

Public Library Bridgetown

On 21 October 1847 the Barbados Legislature enacted a statute for establishing a free public library. It is noteworthy that this predated Britain's Public Library Act, dated August 1850, by almost three years.

The Barbados Public Library finally opened in October 1849 in premises located on the ground that is now the Coleridge Street Car Park. In 1853 it was transferred to another address in Bolton Lane, and then in 1875 to the room beneath the chamber of the House of Assembly in the newly erected east wing of the public buildings (now parliamentary buildings).

In 1904, with a special grant of £4,800 donated by the famous American industrialist and philanthropist Andrew Carnegie, the island's Governor Sir Frederick Hodgson, had the present edifice in Coleridge Street built as the home of the public library. The plans were prepared by E F S Bowen, the then Superintendent of Public Works and the first stone was laid on 15 September 1904. The completed building was opened on 26 January 1906.

Government House

The residences of several of this island's early governors were located at different places in or near Bridgetown. But finally, in 1674, when Sir Jonathan Atkins came, a mansion, later called Holborn, at Fontabelle where the oil tanks now stand was rented by the government of the day as a first residence for governors.

Sir Bevil Granville, who came in 1703, however refused to live so close to the seaside because he had a fear of being kidnapped by pirates, so 'Pilgrim' plantation house, just east of Bridgetown was leased for his residence at £120 per annum. There, one day in June 1704, an attempt was made on his life by someone who shot at him from the roadside.

In 1734, when the lease expired, the government bought the property outright for £1,350. The house has since undergone some alteration and even reconstruction from time to time, usually after suffering damage by hurricanes. The last major reconstruction was in 1857-1858 when most of the walls had to be taken down and rebuilt to carry the extra weight of a third storey.

Since then Government House has not been radically altered, but in 1963 with the concurrence of the Cabinet, the then Governor, Sir John Montague Stow had some three-and-a-half acres detached from the grounds to provide a site for a new school.

Fountain Gardens

Shortly after piped water was introduced into the City of Bridgetown in March 1861, a number of influential persons suggested that this historic development should be commemorated

by the erection of an ornamental fountain in some conspicuous spot.

The following year, on the initiative of Edward Carpenter the manager of the local branch of the Colonial Bank (now Barclays Bank, Plc) a subscription list was opened for the purchase and installation of a fountain. The government donated a site in Trafalgar Square and the Bridgetown Water Works company agreed to provide the water free of charge.

The fountain manufactured in Britain, arrived in Barbados in early 1865, but the large basin at its base was made locally of limestone. The entire structure was erected upon a circular block of masonry resting upon 44 hardwood piles driven ten feet into the ground. On 17 July the fountain was inaugurated with ceremony befitting a national occasion, at which the Acting Governor, Major Robert Mundy presided.

The garden around the fountain was laid out in 1882, and in 1888 when it had reached an appropriate stage of development it was thrown open to the public as a place of recreation.

DEPARTMENT OF ARCHIVES

The Department of Archives, currently a part of the Ministry of Education Youth Affairs and Culture, was established in 1963 by an Order-in Council. The creation of the department followed a 1961 survey of records in Barbados conducted by Englishman Michael J Chandler, of the Corporation of London Record Office, under the auspices of the University of the West Indies, with funding from the Rockefeller Foundation. Mr Chandler was appointed Archivist in 1964 and concluded his contracts with the Barbados Government in 1976. Christine Matthews was appointed Chief Archivist in 1977.

The department's responsibilities include preserving and restoring valuable original documents and producing microfilm copies where advisable and placing copies of historical material at the disposal of centres of learning. The 1988 Archives Act gives the department responsibility of co-ordinating records management procedures in the public service.

The basic infrastructure typical of a small archive service has been established with environmentally controlled buildings, fumigation chamber, conservation facilities and a reference service. The department began providing reference service to the archives in 1965 as it was felt essential to show the value of preserving and exploiting the information in the old records which date back to 1647. A significant amount of the research in current publications and audiovisual presentations regarding Barbados' historical, cultural and architectural heritage has been researched at the department. Among the records are the earliest deeds registers, levy (tax) books and population records, the 1834 Emancipation Act, 18th and 19th Century records of Drax Hall Plantation, governors' correspondence, the 1966 Independence Order (the Constitution of Barbados) and the private collections of the late Sir Grantley Adams, Frank Collymore and H A Vaughan, as well as many small private manuscript and photographic collections. There is also a library of official and unofficial Barbadian and Caribbean memorabilia and paraphernalia which includes some significant rare items. Over 2,000 visits and 150 overseas letters and many local telephone enquiries are serviced by the department annually.

In addition to information dissemination, the department places great emphasis on preservation and conservation, to this end it was instrumental in the creation of conservation and microfilm services. Along with the main library, the Law Faculty library, History Department of the University of the West Indies, Cave Hill and the National Library Service the department has participated since 1976 in a co-operative for the purchase of microfilm of archival material relating to Barbados in the custody of overseas repositories. Because of the former colonial relationship, the majority of such materials is in British official and private archives, although a considerable amount of material is also in the United States.

Parish guide

St Lucy

Population: 10,000. St Lucy is the northernmost and least populated parish of the island. Neighbouring parish is St Peter to the south. From the northern tip, the land gradually rises to form wall-like cliffs, reaching 449 feet above sea level at Mount Gilboa.

Great Houses

Fustic House - Designed by the famous stage and film designer Oliver Messel, this colonial style coral stone residence is surrounded by 11 wooded acres.

Churches

St Lucy Parish Church - dating back to 1629, when St Lucy was constituted as one of the six original parishes, this church is Georgian in style and made of sawn stone and has a tower and a running gallery on three sides.

Places of interest

Checker Hall's Fort - now disused, was built to guard Hangman's Bay. There are examples of Barbadian vernacular yard art around this and other sites in this parish.

Halfmoon Fort - Although the fort has all but disappeared, one can see boat building, a fishing fleet and market and a fish farming enterprise. There are good opportunities for snorkelling along this stretch of coast.

Animal Flower Cave - A series of caverns that open onto the Atlantic. This is home to the colourful Animal Flowers - Sea anemones and tube worms. A bar offers refreshments and there are gifts shops, some which specialise in Arawak-related art forms.

Mount Gay Distillery - with 330 years of history behind it, Mount Gay lays claim to the world's oldest rum. Guided tours around the distillery: 9 - 4 pm Monday to Friday; 10 - 1 pm Saturday.

Nearby on a plateau is a huge wind turbine generator which is visible from most points in St Lucy.

River Bay - an archeological site of the Arawaks, and now a picnic site with toilet facilities among the casuarina trees by the mouth of a dry, shallow river bed.

The Animal Flower Cave

OPPOSITE: North Point

170

Cove Bay - near a stud farm is a dramatic view of the Atlantic known also as Gay's Cove. Interesting geological formations such as Pico Teneriffe and a chance to observe sea turtles in the water.

Beaches

Maycock's Bay - a sandy beach surrounded by cliffs inhabited by monkeys. There is a ruined fort and a coconut tree lined meadow to explore and have a picnic. Nearby is Harrison's Point - a disused naval base and Harrison's Point Lighthouse.

Archer's Bay - sandy and uncrowded beach which is popular locally for picnics.

Major industries

Primarily agricultural, there is also fishing along the western coast of the parish, Arawak Cement Plant, a lone garment factory and a rum distillery.

Famous people

Errol Walton Barrow, (1920-1987). Founder of the Democratic Labour Party (DLP). He became the first prime minister of Barbados when he led the country to independence in 1966. He founded the Caribbean Free Trade Area (CARIFTA) forerunner of the Caribbean Community (CariCom).

Dame Ruth Nita Barrow, (1916-1995), was the first woman to be appointed Governor-General of Barbados. She was internationally respected for her community service, her work in the womens movement and her involvement in the struggle against apartheid.

Charles Duncan O'Neal, (1879-1936). Founder of the Democratic League and campaigner for important social and political reforms. O'Neal's portrait appears on the $10 note.

St Peter

Population: 11,500. Main town - Speightstown. Neighbouring parishes clockwise from the north are St Lucy, St Andrew and St James. St Peter is a rural parish known for it's fishing and superb beaches.

172

Speightstown's name came from William Speight a wealthy merchant, landowner and member of parliament in 1639. The town was built on land he owned and developed. It is a busy town with shops, restaurants, hotels and banking facilites. Speightstown is the second largest town in Barbados. There is also an ultra modern shopping mall and many remarkable old buildings.

Mullins Bay & Beach

Great Houses

Nicholas Abbey is the oldest house in Barbados. An example of Jacobean-style architecture. It is thought that the house was built in 1650 by Colonel Benjamin Berringer, a landowner.

Alleynedale Hall was once called Cabbage Tree Hall, the three storey house is part of the 350 acre Alleynedale sugar estate

Arlington House was built to resemble the houses in South Carolina, US.

Farley Hill Plantation and National Park was built around 1818. It had a reputation as one of the most lavish plantation houses. In the 1950s it was used in the Hollywood film 'Island in the Sun' starring Harry Belafonte.

Speightstown has changed little over the centuries, and is unique because it has retained much of it's original street systems.

Speightstown Esplande overlooks the sea.

Speightstown Mall, opened in 1980, is one of the most modern shopping malls on the island.

Heywood, a modern complex for tourists, is built around an old sugar plantation on 30 acres. This government development cost BDS$60 million and has a 250-seater conference centre.

Farley Hill Plantation and National Park

Famous people

Owen Arthur (1949) Labour Prime Minister of Barbados in 1994, was born in Rose Hill, St Peter. He is the youngest man to become prime minster of Barbados, aged 44.

Churches

St Peter's Parish Church, All Saints, was built in the 1630s. It was partially rebuilt in 1837 and eventually restored to it's original glory in 1980 after being damaged in a fire. St Philip the Less Church was built in 1861.

Schools

The Alexandra Girls School is the oldest school in St Peter. Founded on the 24 September 1894. It was set up to educate poor girls who would not otherwise receive an education. The school was named after Alexandra, the Danish wife of King Edward V11.

Places of interest

Whim Gully is one of the easiest to reach of the 12 or so gullies in Barbados

Sailor's Gully, home to Barbados Wildlife Reserve, is where you will find green monkeys living in their natural habitat.

Pleasant Hall Hill Cave is where the ealiest Amerindians once worshipped.

Pico Teneriffe, the well known landmark in Boscobelle, is a tall pillar of rock that can be seen in St John.

Eastry House Hotel is located on six acres of landscaped gardens on a cliff-top 200 feet above the sea.

St Andrew

Population: 6,500. Neighbouring parishes anti-clockwise from north are St Peter, St James, St Thomas and St Joseph.

Churches

St Andrew's Anglican Church was one of the few churches to survive the hurricane in 1831. The present building was built in 1846.

Major industries

Chalky Mount is where large reserves of clay are found. It is also home for many of Barbados' most famous potters. The soil is reddish-brown in this part of the parish.

Places of interest

Morgan Lewis Mill was the last working windmill in Barbados, ceasing operation in 1947. At one time there were over 500 windmills in Barbados

View from Cherry Tree Hill

174

all grinding sugar cane.

Turner's Hall Woods is the only place to visualise Barbados as it was in 1627. This small forest is one of the few remaining original forest areas in Barbados.

Haggatts Estate is the location of the government's agricultural station, the headquarters of the Soil Conservation and Rural Development Scheme in the Scotland District which started in 1957. The station is well known for the research it does into fruit tree production. It also has extensive orchards which produce many fruits including the Barbadian cherry. One cherry can supply the body with a full days requirement of vitamin C.

Mose Bottom is ideal for a view of the deep ravine in this area.

Mount Hillaby is the highest point on Barbados at 1160 feet above sea level.

Cherry Tree Hill, where an avenue of mature mahogany trees leads to a spectacular view of the rugged Scotland District.

Barclays Park is a 50 acre park on the east coast road which was a gift to the Barbadian government from Barclays Bank International Ltd to commemorate Independence in 1966.

St Andrew's Anglican Church

Beaches

Morgan Lewis Beach is an isolated two-and-a-half-mile long beach with beautiful white sand.

Great Houses

Bleak House is located on a limestone ridge at the western point of St Andrew and was built in 1886. It is set in 166 acres of land and provides a great view of the area.

St James

Population: 21,000. The main town is Holetown. The parish of St James is the island's smallest parish. Some of the most luxurious hotels and sumptuous homes are located in this parish. St James was discovered' in 1625 by Captain John Powell of the *Olive Blossom* ship. He claimed the island in the name of King James 1 of England. The area was first named St James in honour of King James, later it was changed to Holetown. St

175

James' neighbouring parishes are clockwise from the north; St Thomas, St Andrew and St Peter.

Great Houses

Porters House - one of the few great plantation houses still standing from the earliest settlement of the island. Though not completely preserved as it was originally built, new parts were added in the 17th, 18th and 19th Centuries. The Great House was once owned by Sir John Gay Alleyne, today it's owned by the Honourable Murtogh Guinness.

Heron Bay Great House - was built by Ronald Tree in 1947 in 20 acres of parkland and was designed to represent the Italian Palazzo style.

Churches

St James's Church in Holetown, is one of the four oldest churches on the island, dating back to the early settlers it was originally built with wood. The church that stands there today was built in 1847, on the same site as the first church. A bell dating 1699 from the old church is still being used and has an inscription on it 'God bless King William.' This bell is older than the Liberty Bell in the United States, which was cast in 1750.

St John the Baptist Church was built around 1867.

Famous buildings

St James's Fort once protected Holetown and its coastal areas. Not much of the fort is left today apart from a bit of wall and a cannon.

Folkstone House was turned into tennis courts and a playground by the Rotary Club.

Folkstone Underwater Park and Museum

Famous people

Arthur Felix Haynes (1873-1941) Born into a well known Barbadian planter family. He did much to encourage the visual arts by teaching drawing to junior children.

Sir John Gay Alleyne (1724-1801) was the longest serving representative in the House of Assembly entering the House in 1757-1797. He founded the Alleyne School.

Places of interest

Folkstone Underwater Park and Museum. Snorkeler's can follow an underwater trail around Dottin's Reef which is seven miles long and just offshore. Visitors can also view the reef and marine life in a glass-bottomed boat. The museum includes corals, artefacts, sponges and photographs of marine life.

Discovery Bay Hotel

Portvale Sugar Factory produces approximately 1,500 tonnes of sugar each week. It also generates electricity for the national grid.

Bellairs Research Institute is off the main highway that runs through St James. The institute studies Caribbean marine biology focusing on Barbados. Set up in 1954 it is affiliated to McGill University, Canada. The aim of the institute is to improve the agriculture and fisheries in Barbados.

Holetown Monument commemorates the landing of English Captain John Powell in 1625, who claimed Barbados in the name of King James I. The monument has the wrong date of that landing on it (1602).

Farmer's Market, Sunset Crest is where fruit and vegetables are sold.

The Sugar Museum tells the story of sugar through its unusual collection of artefacts. The items in the museum were collected by Sir Frank Hutson a Barbadian engineer. The museum is open Monday to Saturday, except public holidays.

Beaches & Sport

The beaches on the coast of St James are known as the platinum beaches because of their shimmering silvery colour.

Golf - Royal Westmorland Golf Club.

Scuba diving - the reefs are safe and exciting all along the coast making them ideal for scuba diving.

Shops

Shell Gallery offers a spectacular display of shells, which are made into gift items, pictures, jewellery, ceramics and china.

Major industries

Portvale Sugar Factory - Barbados' newest sugar factory. There are factory tours during the sugar cane harvest season.

St Thomas

Population 12,000. St Thomas is in the heart of Barbados. Highways 2 and 2A from St Michael and Highway 1A from St James, pass through St Thomas. This parish is ideal for hiking and exploring. It has limestone caves, ravines and farmlands. St Thomas is an agricultural district for sugar cane and a wonderful way to view this parish is on horse back. Neighbouring parishes clockwise from the north are St Andrew, St Joseph, St George, St Michael and St John.

Churches

St Thomas Parish Church was one of the original six parish churches in Barbados. The first church was destroyed in 1831 by hurricane.

Sharon Moravain Church built in 1799 by Moravians who settled in Barbados in 1765. These missionaries who came from Germany wanted to bring Christianity and education to the slaves. They were the first Europeans to encourage slaves to join their congregation. The church, unspoilt by alterations, shows the architectural influences from Europe where the Moravian faith began.

Holy Innocents Chapel was built in 1838 to replace the previous chapel of ease that had been destroyed by the hurricane of 1780.

Clifton Hill, a Moravian church ,was, built in 1839.

Places of interest

Welchman Hall Gully is home to tropical trees and plants that grow in this quarter-mile ravine. The gully is a deep crack in the coral limestone cap which covers most of Barbados. The name came from General Williams, an early Welsh settler, who owned the land. Welchman Hall Gully has been run by the Barbados National Trust since 1963.

Harrison's Cave is the only one of its kind in the Caribbean. The cave has electric trams to ferry visitors through the limestone caverns which have been formed by underground streams over the centuries. The cave is a popular tourist attraction. In 1970 a Danish cave expert Ole Sorenson discovered another section of the caves known as the crystal caverns. In 1981 the National Trust opened the caves to the general public. The caves contain stalagmites and stalactites. At the lowest point of the cave there is a 40 foot waterfall which flows into a large blue-green pool. In 1985 the

Welchman Hall Gully

cave's started opening for night tours.

A baobab tree, believed to be one of only two on the island, can be found in St Thomas. This African tree with a massive trunk and large edible pulpy fruit is thought to be over 250-years-old.

Harrison's Cave

Great Houses

Welches House and plantation is owned by Jill Walker, a local artist. The plantation was built in 1627, however the existing house dates back to the mid-1800s. The plantation's buildings have been turned into administrative offices and studios. The company produces 'Best of Barbados' crafts and gifts that depict the culture of Barbados.

Bagatelle Great House is now a restaurant with a worldwide reputation for its gourmet foods. This plantation dates back to the 1650s, the same time as St Nicholas Abbey and Drax Hall, two of the oldest buildings in Barbados.

Rock Hall Village was the first black freehold village in the country. The area was part of Mount Wilton Plantation and managed by Reynold Alleyne Elcock, a young white planter with moral values. He made a will in 1820 leaving £5 sterling per year to each of his 120 adult male slaves and making provision for repairs to their living quarters. Somehow, the news of Wilton's will got out and his valet, a slave named Godfrey, slit the planters throat as he slept one night in 1821. Godfrey was hanged and the estate's slaves had to wait 17 years, until Emancipation in 1838, before they benefited from the will. They used the money to buy plots of land at Mount Wilton Estate, the village became known as Cut-Throat Village. Today it is called Rock Hall. Other planters in St Thomas willed their plantations to their coloured children born to slave mothers, an example of this was William Ellis whose son Thomas was the first coloured man to be elected to the House of Assembly.

Warrens plantation house was built in 1686.

Sport

The Sandy Lane Golf Club boasts an 18-hole professional course.
Scuba diving at the West Side Scuba Centre.

Shops

Earthworks Pottery is a family owned and operated business which produce beautiful and functional wares.

St Joseph

Population: 8,000. The main town is Bathsheba. Neighbouring parishes from north anti-clockwise; St Andrews, St Thomas and St John. St Joseph, on the east coast of Barbados, is blessed with a rocky and dramatic coastline.

Churches

St Joseph Anglican Church at Horse Hill was built prior to 1640 and was rebuilt in 1839 after being destroyed by a hurricane in 1831.

Little St Joseph's chapel was built in Hillcrest in 1837. At the end of the century it was restored and dedicated to St Aiden. Then in 1884 it was demolished in a landslide caused by the building of the nearby railway line and subsequently rebuilt around 1904-1909.

Places of interest

Bathsheba just off Highway 3 . This fishing village is surrounded by rolling and magnificent landscape, with huge boulders rising out of the bay.

Flower Forest a beautiful area with strikingly attractive flowering plants and tropical trees, is open every day.

Cotton Tower presents a wonderful view of Scotland District. The area is known for it's breathtaking scenery. The site is commonly used as a picnic area.

Bathsheba

Andromeda Gardens, the name coming from Greek mythology, are owned by Mrs Iris Bannochie, Barbados' foremost horticulturist.

Joe's River Tropical Rainforest is 85 acres of woods and rainforest with giant ficus, citrifolia, fid woods, white woods, cabbage palms and mahogany.

Sport

Surfing - The 'Soup Bowl' is where local and international surfing championships take place every year. The area takes its name from the foaming surf that collects there.

OPPOSITE: The Andromeda Gardens

180

St Michael

Population: 98,000. Capital city: Bridgetown. Neighbouring parishes clockwise from the north are St James, St Thomas St George and Christ Church. Bridgetown is the capital of Barbados. The name comes from a bridge that was built by the Arawak people, the original inhabitants of Barbados. There are two bridges in Bridgetown the Charles Duncan O'Neal Bridge and the Chamberlain Bridge, both span Constitution River. This is not so much a river as a basin where the sea comes some distance inland. The careenage is located near the entrance to this basin where, schooners were careened and had their hulls cleaned and repainted.

Places of interest

Trafalgar Square the statue of Lord Horatio Nelson stands looking towards the city. The bronze monument was erected in 1813, years before Nelson's Column was erected in Trafalgar Square, London.

The water fountain was built in 1861 to celebrate the introduction of piped running water to Bridgetown. The fountain is surrounded by gardens.

War Memorial Bridgetown has a memorial for those who fought in World War's I and II. Many Barbadian's lost their lives in the wars and bronze panels on the memorial list the dead of both wars.

Broad Street is the main commercial street. There are banks and a huge variety of shops which rival any duty free port in the world. Trading in Broad Street dates back to the mid 17th Century.

The Jewish synagogue, 200 yards from Broad Street, is the same site where the first synagogue was built in 1664 and damaged by the 1831 hurricane. Jews settled in Barbados in 1654, mostly in Swan Street.

The Barbados Museum, a former British military prison, houses extensive collections of the country's flora and fauna. Amerindian artefacts from Barbados and neighbouring islands, artefacts from the period of slavery and sugar, Barbadian craftsmanship, porcelain and silverware, toys, dolls and games from the Victorian era, antique maps, historic portraits and landscapes and unique Westindian prints along with a fine Museum library, shop and rest rooms.

Baxter Road is known as the street that never sleeps. The restaurants and rum shops open all night, the wonderful aroma of chicken, pork-Bajan style and fish constantly fill the air.

The Barbados Museum

OPPOSITE: Aerial view of central Bridgetown

Medford Craft Village near Baxter Road for a wide selection of genuine Barbadian souvenirs and gifts while you watch the craft-men work with mahogany.

Parliament Building is the third oldest parliament in the Commonwealth.

Lazaretto Gardens is a beautiful landscaped garden with a wonderful waterfall cascading from the rock face.

Verandah Art Gallery is located in Bridgetown and is considered one of the largest galleries in Barbados where there is a wide selection of paintings, carvings, batiks, ceramics and custom jewellery. Open Monday to Saturday.

Parliament Building

Major industries

Banks Breweries is where the famous beer is produced. There are regular tours so that visitors can see how Banks beer is brewed and bottled.

Cockspur Fine Rum at Brighton, St Michael, have a midday tour of their distillery.

Mount Gay Rum is the worlds oldest rum dating back to 1663. There is a Visitors Centre in Bridgetown on the Spring Garden Highway.

Cockspur Rum factory

Shops

Plenty of stores to choose from: Harrisons, Colombian Emeralds, Cave Shepherd, Correia's, The Royal Shop and Little Switzerland offer duty-free goods at prices 30-50 per cent cheaper that regular prices in Europe and US.

Great Houses

Ilaro Court was designed in 1919 by Lady Carter, the wife of Governor Gilbert Carter. Built from coral stone the house combines varied architectural features - garden, courtyard, Greek styled columns and an enclosed swimming pool. The house was purchased by the government in 1976 and is the official residence of the prime minister.

Tyrol Cot House was built in 1854 by William Farnum one of the outstanding Barbadian builders of the last century. It was the home of Sir Grantley Adams, the first Premier of Barbados and the only Prime Minister of the Federation of the West Indies. It is also where his son, Tom Adams was born, and who also became Prime Minister of Barbados. The house now belongs to the Barbados National Trust.

Harmony Hall pre-dates the 1700s, and shows the very best of 17th Century architecture. For almost 100 years it has been associated with medicine, being the home and surgery of Sir John Hutson from 1893-1946

and of Dr Will Kerr from 1946 until 1981.

DeLodge Inn, Belleville, St Michael is one of the oldest houses built in this area. The 1890 two-story suburban villa has a curved parapet which was copied by almost every house built in Belleville over the following 30 years.

Queen's Park House in Bridgetown was a military house bought by the Barbados government in 1906 after the withdrawal of the British troops in 1905.

Churches

St Michael Cathedral was built in 1628, where the present St Mary's Church stands. It was rebuilt in 1660 by Robert Cullimore who had disputes over standards and money with the vestry of the Church. The work was finally completed by John Hallet. It is believed brick, instead of stone, was used in the building and only the roof was damaged during the 1831 hurricane.

St Mary, built in 1825, is one of the finest churches in Barbados. This large brick built church is Georgian in design, and was one of the few churches left standing after the 1831 hurricane.

St Matthew's chapel was destroyed by the 1831 hurricane and rebuilt in 1832.

St Paul's chapel was built in 1830-31 and on completion was destroyed by the 1831 hurricane it was rebuilt in 1832.

Calvary, this Moravian church was built in 1894.

Sir Garfield Sobers Sports Complex

Sport

The Aquatic Sports Centre houses an Olympic-sized pool that can be used for water polo. There is also a multi-purpose gymnasium, tennis court, hockey and football fields.

The National Stadium was opened by Prince Charles in 1970.

Roadways

The Adams, Barrow, Cummins Highway is Barbados's most modern highway. It starts from the airport and runs to the west coast. Called the ABC Highway it is named in honour of three of Barbados' great statesmen.

Yachts in the Careenage

University

The University of the West Indies (UWI) is located in Cave Hill, the other UWI campuses are located in Trinidad and Jamaica.

St George

Population: 18,000. Neighbouring parishes clockwise from the north; St Joseph, St John, St Philip, Christ Church, St Michael and St Thomas. St George is a flat parish and is known as sugar cane country. There are many great estates and plantations in this parish. Highways 3, 3B and 4 run through St George linking the surrounding parishes.

Great Houses

Drax Hall Estate on Highway 4 is where sugar cane was first cultivated in Barbados around 1642, is one of only two Jacobean houses remaining in Barbados. This estate has belonged to the Drax family since the 17th Century. It was built in the 1650s by James Drax and his brother William. It is a private home, not open to the public. The estate dominates the eastern section of St George.

Valley Plantation spans 254 acres and is open to the public.

Brighton Great House is one of the oldest houses in Barbados. It has been owned for over 100 years by the Piles family. In 1804 John Gittens Archer owned the house. He was the first white Barbadian to be convicted for the murder of a slave (sentenced for a year). He sold Brighton Great House to Conrad Pile. The house is supported by four grand columns and 20 foot beams.

Francia Plantation House is located on a wooded hillside overlooking the St George valley. The house contains examples of mid-19th Century craftwork. The name comes from the Portuguese word 'franc' meaning France. The original owner was French.

Byde Mill plantation

Byde Mill plantation was the home of Joshua Steele, who tried to improve the conditions of poor whites among other things. The 1876 Confederation Riots started on this plantation.

Places of interest

Gun Hill is the site of the giant limestone lion sculptured in 1868 by Henry Wilkinson out of a single piece of rock. Wilkinson served as a military commander at the station, which was also used as a communication post and a convalescent station for the Imperial troops.

Bulkeley Sugar Factory is one of the oldest factories in operation in

186

Barbados and the last one in St George still working. Visitors are welcome for night-time tours.

Churches

St George Church was built in 1784 and cost £600. It survived the 1831 hurricane and contains monumental sculpture work by Richard Westmacott, who also sculptured the statue of Nelson in Bridgetown.

St Augustine was built around 1858 on what was the Groves Plantation.

St Jude's chapel was built in 1834.

St Luke was built in 1830 on land that was a gift from Conrad Pile. It was destroyed in the hurricane of 1831 and rebuilt in 1832.

Lion statue at Gun Hill

St John

Population:10,500. Neighbouring parishes from the south clockwise; St Philip, St George and St Joseph. St John is served by Highways 3B and 4. This delightfully hilly parish is steeped in history.

Places of interest

This parish is dominated by Hackleton's Cliff, 1,000 feet above the sea and providing picturesque scenery of the east coast, spanning from Pico Teneriffe in the north to Ragged Point in the south.

Ashford Bird Park is a sanctuary for birds and animals as well as being part of the Ashford Plantation, which is a working estate set in 197 acres.

Martin's Bay - from the end of the 1800s until 1930 the Barbados Railway travelled through this area, though all that remains of the railway today are some old railway tracks. The road into Martin's Bay also passes a popular picnic spot.

Bath used to be a plantation estate when 'sugar was king' but now it is famous for the satellite dish, that links Barbados to the world. There is also a park in this location.

Consett Bay is a beautifully sheltered bay where local fisherman land their daily catch.

Codrington College is a complex of buildings standing on a clifftop 360 feet above sea level. It provides a spectacular view of Consett Bay.

Codrington College

The college was originally the plantation home of Christopher Codrington.

Famous people

Christopher Codrington III was born in 1668 and died in 1710 . In his will he left £10,000 pounds to establish an educational institution in Barbados. The will was contested by relatives in England and the college was not built until 1748, nearly 40 years after his death.

Churches

St John's Parish Church overlooks the coast of St John and the Atlantic ocean, it is 825 feet above sea level. The first church was built from stone and dates back to 1660. The existing church was built in 1836 after the original church was destroyed by the hurricane of 1831. The pulpit in the church is made from six different kinds of wood.

Mount Tabor Moravian Church was built in 1825 and is surrounded by mahogany trees.

The Chapel of the Holy Cross and St Marks were originally built as chapels of ease.

St Margaret is one of the later churches built in 1862.

St John's Parish Church

Great Houses

Villa Nova was built in 1834 and is open to the public five-days a week.

Wakefield Vegetable Estate is on a hill beneath a canopy of trees which overlook the estate. Most of the vegetables eaten in Barbados are grown here.

Clifton Hall is another Great House with a fine example of Georgian architecture, unfortunately it is not open to the public.

Eastmont is a private house built in the 19th Century. This plantation was bought in 1895 by Miller Austin, a mulatto blacksmith and entrepreneur, who broke the monopoly of the white plantocracy in St John. His grandson, the Hon H Bernard St John, became the third Prime Minister of Barbados in 1985. The house has remained in the family ever since.

Newcastle Great House is a well planned Georgian house built in the 16th Century, though sadly, it has now fallen into disrepair.

Bath Plantation House, surrounded by magnificent cabbage palms, has been unoccupied since it was purchased by the government.

Clifton Hall

Christ Church

Population: 47,500. The main town is Oistins. Christ Church was the first parish to develop it's tourist industry, mainly because of its healthy environment, a most picturesque coastline and its many white sandy beaches. It is now the most built-up area in Barbados. The main Highway 7 runs parallel to the sea from Hastings to Oistins. Christ Church is home to Grantley Adams International Airport. Neighbouring parishes clockwise from north; St George, St Philip and St Michael.

Famous buildings

The Grantley Adams International Airport is an efficient and modern airport serviced by banks, restaurants, shops, car-hire, public telephones and a tourist information bureau. The airport is 11 miles from Bridgetown.

Famous people

Richard B Moore (1893-1978) born in Hastings, was the son of a lay-preacher, he became a teenage evangelist and emigrated to New York in 1909 at the age of 16. He worked tirelessly for African-American consciousness, Pan-African politics and Caribbean freedom. He was responsible for the term Afro-American. (Later replaced by African-American).

Churches

There have been five churches of Christ Church:

Christ Church the first church and chapel of ease was destroyed by rains and floods in 1669. The present church contains some of the oldest memorial ledgers on the island and the church yard contains the famous Chase Vault.

St Davids is a chapel school.

St Patricks chapel school was built around 1839.

St Matthias was built in the 18th century.

Beaches & Sport

The coastal stretch from Hastings to Oistins has many of the best

View from St Lawrence Gap

swimming and bathing beaches. Efforts are being made to protect the coastline and marine life by laying artificial reefs.

Golf at the Rockley Golf Club, parasailing at Carlisle Bay, and diving can be enjoyed at St Lawrence Gap and along the coast in this parish.

Rockley Beach

Places of interest

Hastings has a colourful military history. The old red-brick buildings scattered along the coast road from Carlisle Bay to Hastings used to provide accommodation and administrative facilities for St Anne's Fort, many have now been converted into homes.

Harry Bayley Observatory was built in Christ Church in 1963. It is the headquarters of the Barbados Astronomical Society and the only observatory in the Caribbean.

Oistins is the main fishing port in Barbados.

St Philip

Population: 21,000. Neighbouring parishes anti-clockwise from the north are St John, St George and Christ Church. St Philip is the largest parish and was one of the original six parishes. Highway 4B and 5 are the main roads to St Philip.

Churches

St Philip's Parish Church, like many other churches, has been destroyed several times by hurricanes.

St Martin was built in 1859 on land that had previously been occupied by a chapel school.

St Catherine was a chapel school in 1922.

Shrewsbury Methodists Church has an 18th Century Georgian appearance.

Places of interest

The infamous Sam Lord's Castle can be found off Highway 5 at Long Bay.

The Emancipation Statue at St Barnabas Roundabout, ABC Highway.

Three House Park was where the railway station stood when trains ran

Bottom Bay Beach

from Bathsheba and Belleplaine on the east coast. All that remains is the ruins of a sugar cane factory. The area has been turned into a popular picnic site.

Culpepper Island is a tiny island, 25 by 35 yards and 20 feet above sea level, it is Barbados' only island.

Coral Stone Quarry produces most of the cut coral stone used for building in Barbados for the past ten years.

Crane Beach Hotel is situated on the cliff edge and was opened in 1867. The hotel is one of the oldest on the island and is a favourite with honeymooners. Stunning views await the visitor.

The Barbados Zoo at Oughterson House was until recently a working sugar cane plantation. Now visitors can walk around the Great House and stroll through the nature trail. Officially opened in 1983, it is still expanding.

Crane Beach Hotel

The Barbados Zoo

Beaches

Crane Beach is a wonderfully romantic white sandy beach and picnic area, once ships unloaded their cargo by a crane from the cliff top. Many say it is the most beautiful beach in the Caribbean.

Other bays along the coast of St Philip are Ragged Point in the east, best known for its limestone cliffs and Salt Cave Bay in the south.

Great Houses

Harrismith House stands on the cliffs of St Philip and was built in 1920 from coral stone by Roland Henry Taylor, a planter from Wakefield (St John). Harrismith was used as a seaside house.

Major industries

General Crude Company struck oil in Woodburne in 1972. The Woodburne oil fields were nationalized by the Barbadian Government in 1982. The oil wells are important to Barbados and supply 50 percent of the country's petroleum as well as much of its gas needs.

Tourism

CRUISING THE WATERS OF BARBADOS: The Jolly Roger (above) and the Bajan Queen (below)

The *Jolly Roger*

The pirates and privateers of the late 18th Century flew the dreaded skull and crossbones flag to strike fear into the hearts of their intended victims. These days, the *Jolly Roger* flag is flown from the masts of the world famous pirate schooners of the same name in their home port of Bridgetown, Barbados. The modern day pirate crew is now intent on providing a top-class sailing excursion, where walking the plank and swinging from the yard-arm are done purely for the pleasure of jumping into the beautiful crystal waters of the Caribbean Sea.

For over 30 years, these ships have become synonymous with tourism in Barbados and continue to symbolise the very essence of a carefree tropical holiday. The unbeatable blend of sea breezes, calypso rhythms and the expertly concocted rum punch, bring out the smiles and the sense of adventure in everyone who sails with the *Jolly Roger* crew. The captain sets the mood from the outset and soon everyone is joining in the seafaring antics, which include a pirate wedding and choosing an unsuspecting 'victim' to 'walk the plank.'

The ships are of a type known to have sailed the Caribbean waters for the past 300 years and apart, from a few modern conveniences, are authentic wooden schooners with real cannons and blood red sails. A wealth of information about pirates who sailed the Caribbean is tastefully displayed below deck as a 'Rogues Gallery'. All of the famous pirate flags are on display and on the main mast flies the dreaded skull and crossbones.

The success of these famous ships has not gone unnoticed and many copies have been attempted in other resort areas around the world. None have been able to recreate the charm of the originals in Barbados and the award-winning format of this type of excursion. Well over two million satisfied clients have experienced the uniqueness of the *Jolly Roger* cruise.

The *Bajan Queen*

For over a decade the *Bajan Queen* has earned an excellent international reputation for being the best dinner cruise vessel in the region. The three deck layout of the ship with ample table seating and open areas lends itself well to creating the breezy setting for a moonlight cruise. The placid Caribbean waters along with the starry skies make a dreamy combination as the boat glides along the sparkling west coast. Add the music from the top local bands and an unforgettable voyage is the reward for all those who sail on the *Bajan Queen*. The vessel itself is quite large and offers a very stable cruise so passengers travel in comfort in an atmosphere that guarantees fun and enjoyment.

Bajan Helicopters

A wonderful and exciting way to see Barbados is by helicopter. Bajan Helicopters, the only helicopter operator in the Eastern Caribbean, is located in Bridgetown at picturesque Carlisle Bay from where this service starts.

This family - run company started in 1989, by leasing one helicopter. They now own two aircraft and plan to purchase a third AS355 Twin Star for all-weather night/day trips.

Bajan Helicopters provide aerial film and photography services as well as ship transfer services for oil tankers and exploration vessels.

The staff of this company are highly-trained professionals with all pilots taking exams at six-month intervals, under the same stringent requirements as airline pilots. The company's engineers undergo training in Dallas, and they must already have met the rigorous standard for obtaining an Engineers License with experience of rotary wing transport.

Over the six years the company has been in operation it has won numerous awards, which are on display at their sales office. The company is a member of the Helicopter Association International, a worldwide body representing the professional helicopter industry.

Bajan Helicopters operate Astar jet helicopters, one of the most successful 'flight-seeing' aircraft. Flying up to seven passengers in a spacious air-conditioned cabin. This highly reliable aircraft, is capable of flying at 170mph at 15,000ft above sea level.

Flight- seeing, offers a unique way of touring Barbados. You can see familiar sights from a different perspective. Bajan Helicopters offer two tours, 'Discover Barbados' which lasts for 20 minutes. This tour takes you on a breathtaking flight of the tranquil west coast beaches. Or you can travel on the more expensive 'Island Tour' which lasts 30 minutes, this tour covers the whole coastline. The pilot gives informative commentary and special rates are available to children and honeymooners.

The *Harbour Master*

The *Harbour Master*, a custom-built four-deck vessel, with its own semi-submersible, restaurant, theatre, night-club, corporate entertainment area and one of the largest bars in Barbados, is the newest attraction in Barbados. The boat is luxuriously furnished with its main deck elegantly appointed with brass and mahogany finishes and gilt-edged mirrors.

The *Harbour Master* offers lunch and dinner cruises, and provides a 'floating entertainment facility' catering to product launches, private parties, weddings, office functions, trade shows and conventions. The boat can hold 800 people and comfortably seat over 400 guests on two decks, during lunch and dinner. *The Harbour Master* cost over BDS$6 million.

The vessel will be 'beached' to operate as any other restaurant offering Bajan brunch on Sunday, a businessman's lunch on Monday and Friday, Caribbean dinner on Monday evening and theatre on Friday evening.

The Harbour Master can also be transformed into a beach facility with restaurant, bar, freshwater showers and changing rooms.

193

The tempo, colour and enthusiasm of the cast make this show an evening of total pleasure only to be experienced in Barbados

Tropical Spectacular

The Tropical Spectacular dinner show at the Plantation Restaurant and Garden Theatre, Christ Church, is certainly an evening of entertainment not to be missed. In keeping with the successful formula that has made this show a tremendous success for the past 13 years, the producers, have once again, created a glittering extravaganza that draws on breathtaking costumes, exhilerating choreography, backed by in-depth research to produce an authentic cultural Caribbean kaleidoscope. An exotic adventure in music and dance, the show combines the on-stage talents of the versatile Plantation Dancers; the red hot exploits of fire-eater Cassius Clay, and all the excitement of fire limbo expertly performed by Jenny and the Phoenix Dancers.

The new show contains all the ingredients that keep visitors and locals alike coming back again and again, and earning the reputation as 'the show not to be missed and the best value for money.'

Regular fans can nevertheless rest assured that this dazzling new revue retains all the excitement, glamour and professionalism of its predecessors. Similarly the top value package still includes one of the best buffet dinners in Barbados; unlimited free drinks; dancing to the pulsating beat of the steelband and the electrifying sounds of Spice & Company; lots of spirited audience participation and complimentary transport laid on.

Truly Caribbean in every aspect with beautiful costumes and vigorous choreography, music and dance - this unique production spans time from pre-historic to the present, capturing artistic expressions that have emerged from the Caribbean melting pot.

The show begins with a tribute to Barbados' first inhabitants, the gentle Arawaks. Moving back yet further in time and faster in tempo for a dramatic retrospective of the Yoruba dancers of Africa, the descendants of whom were shipped to Barbados as slaves.

The scene then shifts effortlessly into all the gaiety of Bridgetown market on a Saturday morning in bygone days. Backed by a medley of traditional folk music and garbed in delightful creole costumes, characters from the colourful coconut woman and nutseller offer their wares and cast their enchanting spell to bring the curtain down on the first part of the show.

The second segment of the show is a fantastic journey through the celebrations and festivals of the Caribbean. Ablaze with colour and sound and enhanced by artful lighting effects, this cavalcade of cultures begins with the Junkanoo dancers of the Bahamas and includes a show-stopping sequence depicting a 'zombie jamboree'of jumbies (spirits) playing mas' (masquerade).

Next stop is Cuba with its seductive Latin rhythms, matched by the sensuous movements of the lavishly plumed and sequinned cast. The roots reggae dancers of Jamaica then pay tribute to the internationally renowned Reggae Sunsplash festival, moving on to a demure, yet provocative portrayal of a traditional quadrille dance from the French Westindies.

Back in Barbados, Crop Over revelry old and new is showcased in an explosion of exuberance, encompassing everything from the Tuk band and masquerade, folk characters liked Shaggy Bear and Steel Donkey to all the splendour of Kadooment. The show comes to a stunning climax as the entire cast jump-up bacchanal style in a celebration of carnival in Trinidad.

Aerial view of the Barbados Hilton, Needhams Point, Christ Church

The Barbados Hilton's 'Big 30'

The Barbados Hilton was opened on 27 November 1966, the seventh Hilton International hotel in the Caribbean. The hotel's opening was timed to coincide with Barbados' attainment of Independence from Britain.

The function, held in ideal weather conditions, was attended by more than 1200 guests, including the former Governor General - Sir Robert Arindell, ambassadors and foreign dignitaries.

Prime Minister, Errol Barrow, cut a ribbon to declare the hotel open, using a pair of scissors presented to him by John and Peter Finamore, the young sons of the hotel's first General Manager, Louis J. Finamore. The guests were addressed by Mr Conrad Hilton among others.

Over the years the Barbados Hilton has been 'home' to many celebrities and heads of state. In 1994, Barbados hosted the UN Global Conference. The top UN officials, heads of states and ambassadors were accommodated at the Hilton.

The Barbados Hilton is situated on a peninsula on the site of the historic 17th Century Fort Charles, close to St Anns Garrison, on the southwest side of the island, surrounded by beaches on three sides, and 14 acres of beautifully landscaped gardens. It is only 30 minutes from the airport and within walking distance of sightseeing and historical attractions in Bridgetown.

The Barbados Hilton's 158 luxury rooms all offer central air-conditioning, private balcony with sweeping views, private bath with tub and shower, direct dial telephone, minibar, taped music and colour satellite television. Laundry/valet service (available Monday - Friday) and secretarial services can be arranged.

Wheelchairs are available at the hotel. A doctor is on call around the clock and baby-sitting services can be arranged. Electric current: 110 volts, 50 cycles.

The Verandah Restaurant offers indoor/outdoor dining and is open for breakfast, lunch and dinner. The Gazebo Snack Bar serves both local and American snacks and cocktails. Dancing and entertainment are offered nightly at the Flambeau Bar. For those wishing to dine at the beach, picnic lunches can be arranged. Room service is available daily from 7.00 am to midnight.

Stretching along a beautiful white sand beach, the Barbados Hilton is a mecca for water-sports enthusiasts. Equipment for scuba diving, sunfish sailing, boogie boarding, snorkelling, windsurfing and deep sea fishing are available at the hotel's beach club. The Hilton also features an outdoor swimming pool; four chevron-surfaced, night-lit tennis courts, and a health club with sauna and massage. Nautilus equipment, aerobics and calisthenics exercise classes are also available. Slot machines are located on the property. Facilities for horseback riding and golf are available within ten miles of the hotel. Pleasure cruises can be arranged at the Tour Desk.

The Hilton's six meeting rooms can accommodate from 30 to 350 people. Blackboards, easels, spotlights and podiums are available. Simultaneous translation service and extra telephone lines can be arranged on request. A full line of audio-visual equipment is available for rent.

The Barbados Hilton is owned by the Government of Barbados - Barbados Tourism Investment Corporation.

195

The beautiful crescent-shaped beach at Sandy Lane

Sandy Lane

The famous Sandy Lane Hotel on Barbados' St James coast has been setting the standard for elegance and style in the Caribbean for over 30 years.

It has one of the most beautiful beaches on earth, wide and crescent-shaped with powdery white sand shelving into the aquamarine of the Caribbean Sea. The acres of well-tended grounds are a profusion of hibiscus, bougainvillea and frangipani.

Architecturally, Sandy Lane is the most impressive hotel in the Caribbean, sculpted in classical style from the island's coral stone, with 90 rooms and 30 suites overlooking the sea or the gardens. All have private balconies where quiet pleasures like morning coffee and evening cocktails are enhanced by views of ancient mahogany trees leading down to the sea.

Two ocean-front restaurants, one formal and the other more relaxed, provide a wide range of local specialities as well as the highest standards of international cuisine. The choice of Continental or English breakfast can be served on guests' balconies or in the restaurant by the sea. Lunch can be a light affair, or a gastronomic buffet. Evenings mean candlelit dinners with a choice of seafood, prime meats and local fruits and vegetables to satisfy the most demanding gourmet.

Many of the staff at Sandy Lane have worked there for nearly 20 years. From the moment of arrival, their concern for guests' comfort is self-evident, backed up by a standard of service that is unequalled in the Caribbean.

Sandy Lane has long been a mecca for sports enthusiasts with five championship tennis courts plus an 18-hole championship golf course. The fullest possible range of watersports is available to guests, whilst the less energetic have the most perfect surroundings in which simply to relax in the sun.

Sandy Lane is under the general management of Barbados-born Richard Williams whose own particular brand of personality and charm has effortlessly introduced a more personal and approachable feel to this legendary hotel.

Island Weddings of Wonder

Barbados Sunshine Weddings, offer exceptional options to lovers in search of an unforgettable wedding location. A romantic cruise becomes the ideal passage to a Caribbean island wedding; couples disembark and step right up to a same-day ceremony, after a whirlwind tour, relaxed meal, or whatever strikes their fancy.

Setting the scene for a romantic retreat, Barbados offers a distinct advantage for those planning their wedding; a new law allows couples to marry the day they arrive, eliminating the need to wait for licenses or permits.

A personal, on-island wedding co-ordinator awaits couples to arrange all the details, from completing paperwork and obtaining a marriage license, to escorting the bride and groom to the venue where everything has been prepared to perfection.

Each wedding package includes the services of a wedding co-ordinator, ground transportation, a minister, government licenses and fees, location, music and more. Some options include wedding cake, photography and video, live musicians, limousine and flowers.

• This lucky couple pictured were married at Discovery Bay Hotel, which also provide Wedding Services

Atlantis Submarine

There are many ways to put adventure into your Barbados holiday and most of these require a little effort. A trip on the Atlantis Submarine, where everything is taken care of for your comfort and safety, provides a lot of excitement in a one-hour trip under the sea. This is a real submarine that cruises on the sea-bed, rises effortlessly over reefs and manoeuvres around wrecks. Large shoals of tropical fish glide by and they seem to be as curious about the submarine and its passengers as the tourists are about the fish. The submarine dives to a depth of 150 feet and there are side viewing windows and a large front viewport. With the artificial magnification effect which exists underwater, everything seems so close and easy to touch. This trip is spectacular, both day and night, and it will thrill most people regardless of age. No need for a wetsuit or wellies!

THE JAZZ FESTIVAL: Jazz enthusiasts throughout the world equate jazz and January with Barbados

Foursquare Sugar Factory

R L Seale & Company which has been blending and bottling rum since 1926 is establishing the first completely new rum distillery to be built in the south Caribbean this century.

The distillery, designed by the Italian firm of Frilli Engineering Spa, features the most modern advances in distillation technology. It will be the first plant in the south Caribbean to distil under vacuum, with consequential benefits in efficiency and product quality.

Environmental concerns prompted the installation of a European style concentration plant for the recycling of distillery waste as animal feed and fertiliser.

The distillery will supply all R L Seale's brands of rum which include Old Brigand, ESAF White and Doorly's to the Barbadian market, and for export to the US, Canada, Australia, Britain, Japan and several Caribbean territories.

The development of the old Foursquare Sugar Factory into a modern seven-acre centre of general interest, information and education about Barbados for visitor and local alike, will have as its main focus the most modern, high-tech rum distillery, to be known as the Rum Factory, in the entire Caribbean area.

Following a formal welcome, a tour of the premises will begin with a five-minute video on the cultivation and harvesting of sugar cane and the eventual delivery of the molasses to the rum factory for distillation. During the tour through the factory the guide will explain the processes which can be seen. It is planned that on the floor of the distillery will be a functioning exhibit of the way in which rum was bottled in the old days. Following this guests will be invited to enjoy a complimentary drink of rum or fruit punch.

On leaving the distillery the visitors will be diverted to the nearby art gallery. On the top floor of this old building will be four artists' studios and, on the ground floor an exhibition of local art which can be purchased.

People are then invited to explore the many other attractions of the 'All About Barbados' place. These will include:
- An exhibition of photographs of old Barbados.
- Local artisans working in their own studio/shops - basketry, woodwork, hand-painting, cotton garments, pottery, leatherwork, custom-made garments for adults and children with local motifs and jewellery from natural local materials.
- A Best of Barbados shop, a Daphne Hunte Shell Work shop and a shop with other locally produced items will be available - weaving, wireworks, figurines, hats woven from fronds and a multiplicity of locally produced souvenirs.
- Artefacts from the old sugar factory with explanations of their former function.
- Landscaping which will include a wide variety of plants, flowers, shrubs and vines - each one labelled for identification.
- An area in which tropical fruits will be grown.
- A small aviary with such tropical birds as macaws, toucans and parrots.
- A landscaped cage of green monkeys.
- An area devoted to the sale of food and beverage - including a 'Mauby Woman' and a 'Coconut Vendor'. In this area, too, there will be a hair-braider.
- An amphitheatre will be developed in the ground depression where the sugar cane was formerly dumped and which still has the original hoist overhead.
- A bookstore with publications on all topics about Barbados.
- An information booth will provide details regarding tourism attractions, business opportunities and international financial services.
- There will be a public address service throughout the complex providing Westindian music and public interest announcements.

Holetown Festival

The celebration starts in February with the anniversary of the arrival of the first English settlers on 17 February, 1627. The location of their landing, now Holetown, hosts a week of activities. Medieval songs are sung in the churches and the more modern rhythms can be heard on the fairgrounds. This atmosphere of the old and the new combine with folk singing and dancing, sports and games, street parades, street markets, fairs and food stalls offering traditional local foods.

Oistins Fish Festival

by Dan L Lanta

Oistins, the largest fishing port in Barbados, is situated on the south coast. Oistins Fish Festival has been held every Easter weekend since 1978 and started one year after the Holetown Festival in St James on the west coast.

The founders of Oistins Fish Festival were Lady Helen H. John and her husband, Sir Harold Bernard John. As an artist in her own right, Lady John sought to highlight the fishing village by focusing on its cultural and economic contributions to Barbados.

Prior to 1983, when the present modern fishing complex was opened, Oistins was a typical, somewhat quaint and outmoded fishing village where the smell of fish permeated the air. At the small, well-structured fish market, hawkers could be heard crying 'fish, fish' to catch the eye of the buyer. People flocked to the seashore to meet the incoming 'moses' fishing boats where they tussled with each other to buy the fresh catch from the fishermen. A narrow street divided the coastal activities of fish-vending on one side and rum shops, stores and residents' homes on the other. Oistins Fish Festival began, therefore, in old Oistins.

The festival sets out to demonstrate that the fishermen and fish-vendors have careers as dignified as any other, that such people contribute to the economy through the sale of their catches, that they contribute nutritionally to the health of the community and improve their standard of living.

Culturally the festival was to showcase the skills and expertise of the fishing community that have long been a legacy of the trade. Foremost among these skills is fish-boning. Barbadian women are particularly competent at this skill. At the market some of these women get the very popular flying fish, bone them and offer them for sale. These fish are carefully dissected to remove all bone, gut and scales.

In order to retain this skill and to demonstrate its artistry, the festival's premier event is a fish-boning competition which attracts fish-vendors from Oistins. There are usually six to eight competitors who vie for the champion trophy and other attractive prizes. Each competitor has to scale and bone eight flying fish with points awarded to those who bone in the fastest time with the minimum bones left in the fish. This event is watched by hundreds of onlookers on Easter Monday.

Every year the Fish Festival is opened with the blowing of conch shells by two old fishermen. The blowing of the shells is another traditional Bajan art form connected with the fishing industry. The conch is a shellfish found in Caribbean waters. The conch itself is eaten and its shell used as a sort of trumpet. Holding the shell in his hand and raising it to his mouth, he blows until the shell makes a loud sound. Many years ago the blowing of the conch shell meant fishing boats had just come ashore and the fishermen were ready to sell their catch.

At the festival you will see another old Barbadian fishing technique - net throwing. Few fisherman engage in this art today and those who do are retired. The net is made by hand. Armed with his net and small open boat (moses boat) the fisherman goes out by the reef to catch frays - small fish. Each competing fisherman attempts to throw his net covering as wide a circumference as is possible while at the same time keeping his balance in the boat. The festival provides Barbadians with an opportunity to see this particular skill.

Visitors to the festival get a glimpse of some of the ancient fishing boats, particularly the moses - a small, open boat managed by not more than two persons. Owners of these boats take part in the annual moses race where one fisherman per boat paddles his vessel in a racing competition. A cricket competition is also held between the fishermen and other competitors. There are sand-castle building contests, tray-racing and the very popular fish-skinning. This last activity is performed by young boys who offer to skin the larger fish for buyers who do not have the time to do it themselves. On the first day of the festival a competition is organised to see who can skin a fish the fastest.

The festival, in addition to keeping alive those skills associated with fishing, also provides an opportunity for those persons living in Oistins and surrounding districts, including youth organisations, to earn money. They do this by setting up stalls on both days of the festival where they sell fish cooked in a variety of ways. Craftsmen get the opportunity to sell their various leather crafts - shoes, handbags and belts; others display wooden artifacts and straw goods. Stalls and vendors line both sides of the street taking full advantage of this opportunity to sell their goods to locals and visitors.

Overall, the festival is one large street fair, stretching from the Saturday before Easter to Easter Monday. There is music throughout the day with a main stage where visitors are attracted by the variety of entertainment. Thousands of onlookers enjoy the movements of the Barbadian Landship, an imitation of a ship and its crew, on land. They are entertained by Tuk-band music, ballroom dancing, square dancing, poetry reading, creative dance and drama. Popular DJs, keep spectators on their feet with live music.

Originally, no activity took place on the Easter Sunday, but within the last five years visitors have been treated to gospel music lasting about three hours in the evening. This event has grown in popularity and gospel groups from around the country are invited to participate in religious programmes. Oistins Fish Festival now effectively covers three days.

The festival finishes with a prize-giving function on Monday afternoon. The Fish-Boning Queen is given her trophy and a financial award. Other important trophies and financial awards are made to members of the fishing community: to the boats with the largest catches during the season to those with the largest catches during the week of the festival, to fisherman who catch the largest single fish of the season and to the team that wins the cricket match.

Every effort is made to improve the festival each year. Barbadians regard Oistins as the place to be at Easter. Tourist and Barbadians living overseas return each year to visit the Fish Festival. The organisers and locals intend that Oistins Fish Festival will continue to expand and prosper year by year.

The Cohobblopot

Cohobblopot is a 'cook-up' of a large number of ingredients in the same pot. The name has been adopted for one of the yearly events at Crop Over, which takes place on the last Sunday evening of the festival in the National Stadium. Cohobblopot features a wide range of talent including all the top performers - the crowned King and Queen of costumes, the Calypso Monarch and Junior Monarch. Music includes calypso, steel band, Tuk band, reggae, folk and gospel.

Kadooment Day

Kadooment is a Barbadian term referring to an important event. It has been adopted as the name of the final event of the annual Crop Over festival and takes place on the first Monday each

August. It also attracts the largest crowd for any event at one place in Barbados. Kadooment begins at 8.00 am with parades of masquerade bands passing before the judges in the National Stadium and then dancing their way along the roads to Spring Garden Highway, three miles away. The masquerade bands, which will arrive well into the afternoon, are accompanied by trucks with powerful sound systems playing the latest and hottest in local calypso The routes are densely packed with spectators and the highway, which is closed to traffic, is lined with stalls selling food, drinks, tee-shirts, records and cassettes. Many stalls have their own sound systems which add to the explosion of colour, sounds and movements. There is also a sea festival on the beach adjacent to the highway, as well as, activities geared for children's Kadooment.

BARBADOS' FESTIVALS

There are many celebrations and exciting annual festivals that mark the Barbadian calendar for fun-loving Barbadians, tourists and visitors who are welcome and encouraged to participate. Most of these cultural events are unique to Barbados and provide a special opportunity for the visitor to take part in activities that reveal the nature of the islanders.

JAZZ FESTIVAL. Music enthusiasts throughout the world recognise that January and Jazz, when juxtaposed, spell Barbados. This jubilant affair attracts a cast of musical maestros, who represent some of the best jazz talent to grace the entertainment stages. This annual event is a masterpiece of musical art against the intriguing backdrop of tropical Barbadian life.

HOLETOWN FESTIVAL. The celebration starts in February with the anniversary of the arrival of the first English settlers on 17 February, 1627. The location of their landing, now Holetown, hosts a week of activities. Medieval songs are sung in the churches and the more modern rhythms can be heard on the fairgrounds. This atmosphere of the old and the new combine with folk singing and dancing, sports and games, street parades, street markets, fairs and food stalls offering traditional local foods.

OISTINS FISH FESTIVAL. Easter weekend brings accolades to the local people who compete in the two-day festival that pays tribute to the skills of the island's fishing folk. The local fishermen and women demonstrate their abilities in fishing, fish-boning, boat racing and even crab racing, while the spectators enjoy dancing to steel bands and mingling with the thronging crowds on the beaches, in the marketplace and in the quaint rum shops that line the roadside. Food stalls, arts and crafts and an exhibition by the Coast Guard round off the activities.

GOSPELFEST. Gospel is a spiritual celebration used by Barbadians for generations to express their African heritage through music. This cadre of songs is captured for three days in May when local Caribbean and international gospel artists come together for one of the most exciting concerts of its kind. The Gospelfest is a family event which features a myriad of attractions and back-to-back performances by a variety of gospel singers

CROP OVER FESTIVAL. The highlight of the summer is the Crop Over Festival, an all-island jubilation running from mid-July to early August. Crop Over celebrates the completion of the sugar cane harvest. Competition 'Tents' ring with the fierce battle of calypsonians for the coveted Calypso Monarch title award, and the air is redolent with the smells of Barbadian cooking during the massive 'Bridgetown Market' street fair. Rich with the spirit of local culture, 'The Cohobblopot' blends drama, dance, and music with the crowning of the King and Queen of costume bands. An exiting evening is the 'Pic-O-de-Crop Show', when the King of Calypso is crowned. The climax of the festival is 'Kadooment Day' - a national holiday - when costume bands fill the streets with pulsating Barbadian rhythms and fireworks ignite the evening sky.

NATIONAL INDEPENDENCE FESTIVAL OF THE CREATIVE ARTS. During November, Barbadians of all ages match their talents in the fields of music, singing, dancing, acting and writing. Then on Independence Day, 30 November, the final appearances are made along with photographic, arts and crafts exhibitions.

CONGALINE CARNIVAL. The Congaline Carnival is a nine-day carnival which takes place at the end of April. The Congaline Village is the heart and soul of the Congaline Carnival and provides a daily exhibition forum and market place for a myriad of free entertainment, local crafts and culture. It is dubbed the 'World's Greatest Street Party', as it culminates in a one day T-shirt band parade.

HOLDER'S OPERA SEASON. Founded in 1993, takes place in March and has already established itself as the premier cultural event in the Caribbean. Acclaimed nationally and internationally, the season is a unique celebration of opera, music and theatre, a major event on the world cultural calender whose high artistic standards draw audiences from all over the world.

The Casuarina Beach Club

Discovery Bay Hotel, Holetown, St James

The Casuarina Beach Club

The Casuarina Beach Club is a spacious 160-room apartment hotel located on the south coast of the island and adjacent to the St Lawrence Gap. Here there are a variety of restaurants, bars and shops, Bridgetown is only a 15-minute drive or bus ride away. The hotel is set in eight acres of tropical gardens with a wide variety of flora. Flowers and Casuarina trees border the 900-feet white coral sand beach, coconut palms can be seen from the poolside lounger. Fruit bearing Bajan cherry, sea-grape and banana trees provide a taste of the tropics.

Casuarina has won awards from Air Canada, Vingressor and repeat Thomson Gold Awards, with over 50 percent of its clientele returning annually, to bask in the sun and bathe in the ocean.

Casuarina welcomes children and is well equipped to meet their needs. There are high-chairs and cribs, a playground including a slide and a Bajan chattel dolls house. There is also a playroom with toys which is supervised by a trained nursery schoolteacher who, at no charge to the guests, involves the children in activities. In addition to the larger and deeper swimming pool there is a circular shallow pool for children.

The Casuarina exhibits an extensive collection of local and Caribbean art. The collection is not limited to the public areas, there are original paintings in all the rooms. The reception, reading room, television and video room, conference room and piano bar have been furnished with restored antique Barbadian furniture. In this elegant atmosphere guests can enjoy English afternoon tea accompanied by piano music. There is a poolside bar and the 'Dover Reef Restaurant' offers fine dining throughout the day and late into the evening.

Amongst the many features on offer are wedding services, a busy Activities Centre, two tennis courts - free to guest's, free entrance and transportation to the nearby Universal Health Club. There is a gift shop, a mini mart, a duty-free shop, laundry facilities for guests use and a laundry service. Also environmentally friendly, the Casuarina aims to stay abreast with progress.

The all-inclusive Mango Bay hotel at Holetown, St James

Windsurf Village

Windsurf Village is located on the south coast of Barbados. In an ocean front location with an excellent beach and a friendly relaxed atmosphere, this is an ideal spot for a carefree holiday. The property is close to Oistins where there are banks, shopping and nightlife. It is also close to the active St Lawrence Gap.

There are three rooms without kitchenettes. These are small and suited mainly for singles or cozy couples. They have double beds, ceiling fans and baths with showers. The hotel also has 13 studios with kitchenettes. These are spacious, airy and although old-fashioned, are comfortable with tropical furnishings, twin beds, bath with shower and ceiling fan. All studios have an ocean view from their individual balconies. The two bedroom apartments are spacious with kitchen, living room, balcony or patio, and have ceiling fans with air-conditioning available in the bedrooms. There is a card phone in the lobby for general use (cards are sold at the front desk).

The restaurant/beach bar is informal and offers all meals and regular entertainment and there is an happy hour. Meals are available.

Club Mistral Windsurfing operates a centre on the property and offers equipment rentals and instruction. This hotel is ideal for those looking for a moderate (two star) property in an excellent beach front location.

Sea Breeze Beach Hotel

Sea Breeze Beach Hotel offers 47 superior studios with kitchenettes, 25 superior rooms with fridges and coffee makers, and three two-bedroom apartments with full kitchens. Each unit has split system air-conditioning, ceiling fan, radio, IDD telephone, hairdryer, and full bathroom with tub and shower. Cable TV and in-room safes are available for a supplement. Each unit has a patio or balcony with view of the ocean, pool or garden. There are two freshwater pools - one with a children's section - three jacuzzis in the garden, an air-conditioned fitness room (with massages available by appointment), gift shop, laundromat, games area, and the spacious and elegant Mermaid Restaurant as well as the new Fish Pot beach bar. The extensive beaches, gardens, and sunning areas offer ample sunbeds and chairs, while creating a sense of spaciousness.

Located just 15 minutes from the airport and about the same distance from Bridgetown, Sea Breeze is an ideal location from which to sample all that Barbados has to offer. With lovely beaches and gardens and the many excellent facilities on the two-and-a-half acre property.

There is windsurfing, kayaking and dinghy sailing along the beach and scuba diving, golf, horseback riding, para-sailing, deep-sea fishing, and a whole host of other sports and sporting events within a 15-minutes drive. There are also helicopter rides, submarine dives, island sightseeing tours and jeep safaris, catamaran and pirate cruises, and day-trips to neighbouring islands to choose from, as well as a wide selection of places to eat or to sample the vibrant Caribbean nightlife, all within easy reach of the Sea Breeze Beach Hotel.

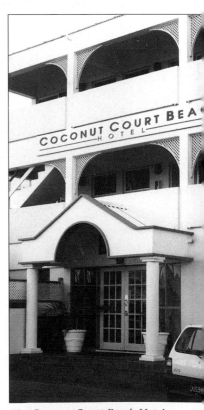

The Coconut Court Beach Hotel at Hastings, Christ Church

203

Conference Facilities

Dover Convention Centre

The Barbados Government's modern Convention Centre at Dover on the south coast resulted mainly from the conversion of three buildings: one of them over 50 years old, was formerly used by Cable and Wireless.

The picturesque complex was originally converted at a cost of BDS$1,086.000 and has since been refurbished to further upgrade the facilities.

The larger building includes a large conference hall, with sound-proof partitions for sub-division when necessary. Total seating capacity is approximately 750 theatre style. There is also provision for simultaneous translation and press booths, committee and staff rooms, office space for supporting services, and an information display area. Attractive lounge and bar facilities overlook the seascape and there is also a handicraft outlet. Overlooking the sea is a restaurant with dining area, as well as office and kitchen space.

The centre falls under the authority of the Ministry of Tourism and Culture and International Transport and is managed by the General Manager, Barbados Tourism Investment Corporation.

Sherbourne Centre

Two miles from the city centre, Bridgetown and adjacent to the main highway linking the south and west coast hotels is the Sherbourne Centre, a fully air-conditioned and well equipped facility able to handle seminars, meetings, international government conferences, trade shows and exhibitions. It is set in well landscaped grounds adjacent to the prime minister's residence overlooking the lush landscape of the St George Valley.

Restaurants and cafeteria facilities are available to seat 120 and 300 persons respectively and these are located directly off the foyers, which also facilitate light exhibition space of 10,000 square feet.

The main hall able to seats 800 theatre style and 450 classroom style. An acoustic partition divides it into two separate spaces, each served with simultaneous translation facilities for six languages. The hall is overlooked by an observer/press gallery and is served by a secretariat which houses 12 offices and a chairman's suite to provide the document production capacity.

There is also a large exhibition/conference hall and three smaller committee rooms which can provide 80 and 160 seats respectively and the usual support facilities required for international conferences such as medical, press, banking and post office facilities.

Frank Collymore Hall

Named after Barbados' distinguished actor, poet and teacher, this is essentially a music hall, but other activities such as conferences, meetings and cultural shows will also find adequate room here. The hall can accommodate 490 people in its 1,180 sq ft of space and the hall is equipped with the latest digital sound and lighting.

ABOVE: Barbadian show jumper, Oliver Skeet at the opening of the newly designed offices of the Barbados Tourism Authority, London, with the Hon. Billie Miller MP, Deputy Prime Minister, Minister of Foreign Affairs, Tourism and International Transport LEFT: The centre piece of the Barbados Tourism Authority's London office - a fresh and vibrant mural which depicts colourful scenes from the island

ABOVE: Frank Collymore Hall OPPOSITE TOP: Sherbourne Centre OPPOSITE BOTTOM: Dover Convention Centre

Barbados...the Sports Paradise

by Mike Goddard

Barbados has long had a reputation for its world class cricket, however, it is also home to a multiplicity of other sports ranging from athletics to yachting.

The exploits of famous cricketing sons Sir Garfield Sobers, Sir Frank Worrell, Sir Everton Weekes, Sir Clyde Walcott, Seymour Nurse, demon bowlers Wes Hall and Charlie Griffith and the opening pair of Desmond Haynes and Gordon Greenidge have forever put the name of Barbados in the mouths and minds of people around the world.

Sir Garfield Sobers, knighted by Queen Elizabeth II in 1975, still has the reputation of being the best cricketer the world has ever seen. His batting, bowling, fielding and all round cricketing genius has written his name indelibly into the history books and in the minds and hearts of every cricket fan. His score of 365 not out in 1958 against Pakistan at Sabina Park, Jamaica, stood until 1994 when it was eclipsed in Antigua by Brian Lara, of Trinidad and Tobago, who scored 375.

Sir Garfield Sobers started his cricket career as a slow bowler but by the time he had retired he had reached the status of being described as the most complete bowler. No one has been as versatile as the tall left hander who could open the innings bowling fast and later return to bowl slow. Sobers had 235 Test wickets and a total of 1,043 first class victims, distinguishing himself as one of the most successful Westindian bowlers of all time.

Sir Frank Worrell one of the famous Three W's, was not only an outstanding player but is best remembered for his captaincy of the West Indies cricket team. On the field he appeared in 51 Tests, scored 3,860 runs, averaging 49.48: captured 69 wickets at an average of 38.73 and took 43 catches.

In 1960 Frank Worrell became the first black captain of the West Indies cricket team. In 15 Tests his team won nine times, lost three, drew two and had that famous tied Test at Brisbane, Australia regarded as the most dramatic Test match ever.

Sir Everton Weekes is among the five Barbadian batsmen who have, over the last 100 years, scored first class triple centuries. The others include his colleagues Frank Worrell, Clyde Walcott and Sir Garfield Sobers. Weekes'

In a Test cricket career which ran from 1954 to 1974 Sobers had a batting aggregate of 8,032 runs, a spectacular achievement for a player who batted only 160 innings. In all first class cricket, Sir Garfield made a total of 28,315 runs and averaged 54.67 per innings, blasting 86 centuries

The Three W's: Frank Worrell, Everton Weekes and Clyde Walcott [team mate Sonny Ramadhin is in the background]

Wes Hall

dynamic batting led him to an enviable Test record. He played 81 innings for 4,455 runs with an average of 58 and 15 centuries.

The other member of the famous Three W's, Clyde Walcott, was just as impressive in his Test career. In 44 matches he played 74 innings, was seven times not out for a total of 3,798 runs. His highest score was 220 and his average was 56.68 with 15 centuries. As a bowler Cyde Walcott took 11 wickets at 37.09 each, at one stage taking off his wicket-keeping pads and gloves to open the bowling but getting his wickets later with his off-breaks. As a Test wicket keeper he took 53 catches and stumped 11 batsmen.

It would be true to say that the success of the West Indies cricket team has in no small measure been built on Barbadian cricketers. These men usually start their careers playing in their village or club teams and as they get better, move on to the competitions organised by the Barbados Cricket Association (BCA).

Organised cricket was started in Barbados in 1892 by the Barbados Challenge Cricket Committee. This body was replaced by the BCA in 1993 and under its guidance the sport has prospered. The other cricket body, the Barbados Cricket League (BCL) was inaugurated in 1936-37 and although playing a secondary role to the BCA, has produced players who have graduated to the BCA competition and later into the Barbados and West Indies teams.

Cricket has over the years grown so rapidly in Barbados that over 150 clubs are affiliated to the BCA and the BCL. The cricket season, runs from May to December and matches are played on Saturday and Sunday afternoons.

The Barbados Cricket team plays in the regional competition which involves the other Caribbean countries of Jamaica, Trinidad and Tobago, Guyana, the Windward and Leeward Islands. This series is sponsored by

207

a Jamaican beer company, and is called the Red Stripe Cup. Barbados has performed well in this competition winning on several occasions.

Barbados is also home to the annual Sir Garfield Sobers Schools Cricket Tournament. Participants have been drawn from cricket loving countries all around the world.

The famous Kensington Oval on the outskirts of Bridgetown is the headquarters for cricket in Barbados. It was the site of the first ever international Test series in the Caribbean, when the Westindies hosted England in 1930.

But while Barbados can boast about the exploits of Sir Garfield Sobers and the other famous cricketers this island is more than just cricket and can easily be described as a sports paradise. With the large number of sports activities available there's something for everyone.

The Cockspur Cup

Since 1982 Barbados has been making an international name for itself in the world of horse racing. The island owes it all to the Cockspur Cup, described as the biggest sporting even in the Caribbean. This race is to the Caribbean what the Epsom Derby and Grand National are to England, the Kentucky Derby is to America, the Queen's Plate to Canada, the Prix de L'Arc de Triomphe to France and the Melbourne Cup to Australia.

On the first Saturday in March each year everything in Barbados, and in some Caribbean islands, grinds to a halt as all attention focuses on the historic Garrison Savannah race-track, just outside Bridgetown. People representing all walks of life from Barbados, the Caribbean and around the world flock to the Garrison for this race. The Cockspur Cup, which brings together horses from Barbados, Trinidad and Tobago, Jamaica and the French island of Martinique is more than a horse race. The pageantry of a marching band, the excitement of the calypso music as the dancing, high kicking, beautiful majorettes bring out the essence of Caribbean colour and excitement in a carnival atmosphere.

The titillating performance by the Cockspur Majorettes sets the scene for a thrilling horse race in which the top thoroughbreds from the islands run their hearts out for the Cockspur Cup, symbol of racing supremacy in the Caribbean.

This race has not only attracted tourists to Barbados but many of the international race-horse owners have either won this great race or are going all out to add it to their successes. One famous owner who has won

Equestrian Sports

Equestrian sports have always been popular in Barbados especially among the more affluent. History shows that the planters always had horses for pleasure whether for playing polo, show jumping or gymkhana. In recent times the sport of dressage has been introduced and this is growing in popularity now that the local organisers have become affiliated to the international governing body, the Federation Equestrian Internationale (FEI).

Polo at one time used to be played at the Garrison Savannah and the owners and managers of sugar plantations would converge there to engage in their favourite sport. Polo moved to a permanent home at Holders, St James, near the west coast in the mid-sixties and participation and interest has widened.

Barbadians play polo to a high standard and some players have reached a four-goal handicap on an international scale of one to ten. This rating system is similar to that in golf.

The Barbados Polo Club has hosted teams from Britain, the US, Canada, Ireland, Jamaica and Australia. One of the major

supporters of polo in Barbados is businessman Mr C O Williams, popularly known as 'Cow'. His string of ponies account for over half of the near 100 active horses playing polo in Barbados. Most of the polo horses in Barbados are retired race horses while there are some imported animals and some local bred ponies. The polo season in Barbados runs from November to May and matches are usually played twice a week.

Show jumping has formed an integral part of the equestrian programme in Barbados for many years, but dressage was not introduced until the 1980s. Both sports are well supported by the several local stables. There are two sand arenas for these sports and several other areas for show jumping on the island.

the Cockspur Cup is Englishman, Robert Sangster. He owns horses around the world and he has won every major race from Australia to north America. Even with his international success, Mr Sangster especially treasures his win in the 1996 Barbados Cockspur Cup with the gelding Rambrino.

Another Englishman, Paul Locke, who has raced his horses successfully in England, Ireland, France and north America considers his Barbados racing stable every bit as important as those in the international arena. His two wins in the Cockspur Cup with Alto Jane in 1994 and Asian Jane in 1995 rate alongside his major victories in Britain and north America.

Champion trainer in Barbados for many years is Bill Marshall who forsook the Newmarket Downs in England and retired from racing there to live in Barbados. His horses have ruled the race-track in Barbados winning every major race including the Cockspur Cup, the United Barbados Derby and the Heineken Stakes.

Marshall, however, has had to share some of the top races with famous Australian, Arthur 'Scobie' Breasley. He too had retired to Barbados after a highly successful career as a jockey and then trainer. 'Scobie' had been champion jockey in Australia before venturing to England and Europe where he continued the trend. He later took up training and saddled winners in Britain, France and north America. While still riding, he purchased a home on the east coast of Barbados and on retirement moved to the island.

When Breasley came to Barbados he brought a few horses with him but was soon asked to train for others. His owners included popular Barbadian David Seale and together they won several of the major races. These included an unprecedented four wins in the prestigious Cockspur Cup, three of these victories going to the legendary Sandford Prince.

The race-track in Barbados is at the Garrison Savannah, less than two miles outside Bridgetown. It has been the home of horse racing since the colonial days of 1845. The officers of the British Regiment who were stationed in Barbados, used what was then the parade ground to match their horses in races and they were later joined by the wealthy merchants and planters.

The Barbados Turf Club, which administers and controls horse racing in Barbados, was established in 1905 and organises three seasons of racing per year. These meetings run from January to March, May to August and from October to December.

The track is a six furlongs oval grass strip and races range in distance from five furlongs (1,000 metres) to 11 furlongs or (2,200 metres) with the horses running in a clockwise direction. The system of handicapping is one which classifies horses from 'A' to 'G' class with 'A' being the highest.

The most important races on the Barbados racing calendar are the Cave Shepherd '5000', run in February, the Cockspur Cup and the Banks Guineas in March, the United Barbados Derby in August and the Heineken Stakes on Boxing Day.

But racing at the Garrison is not only for the race fan and can be a day of family entertainment. Those who want to enjoy the spectacle from the stands can do so while those who prefer an informal picnic atmosphere can lounge in the shade of the tall trees surrounding the track. There's also a play park for the children and the family can enjoy Barbadian dishes like pudding and souse, rice and stew, fried fish and fish cakes. Quenching the thirst is not a problem with drinks ranging from refreshing coconut water to the finest Barbadian rum.

The serious punter has several options for watching the races. They can enjoy the view from the Grand Stand, the Field Stand, the Sir John Chandler Stand or, if they are lucky enough to get an invitation, to the luxurious corporate boxes overlooking the famous paddock bend.

Field Hockey

While horse racing has been in Barbados for 150 years there are other sports which are of more recent vintage. One is the fast paced and exciting field hockey which has been rapidly gaining in popularity. This sport is expected to get even bigger with the laying of an artificial field at the Sir Garfield Sobers Sports Complex. This will bring the facilities for this game in line with international standards.

Organised hockey in Barbados started in 1958 with the founding of the Barbados Men's Hockey Association. This body was merged with the Barbados Women's Hockey Association to form the Barbados Hockey Federation (BHF).

There are some 20 clubs and 600 hockey players in Barbados and from May to October the federation

Photo: M Goddard

Body Building

Barbados has done well in the area of body building having won several titles at regional and international level. People like Roy Callender and Earl Maynard have done well winning *Mr Universe* and *Mr World* while Albert Scantlebury has taken the title of *Mr Caribbean and Central America*. Barbados has also won several other titles at the Central American and Caribbean championships including the team prize on more than a dozen occasions. Pictured is David 'Noddy' Alleyne, perhaps a future *Mr Universe?*

organises its league competition with more than 24 men's and 14 women's teams participating. In addition there are indoor, knock-out, six-a-side and schools competitions.

One of the most successful tournaments organised by the BHF is the annual Banks International Hockey Festival which started in 1986. This exciting series, usually scheduled for August, attracts teams from Barbados, the Caribbean, Britain, Europe, the US and South America and even as far away as Abu Dhabi in the Middle East. The festival has been described as the biggest, single, regular, international hockey event staged anywhere in the hemisphere. In 1996 this tournament expected to attract 42 clubs.

Athletics

One of the highlights of the athletics programme in Barbados is the annual Run Barbados International Road Race Series which takes place in early December. This comprises a ten kilometre race and a marathon and attracts runners from around the world. Participation in this event has been rapidly growing over the years with runners from the US, Canada, Britain, Italy, Morocco, Africa and the Caribbean.

Winners of the Run Barbados Series include 1984 Olympic Marathon silver medallist John Tracey of Ireland, two-time Boston Marathon winner Geoff Smith, world ten kilometre record holder Hugh Jones, Peter Maher of Canada, women's ten kilometre world record holder Judi St Hilaire of the US, Laura Konantz of Canada, Susan Tooby, Jill Clarke and Leslie Watson of Britain.

The Run Barbados programme provides a great opportunity for world class athletes to enjoy the ambiance of a Caribbean holiday with an international series of races. Participants are made up of both professional athletes and the running enthusiasts.

But athletics in Barbados is not only about road racing. The Amateur Athletics Association (AAA) of Barbados ensures a full annual programme for local and international participants. These meetings are held at the National Stadium with its 500 metre international track and modern facilities.

Barbadian athletes have competed on the world scene and one whose name is quickly being recognised is Obadele Thompson one of the top sprinters in the world. He has been impressive on the college circuit in the US and ran the fastest 100 metres ever recorded during

1996. This performance was not officially recognised because it was wind aided. Thompson competed at the Olympics in Atlanta and although not winning a medal, was fourth in the world record breaking 200 metres final won by Michael Johnson of the US, from Frankie Fredricks of Namibia and Ato Bolden of Trinidad and Tobago.

Thompson's performance was commendable considering that he was returning from a lay-off due to injury. Hopes are high for this young man to be a future Olympic medallist.

Volleyball

The game of volleyball is rapidly gaining popularity in Barbados and the country is known as the ruler of Caribbean volleyball. The women's team has won the regional championship three times and the men have been triumphant on five successive occasions including the 1996 tournament.

Through the efforts of the Barbados Volleyball Association this game is being promoted in the schools and communities. This is resulting in an increase in the number of teams playing the game and the number of spectators.

Volleyballers in Barbados have the luxury of a modern court at the Sir Garfield Sobers Sports Complex and this facility was filled to capacity when Barbados defended the Caribbean championships in 1995.

Basketball

Although the standard of basketball in Barbados is nowhere near that of the United States' National Basketball Association (NBA), the local players hold their own in the Caribbean competition. The island has won the title of Caribbean Basketball Champions and the ability of some of the players is now leading them to professional and semi-professional contracts overseas. Some of the young players are also benefiting from scholarships at American universities.

Like many of the indoor sports in Barbados, the important basketball games are played at the ultra modern Wildey Gymnasium, within the Sir Garfield Sobers Sports Complex. The Barbados Amateur Basketball Association (BABA) which administers the sport also promotes the game among the women's teams and in the schools. The United Insurance

Sports Facilities

Barbados can boast of its sporting facilities as most are up to international standards. These include the Wildey Gymnasium and the Aquatic Centre both located at the Sir Garfield Sobers Sports Complex and the National Stadium.

The National Stadium

The Barbados National Stadium was built on a 22-acre site and officially opened in 1970. Recently refurbished, it has a 400 metre eight-lane rubberised track and a 500 metre cycling track.

The five spectator stands are covered and provide seating for 5,000 persons. The main stand which seats 600, incorporates booths for sports reporters as well as radio and television broadcasts.

The stadium and its annexe provide facilities for soccer, hockey, cycling, boxing, shooting, netball and all track and field events. Parking is available for over 1,000 vehicles.

Gymnasium

The multi-purpose gymnasium is part of the Wildey Sporting Complex. Situated at Wildey, St Michael, the gymnasium is one of the most modern sporting facilities in the Caribbean with full air-conditioning and seating for 4,000 patrons. The games hall floor is made of maple parquet timber with concealed rubber grommets which produce a slight spring to absorb the impact and reduce pressure on the athlete's joints.

The indoor facility is designed to cater to 12 sporting disciplines: table tennis, volleyball, weight-lifting, bodybuilding, boxing, basketball, judo, karate, badminton, gymnastics, handball and netball.

There are modern sauna and massage rooms for male and female athletes, and a medical room for pre-medical checks. The gym is fitted with two-timing and electronic scoreboards which are programmed to show international time, current time, correct game and scoring data for basketball games. The Wildey Gymnasium is also available for cultural and religious events, conventions and assemblies.

The Aquatic Centre

This new swimming complex is designed for competitive swimming and watersports as well as other pool-based recreational activities. It was built by the Barbados Amateur Swimming Association with funds raised entirely by its efforts.

The facility boasts a 25-metre by 10-metre teaching pool which is one metre deep and a 50-metre by 25-metre pool which can be used for both short course and long course laps. Daktronic timing equipment is installed and starting blocks and anti-turbulence lane markers are of international standards. A covered stand seats 800 spectators and runs the full length of the 50-metre pool.

Netball

Barbados has always done well in Caribbean netball and has won the championship on several occasions. The game is very popular and attracts large crowds to the Netball Stadium located at Waterford, about three miles outside Bridgetown. This was the venue when Barbados hosted the 1991 Caribbean Netball Championships. The best facilities for netball however are at the all purpose indoor Wildey Gymnasium

Schools Basketball competition is the biggest for junior players and this tournament has for more than ten years been the nursery for the top teams and the national squad.

Golf

The worldwide interest in golf has not been lost on Barbados and this sport is probably one of the fastest growing in the island. The four major courses are at Royal Westmoreland, Sandy Lane, Heywoods and Rockley.

Royal Westmoreland Golf and Country Club was opened in 1995 and its international 18-hole course has been described as one of the finest in the world. Another nine holes are to be added and the facility has been getting rave reviews from golfers from all over the world. The 480-acre Royal Westmoreland Golf Club is a former sugar plantation and is in a dramatic setting of rolling hills with spectacular views.

The 18-hole Sandy Lane championship golf course has also been very popular with Barbadians and visitors alike. It hosts several local and international tournaments with one of the most popular being the United Open, sponsored by the local company United Insurance Company Limited. This competition attracts the best amateur players from the Caribbean and around the world and is enhanced by the inclusion of some professionals.

Rockley Resort, is the oldest golf course in Barbados and regular tournaments are held there. Heywoods in the north of the island is also 18-holes and is ideal for beginners.

Barbados is expected to get another golf course shortly with the resuscitation of Durants in the south of the island. A group of businessmen are working on a project which will see 18-holes opened on this course in the next two years.

Swimming

The warm waters of the Caribbean Sea are ideal for swimming but if you want to be competitive the place to go is the Aquatic Centre, within the Sir Garfield Sobers Sports Complex. The 50-metre Olympic size

213

swimming pool not only provides excellent facilities for the local swimmers but has been attracting teams from the US, Canada and Britain.

Swimming has always been popular in Barbados and at one time the island held the championship in water polo. The Aquatic Centre is usually a hive of activity with the various clubs training their members until late at night.

There's great excitement in Barbadian swimming circles following the performance of local girl Leah Martindale at the Olympics in Atlanta. She did not win a medal but performed well enough to give Barbadians strong hopes for a future Olympic medal.

Soccer

Whether you call it soccer or football this game generates tremendous excitement in Barbados as it does the world over. Teams from the island participate in several regional and international tournaments including the World Cup. Although the national team has not made a significant impact on the international scene, some players have been gaining recognition in places like Britain. One Barbadian who has played in the English Football Association competition is Gregory 'Lalu' Goodridge who was a professional with the London-based team Queen's Park Rangers.

Barbados Football Association, the governing body for the sport is affiliated to all the international football organisations.

Motor Sports

Motoring is one of the most popular sports in Barbados and whether its racing or rallying the crowds are large. There are year-round competitions ranging from speed events, through rallies, dexterity tests, hill climbing and acceleration tests.

Barbados did have the famous Bushy Park race circuit which attracted thousands of spectators and competitors from across the Caribbean to a variety of motor sport competitions - unfortunately this has closed. There are no plans at present to revive this venue.

Cycling

The velodrome at the National Stadium has greatly boosted the standard of cycling in Barbados. The 500-metres track is of international standard

Draughts

Barbados is an independent island but there's a saying that the country has an unofficial 'king'. The man in question is Ronald 'Suki' King, World Draughts champion.

Like Muhammed Ali, 'the king of draughts' tells the whole world that he is the best and then goes on to prove it by beating all challengers. He holds the titles of World's Go-As-You-Please Champion and World's Three Move Restrictions Champion. He has won in the United States and the United Kingdom and has successfully defended his titles at home.

Dominoes

Dominoes is more than a game in Barbados and could be described as a national past-time. Nearly every Barbadian can play the game and there's hardly a time when anyone would turn down the opportunity to slam a dom or 'play a six'. Barbadian domino players participate in national and regional competitions.

Bridge

For more than half-a-century the game of bridge has been played in Barbados. The Barbados Bridge League which administers and organises tournaments was formed in 1965 and since then has been attracting serious players. The Bridge League has also been presenting international competitions including the annual 'Sun, Sea and Slams' which is held in October. This tournament is geared for the bridge players who also want to enjoy a holiday on a beautiful Caribbean island.

214

Lawn Tennis

Nearly everywhere you go in Barbados you are likely to find a lawn tennis court. This is testimony to the popularity of the sport. With most hotels offering this facility and the islands eight tennis clubs operating courts, there are adequate opportunities to have a game of tennis.

Barbados competes in the Davis Cup and several other regional and international lawn tennis tournaments and the standard of the game continues to improve.

Among the clubs, Pragon has done well winning several titles but others like Summerhayes, Barbados Yacht Club, Barclays and Windward have also been playing good tennis.

Table Tennis

Table tennis, although not drawing as large a number of players and supporters as lawn tennis has been quietly making a name for Barbados. Players like Kibbi Moseley have made Barbadians proud by winning regional titles. Miss Moseley has ruled the Caribbean and Central America as the Junior and Senior Women's Champion.

Squash

Facilities at several hotels and those established by the Barbados Squash Racquets Association has helped to rapidly promote the game of squash in Barbados. This game is a recent addition to the sports calendar but is avidly played by visitors and locals alike. Barbados has had the pleasure of winning the Caribbean squash championship.

and has attracted several world class riders. Barbadian cyclists have been able to compete with their counterparts from the US, Canada, Britain, France, Italy, Australia, Germany, Venezuela, Jamaica and Trinidad and Tobago. Cycling is making a resurgence in Barbados with a crop of young talented riders. The Barbados Cycling Union organises several competitions each year including road races and track meetings.

Water Sports

The seas around Barbados, ranging from tranquil on the west coast to pounding surf on the east coast are ideal for watersports. Surfing, windsurfing, deep sea diving, snorkelling, yachting and game fishing are enjoyed around the island.

Barbados figures prominently on the international surfing circuit and has hosted several international competitions. The constant high-rolling waves at the bay they call the 'Soup Bowl' at picturesque Bathsheba is well known throughout the surfing world. Kellogg's, the American food company, has used the breathtaking scenery of the 'Soup Bowl' in some of its commercials.

Windsurfing, has its base at Silver Rock on the south coast and this windswept area has attracted some of the best windsurfers and board sailors in the world. The International Mistral Class held its 1983 championship in Barbados and a Barbadian, Rodney Marshall was the free-style champion. The top Barbadian windsurfer is Brian Talma who competes around the world.

The period between December and April is considered the best time for windsurfing in Barbados because the steady trade winds are at their strongest.

Yachting

Barbados has long been a haven for yachtsmen from around the world. Being the most easterly of the Caribbean islands, it has become the first stop for sailors crossing the Atlantic. This is one of the reasons why the island has been chosen many times as the finishing point for Cross-Atlantic races.

Besides being a stop-over for visiting yachts, Barbados has its own fleet of boats and offers sailors the best of both worlds. They can enjoy just a quiet sail along the coast in their dinghy, compete in races or they can sail across the Atlantic in their big yachts.

There are two boating clubs in Barbados, one being the older and larger Barbados Yacht Club and the other the Barbados Cruising Club. Both organisations have racing and cruising craft. Several types of crafts can be found in Barbados including sail and motor.

The Spirit of Sailing

For more than a quarter century, Mount Gay Eclipse Barbados Rum has played a central role in the enjoyment of yacht-racing and cruising in the Caribbean, the US and around the world. From its active involvement in top regattas such as the America's Cup, Storm Trysail Club's Block Island Race Week and *Yachting* Race Week at Key West, to its ubiquitous presence in the grog-lockers of countless cruising boats, Mount Gay Rum has become almost as much a part of the world sailing scene as the wind. The brand's trademark, with its yellow map of Barbados, has become an unofficial symbol of the sport itself, visible wherever sailors gather, from Annapolis to Auckland to Antigua.

Mount Gay Rum has been exported to the US since the early 1900s, but its association with sailing events began in the early 1970s. Around that time, the US importer observed that a considerable quantity of rum was being sold in sailing towns on the east and west coasts - Marblehead, Annapolis, the towns along Long Island Sound. Rum is acknowledged worldwide as the official beverage of the Caribbean and the Caribbean has always embodied the spirit of sailing and instant escape from worldly pressures.

Today, Mount Gay sponsors around 50 regattas in 50 countries, worldwide. Between 50 and 60 regattas in the US receive support from the brand.

Major international regattas supported by Mount Gay include the Sydney Hobart Race, CORK (Canada), Antigua Sailing Week and Cowes Week (Britain). In 1995, Mount Gay entered an arrangement with *Yachting* magazine to sponsor three major racing events. *Yachting* Race Week at Key West, the Chicago-Mackinac Race and Annapolis Race Week. Each event carries the Mount Gay Rum brand name in its title.

At the regattas, Mount Gay and its distributors provide a broad range of in-kind support and services. Mount Gay Rum often is an integral part of the festivities. The Mount Gay logo is ubiquitous at many of these events, on T-shirts, cups, flags and on-site promotions such as the Mount Gay Grinder, where crews compete to hoist an imaginary - and very heavy - mainsail up a short mast in the quickest time.

Mount Gay logo items are hot properties at venues such as Key West, but none are in greater demand than the red hats. Mount Gay hats have become badges of honour for racers the world over. Usually embroidered with the name of the regatta and available only to participants, they have become cherished keepsakes and collector's items. The more weathered they become, the better.

Mount Gay intends to continue to support yacht-racing worldwide. Recently Mount Gay entered a license agreement with the British brewer Whitbread to develop rules for classes of offshore racing yachts of 25, 30, 35 and 40-feet. The Whitbread 60 rule will serve as a basis for the formulation of the new classes to be known as the Mount Gay 25, Mount Gay 30 and so on. All racing yachts will carry the Mount Gay logo on their mainsails. Mount Gay will also provide assistance for the management of class rules.

Whether its cruisers winding-up a relaxing afternoon on the bay, or racers winding-down after an intense battle around the buoys, wherever the day takes sailors, it always ends with Mount Gay Rum.

Dive Barbados

by Mike Seale

The beauty of Barbados extends beyond its lush land mass, its sights and friendly people, to the nutrient rich waters that surround it. Fed by Atlantic currents, this green emerald island proudly displays itself against the vast blue waters of the Atlantic Ocean, which pale to powder blues as you reach her white sandy beaches and near shore reefs.

Once you've got over your initial surprise as to how a small, independent Caribbean country can have such a rich marine culture, (and one of the world's best drinking water supplies), its time to don your scuba tank, snorkel or even take a ride on a semi-submersible or submarine and discover Barbados' other secret, her underwater world.

Once underwater you will find ridges totally encrusted with corals and plant life, much like those, that formed Barbados over 700,000 years ago. Still reaching for that brilliant sunlight above, these coral reefs are swarmed with a kaleidoscope of living colour and both Atlantic and Caribbean marine life are found here. If you haven't yet seen your first sea-horse, flying gurnard, frog fish, giant sand eel or batfish, then pack a camera and experience the dive of a lifetime..

Reef diving

Barbados has two basic types of reef structures, the fringing or patching reefs and the banking reefs. Fringing or patching reefs form an almost complete ring around the island, these are near-shore reefs and vary in depth from 25-30 feet depending on their distance from the shore. West coast fringing reefs tend to be wider with very few drop-offs, and little variation in depth, where as, south coast fringing reefs tend to drop-off much more dramatically away from the shore. These make a good second dive of the day as these reefs are busy nurseries for hundreds of species. Around these you will find your frog fish and sea-horses.

Located between half-a-mile to a mile from the shore, you will find the banking reefs, that seem to pop up from the deep to a depth of about 60 feet below the surface to form ridges running parallel to the shore, some as small as 30 feet wide and up to a mile long.

An ideal first dive of the day. Big coral heads, large sponges, hundreds of schooling fish and the chance to see the big ones come to feed. Hawksbill turtles are a common sight on these reefs and can usually be approached for close-up photographs. Banking reefs on the south coast are good for multi-level diving as well as drift-diving.

Wreck diving

Barbados has many great wrecks, some in only 20 feet of water. In Carlisle Bay, over 200 ships were lost in storms, some dating from the 17th Century. Cannon, anchors, pottery and old hand-blown glass bottles are all that remain of these once proud ships. Designated as a marine park, Carlisle Bay also offers great macro-photo opportunities with its rare and diverse marine life.

Listed as one of the world's best recreational wreck dives, the (360 feet) S S Stravronikita, is Barbados' premier wreck. Gutted by fire in the early 1970s, this Greek freighter was sunk purposely in 1978. The wreck has been made safe for divers and her main cabins and cargo areas have become a favourite for even the most inexperienced wreck diver. Laying at a maximum depth of 137 feet with her uppermost mast reaching to within 18 feet of

the surface, she is ideal for multi-level diving (dive computers advised). Wide angle photography is great everywhere on this wreck, her masts and huge prop have become hot spots for underwater photographers. The latest edition to Barbados' wreck collection is the *Eillon Kingstown* which was sunk at Carlisle Bay Marine Park. The former cargo vessel is laying at 110 feet and already has a resident barracuda.

Diving conditions

Barbados offers excellent diving all-year round, however the summer months produce the best opportunities for diving the north and east coast reefs. Visibility varies from 40 feet to 100 feet in summer. Water temperature is fairly constant at 81 degrees Fahrenheit.

Best wreck dive: S S *Stravronikita* (west coast).
Best night dive: the *Berwyn* (south coast).
Best drift dive: the *Muff* (south coast).
Best naturalist dive: Close Encounters (south coast).
Best eco dive: Clarks Bank (south west).

Facilities

There are more than 20 locations providing diving facilities in Barbados, varying in size from small to the large internationally recognized PADI five star facilities which offer full tuition in diving (including one-day courses with a dive), equipment sales, service and rentals. Most established dive-operators are members of the Professional Association of Dive Operators (PADO Barbados). The locally formed association is responsible for the implementation of safety standards, the protection and enhancement of the marine environment and its Rescue the Reef's programme. Their efforts should be supported, so shop around for member facilities.

Chamber

Barbados has one decompression chamber which is situated at St Ann's Fort midway between the major dive sites. The chamber is staffed 24 hours a day by four specially trained full-time doctors, as well as with chamber attendants from the Barbados Defence Force personnel.

Animal Flower Cave, North Point, St Lucy

Caves of Barbados

One of the earliest references to caves in Barbados comes from the pen of the historian Richard Ligon (1647) who describes: "......a Cave large enough to hold 500 men and the mouth of it covered with a green Curtaine, 40 foot high and 200 foot long and so close a Curtaine it is (the vine being wrapt and interwove one into another) as without putting it aside, you can hardly have light to read."

We shall probably never know whether the cave we now know as Harrison's Cave was known to Ligon.

In his *Natural History of Barbados*, published in 1759, the Reverend Griffith Hughes records that although his inquiries into the remarkable caves in Barbados *"were the most laborious and dangerous, they were also by far the least pleasing to myself and the description of them (Cole's Cave excepted) will prove the least instructive or amusing to my Readers."*

Reverend Hughes describes Cole's Cave *"by far the larger and most worthy of our Notice"* in some detail but he makes no mention of Harrison's Cave and appears not to have known of its existence.

A medical doctor, George Pinckard visited Barbados some 50 years after Hughes and rescued Harrison's Cave from obscurity. Writing in a letter of 27 February 1796, Dr Pinckard, a careful and attentive observer, described an excursion into Harrison's Cave which he made with a number of companions and slaves.

Harrison's Cave

For many generations of Barbadians, Cole's Cave in the parish of St Thomas, remained the only cave in the island worthy of mention until the re-discovery in 1970 of Harrison's Cave by the Danish speleologist, Ole Sorensen, who was commissioned by the Barbados National Trust to make a survey and map the cave. Even the otherwise careful and meticulous Sir Richard Schomburgk, whose *History of Barbados* published in 1848 is a standard text, appears to have dismissed Harrison's Cave as of *"less extent an interest"* than Cole's Cave. He could not have been aware of Dr Pinckard's exploration in 1796.

It was immediately obvious to Ole Sorensen that the fascinating formations and extensive rooms would make Harrison's Cave a great attraction. He had little difficulty in convincing the government authorities that the cave should be landscaped and developed.

Work on the development of the caves began in earnest in 1974. It required the application of science, art and technology and their careful integration in the development effort. The tunnels had to be dug, the cave area meticulously surveyed and detailed plans for drainage and lighting prepared.

The work had to be based on close geological study of the surrounding area. Surveys were necessary to establish the thickness of the limestone (between 52m and 66m - 175 to 215 feet), which, is very near to Dr Pinckford's estimate made nearly 200 years earlier of 180-240 feet.

The rate of infiltration of rain water had to be calculated from observations and the maximum amount of water that could flow through the cave had to be estimated.

The most difficult task underground was that of diverting the water of two streams from the centre of the passageways, where it had run for hundreds of years, to a course alongside the roadway. The first months were spent in building a dam to hold and measure the thousands of litres of water that flowed in the cave each day. The dam allows part of the flow to continue over waterfalls and through the stalagmites in

Animal Flower Cave

Ask what is St Lucy's main tourist attraction and most Bajans will reply 'the Animal Flower Cave'. These dramatic, adjoining caverns open on the Atlantic in the rugged sea cliffs off the north point where the Atlantic and Caribbean seas meet. A stairway through a blow-hole in the bedrock provides safe access to them.

At first glance, the suite of caverns looks like the abandoned habitat of an unkempt troll; in places, the sea has smoothed and flung a blanket of stones underfoot, while the presence of copper and iron is visible in the encrusted ceiling's hues. Diminutive stalactites provide a first-hand view of how the island's groundwater supply is filtered by the porous coral limestone, as fresh water drips from them. The animal flowers are in the Carpet Room, a division of the cavern that must be reached by wading through a pool under a fissure. Another clear, tranquil pool is good for swimming. Both are only possible to enjoy when the sea is low and calm. This condition is most consistent from June to November.

Some of the colourful animal flowers are actually sea anemones, while others are filter-feeding tube worms that are otherwise known as seafeathers or *Sabellastarte Magnifica*. By 1850 they were considered one of the wonders of Barbados. Though now an eroded moon-scape, the area around the cave was then a sugar plantation. To stop visitors from trampling his crops, the irate owner drilled into the holes from which the flowers protruded. They returned in a few weeks. A succeeding century or so of careless plucking, however, has nearly accomplished his aim. Although the flowers are now less abundant, the cave is still a thrill to enter.

Above ground there is a friendly bar where you can quench your

Harrison's Cave, St Thomas

thirst and have a snack, as well as two tiny cabins where you can purchase mementos. Artist Laura Ward sells her clay creations and other attractive items from one of these. Among them are finely-crafted masks in which she has Creolised the Arawak-related art forms of her native Venezuela with those of Barbados's African roots. Their peaceable but vivid presences resonate the same positive energy that she herself does.

The Hobbit-style, rock-faced, A-frame house across the road houses Laura, her workshop, and some of the Arawak artifacts she has discovered on the island. This area was once the site of a thriving Arawak village, and the ground a mere two minute's walk east is still littered with fragments of their rough clay pots.

the upper passage of the cave, while the rest is carried off down the central drainage pipe system which covers a mile of passageways.

There was the work of constructing the various rails to facilitate access and viewing - the shape of the tunnel had been earlier determined, during this work and much thought was given to the material to be used: there was to be a minimum of metal and no wooden fixtures since wood encourages the growth of fungus which, in a warm climate, could be excessive.

Underwater lighting has been used to bring out the brilliant colours of the pools and a waterfall has been highlighted as it plunges into a pool at the lowest point of the cave. The white formations of the rocks have been illuminated so as to create a sense of mystery. Harrison's Cave is a spectacle of galleries of stalactites and stalagmites, streams of running water, waterfalls and deep pools - a magnificent tableau of nature's elements.

Visitors who are unfamiliar with caves may ask whether there is any danger. Although Harrison's Cave is stable and rockfall and ceiling collapse do not constitute a significant danger - visitors must wear hard hats.

So far as ventilation is concerned, rigid tests

and measurements of air movement have established that the cave has more than adequate ventilation to protect the health of visitors.

The vehicles used for transportation with the cave are powered by battery.

Cole's Cave

The calcareous rock of these ravines (in the Parish of St Thomas) frequently juts out and forms considerable caverns, resembling in their structure deep recesses. The roofs of these caverns and recesses are hung with stalactites, which, increasing in size frequently reach the ground and unite with stalagmites on the floor to form pillars... A similar instance has occurred in Social-Rock Gully on a large scale, where a column has been formed which supports the canopy-like recess.... It unites near the estate called the Spring and within a short distance of that junction is Cole's Cave. The division of these two caves is called the Fork.

The roof of the larger cave presents a most remarkable appearance in consequence of its being studded with numerous cavities or pits of a rounded form, resembling inverted saucers or calabashes.

GEOLOGY AND LANDSCAPE

Text and illustrations by Leslie Barker

Barbados' landscape can be divided into two distinct regions: These are the limestone lands and the Scotland District terrain. The limestone lands cover about 85 percent of the island and as a region is exposed over most of the country as a gently rolling landscape. These limestone lands can be further divided into five sub-regions as follows:

St Lucy Flatlands

This area represents a broad flat region extending completely across the northern section of the island.

Western and Southern Terraces

This is a topographically distinct zone on the western and southern side of the island stretching from St Lucy in the north to Chancery Lane in the south. Generally this region shows a series of terraces and cliffs, which rise from the coast up towards the central region of the island. This cliff-and-terrace or 'staircase-like' topography is better developed on the western side of the island. On the southern side, the cliff-and-terrace topography is interrupted by the presence of the St George valley meeting the coastline at the Carlisle Bay area. A more poorly developed cliff-and-terrace topography however continues southward of Bridgetown.

Two major cliffs known as 'the first and second high cliffs' run almost continuously around the island (except in the Scotland District) at the respective heights of approximately 40 metres (125 feet) and 158 metres (494 feet) above mean sea level.

Central Uplands

Generally form the spine area of the island and stretches from Mount Gilboa in St Lucy to Chimborazo in St Joseph, where it reaches a height of 340 metres (1,116 feet) and then slopes off southward to the St George Valley.

St George - St Philip Valley

Is a broad lowland area which traverses the broadest section of the island and separates the higher central uplands from the southern region.

Christ Church Dome

Is a low dome shaped upland in the south of the island which rises to about 122 metres (400 feet) just south of Mount Friendship in St Michael.

Scotland District

Is situated on the eastern side of the island, and exhibits a distinctly different topography from the rest of it. It is an area of typical bad-land type topography characterised by deep, steepsided river valleys with sharp, intervening, ridges which gives it a rugged scenic beauty. This area is a favourite with local and tourist nature lovers and picnickers.

Geology

Barbados is well known as a coral limestone island, with extensive, white sandy beaches. This is a direct consequence of the geology of the island, which indeed makes it somewhat of an enigma among the volcanic group of the Lesser Antilles. There are no volcanic rocks in Barbados, except for a few thin ash deposits seen on the eastern side of the island, embedded in some of the clay formations.

Modern science has shown that the earth's crust is divided into a number of plates, which are being pushed together by the internal forces of the earth. This feature is called plate tectonics.

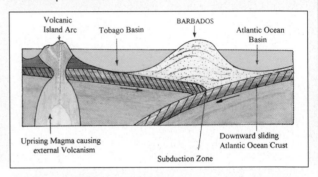

We now know that the Atlantic plate is being pushed under the Caribbean plate (**above**). This has caused a variety of movements at the junction between the two plates and as a result sediments from South America which has been deposited in a trench at this junction, have now been buckled upward to form the island of Barbados and indeed has also been the cause of the formation of the volcanic islands in the Lesser Antilles island arc, by creating the vents and fissures to allow the earth's internal molten material to reach the surface.

Rocks of Barbados

Generally in geology the older rocks are found at the bottom of the pile and as progress is made upwards the rocks become more recent.

In Barbados, the oldest rocks are exposed in the Scotland District in St Andrew and St Joseph, where much of the younger rock has been eroded away. These rocks are known as the Scotland Formation and are mainly sandstones and claystones which may range from hard, indurated rocks to soft, friable material. They are well exposed along the East Coast Road, and can be easily seen just of the highway.

The Scotland Formation rocks are sedimentary deposits formed over 45-million years ago.

Overlying these older rocks are a group of greyish-green clays known as the 'Oceanic Series'. They are a set of deep sea deposits, formed mainly from minute marine organisms. These clays are exposed all along the rim of the Scotland District, stretching from the coast at Bath, St John, through to the higher regions of Mount Hillaby and again descending to the coast at Gays Cove in St Lucy.

Even though the Oceanic clays lie above the Scotland Series, they are of the same age. This strange phenomenon has caused much geological debate over the years, but it is now thought that these rocks were formed at the same time at different locations, and were pushed together with the Oceanics ramping above the Scotland Formation.

The Joes River mudstones (**above**) are best represented in Frizers Valley. These are old oil and gas reservoirs, which have intruded the Scotland and Oceanic Series and they most probably were originally part of the same Scotland Formation.

The youngest group of rocks which lie on top of these older rocks is the Coral Limestone Series.

As the plate movements raised the island into relatively shallow waters, coral reefs began to form. These grew in the shallow waters around the island, and as it continued to emerge, this produced fossil coral limestone reefs on the island itself, while the living reefs grew offshore in the shallow waters. The oldest limestone rocks are about 700,000 to 800,000 years old, and are found in the Central Upland area.

The present day offshore reef is the subject of much study by government, since it is the foundation resource upon which much of our economy depends. It provides the sand for our beaches; it is a source of protection for them during storm waves; it is a source of recreation for tourists and locals and it provides a habitat for fish and other marine organisms.

Originally, the limestone would have covered the entire island, but the higher north-east area of the island was subjected to more severe stress and there was much fracturing of the cap rock in this area. This segment was then exposed to severe weathering and erosion.

Most of the limestone in this area has now been removed, except for a number of small patch reefs, and numerous huge limestone blocks. The latter occur widely, from the higher parts of the gullies and valleys, down to the Cattlewash and Bathsheba coast, where they form spectacular mushroom-shaped blocks.

One of the more spectacular features of the coral limestone occurs at the rim of the Scotland District, and can be viewed looking northward from St John Parish Church. Here a major fracture in the coral limestone has formed Hackleton's Cliff (**above**) a steep cliff - where the limestone drops off for 61 metres (200 feet) down to the Oceanic clays below.

The coral limestone covers 85 percent of the island and is therefore the most visible rock type. This rock, though subject to erosion and weathering like all other rocks, however, shows a peculiar response, producing a distinct group of features referred to geologically as "Karst" topography. Features include gullies, sink holes, caves and the rolling topography which is so characteristic of much of the island.

Rainfall does not remain on the surface due to the very porous and permeable nature of the limestone. Thus there are no permanent rivers on the limestone section of the island. The rain water however runs underground and on account of its slightly acid nature, it corrodes the limestone along cracks and joints. Over thousands of years, this corrosion formed underground caves, which have been further enlarged by the additional action of underground streams. Harrison's Cave, well known to tourists and locals, is a spectacular example of such a cave. Here we see a harmonious blend of the natural and the artificial providing an excellent tourist attraction.

U-shaped river valleys with steep sides, which only contain water after heavy rainfall, are also a natural feature of our landscape. These are locally known as gullies. Many of these may have been formed from the collapse of the roofs of former near-surface caves. Nowadays, the gullies are some of the few remaining sites of indigenous flora and fauna. Sink holes are the most ubiquitous feature of the limestone landscape. They are small circular depressions, which represent centres of inland drainage through which the water drains underground.

Barbados' fascinating geology can be of interest both to the casual nature lover, or the serious student of the subject.

GREEN BARBADOS

by C M Sean Carrington

Like other islands of the Westindies, Barbados was once densely forested but within 40 years of European arrival most trees had been felled and the country transformed into a giant sea of sugar cane. Botanically, Barbados is part of the Lesser Antilles, an archipelago of small islands flanked by Puerto Rico in the north and Trinidad in the south. Some 2,100 species of flowering plants are native to the Lesser Antilles with 13 percent unique or endemic to these islands. By comparison, Barbados is home to about 700 species of native and naturalised flowering plants, three of which are unique to Barbados. This relatively impoverished flora can be explained by the early land clearance for agriculture, the low-lying, coralline nature of the island with its limited ecological diversity and the fact that Barbados is much younger geologically than its volcanic neighbours.

For such a small spot on the earth, Barbados' flora is remarkably well-documented. Richard Ligon, arriving in the early years of European settlement, described in his *True and Exact History of the Island of Barbados* (1657) an island very different to the one we know today, *"... so grown with wood as there are no champions or savannas for men to dwell in..."* He described many local plants including the cabbage palm *(Roystonea oleracea)* which towers 30 metres high and still abounds in gullies to this day. He termed this plant the palmeto royal or royal palm, a name used today for a related Cuban palm. Many prominent European botanists published descriptions and illustrations of Barbadian wild plants but one of the most useful early works is *The Natural History of Barbados* (1750) by a Welsh clergyman, the Reverend Griffith Hughes, which provides much information on folk uses and plant lore. The sterling efforts earlier this century by Barbadian scientist Graham Gooding produced his authoritative *Flora of Barbados* (1965) on which all modern studies have been based.

Of the island's three endemic species, the maypole *(Agave barbadensis)*, is the best known. It is found in dry coastal areas especially on the eastern side of the island. As it is a succulent, some Barbadians refer to it mistakenly as a cactus. Agaves are often termed century plants as they take ten or more years (but not a century!) to flower, producing an impressive pole-like structure, topped by attractive flowers. Why this common name? Maybe in the past Bajans danced around this as a maypole or perhaps its just the fact that these flowers appear around the month of May. Whatever, to this day the flowering 'pole' is used as a float by fisherfolk diving for sea eggs (urchins) while youngsters scratch the names of their sweethearts on the stiff, fleshy leaves.

From a horticultural standpoint Barbados has also given the world two unique plants. The grapefruit, originally called by the rather ominous name, forbidden fruit, arose in Barbados as a hybrid of the introduced sour orange and shaddock. No less a visitor than George Washington described eating this unique fruit while visiting Barbados in 1751. Our other gift to horticulture is the farleyense fern, a unique kind of maidenhair fern with delicate ruffled fronds found in the late 19th Century at Farley Hill. This site is now a park but once boasted one of the island's finest Great Houses and gardens.

Like anywhere in the world, a strong tradition of herbal medicine developed in Barbados. Barbadian 'bush teas' combine the knowledge brought by slaves from Africa with elements of the European and Amerindian pharmacopoeia, as well as further expertise developed in the Caribbean. Barbadian herbal medicine in the past was often seen as connected with superstition and obeah, perhaps because some plants and 'bush baths' were advocated as having magical powers. As alternative medicine gains respectability and people recognise that plants provide almost half of modern-day prescription drugs, interest in herbal medicine and 'bush teas' has increased. Cerasee *(Momordica charantia)*, a kind of wild cucumber, is perhaps our best-known medicinal plant, widely respected as a remedy for flu. Other notables are fingle-go *(Zanthoxylon spinifex)* which is claimed to be an aphrodisiac and soursop *(Annona muricata)* which is used to make a calming tea.

Despite extensive development and intensive agriculture, a range of natural plant communities survive. These range from beach and dune vegetation to mangrove communities, like Graeme Hall Swamp in Christ Church. Back from the beach, most of the littoral forest and dry woodland have long disappeared but, tucked away on a hillside in the north-east of the island, a 30 hectare tract of original forest, Turner's Hall Wood, has miraculously survived. Botanically, this is the most species-rich site on the island, with several plants that are found no where

else in Barbados. Several of the tree species in the upper, emergent canopy are deciduous dropping their leaves in the dry season. This type of forest comprising evergreen and deciduous trees and with few epiphytes is too dry to be considered rainforest but it gives some idea of the tropical mesophytic forest which in pre-Colombian times covered most of the country.

In fact, one positive aspect of the decline of 'King Sugar' is that areas which have fallen out of cultivation are gradually returning to forest. Of prime mention in this regard is the island's gully network. These forested chasms in the coral cap, up to 60 metres deep, total some 160 kilometres in length and also serve as watercourses from the high rainfall areas to the coast. In this sheltered environment, a unique forest community has developed comprising mainly native trees and shrubs. Of particular interest is the balsam tree *(Clusia plukenetii)* which grows along the gully rim, its long hanging roots being used for basketry. Woody vines or lianas bob and weave through the canopy while the high humidity supports delicate sprays of ferns and mosses. One of the easiest ways to explore a Barbadian gully is to join the Sunday walks, organised by the Barbados National Trust, an association committed to the preservation of the island's natural and man-made heritage.

Barbadians are, of course, great gardeners and a vast number of plants have been introduced to the island for their beauty. Andromeda Botanic Gardens and the Flower Forest are public gardens with fine collections of these exotic ornamentals.

Maypole (Agave barbadensis) a Barbadian endemic

Barbadian fauna

by C M Sean Carrington

The Green Monkey of Barbados

With no dangerous snakes or other beasts to lose sleep over, unless you count the occasional centipede, you may well be lulled into thinking that there is no noteworthy animal life in Barbados.

The only wild animals of any size in Barbados are both exotics, namely the green monkey and the mongoose. The green monkey (*Cercopithecus aethiops sabaeus*) was brought from West Africa some 350 years ago and today, despite a bounty on its tail for all the crop damage it can cause, an estimated 8,000 monkeys roam the island in small troops. A visit to the Barbados Wildlife Reserve will guarantee you a close-up look at some of these.

We know a little more about the importation of the mongoose (*Herpestes auropunctatus auropunctatus*). These were brought from India in 1878 to control rats in the canefields. Unfortunately, they soon turned their attention to other animals and are especially partial to fowls and their eggs, as many a farmer soon learns. The plural of the word mongoose is a contentious point on which much time can be spent (mongoose, mongooses or mongeese?)! For completeness it must be added that raccoons, probably the north American *Procyon lotor* were once found in Barbados, living in caves, but these now appear to have disappeared.

While not an exciting wild beast, there is one large animal of the farm variety, which is uniquely Barbadian. The black belly sheep, which many northern visitors mistake for a goat, is a hybrid variety derived from an African hair sheep and the European wool sheep. It is a breed that developed on the island hundreds of years ago and provides the most tender, tasty lamb - more than can satisfy local demand.

A lack of adequate forest cover goes a long way in explaining the rather unimpressive number of birds resident in Barbados. There are probably 36 residents, 12 of these being exotics, released or escaped, but with established breeding populations. Many of the indigenous species like the wood dove, blackbird, sparrow and yellow-breast are common but the yellow warbler (*Dendroica petechia*) is on the endangered list. A unique breed of this bird is endemic to the island and no more than 20 pairs of these survive at the island's only mangrove, Graeme Hall Swamp.

In addition to these resident species, large numbers of migratory birds use Barbados as a watering hole each year. The shooting of these has been a pastime among the well-to-do for over 200 years and continues to this day.

There may be no song birds in Barbados but the pleasant 'coqui' sound, characteristic of nightfall in Barbados is thanks to the whistling frog (*Eleutherodactylus johnstonei*). This indigenous species, no bigger than a

Green monkeys *(cercopithecos)* were brought to Barbados from West Africa on slave ships over 350 years ago. The green monkey is the only species of monkey in Barbados.

The green monkey gets its name from the colour of its coat which is brownish-grey with specks of yellow and olive green. In some lights, this combination gives the overall impression of a green monkey.

The ability to incorporate new foods into their diet is one of the main reasons the green monkey can successfully move into new environments.

After 75 generations occurring over 350 years the Barbados green monkey has evolved some physical differences from the West African green monkey. Most notably is the shape of the face - the Barbados monkey has a more 'dog-like' look than the West African monkey. There is also less white fur around the eyes of the Barbados monkey and the vocalisations differ between the two populations.

Troops of green monkeys can be as large as 15 members, usually consisting of two senior males and five to six mature females, with the remainder being aged two-months to five-years-old. Females mate every year and, after five and a half months gestation, produce a single baby monkey.

There are estimates that the number of green monkeys in Barbados is at least 5,000 and perhaps as many as 8,000. The parishes of St John, St Joseph, St

Thomas, St Andrew and St Peter have the highest densities of monkeys. Areas of high rainfall and numerous gullies and cliffs provide ideal cover. Although more monkeys may be present in these parishes, they are less visible because of the high amount of tree cover. The flatter parishes which have been deforested, cultivated and developed provide little cover for monkeys.

However, monkeys move around quite a lot in search of food and can be seen all over the country, crossing roads and gardens. They become more visible in the dry season as they have to forage further for their food.

Green monkeys have a varied diet that changes seasonally with the availability of different foods. Much of their diet consists of cultivated foods such as bananas, mangoes, papaya, corn, cucumber, guavas, sweet potatoes, tomatoes and even sugar cane.

They eat leaves, fruits, flowers and the bark from a range of non-cultivated plants such as flamboyant and hibiscus flowers, tamarind fruits, clammy cherries and sea grapes.

They also eat animal matter like lizards, many insects, bird's eggs and nestlings. They have been seen to chase rats and mice.

Green monkeys like to eat fruits at the same stage of ripeness as human beings and in order to assess how ripe a fruit is, a monkey may take small bites out of many fruits, spoiling it in the process.

It is unlikely that green monkeys are more serious pests to farmers than insects, fungi, rats or birds.

The monkey population in Barbados is more dependent on the amount of vegetation cover available for its survival than its exposure to man, its main predator. Green monkeys rarely stray far from wooded areas, they prefer to take refuge in the trees when danger threatens. They sleep, mate and give birth in the trees.

The monkey has become an integrated part of the Barbados ecological system.

finger nail and living in damp shady places, is also found in four other islands of the Eastern Caribbean. Unlike most amphibians it does not need to return to water to reproduce, but lays its eggs in some damp spot with the young frogs hatching directly, without passing through a tadpole phase. This is not to be confused with the large toad *(Bufo marinus)* called a frog or crapaud by most Bajans. This was introduced to the island in 1835 to control insect pests of sugar cane. It can exude a foamy irritant when disturbed and should not be handled.

Of all animals, however, it is the reptiles which put Barbados on the map. Our tiny, blind or worm snake is the smallest snake in the world and is found only in St Lucia, Martinique and Barbados. It lives in leaf mould and might well be mistaken for a worm. In the wetter, inland region of St Joseph a harmless, thin-bodied colubrid or 'racer' snake *(Liophis perfuscus)* is occasionally seen. This is unique to Barbados and the focus of conservation efforts to ensure it does not suffer the same fate as the closely related *L. cursor* and *L. ornatus*, single island endemics of Martinique and St Lucia respectively. The St Lucian species is now claimed to be the world's rarest snake and survives only on the small offshore islet of Maria Major while the Martiniquan species is probably now extinct. Barbadian lizards are also of note, with two of the five species present unique to the island. One of these is the common green *Anolis* lizard seen everywhere. The other is a less common gecko-like lizard *(Phyllodactylus pulcher)* often found indoors. This surviving herpetofauna, with its relatively high endemism, is the more remarkable for a geologically young island, and one which was virtually denuded of forest within 40 years of settlement.

Barbados Wildlife Reserve

The Barbados Wildlife Reserve was developed primarily as a monkey sanctuary for animals to roam freely in a well-provisioned natural environment. The monkeys mingle with other Barbadian fauna (hares and tortoises) and are sheltered from the day-to-day encounters they would normally face when raiding crops and competing with the island's farmers for the same food resources. The reserve is also an escape for people to enjoy a unique opportunity to relax and simply watch wild animals.

Set in a lush natural mahogany woodland, a footpath enables people to observe the monkeys and other animals at close range. In this natural environment, the needs of conservation, research, education and recreation are all met. It provides a sound base for visitors to learn more about the natural history and behaviour of the precious Barbadian fauna.

The Barbados Wildlife Reserve is a project of the Barbados Primate Research Centre and was made possible through seed money generously provided by the Canadian International Development Agency (CIDA).

The Birds of Barbados

by Karl Watson, PhD

The visitor to the island quickly notices that Barbados does not have many species of birds, on the other hand, large numbers of the most common Eastern Caribbean species inhabit the island and are easily seen.

All islands tend to be poor in species variation and for two reasons, Barbados is poorer than most. First, it is relatively isolated from other islands in the region and secondly and more importantly, complete destruction of native forests in the middle of the 17th Century to accommodate the sugar industry, led to loss of habitat and species extinction.

At the beginning of the 20th Century, Barbados had only 18 resident species of birds, complemented during the period July to December, by some 130 migratory species of mainly north American birds. In this century however, some changes have taken place, leading to an increase in resident species and to growth in numbers of most of these species.

Caribbean parakeet

The sugar industry has receded giving way to a greater variety of crops, marginal land previously used for sugar has either reforested naturally or has been used for suburban developments with their attendant gardens and flowering shrubs. The gullies that traverse the island are no longer combed for firewood, since a more affluent population uses modern cooking appliances, so they have also reforested. This change is an important one, since the sugar-dominated landscape of 1850-1950 was quite sterile and offered little in terms of food or shelter for birds.

There has, therefore, in the last 50 years or so, been a marked improvement in the variety of habitats and food sources for birds which co-exist best with humans or can alter their behavioural and feeding patterns to accommodate a modernizing Barbados, whose landscape is now characterized by rapidly spreading suburbia. The number of resident species has now increased to approximately 40 due to species either expanding their range, being deliberately introduced, or some exotic species have escaped captivity and are now establishing resident populations. Examples of these include the Indian ringnecked parakeet, the budgerigar and the love bird.

Bananaquit

The migratory birds which pass through Barbados in large numbers during the last six months of the year are almost all north American birds on their way to winter in South America. Since Barbados lies at the edge of the eastern flyway, the island makes a convenient stop for birds which want rest and water. The vast majority of these birds are shore and marsh birds, warblers, swallows, and raptors (mostly ospreys, peregrine falcons, merlins, northern harriers and American kestrels).

The best time to spot migratory birds and see unusual vagrants from Europe or Africa is during the passage of tropical storms or hurricanes when

Antillean crested Humming bird

Illustrations by Don R Eckelbury and Arthur B Singer, courtesy of 'Birds of the West Indies' by James Bond, Collins, 1988

230

flocks numbering thousands of birds seek refuge here. Unfortunately, this is when they are at their most vulnerable from man, the predator. Most of the island's wetlands have been drained. Only Graeme Hall Swamp remains, which conservationists are now attempting to rescue and use as a bird sanctuary. Therefore, the only places for migratory birds to land for a brief respite, are at artificially constructed shooting swamps. But there they often meet their doom. They are lured by decoys, live birds and recorded calls and shot by the thousand, since no bag limits exist. Even small species such as the pectoral sandpiper and the semipalmated sandpiper are shot. The last two confirmed specimens of the Eskimo curlew, (which may now be extinct) were both shot in Barbados in the 1960s. If this species still survives, then Barbados is ideally situated to provide confirmatory sighting records.

A hasty reaction to the previous observation would be to ban shooting. However, this would be a counter-productive move which could prove even more disastrous to the birds. Because of wetlands drainage, the only suitable habitat left for migratory shorebirds are the artificially created swamps, which are expensive to build and maintain. Without them, there would be no reason for birds to land here, greatly impoverishing the bio-diversity of the island. The solution certainly is to encourage controlled shooting, with bag limits, strict policing of young or inexperienced shooters, and the inculcation of conservationist attitudes through education. Also, the potential of these artificial swamps for niche eco-tourism is considerable. According to ornithologist Dr Paul Buckley, Barbados, because of its geographic location and accessibility, ranks as one of the best places in the world to observe waders and the other species of water foul.

The most pleasant aspect of birding in Barbados is the greater acquaintance one makes with the surprisingly varied terrain of this compact island, which at the same time, is not so challenging, thus allowing any moderately fit individual, of any age, the opportunity to enjoy nature's bounty.

BIRDSPOTTER'S GUIDE

SPECIES	DESCRIPTION	STATUS	PLACES SEEN
Audubon's Shearwater	Sooty back, white belly	Rare	Sea coast, nocturnal bird
Yellow Warbler	Bright yellow medium-sized bird	Rare	Inlets on coast, Mangroves, Graeme Hall Swamp
Grackle (Blackbird)	Black plumage, yellow eyes	Very common	Gardens, pasture land
Bullfinch (Sparrow)	Brown with thick beak	Very common	Enters houses, gardens
Blackfaced grass Quit	Brown bird with black head	Very common	Large gardens, grassland
Grassland yellow Finch	Olive mottled back, yellow belly	Endangered, uncommon	Grasslands
Scalynaped Pigeon	Large slate grey pigeon	Very common	All over
Zenaida Dove	Brown, medium-sized dove	Very common	All over
Violet eared Dove	Smaller than zenaida, same colour	Uncommon	Grasslands, scrub in southern parishes
Ground Dove	Small, with reddish wings	Common	All over
Bananaquit	Small, black back, yellow breast	Common	In gardens
Grey Kingbird	Medium-sized, white breast, grey back	Common	Town and country, perches on telephone lines
Caribbean Elaenia	Small fly catcher, grey back and yellowish belly	Common	All over
Caribbean Martin	Small, white breasted swallow	Common	Town and cliffs on sea coasts
Black whiskered Vireo	Greyish bird with white stripe over eye	Common	All over, in tree tops
Scaly breasted Thrasher	Greyish brown	Rare	Forested areas on east coast
Antillean crested Humming bird	Smaller of the two resident species	Common	All over
Emerald throated Humming bird	Dark green	Common	All over
Glossy Cow bird	Male - gun metal Female - brown	Common	All over
Cattle Egret	White bird, with yellow beak and legs	Very common	All over
Eastern green Heron	Small heron with reddish throat	Fairly common	All over
Snowy Egret	White with black bill and legs, yellow toes	Uncommon	Graeme Hall Swamp
Little Egret	Small white egret	Uncommon	Graeme Hall Swamp
Gallinule/Moorhen	Black water bird with bright red frontal shield	Fairly common	Graeme Hall Swamp, ponds in countryside
Masked Duck	Small, shy diving duck, with blue bill	Rare	Isolated ponds in countryside
Cayenne Nighthawk	Brown, inconspicuous on ground	Rare	Eastern parishes
Orange-winged Parrot	Medium-sized green parrot	Small numbers	(IN) Bridgetown
Yellow shouldered Parrot	Medium-sized green parrot	Small numbers	(IN) Bridgetown
Blueheaded Parrot	Medium-sized green parrot	Small numbers	(IN) Bridgetown
Indian ring-necked Parakeet	Medium, long-tailed green parakeet, with ringed neck	Small numbers	(IN) Bridgetown
Budgerigar	Small, long-tailed, green parakeet	Rare	Bridgetown, St. James, St. George
Lovebird	Small, green parakeet, short-tailed	Rare	(IN) Countryside
Guinea Bird	Large black/white speckled bird	Rare	Feral birds in some (IN) country areas
Bobwhite Quail	Small, brown ground forager	Rare	(IN) Countryside
Laughing Gull	Small gull, black head, white body	Uncommon	Coasts, Bridgetown Harbour
Yellow crowned night Heron	Small, brown and white heron	Uncommon	Graeme Hall Swamp, nocturnal bird
Mallard	Medium duck	Uncommon	(IN) Ponds in countryside
Caribbean Parakeet	Green back, orange throat	Uncommon	(IN) Bridgetown
Quaker Parakeet	Medium, green-backed parakeet with cream front	Uncommon	(IN) Bridgetown

(IN) = Introduced and nesting locally

Aerial view of Graeme Hall Swamp where some of Barbados' more uncommon birds can be seen

The Future Centre

by Sarah Venable

Sustainability, or long-term resource management, is a life or death issue for many small island nations. With its image as an upmarket tourist paradise, a resident population upwards of 264,000, and almost 900,000 visitors a year to its ecologically-fragile 166 square miles, Barbados has begun to take the matter seriously. One local organization, the Future Centre Trust, makes an holistic approach to sustainability its entire raison d'etre. In addition, the government, the University of the West Indies and various research agencies, along with international

organisations, are working to forge a coordinated approach to keeping the environment healthy and productive in the long term.

In 1994, Barbados hosted the global UN Conference on Sustainable Development of Small Island Developing States. In the spirit of its Barbados's motto, 'Pride and Industry', the people also erected a Village of Hope that attracted 45,000 visitors as a parallel activity. Out of all this energy the ongoing Future Centre Trust was born, to keep sustainability at the forefront of Barbadian consciousness.

The Future Centre Trust (FCT) is a tenacious centre of hope with big ambitions. It is working in partnership with existing organizations to set up the Future Centre to provide a permanent stimulus to a happier more sustainable lifestyle.

The Future Centre is envisioned as a spectacular, self-financing exhibition and resource centre that will educate, entertain and exhort its visitors. It will include exhibits created by young people as well as by noted environmental experts; a job centre to combat the ills of unemployment; a library and reading room complete with Internet terminals; an intellectual property centre to promote and protect appropriate technology knowledge; a shop where environment-friendly tools and information can be purchased; and a supermarket designed to eliminate needless packaging.

The Future Centre is slated to occupy a portion of the enormous A-frame warehouse near the deep water harbour in Bridgetown. Once taken up by bulk sugar storage, the building can now be put to other uses. Situated at this point of entry for cruise ship passengers, the Future Centre could expect to host a quarter of a million visitors from overseas in addition to enthusiastic Barbadians. It is hoped that the Centre will be in operation by 1998.

The Future Centre Trust is blessed by government approval and run by innovative agronomist Colin Hudson with the help of dozens of volunteers. However, it is sorely underfunded at present, receiving only occasional cash grants from inspired foreign visitors and donations of material and services from concerned local businesses.

Visitors are welcome to the present Future Centre Trust headquarters at the Tyre Garden Centre, Edgehill, St Thomas. Regular presentations and rap sessions, complete with refreshments and a tour of the tyre garden, takes place every Thursday and Friday evenings.

Modern Barbados: AGRICULTURE

by Mark A Byer

The economy of Barbados has for centuries been based on agriculture. Agriculture was the engine for development. Agriculture during this period was synonymous with sugar cane production. In 1960, agriculture provided 33.6 per cent of GDP (Gross Domestic Product) with its nearest competitor being the distribution sector 27.6 per cent. Sugar cane contributed 25.5 per cent of GDP.

In 1993, sugar contributed BDS$46.8 million (US$23.4 million) to GDP while non-sugar agriculture contributed BDS$99.9 million (US$49.95 million). Agriculture as a whole contributed 5.3 percent of GDP; while sugar contributed 1.6 percent of GDP. Sugar was dethroned by a vigorous diversification programme over the last two decades, geared to expanding non-sugar agriculture, exports, reducing food imports and strengthening the inter-sectorial linkages between agriculture and the other sectors of the economy.

Barbados enjoys an excellent climate for agriculture production, maintaining an average temperature of 85 degrees Fahrenheit (25 degrees centigrade) with basically two seasons: the 'dry season' (December to June) and the 'wet season,' (July to November). The average rainfall varies from about 30 inches (76.2mm) in the coastal areas to 80 inches (2,032mm) on the central ridge. The average annual rainfall is 60 inches(1,524mm).

Some 21,500 hectare (50 percent) of Barbados' 43,000 hectare is in agricultural use. This is characterised by large plantations and numerous small holdings. Some 95 percent of all holdings occupy farms of under one hectare in size.

A drive through the heart of the island reveals large plantations dominated by sugar cane with several oasis of non-sugar crops like yams, sweet potatoes, vegetables and cotton. A more diligent search reveals a relatively newcomer: flower growers producing mainly orchids, tube roses, anthoriums and ginger lilies. Winning several major awards at the Chelsea Flower Show in England serves to demonstrate the exceptional quality of Barbados flowers.

Barbados' soils are mainly coral-based. One-seventh of the island is on oceanic clays. The topography is more rugged over the oceanic clays; this area is referred to as the Scotland District. It is used mainly for fruit production, papaw, citrus, bananas, mangoes, coconuts, golden apples and many more tropical fruits can be found scattered throughout Barbados.

Production

Barbados is self-sufficient in vegetables and root crops offering a wide variety such as onions, the crucifers and cucurbits, tomatoes, string beans, carrots and okras being the main crops of interest, but most tropical vegetables are grown. Some 60 hectares of bananas and 18 hectares of plantains are also grown.

At least 300 hectares of sweet potatoes is usually grown with yams accounting for over 150 hectares. Some cassava and eddoes are grown as well.

Barbados exports an array of agricultural produce. These include sheep, pork products, milk, yogurt, fish, fruits and vegetables. Approximately 250,000 kg of breadfruit, 350,000 kg of hot peppers and 250,000 kg sweet peppers were exported in 1993.

Sugar

When Independence came to Barbados on 30 November 1966, the sugar industry had reached a peak of prosperity. During the previous 20 years it had been transformed by new technology. Tractors and mechanical implements replaced cattle, mules and forks; cane-holes were abandoned in favour of furrows. Mulching, weedicides and new manurial methods had increased sugar cane yield per acre. By 1946 windmills had disappeared and central factories equipped with vacuum pans and automatic centrifugals produced high grade crystals, reducing the tonnage ratio of cane needed for a ton of sugar from 10 to 8.5.

The acreage under sugar declined from 44,778 acres in 1961 to about 25,800 acres in 1991. Although non-sugar agricultural production now surpasses sugar production, sugar still dominates the agricultural exports of Barbados.

The government has recently been encouraging increased sugar production through the Barbados Agricultural Management Company (BAMC). In 1993 the government started to restructure the sugar industry and over 40 plantations have been placed under the BAMC management. BAMC retained the services of the British firm of management consultants, Booker Tate Ltd, for a period of five years, to manage the plantations on their behalf. Since this restructuring, production has grown to over 60,000 tonnes sugar in 1995-96. There are three sugar factories located at Portvale, Bulkeley and Andrews.

Non-food Crops

The latest phase of Barbados Sea Island cotton cultivation started in 1984. Since then production and acreage planted has fluctuated. In 1995, 147,315 kg of lint was produced from 485,126 kg of seed cotton, with Japan as the major market for this highly esteemed product.

Floriculture, commercial flower production, started in 1985; by 1988 there were 37 acres in production and by 1991 there were 57acres. Most are planted in ginger lilies and heliconias.

A private sector organisation with assistance from government, FLORAPEX, has been formed to coordinate production and marketing. Mainly ginger lilies are exported. The latest varieties of anthuriums and orchids are imported from Europe in tissue culture by laboratories, which handle their reproduction and preparation for planting.

Livestock

Prior to the 1960s, livestock production did not occupy a place of importance in the agricultural system of Barbados. In 1962 the government outlined an agricultural diversification programme in its National Development Plan, in which import substitution of animal products (beef, milk, mutton, pork, poultry and eggs) was stated policy objective. By 1966 government had completed arrangements for the establishment of Barbados Dairy Industries Ltd (Pine Hill Dairy), and built the Animal Nutrition Research Unit at the Pine - including the installation of irrigation facilities to assist grassland research.

These initiatives facilitated rapid development in the dairy industry. In fact, by 1967 milk receipts by the Pine Hill Dairy had grown from 1,364 litres per day to 4,546 litrer per day and the dairy was already reporting a surplus, which it converted into condensed milk.

At the same time government continued to expand and upgrade the dairy herd at the Central Livestock Station, and to further demonstrate its commitment to the development of the dairy industry, imported 60 pure-bred cows for the Barbados Agricultural Development Corporation (BADC) in 1968, to establish a dairy at Greenland.

In 1976 Barbados had reached virtual self-sufficiency in whole chicken and table eggs (except during seasonal peaks in demand); and by 1986 there were at least three processing plants, and all the pork for local fresh consumption and a substantial portion of the requirements for the processing sub-sector were being met from local production.

Local production of beef and mutton lagged behind all the other livestock products. The limited land available for pasture resulted in successive governments pursuing a 'beef-from-dairy' policy, where beef production is seen as a by-product of the dairy industry, in the form of bull-calves and cull-cows. Its expansion has therefore lagged behind the dairy industry. Sheep and goat production have essentially remained in the hands of small and landless producers.

Recently, as a result of research work done by the Ministry of Agriculture - in collaboration with some private producers - in the production and marketing of feed-lot lamb, the demand for fresh lamb has been increasing. With local production still accounting for less then ten percent of the demand for lamb, the opportunity for import substitution is tremendous. Given the prolificacy of the Barbados blackbelly sheep (**below**), sheep farming seems to be the

livestock enterprise with the greatest growth potential for the future.

Fresh milk supply at current market prices is already in excess of demand. Indeed, from about 1990, the Pine Hill Dairy placed

milk production under quotas. This caused many of the dairy farmers to cull heavily, in order to reduce stock. The result was an increase in beef production. Thereafter, however, the reduction in numbers of calves and cull heifers for beef, resulted in lower beef production, such, that by 1995 it was estimated at 860 tonnes.

In contrast, mutton production increased from 38 tonnes in 1992 to 67 tonnes in 1995; but pork production declined slightly, from 2,018 tonnes to 1,928 tonnes over the same period. The forecast is for sustained increases in mutton production. The pig industry is already satisfying the fresh market demand for pork, but production costs have to be reduced if producers are to gain a greater share of the market in the processing sub-sector.

Fisheries

The average contribution of the fishing industry to the economy is about one percent of GDP. This is equivalent to about BDS$30 million per year (US$15 million). This is from total fish landings of 3,000 - 5,000 metric tonnes.

Fishing employs less than two percent of Barbados' labour force, but about 17 percent of the agricultural work force. Ice boats and longliners have been introduced even though existing fleet capacity is under-utilised. Processing, marketing and distribution of fish and fish products show the most potential for expansion and income earning.

In 1995, the fish harvest was established at 3,285 tonnes representing approximately an eight percent increase over 1994. Flying fish, the local delicacy, accounted for over half the total catch. In 1995, the local fishing fleet totalled 763 vessels of which 93 were iceboats and 13 were longliners. There were 355 moses and 303 launches.

There are 26 landing sites. Government has significantly improved the landing and marketing facilities in the south of the island and is in the process of improving the facilities in the north and east.

The CariCom Fisheries Resources and Assessment Programme (CFRAMP) was initiated through the signing of an agreement between the Caribbean Community (CariCom) and the International Centre for Ocean Development (ICOD) in January 1991. It is scheduled to terminate in 1998.

This BDS$20 million (US$10 million), regional programme has as its main objective the promotion of the management, conservation, and optimal exploitation of the fisheries resources of CariCom countries.

Marketing & Processing

The government department responsible for agricultural marketing is the Barbados Agricultural Development and Marketing Corporation (BADMC). Marketing of agricultural produce, both export and local, is carried out by a number of private businesses. Most of the local marketing is carried out by supermarkets and various farm outlets.

There are well-established poultry, pork and fish processing plants. The processing of various herbs and hot peppers for the local market and export is a growing business. Packaging and primary processing of a number of vegetables is in place for the local market and the hotel sector.

235

Bathsheba and the east coast. Barbados enjoys an excellent climate for agricultural production

Resources and Infrastructure: Land

There are over 17,000 farm holdings in Barbados, 95 percent of these are less the one hectacre in size. Most are part-time farmers who produce vegetables and livestock mainly for domestic consumption; surpluses are sold for cash.

There are 1,600 farms (9.2 percent of the farm holdings) between one and ten hectares in size. These farms produce mainly non-sugar crops, vegetables, fruits and some livestock, and are under intensive management using a high level of technology. Most of these farms are mechanised and usually irrigated.

There are about 144 farms which are over ten hectares (25 acres) in size. These farms are mainly in sugar production, root crops and some vegetables.

Water

Most of Barbados' rainfall, 60 inches (1,524mm), falls between July and December. It is estimated that agriculture uses around six-million gallons per day. Some 67 percent is estimated to come from the public supply system, while 33 percent comes from private wells. There are some nine irrigation schemes scattered around Barbados. These are managed by the Barbados Agricultural Development and Marketing Corporation (BADMC).

Over 25 percent of the non-sugar producers use irrigation with drip irrigation being the most common method. Various fertigation systems (the application of fertiliser through the irrigation system) are used.

Machinery and Equipment

All the farmers in Barbados have basic hand tools. Those in the 10-20 hectares category have cultivation equipment. Some 81 percent also have tractor-mounted spraying equipment, while all farms above 20 hectares have tractor-mounted spraying equipment.

Barbados has access to two tissue culture laboratories: one owned by government and a regional laboratory owned by the Caribbean Agricultural Research and Development Institute (CARDI). These are mainly used in root crop and banana production and in floriculture.

Small farmers are provided with tractor services by the Motor Tractor Cultivation Scheme of the BADMC and by private operators.

Capital & Human Resources

The main source of capital for agricultural development is the Agricultural Division of the Barbados National Bank (BNB), Barclays Bank, and the Barbados Development Bank (BDB). Commercial bank credit to agriculture is in excess of BDS$30 million (US$15 million).

The Agricultural labour force has declined substantially over the years, it decreased from 9,000 in 1980 to 6,900 in 1987, by 1991 the figure had declined to 5,900 people. This downward movement is also aggravated by the high age structure of the labour force. Approximately 50 percent of the labour force is in excess of 50 years of age.

In the Ministry of Agriculture there are a number of agricultural professionals and technicians: etymologists, agronomists, pathologists, tissue culture specialists, animal nutritionists, veterinarians, marine biologists and meteorologists. Some of these professions are available in the regional and international organisations based in Barbados.

Agricultual training to diploma level is available at Samuel Jackman Prescod Polytechnic; Barbados Community College provides an associate degree in agriculture. Degree level education in agriculture is available at the University of the West Indies.

Sources of Information

The Ministry of Agriculture and Rural Development
Barbados Agricultural Development and Marketing Corporation
Barbados Agricultural Management Company
Barbados Sugar Industries Limited
Barbados Pig Producers Cooperative
Barbados Agricultural Society
Caribbean Agricultural Research and Development Institute
Inter-American Institute for Co-operation on Agriculture,
Soil Conservation Unit

Barbados Horticulture

The Barbados Horticultural Society was formed in 1927 by 13 horticultural enthusiasts to encourage and further the study of horticulture on the island. Rules have changed little since then. In 1976 with the help of many fund-raising activities the society bought Balls Plantation as its own headquarters on the site of an old plantation boiling house, complete with a mill dating from 1866.

Now, with a membership of over 300, the ground surrounding the boiling house and mill, initially rough and overgrown, is covered in

smooth lawns with a luxuriant and colourful rock garden of riotous coloured bougainvillea sprawling towards the nearby highway and making its way up some of the trees.

The Barbados Horticultural Society has exhibited at the Chelsea Flower Show every year since 1988, winning four Silver and four Gold Medals. Various organisations in Barbados fund the team, paying some of the many costs involved in mounting the exhibit at Chelsea Flower Show, 40 to 50 large boxes of flowers, foliage and props are transported, courtesy of British Airways each year.

Private gardeners and flower farmers from all over Barbados bring flowers and foliage to the society to be cleaned, sorted and packed - after first having everything passed by the Plant Quarantine office as being free from any insects or blight.

Before transport, however, tremendous activity takes place. Private members and friends do all the work the day before and, on the day of departure taking infinite care to wrap the fragile cargo before packing the boxes.

(L-R): Mrs Jean Robinson, President of the Barbados Horticultural Society. proudly showing the 1996 Chelsea Flower Show Award with HE Mr Peter Simmons, High Commissioner for Barbados in the UK and Diedre Cumberbatch, UK Manager of the the Barbados Tourism Authority

Full support from the Barbados Tourism Authority, the Ministry of Agriculture, Food and Fisheries, flower farmers and amateur gardeners make the entry at the Chelsea Flower Show possible. As a result of the society's efforts, thousands of gardening enthusiasts visit this extravaganza each year to savour and enjoy an unsurpassed display of beauty and creativity. Meanwhile the flower growers go from strength to strength and the exposure gained at the show provides a boost towards the marketing of the rich and vibrantly coloured blooms.

THE HELPFUL ALOE PLANT

Aloe, one of the most popular ingredients of hair and skin-care products grows in Barbados, where it is commonly referred to as 'aloes', and pronounced like 'alluss'. It is a handy plant that is effective for a number of uses. As a sunburn remedy it is unparalleled. Its thick, cool, soothing juice can be applied straight from the plant to the skin.

Barbados could be regarded as a trailblazer of aloe cultivation in the Western world. A succulent member of the lily family native to Africa, aloes were once farmed heavily in St Philip, and were a Barbadian export crop from as early as 1693. The thick, juicy leaves were cut and set upright to drain. The juice was reduced by boiling or sun exposure, and was shipped, primarily to England, in gourds. There it was a popular purgative for clogged digestive systems and came to be listed in the pharmacopoeia as Aloe Barbadensis. This business prospered until the mid-19th Century.

The aloe has been known and used for millennia as an effective skin soother and healer, as well as a tonic and powerful purgative of the digestive system. The dried crystalline product is 'aloin' and has many medicinal uses for its bactericidal and fungicidal properties. The plant was cultivated for medicinal use as far back as ancient Egypt and was used in Biblical times.

Many Caribbean islanders today use aloe internally as a tonic and to 'clean out the insides'. Bajans also find its bitterness useful in discouraging children from thumb-sucking.

The aloe's long, pointy, pale green leaves are succulent as those of a cactus and grow nearly straight upwards from the ground in a clump that can reach a height of about 18 inches. At times, it bears a central stalk of pale yellow flowers. There are over 200 species of aloe, and there are three medicinal species of which the aloe vera is but one.

To use: strip away and discard the sharp edges. Open the fleshy leaf, and score or bash the dark yellowish, gelatinous matter inside to release the juice. It can then be smeared liberally on the skin for instant relief of burns or taken internally in small quantities for other results. In this unprepared form, it will badly stain clothing or any porous surface onto which it seeps.

Tyre Gardens

by Winnie Merritt

Dr Colin Hudson with a visitor and (below) with the late Governor General Dame Nita-Barrow

Container gardening is a common practice in northern cities where soil is limited, space at a premium and growing seasons short. But why the trend to grow things in tyres in sunny Barbados - land of rolling fields of sugar cane? The answers are found in the parish of St Thomas in the tyre gardens of agriculturalist and innovator, Dr Colin Hudson.

Tyre gardens are just one of Dr Hudson's many enthusiasms which generally revolve around saving arable land and helping farmers to stay afloat. At the small, problem-solving centre called Carib Agro-Industries Limited the chatter of school-children touring this lush garden mingles with the clang and clatter of the machine shop. As we weave among the neatly painted stacks of white tyres which spout graceful stalks of long beans, the purple gleam of eggplant and fat green heads of cabbage, we hear the whine of a grinder working on equipment for the farms of Barbados and far away places like India, Costa Rica and the United States.

Dr Hudson tells visitors that the gardens need only a half-minute each of hose water twice a week. They get a little chicken litter mulching every two weeks or so. Other than that, reaping the produce is the biggest job! We begin to understand the reason why he has been advocating this form of gardening through television, radio, print and a Saturday morning open house: tyre gardens require minimum attention.

We turn and reach up to pick a crisp green pepper. Why reach up? Another advantage of the tyre garden becomes clear. This kind of garden can save an aching back. With tyres stacked in tiers of three or four high, planting, watering, reaping and pulling the occasional weed are all done from the hip! People in wheelchairs can easily manage this kind of garden. Some already do.

Everything is organically grown, too. We pop a plump cherry tomato straight in the mouth. No '...cides' of any kind on these plants. The usual garden pests and diseases present far fewer problems here. The interplanting diversity of vegetables and herbs produces a variety of odours which confuse most garden pests. Those who find their way in are likely to meet lady bird beetles and other useful predators laying in wait for them. Some insects are further confounded by the white paint on the tyres, since they orient to the sky, they literally cannot tell which way is up! A pleasant bed of white gravel on the paths through the garden further reduces pest problems and makes for clean shoes in rainy weather.

Small islands have a big waste disposal problem. Always concerned with environment, Colin Hudson utilizes what would otherwise be considered waste products as a demonstration of possible solutions for this problem. The gardens are made of discarded bus, tractor and car tyres. To prevent the invasion of tree roots, a sheet of discarded aluminum from a publishing house is placed under each tyre. The white 'paint' on the tyres is actually a carbide by-product from the local gas plant, and the unique watering system is fitted with a series of small plastic drink bottles, cut and made into a tube, which are inserted through holes in the tyre rim to rest on a bed of gravel in the bottom rim. A garden hose is then directed into this tube for watering.

The growing medium utilises by-products from the Barbados sugar factories. Compost is made of filter mud, fly-ash and furnace-ash, all mineral-rich substances, which are added to bagasse, a fibrous matter remaining after the cane juice has been squeezed. Some chicken-litter and soil is added and the mix becomes a gardener's dream. It is loose, loaded with plant nutrients and water conservative. No wonder the carrots fairly leap into the basket when pulled!

Interest in agriculture has waned as white-collar jobs become more attractive all over the Caribbean. Schools which have recently become involved with tyre garden tours and projects are attempting to rekindle the interest of young people in agriculture. The youngsters begin to appreciate the dignity of the farming profession and the variety of managerial skills required to produce food. They also learn that if they grow what they eat, they can know it is safe from harmful chemicals, and fresh with nutritious vitamins and minerals. As a result, many young people are now setting up their own tyre gardens - perhaps their first step to a future in Caribbean agriculture.

Fishing Industry

The Barbados fishing industry provides employment for an estimated 4,000-5,000 workers including fishermen, vendors, hawkers, boat builders, cleaners and processors.

Barbados has a 12-mile territorial sea and a declared 200-mile Exclusive Economic Zone (EEZ). The island has only a small shelf area of 320 sq km with a 180 metres contour some 1.8 km from shore. The EEZ of Barbados includes an estimated 166,600 sq km of inshore and offshore waters.

Eight to ten km south-east of the island is a shoal 'London Shallows' which measures eight km at its widest and 18 km at its longest. Its depth varies from 50 - 60 metres. There are other shoals such as 'Trader Banks' located to the south-west of Barbados.

The pelagic fishing season extends from November to July, with January to June being the months for the largest catches made up of flying fish, billfish, tuna, kingfish and shark.

August to October are the months for pot and snapper fishing. Jacks and sprats are caught using cast nets.

The island's fishery resources are generally divided into three categories.

(a) **Inshore coral reef resources** - which surround the island and provide shelter for a number of species that are caught in pots and traps. These include sea eggs, turtles, lobster and conch. Trap fishing is the main inshore method of catching parrot fish, surgeon fish, grunts and squirrel fish.

(b) **Offshore resources** - located on offshore banks and slopes is the snapper or red fish as it is locally known. The queen snapper or brim is the most common snapper. Groupers and hinds are also caught on these banks.

(c) **Pelagic resources** - pelagics are the main catch and consist mainly of flying fish, billfish, shark and tuna. Tunas include yellowfin, bigeye, skipjack and blackfin. The yellowfin and bigeye are known locally as albacore while skipjacks and blackfins are called bonita.

Landing sites

There are 26 coastal sites where fish are landed. These are divided into three categories according to the type of physical infrastructure present.

(1) Primary landing sites:- There are three such sites - Bridgetown, Oistins's and Speightstown Fish Market, together these account for a

Large pelagic fish can be bought fresh at roadside vendors

Sea eggs

Known to sushi fanciers as "uni," the sea egg is the variety of sea urchin that bears short white spines. Denuded of this outer covering, the pretty white shells have an embroidered looking pattern and can occasionally be found whole or in fragments along the beaches.

Many years ago, each sea egg season (September to April) saw the harvest of thousands of these creatures. Since then the sea egg population has declined due to overharvesting and damage to the inshore reef. A half gallon container of sea eggs now sells for BDS$100 but is seldom available even in season. It is illegal to harvest sea eggs in other months.

Fishermen used to dive the inshore reefs to get the sea eggs, using a scraper to deposit them in nets. Once the sea eggs reached the shore, the hawkers took over. They broke each shell, shook out the gut then packed the rows of eggs into an empty shell in the bottom of a cone made from a sea grape leaf.

Fishing village, Fowl Bay

All vessels must be registered with the Fisheries Division each year

large proportion of the total catch. Major structures are provided for the landing and sale of fish. Cold storage and chilling facilities are located at the two complexes while blast freezers are located at the Bridgetown complex.

(2) Secondary landing sites:- There are nine secondary landing sites and the type of infrastructure present is a simple shed which provides shelter for the processing and retailing of fish. In the case of Consett, a jetty is provided.

(3) Tertiary landing sites:- These are simply open bays where fish are landed. There are no physical structures for the processing and sale of fish or amenities. However a diesel storage tank is loacted at Sixmens Beach to facilitate fueling the boats.

Fishing Vessels

The four types of vessels used are:-

(1) The Longliner:- These boats mainly target the yellowfin, tuna and billfish fisheries.

(2) The Iceboat and (3) Day boat:- These catch mainly flying fish and pelagics. The iceboat has an ice hold where fish are stored allowing it to remain at sea for up to ten or more days.

(4) Moses or pirogues:- These are used as tenders or in-shore reef or handline fishing.

Fish Imports

There are nine registered importers of fresh fish (processors not included). About 2,000-2,500 metric tonnes of fish are imported annually. The main countries of origin for fresh/chilled/frozen fish are Trinidad and Tobago, Grenada and Guyana. Preserved/prepared fish is imported mainly from Canada, UK and US.

Exports

There are four major exporters of fish. Between 12-25 metric tonnes of fish are exported annually. Destinations include Canada, UK and US.

Contribution to GDP

The fishing industry contributes between BDS$20 million and BDS$40 million per year or between 0.6 to 1.0 percent to GDP.

Fisherfolk

There are an estimated 2,200 fishermen, 80 percent operate on a full time basis while ten percent are part-time. There are approximately 800 boat-owners of whom about five percent are female. Fish vendors, boners and cleaners number about 400 and more than 75 percent are female. There are 30-40 hawkers, the majority being men.

Processors

There are seven major processors and three smaller ones which employ over 125 workers, 95 percent of whom are women. The products are mainly vacuum packed fillets, frozen flying fish and other large pelagics. Additional products include salted fish and fish burgers.

Role of government

There are an estimated 2,200 fishermen in the industry

Government plays a major role in the administration and management of the fishing industry and includes the following:-
* To provide the administrative and technical personnel required to manage the fishing industry.
* To provide onshore infrastructure to facilitate the landing and storage of fish.
* To provide loan portfolios, subsidies and services.
* The management of the local fishing industry falls under the portfolio of the Ministry of Agriculture and Rural Development. The Fisheries Division is the agency of the ministry which has to manage and develop the fisheries sector - to ensure the optimum utilisation of the fisheries resource in the waters to the benefit of the people of Barbados, as well as keep available up-to-date information on the fishing industry of Barbados, to be used in government and private sector for decision-making.

The Markets Division manages the major physical infrastructure provided for the landing of local catch at Oistins's and Bridgetown Fisheries, which have ice machines, cold storage facilities, freezers, fish processing areas and fish selling booths - and Speightstown Fish Market. A tax must be paid on all fish landed at markets. Simultaneously fish landing statistics are recorded by landed weights of species and species groups. Government also provides personnel at other secondary landing sites to collect fish landing statistics.

The analytical services carry out any chemical analysis required by the

Flying Fish

Flying fish is widely distributed in tropical waters, and abounds off Tobago where it is heavily fished by Barbadian ice-boats.

The most economical way to catch flying fish is by large gill nets, with mesh wide enough to allow immature fish to escape, while trapping the larger ones.

There are two small species about 12 inches in length, and a larger one, rarely seen, locally called a guinea-man, about 18 inches long.

The fish glides rather than flies: rapidly vibrating its tail, it accelerates to around 40 miles-an-hour, and then leaps from the water, spreading its large lateral fins, on which it glides for up to 100 feet. It flies solely and in groups, in a straight line or an arc, day or night, almost always taking off into the wind, the body forming an angle of approximately 13 degrees to the horizontal.

The fish's skeletal structure allows an expert filleter to strip one to a boneless steak in less than 90 seconds.

December to May is the fishing season in Barbados, when more than 450 fishing boats, including ice boats, make the largest catches.

A plentiful supply during the season, its relatively cheap price, the ease with which it can be prepared, and its delicate taste make the flying fish the single most important fish in Barbados.

industry. The Ministry of Health through the Public Health Inspectorate ensures that sanitary conditions are maintained at all landing sites as well as vessels involved in the trans-shipment of fish. This ministry also issues phytosanitary certificates which may be required by exporters of fish.

Statutory Corporations

The Insurance Corporation of Barbados underwrites the local fishing fleet. The Barbados Development Bank provides a loans portfolio for the local fishing industry, and Barbados National Standards Institution provides standards for local fish products.

Fisheries Division

Besides the management and administration of the fishing industry the following services are offered to local fishers.

Boat Haul-Up System. The Division offers an island-wide subsidised haul-up service for fishing vessels to facilitate routine and emergency repairs of commercial fishing vessels.

In the event of a hurricane or bad weather the haul-up service is offered free of cost to fishermen and boat owners.

Fishing Facilities. Facilities for the processing and sale of fish are provided in the form of eight sheds. The Markets Division is responsible for the administration, staffing and maintenance of the Oistins, Bridgetown and Speightstown fish markets.

The Division provides both water and electricity services to the fish sheds and open bays around the island. Caretakers are employed to clean existing fish sheds and record the species and weight of fish caught at a number of fish landing sites.

Boat Inspection and Registration. Under the Fishing Industry Act 1993, all fishing vessels must be registered with the Fisheries Division. The certificate of registration is valid for one year only. The vessels are inspected for seaworthiness and suitability for fishing. The inspection service is island-wide and is serviced by a fisheries assistant and three mechanics. Inspections and certifications are done on a daily basis - the information gathered is computerised. A subsidy is offered to fishermen to defray some of the cost of vessel maintenance.

Modern Barbados: INDUSTRY

Airport

The forerunner of Grantley Adams International Airport, known as Seawell Airport, came into being when a Royal Netherlands Airlines (KLM) plane landed on a grass runway in 1938. The outbreak of World War II brought some assistance from the US government and the rainy season of 1940/41 made it clear to the Barbados' government that if an important and vital link was to be maintained between Barbados and the outside world, a paved runway was an absolute necessity.

Early in 1940 the occupation of Holland by German forces brought the Dutch service to Barbados to an end, and soon after, the British West Indian Airways service was inaugurated.

The US government assisted in the change-over from grass to concrete as the US military maintained a small signal station at Seawell during the war. A small terminal building and control tower were built to service the budding airline movements. In those early days, people used the airborne method of travel with some trepidation and only the most hardy would brave the inconvenience and discomforts experienced in travelling by airplane out of Barbados.

At the end of World War II with the world moving swiftly to formulate plans for recovery, reconstruction and expansion, the government of Barbados realised that air traffic was becoming vitally important to the economy of the island. The first step was taken by Air Canada when a service from Montreal to Barbados was started in December 1949. Immediately after, major reconstruction of Seawell Airport started in earnest. New terminal buildings were erected to replace the old shed-like structure, and the old paved runway was replaced by a new one on foundations in a slightly different direction.

The new building was opened in 1956 and though it served Barbados well for 23 years, it became outdated almost as soon as its doors were opened because of the rapid growth in air traffic.

During the 1960s, the runway was extended to 9,000 feet and an addition was made to the terminal building to serve as an arrivals section. These were merely 'patchwork' efforts intended to meet the demand created by a passenger traffic which was increasing by an annual rate of 16 percent.

By 1970 the government realised that this 'patchwork' type expansion programme could not handle the anticipated traffic of the next three decades. A feasibility study of the airport expansion through to 1990 was commenced; it was conducted by Howard Needles, Tammen & Bergendoff International who found the expansion was both feasible and economic and recommended a development programme.

The Airport Project stretched across a time span of eight years: 1971 - 1979. The runway, extended to 3,352 metres can now accommodate wide bodied aircraft and is one of the longest in the Caribbean. There is parking space for 16 aircraft of the largest size, but as many as 77 aircraft of varying types have been accommodated on the two parking aprons.

Barbados was thus brought in line with the most modern airports around the world. A cargo facility was erected on the south-west side of the old terminal building and an ultra modern flight kitchen was developed to serve the needs of a growing number of airline customers.

The new air traffic control tower was completed in 1976. In that year the airport acquired a new name. It was renamed in honour of a great patriot, Sir Grantley Adams, father of the late Prime Minister, Mr J M G M, Tom Adams, then Prime Minister of Barbados. In October 1976 Seawell Airport thereafter became known as Grantley Adams International Airport (GAIA).

The landmark occasion for GAIA was November 1979 when the new terminal was opened. The building was constructed at the budgeted capital cost of BDS$28 million.

At Grantley Adams International Airport the ingredients of location, climate, a well developed infrastructure of local services such as roads, communications, beach front hotels and one of the most liberal foreign exchange policies in the Caribbean serve as an impetus to the leisure traveller and business tycoon alike.

In Barbados the passenger's safety is of prime importance. Safety and security procedures are continually upgraded to equal or surpass those at many of the airports in this hemisphere.

It is recognised that the provision of the best runways and ground aids must be supported by adequate parking aprons and ground handling services. Grantley Adams International Airport has already projected into the 21st Century its needs for these support services. An

Building the Caribbean

Since 1975 Structural Systems of Barbados has played a significant role in the development of the Caribbean by providing creative, attractive, functional, and economical solutions to the building needs of the region's people and governments.

Across the region, in towns, and in country fields for every purpose - churches, schools, retail stores, factories, warehouses, hotels, offices, sports complexes; - Structural Systems' custom-engineered buildings and fabricated-steel structures are daily providing satisfaction to the architects, the engineers, the building contractors, the developers and ultimately the people who live, work in and frequent these buildings.

From design to manufacturing to inventory control and delivery. Structural Systems has invested in state-of-the-art technology. Using Computer Assisted Design Structural Systems' operation is one of the most advanced in the Caribbean. Costing and inventory control departments are also fully computerised. All manufacturing processes, from the shot-blasting of all steel entering the works, through to the continuous loading of trailers are fully mechanised.

Structural Systems believe that a metal building must be a solid, lasting investment. Buildings are designed to withstand hurricane-force winds and the corrosive affects of the climate.

Every step of the manufacturing operations, from sourcing the finest quality materials to careful, precision engineering processes to meticulous installation, is focused on delivering buildings and steel structures of strength, and long-lasting durability.

Grantley Adams International Airport is served by an all cargo air carrier operating to major north and South American cities

extention to the existing parking apron will be completed by November 1996.

To complement the Barbados government's industrial programme, a major highway was constructed to link the airport with the seaport to facilitate the supply of imported raw materials and the air shipment of finished products.

Grantley Adams International Airport is already served by an all cargo air carrier operating to major north and South American cities.

The Caribbean Basin Initiative announced by the United States government make the island of Barbados therefore an excellent choice for the investor seeking to use this incentive programme for exports to the United States.

GAIA was also the home base for a major regional airport programme development which was concluded in 1992. This Canadian government sponsored programme was designed to upgrade 22 Caribbean airports in 13 countries; Barbados airport personnel participated in this programme. The Canadian government contributed funding of CAN$80 million over five years, and based the techincal and adminstrative staff at Terminal II (the old terminal). Barbados with its already well developed airport and excellent air services was the ideal base for this project.

It is also easily accessible for Fly/Cruise charters and is the sole airport in the Caribbean through which Fly/Cruise charters may operate with the easiest transfer available to such passengers. The transfer from GAIA to the Bridgetown Port or vice versa is done in a smooth operation with a minimum of red tape. Intransit passengers are processed without customs and/or immigration checks. By this means the full passenger load of a wide bodied aircraft can be processed through the airport in less than 20 minutes.

247

Bridgetown Port

The Bridgetown Port was officially opened on 1 July 1961 with the enactment of legislation to establish the Port Department. The main functions of the Port Department were to administer a coordinated and integrated system of harbour facilities, lighthouses and other port services within the island.

The Port Department was organised into four divisions, marine, marine engineering, administration, maintenance and shipping office.

The cargo handling activities were conducted by a private company, Port Contractors (B'dos) Ltd., of which government owned 25 percent shares. Port Contractors operated under contract as agents of the Port Department, and had as its primary function the responsibility for organising shore activities and the management of all transit sheds.

Port Contractors was divided into four sections cargo, handling and shed management, main administration office, and maintenance and security.

Since 1961, the port has gone through revolutionary changes generally associated with the dynamics of the maritime industry. With these rapid technological changes imparted on Barbados' limited resources, it was therefore evident that the need had arisen to expand and streamline procedures to meet the ever-changing demand for additional port services particularly, as the container revolution had arrived.

By 1972, the government had secured the services of the Canadian International Development Agency (CIDA) to develop a study which interalia would recommend the development needs of the port. Out of CIDA's recommendations, the Barbados Port Authority was established by an Act of Parliament entitled the Barbados Port Authority Act 1975.

The Act provided the amalgamation of Port Contractors and Port Department into an authority which was a fully autonomous body.

The container revolution, by then, was gaining in momentum, thus propelling the port to expand to meet the new box era. This expansion was completed in 1978 and saw the following improvements in the Port:- the extension of the quay wall by 183 metres; the completion of a modern two-storey administration building; the reclamation of 6.5 hectares of land; the completion of the shallow draught; the construction of a bulk grain facility; and a shallow draught facility.

In 1979, the Barbados Port Authority was formed. The function of the authority as a statutory body is to plan, build, develop, manage, maintain and operate the port.

Faced with the high demands in the handling of containers, as well as

Giant gantry crane

Bridgetown Port wins 'Port of the Year' award

For the second time in three years, the Barbados Port Authority (BPA) has won the Port of the Year Award. The prestigious title was bestowed during the Caribbean Shipping Association's annual banquet at the Sherbourne Centre. The Bridgetown Port first took this eight-year-old award in 1993 for its achievements in 1992.

In 1995 Barbados competed against the ports of The Bahamas, St Lucia, Dominica, Jamaica, St Vincent and Trinidad and Tobago.

During 1996, cargo handling at the Bridgetown Port increased by 15 percent, and there has been an increase in profit from the BDS$3.5 million in 1995. An increase in cruise ship activity and provision of better facilities for cruise ship passengers also led to the overall success of the port which is undergoing improvements.

Bridgetown Port: Winner of 'Port of the Year' award for the second time in four years

SHIPPING ASSOCIATION OF BARBADOS

The Shipping Association of Barbados (SAB) has enjoyed significant growth since its inception in 1981. Membership of the association is made up primarily of ship's agents and stevedore companies, who regularly meet to discuss common problems, share information on new technology and analyse trends in the market-place.

As a member of the Caribbean Shipping Association (CSA) SAB enjoys automatic links with the French, Spanish and Dutch-speaking Caribbean countries, three of the four major language groups embraced by the CSA.

As the voice of shipping in Barbados, the SAB seeks, among other things, to provide for consultation between members to ascertain their views on matters of common interest and also to collect and circulate statistical and other information relating to the shipping industry.

Having experienced sustained growth over the years, the association's links with the CSA include training, research and representation at government and CariCom Secretariat level.

To meet the competition, the Bridgetown Port will move in the direction of trans-shipment business, according to the President of the Shipping Association of Barbados and Vice-president of the Caribbean Shipping Association, David Harding. Any further development of the Bridgetown Port has to take into account the possibility of increased trans-shipment.

"Barbados must look specifically to the area of hub activity, where, if we see a trade lane from South America to north America we could target the particular line and convince them of the increased benefits of using Barbados as a relay station for their product. Barbados had reached a level of sophistication in cargo-handling technology where it can go and actively market the port as well as target specific shipping lines."

the growth of the cruise industry, emphasis was placed on improving the efficiency of the port by the purchase of equipment to handle containers.

The first type of equipment employed was Lancer Boss Side Loaders along with forklift trucks capable of handling containers. In 1987, the port purchased a gantry crane supplemented by straddle carriers which were in use prior to the purchase of the gantry crane. In addition, the gantry crane was supported by a mobile crane which was used on a rental basis.

A small cruise terminal was constructed in the western section of a former cargo shed and officially opened in May 1986. However, by the late 1980s and early 1990's indications were that there was a need for a larger cruise terminal to meet the rapid growth of the cruise industry. This heralded the commencement of the plans to construct a modern cruise terminal.

Cruise ships arrive every day

On 1 January 1994 the modern and spacious passenger terminal was officially opened providing 20,000 square feet of floor space accommodating:- over 20 tax free shops, modern telecommunications system, customs, immigration, security and health offices, a tourism office, post office, and a chattel house village to accommodate small vendors.

However, the most significant development in the port's history was the conclusion and implementation of the port rationalisation programme in 1992. With the support of all the social partners, it was agreed that all direct labour and some categories of supervisory and other staff should be severed.

It was generally considered that in the interests of all parties concerned, the following major changes were necessary:-

• All direct labour was styled dockers;

• Workers operating equipment were referred to a operators. These workers must work on board or on shore when posted to work on any particular day. This allows management the necessary inter-changeability and flexibility to better utilise the direct labour force. The direct labour force was reduced to 140.

• All dockers were guaranteed a weekly rate of pay dependant on category.

The port now operates on a 24 hour basis for container vessels. There was also a reduction in the number of dockers engaged on container vessels. Productivity increased as there was no limit in the number of containers lifted during a given period.

Regarding the need for the protection of the marine and natural

A modern 20,000 sq ft cruise terminal with duty-free complex and a 200-fleet taxi service

BICO keeping cool

Since 1972, BICO Limited have handled all refrigerated cargo landed at Bridgetown Port as sub-contractors to the BPA. Refrigerated containers are off-loaded from the shipping vessel by the BPA's gantry crane and moved by side loader or straddle carrier the short distance to BICO's receiving ramps in Bridgetown Port. The company's employees strip the containers, sort the cargo and store at the appropriate temperatures. Meanwhile, the empty containers are taken away by the BPA, cleaned and returned to the vessel on the same day.

This service allows shipping lines to immediately re-use their containers instead of waiting to collect them on their next Barbados voyage several weeks, or even months later.

BICO's 750,000 cu.ft. facility is fully mechanised and racked, which allows the firm to redeliver any commodity, from any shipment, to consignees.

For consignee/customer convenience, BICO has a customs office on the premises, as well as inspectors from both the Port and the Ministries of Agriculture and Health.

All refrigerants used in the facility are 'green' (CFC free).

Another benefit to consignees is that they may pre-sell all, or any part, of their reefer cargo prior to its arrival in Barbados, and issue customers with a delivery note for collection of the goods at BICO's facility within the 'free' storage period included in their freight charge.

BICO's warehousing operation started at Bay Street in 1910, and the company is a member of the Shipping Association of Barbados, the International Association of Refrigerated Warehousemen and the Refrigeration Research Foundation.

environment the port installed a Hoskinson Pyrolytic Smokeless Incinerator in 1993 to handle the disposal of all ships waste in an environmentally friendly manner.

There is indeed reason for great optimism about future prospects for Bridgetown Port. Indications are that the number of cruise liner passengers will continue to grow. A greater effort will be made to capitalise on Barbados' advantageous geographical location as it relates to the handling of trans-shipment cargo. Indeed, Barbados is well positioned to serve as a major trans-shipment hub for cargo trade plying between north and South America and Europe and the Caribbean.

The newly established marketing department within the authority was a positive step in the right direction towards the achievement of this objective.

The future of cruise tourism looks most promising for Barbados. There is also tremendous potential for the increased home-porting of cruise vessels and with the expansion of the port, this aspect is achievable.

Barbados Port Authority is also committed to improving the general welfare of all employees through human resource development, enhanced operational systems, provision of improved health and safety standards.

Berthing facilities include, berthing capacity for eight vessels; Guaranteed berths for five cruise liners on any given day; water; bunkering; and telephone service supplied at all berths.

Cruise Arrivals

Unlike many destinations, cruise passengers find Bridgetown hassle-free and friendly

The Port of Bridgetown can provide berths for five mega-cruise ships with up to 9.6 metre draughts. All berths provide telephone lines, water, bunker and waste disposal services.

The port has a very modern cruise terminal offering 20,000 square feet of space of ultra modern duty free shops, providing a wide variety of local and overseas goods.

There is a restaurant and bar, as well as immigration, health, customs and security officers.

Full banking services are provided with a communications centre offering international calls and facsimile services.

Other services available within the terminal are scuba diving, horse riding, bicycle rentals, car rentals and rum tours.

In addition there are fully organised ground tour operations to heritage sites, beaches and other attractions.

A reliable taxi service with a fleet of 200 taxis is also available for those who did not pre-book tours.

To meet the growing number of mega-ships being constructed, the Port has purchased a Damen 4,600 horsepower tug. This allows greater capacity in providing towage and berthing services to large vessels which call at the Port of Bridgetown.

The Port of Bridgetown is also one of the few ports in the eastern Caribbean through which Air/Sea charters operate with convenient airlift to the United States and Europe.

To facilitate the speedy processing of passengers prior to entry into Barbados, an immigration officer can meet the vessel at the last port-of-call before arriving at Barbados, thus clearing passengers en-route and saving them valuable time.

However, to meet the anticipated growth in the cruise line industry, there is a port reform and expansion project under construction to provide: six additional cruise line berths; separation of cruise line activity from cargo handling activity; further development of air/sea transfers particularly for cruises commencing at the Port of Bridgetown and encouragement for home-porting and the development of cruising along the South American coastline and the Caribbean Sea.

The hurricane of 1694 that destroyed the first man-made harbour

IN February, 1686 the government, under the administration of Lieutenant Governor Edwyn Stede, commissioned John Stewart, a Bridgetown merchant, to construct new harbour facilities. The terms of the contract required him to build two piers of stone capable of accommodating and protecting ships of 200 tonnes. One pier was to begin from Willoughby Fort and extend westwards into the sea for a distance of over 150 metres. The other was to begin from Stewart's Wharf and extend in a southerly direction. Each pier was to be nearly ten metres wide and the entrance to the harbour nearly 40 metres across. Additionally, Stewart had to remove a sandbar located near the entrance to what is now called the Careenage, dredge the channel and maintain it to a depth sufficient to enable boats to move to and from the wharfs above.

Work on the project started in July 1687 and by March 1690 had made sufficient progress towards completion to enable shipping to berth within the anchorage. Lieutenant Governor Stede appointed Stewart Harbour Master and issued him a set of rules for the orderly operation of the new harbour.

Unfortunately, in late September 1694, just as the final touches were being applied, the entire harbour was destroyed by a violent hurricane. The cost of reconstruction being prohibitive, the government was forced to abandon the scheme altogether.

Warren Alleyne

Mount Gay: The oldest rum in the world

by Arti Meyers

Mount Gay Extra Old Barbados Rum

Cane-cutting during the harvest

The story of rum dates back to the very birth of Barbados, since the first harvesting of sugar crops, Bajans have been producing a spirit from its byproducts. In fact, the name 'Rum' was born on the docks of the Bridgetown harbour as early as the 17th Century. It was originally called 'rumbullion' because a 'rumpous' occasion usually followed the consumption of this celebrated beverage. Of course rum has evolved over the years, but the key ingredients of fine Barbados sugar cane, and pure coral filtered water remain the same to the present.

The history of Mount Gay rum is packed with personality, heritage and history. The first surviving written evidence of rum production on the Mount Gay estate is found in a legal document in the Barbados archives, dated 20 February 1703; it outlines property (then owned by Michael Terrill) and the equipment essential for rum-making, that was found there.

'two stone windmills....one boiling house with seven coppers, one curing house and one still house....'

This confirms that rum production was already well underway by 1703 and has continued for almost 300 years, making Mount Gay rum the oldest rum in Barbados, and equally important... the oldest rum in the world

In the early 18th Century the plantation comprised of many very small, separately-owned, sugar plantations; these were named after the families that owned them. Today some of the 54 fields at the Mount Gay Plantation still carry their names, including: Tyrell, Jemmot, Jones, Hussy, Gray and Pickering. These names have lived on in the canefields of Mount Gay for nearly three centuries. Before being called the 'Mount Gay' plantation in the early 1800s, this stretch of land was named Mount Gilboa after the ridge to its north.

The plantation was renamed 'Mount Gay' in 1801 in honour of Sir John Gay Alleyne, a close friend of the owner, and eminent Barbadian of the 18th Century. Because a Mount Alleyne already existed in St James, the land was named 'Mount Gay Plantation'. Sir John was a member of parliament for 40 years, and was unanimously elected Speaker of the House of Assembly in 1767 - a position he maintained, unchallenged, for 30 years. His industry and service to Barbados were recognised and rewarded by King George III, who granted him a knighthood in honour of his outstanding achievements.

Sir John Gay Alleyne was a respected member of society, and indeed a colourful character! He was married twice and had eight children. He first married Christian Dottin, whose father owned St Nicholas Abbey. It

is rumoured that, for a bet, Sir John rode his horse up the stairs of this historic home! Four years after the death of Christian, Sir John, at the age of 62, remarried 21-year-old Jane Abel. In the next 14 years, she gave birth to seven children, and sadly pre-deceased Sir John by a few years.

A much admired and deeply respected man, Sir John Gay Alleyne was not without fondness for fine wine and spirits. In his will he bequeathed 'two cases of extraordinarily fine Noyau... Malmsey wine... and all the Madeira and Port wine that may not be required for my funeral'. It is therefore fitting that after his death in 1801 his name became synonymous with the finest Barbados spirit, Mount Gay rum.

The past 100 years at Mount Gay have been years of pride and growth. In the early 1900s the Mount Gay plantation was bought by prominent Barbadian businessman Aubrey Ward. He introduced new methods to meet the increasing demand for Mount Gay rum, while insisting that its traditional character be maintained. Along with his business partner and marketing specialist John Hutson, they introduced Mount Gay rum to an international market. Today the Ward family continue to be involved in the business and the international sales development is handled by the Remy-Cointreau Group.

The 'master blender' carefully checks the rum

Making Mount Gay Rum

It all starts with lush, green fields of high quality Barbados sugar cane...after planting, the young cane takes 12-18 months to mature and is harvested when the sugar content reaches its peak. Most of the cane in Barbados is still cut by hand, and one person can cut and stack as much as 500 tonnes during the harvest season, which lasts about five months. The cane is taken to a sugar-refinery where the juice is squeezed from the sugar cane fibers and heated to produce sugar crystals. A residue of thick black syrup, known as molasses, remains. The molasses is returned to the Mount Gay plantation, where it is mixed with pure Barbados water in huge oak vats and allowed to ferment into alcohol.

It is this alcoholic base which is carefully distilled and then double distilled, to produce two distinctly different types of spirit. A rich, full double-distilled spirit results from the traditional copper pot stills, used since the 1700s. The modern "coffey still" produces a more neutral, single-distilled spirit. These two spirits must be aged for several years before they are blended to achieve the inimitable flavour of Mount Gay rum.

Mount Gay distilleries use specially imported barrels from Kentucky to

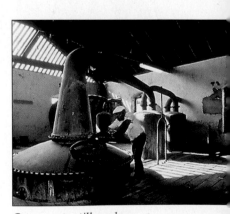

Copper pots still produce "double distilled" rum

The home of Mount Gay Rum in Barbados

Mount Gay's ageing cellar in Brandons, Barbados

age this delicate spirit. The barrels, once used to mature fine American bourbon, are made of a soft mellow seasoned oak. The inner surface which is slightly charred, imparts a distinctive smokey flavour and rich colour to the spirit - a unique feature of Mount Gay rum. When ageing is complete, the single and double distilled spirits are 'married' by the master blender according to the Mount Gay secret recipe. It is then diluted and placed in huge vats and allowed to settle before bottling. Here the individual characteristics of the spirits mingle and take on a smooth rounded nature and rich bouquet of a premium quality, well-aged rum. This process has been carefully handed down from generation to generation for almost 300 years.

Today Mount Gay rum is exported to 66 countries worldwide. Mount Gay rum has got a special place in the hearts of yachtsmen and in fact, sponsors over 100 sailing regattas around the world - in America, Europe, Asia and Australia. It's global recognition and appreciation is growing year by year. In 1995 Mount Gay's Extra Old Rum won a gold medal at 'Selection Mondiale de la Qualite', a wine and spirits competition held in Brussels.

The Visitor's Centre

Tourists are warmly welcomed to the Mount Gay Visitor's Centre on the Spring Garden Highway overlooking the magnificent west coast. The centre's friendly and knowledgeable staff share the story of the world's oldest rum and treat visitors to a wonderful Barbadian experience. The tour begins as guests are escorted into an air conditioned theatre, which is designed to resemble a traditional Barbadian rum shop, following a ten-minute presentation, guests are taken on a tour which involves the different processes and stages of rum-making from refining, ageing, blending to bottling.

A tour lasts between 30-40 minutes and concludes at the centre where guests are invited to indulge in rum 'tasting' and getting tips from the experts. Regular tours take place from 9am to 4pm Monday to Friday for a small fee. Special luncheon tours are also available daily. The Mount Gay Rum tour experience is an integral part of the culture, history - and the fun of Barbados; a Barbadian experience that should not be missed!

Oil and Natural Gas in Barbados

by Robert Weekes

The petroleum industry in Barbados has its origins around 1860 when the first records of oil production were noted from hand dug wells, no more than 100 feet deep in the Cattlewash area. These wells were known as the Lloyds Oil Wells and, although production was very small, they generated tremendous interest. Between 1890 and the first half of this century, the West Indies Oil Company and British Union Oil Company focused their exploration and production efforts on the Turners Hall area in search of an oilfield. After drilling a number of wells in 1920s and 1930s, 40 wells were established in the area, producing 250,000 barrels of crude oil. Between 1940 and 1960 several efforts were made in vain by various companies to find another oilfield.

In 1966 the first well was drilled in the Woodbourne area and this signalled the discovery of the Woodbourne field. This area has been the most productive on the island. It contains more than 150 wells, ranging in depth from 2,700 to 8,000 feet, and has produced more than five million barrels of oil, and is currently averaging 450,000 barrels per year.

The island's only refinery is located at Aquatic Gap, St Michael between two of the island's larger hotels. It is owned and operated by Mobil Oil and provides a range of products, including leaded and unleaded gasoline, kerosene, fuel oil and asphalt for the local market. Due to be closed at the turn of the century, the 5,000 barrel per day refinery uses both local and Venezuelan crude oil as its feedstock and produces exclusively for the local market.

In the marketing segment of the local industry, four multinational companies; Esso, Mobil, Shell and Texaco; have operations on the island. Barbados has the only domestic natural gas distribution network in the Caribbean. Over 14,000 households, commercial enterprises and the local electricity company are connected to the network and receive a quality of service comparable to international levels. The price of local natural gas is very competitive with alternative sources, and consequently most households connect to the network where it is available. The National Petroleum Corporation, a statutory organization, is the sole distributor and is currently expanding its 208 mile network. The island has a liquefied petroleum plant which was commissioned in 1988 and has the capability to produce 58 percent of the island's demand.

Whilst the petroleum industry in Barbados is relatively small by global and regional standards, it is certainly an emerging industry. As the next millennium approaches, the local industry will be faced with some critical challenges, including an alternative to the closure of the sole refinery, the exploitation of its offshore resources as well as the maximization of the onshore production. Of necessity, rationalization within the marketing segment of the industry must be a goal if only because of the changing demographics and economics.

Oil refinery at Aquatic Gap, St Michael

Alternative Energy Resources

Although the island is endowed with modest supplies of oil and natural gas, these cannot meet Barbados' combined domestic and industrial demands for energy. Some fossil fuel is imported, but alternatives are also in use.

Animal and plant material known as biomass can be used to produce fuel. Biomass is the leading alternate energy source in Barbados and has long contributed to the energy sector. Bagasse, the squeezed-out shreds of sugar cane, has been used in the sugar industry for centuries to run factories and until 1962 supplied more than half the fuel energy used in Barbados. The manufacture of sugar uses approximately 80 percent of the bagasse it produces. In 1992, the industry also sold 15 mwh of surplus electricity from bagasse to the utility.

Solar power is increasingly used as other fuels become less economical and environmentally benign. The number of installations increased from 545 in 1979 to 2,857 in 1989. Solar water heaters are very popular in Barbados and their collectors and tanks can be seen reclining on many a Bajan roof. Three local firms presently manufacture these systems for both the domestic and a limited export market. Solar crop drying, solar distillation and solar air conditioning are other examples of solar energy utilization on the island.

Oil wells in Barbados range in depth from 2700 feet to over 8000 feet

Biogas, also derived from organic material such as pig faeces, is not used on a large scale in Barbados. Biogas digesters are located at a few farms such as Hoad's Dairy Farm at Morgan Lewis and Barnwell Farm at Rock Hall, St Thomas. These farms produce enough biogas to provide for their domestic and agricultural energy use.

Wind energy was used heavily into the 1930s for grinding cane and pumping water to the surface, especially near the coast. The last windmill for grinding cane closed in 1947. With the change to oil-generated electricity, there was a gradual demise of both Barbados' windmills and their newer cousins, the fanmills, hastened by Hurricane Janet in 1955. However, during the period 1986-90 the harnessing of wind energy was conducted on an experimental basis by a UK aid programme and an enterprising factory. Production levels peaked at 300,000 kwh in 1988, after which the experiment was discontinued because of high costs.

There are a number of sites that would be suitable for the establishment of wind farms. According to a 1988 study, the electricity system could accommodate 20mw of wind farms by the end of the century.

Barbados' famous Banks Beer

Hot, sunny days and cool nights, tempered by the northeast tradewinds and the occasional refreshing shower. That's Barbados.

A myriad of colours, aromas, tastes, events, experiences and people that produces a cultural experience that's Bajan.

One gem - treasured by Barbados for its taste - is Banks Beer, whose fame has spread far beyond Barbados. It has garnered international distinctions in prestigious world brewing competitions. Monde Selection of Brussels, in Amsterdam, Rome, Paris and Brewex of London are just a few. For English beer-drinkers, at least, Banks is available - as Bajan Beer - at Sainsburys and Tescos supermarkets in the UK.

Despite its international stature, Banks Beer is very much at home in Barbados. Indeed, its fortunes are intricately bound to those of the Barbadians.

Back in 1959, it was decided that a brewery would be established in Barbados. Unlike most ventures of the day, or indeed today, it was decided that its shareholders would comprise 'Joe Public' - for BDS$100 any member of the community could buy a stake in the enterprise. The objective was to ensure widespread ownership that would in turn lead to mass consumption. Primarily, those to whom the venture was specifically entrusted were Barbados' shopkeepers. It was they who would sell the product, and their commitment through personal ownership of shares was a necessity. When the share issue was published on 29 August 1959, it had taken a mere seven days to raise just over BDS$2 million in share capital, far

in excess of the amount required. On 7 September 1961, Banks (Barbados) Breweries Limited opened its doors.

To date, many individuals and groups have benefited from Banks Beer through its commitment to the community. In particular, the brewery has pledged its support to several charities including The Challenor School and The Thelma Vaughan Memorial Home. Two days a week, Banks hosts brewery tours and the proceeds are given to charity.

In an hour-long tour visitors are introduced to the brewery through a 12-minute video presentation. Thereafter, a guide takes them to the old brew-house which ceased operation in 1993. Its towering copper kettles are a nostalgic link with the past. The new computerised brew-house with its stainless steel kettles, is the next stop; and finally the outdoor cellars and bottling hall completes the tour. Visitors are taken to the Rachel Pringle Bar to sample the beverages produced at the plant.

The range of products include Banks Beer, Tiger Malt, a health food drink; Bajan Light, a sports drink, the first light beer brewed in the Caribbean; Stallion Stout, a vitalising brew; and Twist, a recent addition to the brews. Ting, a grapefruit-flavoured drink and world famous Guinness Stout, are also brewed under license at Banks Breweries.

A new Xxtra strong brew lager beer was launched in July 1996. Naturally brewed with pure water, barley malt and the finest of imported hops, the golden-coloured Xxtra is slow-brewed for flavour and has an alcohol volume of seven per cent.

For years Banks' name has been associated

with the Crop-Over festival, a two-month celebration of the island's cultural heritage. Calypsonians have competed for top honours in the Banks Pic-o-de-Crop calypso competitions, while Kadooment bands annually receive the support of the brewery.

Banks, in association with its sister company Barbados Bottling Company, have entered into a new partnership with the National Cultural Foundation to host some of the premiere events on the Crop-Over calendar.

These include the Plus/Coca Cola Youth Fest, the Banks/Coca Cola Bridgetown Market and the Banks/Coca Cola Grand Kadooment. Banks and Coca-Cola are also refreshingly present at the calypso tents, where the calypsonians show-off their talents.

There is hardly a sporting discipline in Barbados that has not had the support of Banks Beer. Generations of Barbadian sportsmen and sportswomen have benefited from Banks' involvement and support.

The most outstanding sportsmen with whom the brewery has been associated includes; Sir Garfield Sobers, the greatest all-round cricketer the world has seen; Wes Hall, West Indies fast bowler, who went on to become the brewery's human resources and public relations manager, in the late 1970s.

Mr Universe 1965, Barbadian Earl Maynard

has endorsed Banks' products, as have cricketers Charlie Griffith, Everton Weekes, now Sir Everton, and current International Cricket Council President, Sir Clyde Walcott. Famous West Indies fast bowler Malcolm Marshall, team coach for the 1997 Australia Tour was also on the brewery's staff in his earlier years.

Today's crop of sportspersons who have enjoyed Banks' support include World Three-Move-Restriction and World Go-As-You-Please checkers champion, Ronald 'Suki' King. The sprinter Obadele Thompson, in preparation for the 1996 Atlanta Games, had his training and travelling facilitated by a BDS$40,000 grant.

Sportspersons of national repute are also on the brewery's staff. These include the Caribbean's top riflewoman, Cherly Best and Carmichael Bryan, one of the island's top bodybuilders as well as several young cricketers.

Banks (Barbados) Breweries Limited is particularly proud of its links with the Barbadian community. It welcomes Barbadians and visitors alike to tour the brewery and discover what it takes to produce a world famous beer, through the efforts of a team of brewing specialists, using state-of-the-art technology.

Crop-Over premier events such as the Monarch Calypso Competition benefit from Banks new partnership with the National Cultural Foundation

259

Barbados Exports

Food. The largest quantities of agricultural produce are shipped to Canada, US, and UK markets as well as to other European countries. Agricultural trading companies and the Barbados Agricultural Development & Marketing Corporation (BADMC) are responsible for the bulk of these exports. Live poultry such as broilers are steadily exported within CariCom and the OECS, while exports of fresh chicken parts to OECS countries are showing a slight increase. Snacks and biscuits are a growing market within the region, especially in Guyana and Jamaica.

Beverages. The export success of alcoholic and brewed beverages to the Canadian and UK markets is well known, but exports of drink concentrates have also grown steadily over the last year. These products are well-received in the OECS, Trinidad, Jamaica and Guyana.

Vegetable Oils, Fats & Margarines. The market seems especially good for margarine products in Guyana, but sizeable quantities are also going to other CariCom countries as well.

Chemicals, Paints, Plastics, Medicinal & Pharmaceutical Products. After seeing plastic products being exported primarily to OECS countries for some time, Barbados is now starting to see some exports to the US. In 1995 paint exports to Jamaica alone were up 65 percent. Sizeable shipments are regularly made to Guyana. Paints, chemical, pharmaceutical and other products continue to be exported in steady quantities to other CariCom countries.

Paper Products. A respectable volume of labelling materials, paper products, printed materials are exported from Barbados each month. Trinidad, Jamaica and Guyana appear to be good markets for packaging materials, while printed paper products go most often to OECS countries.

Manufactured Articles. Sanitary napkins and disposable diapers are being exported to Trinidad, Jamaica, Guyana and to the OECS. Because garments are not encouraged under any current preferential trade agreement, trading partners are typically expected to pay duties on Barbadian garments. However, there is an opportunity to export garments under the LOME agreement, but qualifying garments should be manufactured from yarn, or must be manufactured using materials originating from any of the European countries. The export of metal cans to Jamaica and Trinidad continues to put in a strong performance.

Printing Industry

THE printing industry in Barbados is evolving to keep pace with developments in a rapidly changing graphic environment. This quiet revolution has brought significant changes to the ways in which Barbadians create, reproduce and disseminate ideas. At the heart of this revolution is the advent of electronic prepress. While traditional printing methods are still employed, digital technology is primarily today's standard.

The printing process is advancing with every new innovation in electronic prepress. As graphic designers and printers transfer from old to new technologies, new developments challenge and influence the decisions today's printer makes in terms of investment and retooling.

As Barbados' printing firms seek and obtain substantial printing contracts abroad, the continuous change in today's environment demands that local printing establishments keep pace with developments in other countries if they are to realise a competitive advantage in quality, cost and time.

Extract: Business Catalyst '95

Informations Services

THE information services sector in Barbados now ranges from large multi-serviced facilities to small specialised operations.

The sector has one of the largest data processing facilities in the world in the American Airlines affiliate, Caribbean Data Services (CDS), employing over 1,000 workers processing airline ticket data, health claims and myriad payroll related functions.

Modern Barbados: INVESTMENT

United Nations praise

IN AN authoritative report which ranks Barbados ahead of Britain in gender-related development, the island tops a list of Caribbean countries receiving high praise from the United Nations for putting people at the centre of economic development.

For the fourth year running, the United Nations Development Programme (UNDP) has given Barbados the highest rating among developing countries for quality of life.

The yardstick used is the Human Development Index (HDI), first introduced in the 1970s and applied consistently over the last five years by the UNDP as an alternative to traditional per capita Gross Domestic Product (GDP) for measuring a country's wealth.

HDI is a broader measurement; it reflects not only income but takes into account such factors as the level of literacy, infant mortality rates, and citizens' access to health care and education in deciding how 'developed' a country is. Using the HDI, the UNDP's 1995 Human Development Report ranks Barbados 25th overall among 174 countries belonging to the UN system. The Bahamas, ranked 26th, was next, followed by Belize on 29.

Launching the report in Bridgetown, Fernando Zumbado, Director of UNDP's Regional Bureau for Latin America and the Caribbean, said the annual series of reports sought *"to lend a new perspective to development - even to redefine development."*

"The concept of human development," he said, *"places people - rather than income or industry - at the centre of development."*

Barbados offers sun, sand and sea and more incentives for investors than almost any other nation

Barbados Investment and Development Corporation

Barbados is an independent English-speaking Commonwealth country with a modern economy. This most easterly of the Caribbean islands is just over three hours by plane from Miami, approximately four-and-a-half hours from New York and eight hours from London. The 166 square mile island, slightly smaller than Singapore, is home to a population of over 264,000.

Continuing political stability and the rule of law are standard to Barbados. Noted also for its economic stability and commitment to free enterprise, Barbados is seeking to attract skill-intensive enterprises and international business companies in order to accelerate the rate of economic growth.

Its judicial, administrative and political systems are closely modelled on the British system of government. Fiscally, however, the Barbados dollar is tied to the US dollar.

The island has a well-developed infrastructure with reliable electricity; natural gas and water distribution systems; modern airport and seaport facilities and outstanding international telecommunications. In addition to its 'first world' infrastructure, Barbados also offers:

- Highly productive workforce: low rate of absenteeism and turnover
- Literacy rate of over 98 percent
- High standard of health care
- A welcoming environment for foreign investment
- A government policy which is oriented towards the facilitation of private sector business initiatives.

Ideal for Manufacturing and Information Processing

Barbados is an ideal location for reducing your manufacturing or information processing costs, increasing your profits and benefiting from duty-free exports to major international markets.

Among the advantages of establishing a manufacturing or information processing facility in Barbados are:

- Ten year tax holiday for approved export-oriented manufacturing projects
- Exemption from import duties on production machinery, equipment, spare parts and raw materials
- Full repatriation of capital, profits and dividends
- Income tax concessions to employees of offshore companies
- Low-cost, subsidized factory space available within ten fully

Political stability and rule of law are standard to Barbados

Cuba and Barbados sign deals

Cuba and Barbados have signed an investment promotion and protection agreement, the first of its kind between the communist-ruled island and another Caribbean state.

The agreement was signed by visiting Barbadian Trade Minister Philip Goddard and Cuban Foreign Investment Minister Ibrahim Ferradez. Goddard also signed an agreement with Cuba's Foreign Ministry abolishing the need for entry visas for citizens of each country making short visits.

First class hotels and year round leisure and sports facilities make Barbados a number one choice for investors

serviced industrial parks
- Cash grants for worker training
- Low corporate tax rates of 2.5 percent maximum to 1 percent minimum for information processing companies
- Duty free access to the US, Canada, the European Union, Venezuela, and the CariCom Common Market for qualifying products
- Low operating costs: savings of 40 percent or more
- Economic, political and social stability and integrity
- Literate, skilled, trainable and productive workforce
- Official welcome from a government committed to private enterprise
- Cooperative and efficient customs service
- Free consulting services of the Barbados Investment and Development Corporation

A World Class International Business Centre

In the relatively short period of 15 years, Barbados has established itself as a major international financial centre.

All of the leading international accounting firms are well represented on the island and provide a full range of accounting and management consulting services for international clients.

In addition to a number of international commercial banks which provide a complete range of commercial and personal banking services, Barbados is home to over 34 offshore banks with total assets of US$2.4 billion.

Barbados introduced its Exempt Insurance Act in 1983 and in 13 years the island has become one of the top five domiciles for captive insurance activities with over 313 registered captives.

Barbados is the only international business centre which offers all of the following in a single location:
- Exempt Insurance Companies
- Offshore Banks
- International Trusts
- International Business Companies
- Societies with restricted liability
- Foreign Sales Corporations
- Ships Registration
- Double taxation treaties with seven countries, including the US, Canada and the UK

- Tax holidays and other incentives for export manufacturing and information processing
- Duty-free concessions on import of equipment and raw materials
- Exemption from exchange control
- No withholding taxes on dividends, interest and management fees and royalties paid
- No capital gains taxes
- Exemption from taxes on transfers of shares and other assets
- Exemption from import duties on equipment and raw materials

Barbados Investment and Development Corporation

The Barbados Investment and Development Corporation (BIDC) is the industrial development agency of the Barbados government. It has special responsibility for export promotion and for promoting and facilitating the establishment or expansion of local and foreign business enterprises in Barbados.

The BIDC administers the government's incentive programme for industry and provides a variety of free advisory services to companies looking to establish business entities on the island especially in the areas of information processing, manufacturing, international business and financial services.

Most hotels provide business services

Services of the Corporation

The BIDC provides a wide range of services to industrialists such as:
- Information on the social, political and economic life of the island.
- Advice on the Fiscal Incentives Legislation and assistance in preparing applications for benefits under the legislation.
- Technical advice on factory location.
- Provision of factory space on a rent or lease/purchase basis.
- Pre-feasibility studies for local companies only.
- Assistance in coordinating joint venture efforts between local and overseas interests.
- Liaison between investor and appropriate government department.
- Consultation to the investor in his initial negotiations with private sector organisations.
- Assistance in the recruitment and training of staff.
- Assistance with the work permit application process.

There are four 18-hole golf courses in Barbados

CIBC's prestigious new headquarters in Barbados reflect the bank's continued success in the region

CIBC in the Caribbean

IN 1920 the Westindies was selected by the then Canadian Bank of Commerce, as the first location for the establishment of new branches overseas.

The Assistant General Manager, Mr V H F Jones, had visited the Westindies in 1919, and, as a result of his recommendations to the Board of Directors, the decision was taken to establish branches in Havana, Cuba; Kingston, Jamaica and Bridgetown, Barbados. The first branch in Barbados was opened on 20 December 1920. Following a merger between the Canadian Bank of Commerce and the Imperial Bank of Commerce, the bank became a branch of the Canadian Imperial Bank of Commerce (CIBC), in June 1961.

In 1963, CIBC began an expansion programme in Barbados, opening branches at Speightstown, Worthing, Rock Dundo, Fontabelle, Marhill Street and Sheraton Plaza. Today, CIBC operates an extensive branch network in Barbados, Antigua and Barbuda, St Lucia and St Vincent and the Grenadines, offering a full range of banking services.

CIBC was one of the first banks to install an automatic teller machine in 1991, which allowed customers access to their accounts 24-hours a day, 365-days a year.

On 1 November 1993, CIBC embarked on a major re-organisation of its operations, including the formation of CIBC West Indies Holdings Limited, which now owns all operations previously held by CIBC in Barbados and the Eastern Caribbean.

CIBC West Indies Holdings recently announced record after tax profits of BDS$24 million for the first half year ending 30 April 1996, up from BDS$8.8 million for the corresponding six month period the previous year.

The company also achieved a return on shareholders' equity of 15.26 percent for the first half of 1996, up from 9.57 percent for the corresponding period in 1995.

Net income before taxes for the first half of 1996 was $35.8 million, and total assets stood at $3.0 billion.

The results for the first half of 1996 reflect the inclusion of four months income from CIBC's new Bahamas subsidiary - CIBC Bahamas Ltd, acquired in January 1996. With this acquisition, CIBC's income streams are now spread between Barbados, Jamaica, the Bahamas, St Vincent and the Grenadines, St Lucia, Antigua and Barbuda and Trinidad and Tobago.

Some of the successful information processing companies

BARBADOS provides an attractive environment for a variety of foreign-owned or joint venture information processing activities. There are also a number of locally-owned subcontractors or service bureaux which provide information processing services for various international clients.

Among the companies with established facilities in Barbados are the following:

COMPANY	COUNTRY OF ORIGIN	PRODUCTS
Confederation Client Services	Canada	Insurance Claims Processing
Semper Holdings	Canada	Direct Main Services
Softkey Products International	Canada	Software Publishing
Scandata Processing	Canada	Data Entry
Cirrus Logic	US	Purchasing & Billing Functions
Caribbean Data Services	US	Airline Ticketing, Insurance
Offshore Keyboarding	US	Data Entry, Type Setting
NDL International Barbados	US	Processing Warranty Cards
Donnelley Caribbean Graphics	US	Pre-Press Operations & Print
International Direct Marketing	Canada	Direct Mail Services
Keydata Service Bureau	Barbados	Data Entry
Secretarial Services	Barbados	Data Entry & Transcription
Bayer Chemical	Germany	Aerosal Products
BEL-Tronics	Canada	Satellite Receiver Assembly
Bondhus Corp	US	Hex Tools
Crompton Modutec Barbados	UK	Panel Meters
Clifford Electronics	US/Barbados	Semi-Conductors
Galt Controls	US	Computers & Timing Devices
Tansitor Barbados	UK	Tantalum Capacitors
International Resistive Co	UK	Wire-Wound Resistors
C T Gamble Industries	USA	Wire-Wound Resistors
Haas Products	Germany	Hairsprings
Imperial Optical Barbados	Canada/Barbados	Spectacles
Tropical Battery Co	Trinidad	Lead Acid Batteries
C'bean Electronics Mfg	US	Temperature Sensors
Kaufel Caribbean	Canada	Small Transformers
I C C Security Systems	Canada	Electronic Security Safes
Atlantic Manufacturing	US	Ladies Lingerie
Vitafoam International	UK	Mattresses & Polyurethane
Caribbean Containers	France	Metal Cans
BRC West Indies	UK/Barbados	Roof Cladding & Steel Mesh

Typical success stories

NDL International Ltd.

IN 1979, National Demographics & Lifestyles of Denver, Colorado, a wholly-owned subsidiary of R L Polk & Company of Detroit, began data entry on the island with only four operators. Today, this international firm has over 250 employees in Barbados.

Company Vice President, Peter Kelly, cites the stability of the country as a major positive factor. "It's unique", Kelly said. "It has an extremely well-educated population leaving school with limited job opportunities and we have been able to recruit a very productive workforce. Our Barbadian workers are more productive, better educated and have a stronger work ethic. The result is a better job with fewer errors at half the cost. In the wake of new technology in data entry, such as imaging and optical disks, NDL has been successfully retraining its workforce", Kelly said.

"We're in Barbados as much for the management skills as for the lower labour costs", Kelly noted. He said there are no US personnel on hand at the Barbados facility.

Caribbean Data Services

THE largest data entry facility in Barbados is American Airlines, Caribbean Data Services (CDS). In 1983, American, a major carrier to Barbados, moved its data entry operations from Tulsa, Oklahoma, to the island. Research had indicated that the airline could reduce its data entry costs by 40 percent and this proved correct with savings of several million dollars during the first two years. However, to management's surprise, it also found productivity and quality to be superior to that of the mainland location.

After beginning with a 150-employee operation, CDS has now increased its payroll to over 1,100. In addition to work for the airline itself, CDS has built a substantial secondary business filling outside contracts. This now accounts for one-third of its work and the Barbados facility has become a major profit centre for its parent company, AMR Corporation.

Donnelley Caribbean Graphics

IN 1987, Donnelley Caribbean Graphics began operations in Barbados providing pre-press services for its parent company, R R Donnelley & Sons, the largest printer in north America.

Donnelley began operations with a staff of 30 and currently employs 135 persons after expanding into a new 31,000 sq ft facility in 1992. Donnelley has been very satisfied with the calibre of its work-force and has invested significantly in the development of its efficient, highly skilled employees.

Donnelley's Barbados facility has built a sound reputation for quality, fast turnaround and competitive pricing. Senior Donnelley executives attribute their success in Barbados to the dedication of the Barbadian worker, the high quality infrastructure and the incentives provided by the government of Barbados.

Softkey Software Products International B V

SOFTKEY, a wholly-owned subsidiary of Soft-Key International Inc, has been operating a software development facility in Barbados since early 1991 and currently employs nine Barbadian professionals.

This company develops and markets low cost software, which offers similar capabilities to the more expensive products, to end users in the US and Canada through budget chains such as Wal-mart.

Michael Nobrega, one of SoftKey's Canadian directors states that although Barbados quality of education was one of the factors which influenced their decision to locate on the island, they were pleasantly surprised by the outstanding talent which SoftKey has been able to recruit in Barbados.

Confederation Client Services

THIS wholly-owned subsidiary of Confederation Life Insurance Company of Canada, started operations in Barbados in January 1991 and currently employs over 100 people processing dental and health insurance claims for its parent company.

The management of Confederation Life reports that Barbados was chosen after a worldwide search for the most efficient and cost effective location in which to process its health claims and the operation in Barbados has been an outstanding success .

Confed's Barbados operation is an on-line process using terminals connected through IBM controllers to a 567Kb line which communicates with Teleglobe in Canada either through a terrestrial circuit or by satellite. Teleglobe then transmits the information into Confed's main computer.

The Information Services Industry in Barbados

THE Information Services Industry in Barbados comprises a variety of companies ranging from a large American-owned facility employing over 1000 people to a small highly sophisticated Canadian software development company.

There are several other foreign-owned enterprises and a diverse group of locally-owned service bureau taking advantage of the skilled workforce, low operating costs, and tax benefits associated with doing business in Barbados.

Port St Charles

Port St Charles is an exclusive private luxury residential Marina situated on the renowned west coast of Barbados where favourable winds and gentle waters make for ideal yachting conditions. The project started in January 1996 and will be completed in five phases over five years.

This exclusive community will be housed within waterfront town houses and condominiums, each with its own berth. A number of premium units are available with beach and waterfront aspects.

Planners have incorporated a number of sophisticated amenities exclusively for the pleasure and convenience of residents. Residence includes membership in the Marina's Yacht Club, which is located on a man-made island and is connected to the beach by a 70 metre bridge with berths capable of accommodating mega yachts.

The eight-acre lagoon has a white sand bottom and is designed to have a daily circulation of six million gallons of offshore water, to ensure the crystal clear water characteristic of the Caribbean.

Recreational facilities include restaurants, bars, watersports, tennis and squash courts, swimming pools and a spa. This exclusive community will be fully enclosed to guarantee privacy and security. Transport to and from the community facilities and to beaches will be provided by a number of complimentary water taxis on constant call.

Each residence is designed by Ian Morrison who is renowned for his distinctive style of timeless island elegance which is apparent on the numerous west coast luxury villas and hotels which he has already designed.

The Port St Charles and their owners have been granted duty free concessions for their yachts, along with all equipment as well as a choice of villa furnishings. Included in each unit will be a refrigerator, cook top, oven, dishwasher, microwave oven and washer/dryer. Bedrooms will be air conditioned and will also have ceiling fans. Normally, all non-residents pay a 10 percent property transfer tax upon purchasing property in Barbados however, the government has waived this tax for residents of Port St Charles.

Port St Charles will become one of the most rewarding investments in the Caribbean

Port St Charles offers a very special retreat where you will experience the pleasures of a luxurious waterfront home, with your yacht just a few steps from your door, as well as the joys of a gracious tropical lifestyle with all the comforts to which you are accustomed.

Innovatively and environmentally planned and designed, Port St Charles will become one of your most rewarding investments and a source of pleasure for years to come.

The project consists of five phases with prices ranging from US$360,000 to US$1.5 million. There is also the potential for magnificent custom built private villas in any phase of the development.

Phase 1 will consist of 28 units and will have one, two and three-bedroom condos which are serviced by elevators and offer single level dwelling. There are also triple level two and three-bedroom townhouses with roof top sun decks complete with outdoor shower. There will also be an option of having a plunge-pool in each townhouse.

Phase 2 will have eight luxury beach front townhouses and several two and three-bedroom condos, along with the breakwater facilities - yacht club with restaurants and bar, swimming pool with areas for sunning and relaxing, a spa, mega berths and heliport, as well as an area to house Customs and Immigration staff.

Phase 3 will be the island - 12 townhouses plus the Sunset Bar. The large administration building is planned in this phase and will consist of reception, sales office, executive offices, complete state-of-the-art gym, mini mart and a few assorted shops. There will also be two flood-lit tennis courts situated in the southeast corner of the site.

Phase 4 will be the townhouses to the south side of the development.

Phase 5 will be further luxury beach/waterfront villas.

Aerial view of Port St Charles location

Yacht facilities can accommodate vessels of up to 60 feet in length and ten foot draft within the lagoon and the breakwater berths will accommodate vessels of up to 150 feet in length.

Your own berth will be directly in front of, or a few steps away from, your townhouse/condo. A 24-hour security service will give added peace-of-mind.

Water taxis are provided to take residents to the lagoon pool, yacht club or beaches and in some cases even into nearby picturesque Speightstown. Two championship golf courses are located just 15 minutes away from the project.

Each one-bedroom unit will have an allotted parking space and each two and three bedroom units will have two parking spaces.

An optional rental and/or management service can be arranged for your home.

The developers are Barbadians who have been involved in construction across the entire Caribbean for over 30 years and have excellent records for quality and reliability.

Returning Nationals

Many Barbadians living overseas look forward to the day when they can return to Barbados to resettle. The process of relocating and resettling can be stressful and requires careful planning if things are to go smoothly.

In order to facilitate the easy resettlement of returning nationals the government has produced a Charter for Returning and Overseas Nationals, which offers a number of generous concessions to returning Barbadians. The objectives of the charter are:

(a) to create the appropriate conditions which would facilitate returning nationals in re-integrating into the society as easily as possible.

(b) to increase the potential human and other resources available to the country, directly through the returning nationals themselves and indirectly through the creation of a more conducive environment for services and investment by nationals remaining abroad.

Facilitation Unit

To achieve the objectives of the charter the Facilitation Unit established for returning nationals in the Ministry of Foreign Affairs:

(a) offers an attractive package of concessions to returnng nationals designed to facilitate their easy re-integration into society;

(b) provides comprehensive and accurate information to returning nationals at both overseas and local locations;

(c) liaises with the relevant agencies, governmental and private sector, on matters relating to returning nationals;

(d) develops programmes of investment opportunities aimed specifically at Barbadians living overseas, and widening local investment opportunities available to returned nationals as well as overseas Barbadians;

(e) maintains a skills bank of overseas and returning nationals both in Barbados and at overseas missions;

(f) develops and maintains a technical assistance programme drawing on the skills of appropriately qualified Barbadians abroad;

(g) maintains contact with Barbadian organisations abroad through the diplomatic and consular missions, with a view to enlisting the organisations support and assistance with various special projects;

(h) liaises with organisations of returned nationals on local projects in which they are or can be involved.

Many Barbadians living overseas can now return and enjoy the new concessions on personal effects and motor vehicles

Definition of a Returning National

A Returning National is:

1. A Barbadian citizen by birth, descent, registration or naturalisation who is returning to Barbados to resettle after a period of ten years abroad.

2. An adult Barbadian/citizen by descent who has never lived in Barbados.

3. An alien spouse of a Barbadian national accompanying him/her to Barbados.

Concessions

Household and personal effects, whether used or new, adequate to furnish a family residence, will be allowed in free of all duties and taxes.

Two motor vehicles per family, but not more than one per person, whether used or new, will be allowed in free of all taxes and duties. The vehicles may not be disposed of under three years.

Tools of trade, whether used or new, will be admitted free of all taxes and duties. One bicycle per person will be allowed in free of all taxes and duties.

Exceptions

The Mininster of Finance will have discretionary powers to waive taxes and duties on personal and household effects, including a motor vehicle, of nationals returning to Barbados after a period of less than ten years.

In exercising this power, the Minister of Finance will take into consideration the special circumstances of the national and/or the contribution the national can make to the development of Barbados.

Limitation

The above concessions will be granted to a returning national only once. To establish your eligibility as a returning national, as defined in the charter, you are required to submit to the Customs Department on clearing your personal and household effects.

• your passport

• such documentary evidence as may substantiate your permanent residence outside Barbados for ten years at least. Short visits to Barbados for vacations, will not affect your eligibility.

Community centre mural at Bathsheba

Importation of Animals

Under the Animals (Disease and Importation) Act and the Animals (Diseases and Importation Control) Regulations, 1961, it is necessary to apply to the Veterinary Services, Ministry of Agriculture and Rural Development, for a permit to import any animal, animal product, bird or meat into Barbados. This applies also to any trans-shipment through Barbados.

The importation of animals and meat is only allowed from certain countries specified in the schedules listed in the regulations.

Import applications must be made at the Veterinary Services Office, The Pine, East-West North-South Cross Roads, St Michael, Barbados.

Dogs and cats are permitted entry into Barbados only from these rabies-free countries: UK; Antigua; St Kitts; Ireland; St Lucia; Jamaica and St Vincent.

Should you wish to bring a dog or cat into Barbados from any other country, animals must first undergo six months quarantine in Britain, during which time an import permit may be applied for to import such animal from Britain.

Horses are allowed in under permit control. Other species may be allowed in from time to time if specific permit requirements are met. Some species (especially birds) are allowed in under very stringent controls for circuses/zoos after a specified period of quarantine in a facility controlled by the veterinary authority of the exporting country.

Other important information

Because in some countries and some locations there are significant concentrations of Barbadians, special Returning Nationals Information Desks have been set up in the following Missions: **UK** - Barbados High Commission (London); **Canada** - Barbados Consulate General (Toronto); **United States** - Barbados Embassy (Washington) or Barbados Consulate General (New York) or Barbados Consulate General (Miami).

In each of these missions an officer is designated to assist returning nationals. You are invited to contact your nearest mission and seek clarification on any aspect of your return to Barbados.

In a country where there is no diplomatic or consular mission, information can be sought directly from the Facilitations Unit for Returning Nationals in Bridgetown. Similarly if you are in Barbados on a visit prior to resettlement, you are encouraged to visit the Facilitation Unit.

LA BARBADE - UNE REALITE QUI DEPASSE L'IMAGINATION

Si vous n'êtes pas encore allé à La Barbade les renseignements suivants vous seront très utiles. Si c'est à La Barbade que vous lisez ce livre, peut-être avez vous déjà fait l'expérience de certains des points évoqués. Quoi qu'il en soit, nous espérons que cette introduction vous paraîtra, de quelque manière, utile et intéressante.

Dès votre première journée sur l'île vous sentirez une différence. Alors que vous vous détendez dans la merveilleuse chaleur du soleil et que vous vous sentez chez vous dans notre style de vie, votre curiosité sera stimulée par la convivialité de ce qui vous entoure. Les secrets de l'île vous sollicitent. Quelles sont ces fleurs aux couleurs vives et éclatantes, qui répandent dans l'air un parfum léger?

Et que fait là ce moulin à vent? Munissez-vous d'une carte et demandez autour de vous. Vous êtes en route pour un voyage de découverte, une fascinante aventure que seule La Barbade peut vous offrir.

Bénéficiant du climat exotique antillais, La Barbade a fleuri comme une fleur originale dans le jardin des îles Caraïbes. Sa beauté ne lui vient pas seulement de sa situation spéciale, mais aussi de l'hospitalité détendue de ses habitants, un peuple intelligent et fier, qui partagent avec enthousiasme leur île avec des visiteurs venus du monde entier.

Les brises marines rafraîchissantes aident à chasser le stress et les soucis de la vie quotidienne. La Barbade éveille votre attention par son originalité frappante: deux rivages distincts et contrastés, distants de quelques kilomètres seulement: l'une des côtes est déchiquetée, spectaculaire, constituant un rempart résistant aux assauts tumultueux de l'Atlantique, tandis que la calme et tranquille Mer des Caraïbes baigne la côte ouest.

Les racines culturelles de La Barbade se sont développées sur plus de trois cents ans, associant l'héritage colonial britannique à l'impact de l'esclavage et des traditions africaines qui survivent. Après l'Emancipation, la puissance des religions européennes a modelé une société saine et aimable, dont le niveau élevé d'éducation est reconnu. Le gouvernement démocratique, assurant la stabilité politique, et un climat très agréable, sont des éléments qui ont contribué à créer un peuple sûr de lui, cultivé, qui apprécie la joie de vivre sur son île autant que vous l'apprécierez vous-même.

Même la langue anglaise, qui est universellement utilisée ici, présente une tonalité particulière. Pour ceux qui ne parlent pas anglais, il existe dans l'île des guides parlant allemand, espagnol, français et italien. La présente introduction a pour but de vous aider à préparer votre grande escapade à La Barbade en vous familiarisant avec cette île très spéciale des Caraïbes, à la recherche d'une réalité qui dépasse votre imagination.

L'indispensable

VÊTEMENTS. Le climat de l'île, chaud et ensoleillé tout au long de l'année, doit guider votre choix de vêtements. Une "élégance sportive" est la règle vestimentaire généralement admise dans la plupart des hôtels et restaurants pour le dîner. Ce qui signifie pour les hommes pantalons longs et chemise à manches courtes ou longues (pas de T-shirts) et chaussures fermées (pas de baskets). Pour les femmes, les shorts ou les ensembles shorts et tailleur ne sont habituellement pas acceptés. Si vous avez l'intention d'aller à la plage, n'oubliez pas votre

BARBADOS BIETET IHNEN MEHR, ALS SIE SICH VORSTELLEN KÖNNEN

Falls Sie noch nie in Barbados waren, werden Sie die folgenden Informationen hilfreich finden. Sofern Sie diesen Reiseführer während Ihres Aufenthalts in Barbados lesen, haben Sie vielleicht hinsichtlich einiger der hier angesprochenen Themen schon Ihre eigenen Erfahrungen gemacht. In jedem Fall hoffen wir, daß Sie diese Einführung hilfreich und interessant finden.

Schon am ersten Tag Ihres Aufenthalts wird Ihnen die Besonderheit dieser Insel auffallen. Während Sie sich in der herrlich warmen Sonne entspannen und sich sofort wie zu Hause fühlen, wird Ihre Neugier durch die freundliche Umgebung angeregt. Die Geheimnisse der Insel locken Sie an. Was sind das für leuchtend bunte Blumen, die der Luft einen leichten Duft verleihen?

Und was macht diese Windmühle hier? Besorgen Sie sich eine Landkarte und hören Sie sich um. Sie befinden sich auf dem Weg zu einer Entdeckungsreise - einem faszinierenden Abenteuer, das nur Barbados bieten kann. Barbados hat sich, umgeben vom exotischen westindischen Klima, zu einer einzigartigen Blüte im Garten der Karibischen Inseln entfaltet. Der Grund für die Schönheit der Insel ist nicht nur ihre hervorragende Lage, sondern auch die herzliche Gastfreundschaft der Inselbewohner, einem intelligenten und stolzen Volk, das seine Insel gerne mit Besuchern aus der ganzen Welt teilt.

Die erfrischende Meeresbrise trägt dazu bei, daß Sie den Streß und die Sorgen des täglichen Lebens hinter sich lassen. Die Insel Barbados verwöhnt Sie mit ihrer schillernden Vielfältigkeit: zwei eigenwillige und völlig gegensätzliche Küsten, die nur wenige Meilen voneinander entfernt sind - einerseits eine bizarre Steilküste, deren Ausläufer den donnernden Wellen des Atlantiks ausgesetzt sind - und das ruhige und sanfte Karibische Meer an der Westküste der Insel.

Die kulturellen Wurzeln von Barbados entwickelten sich über dreihundert Jahre hinweg, und verbinden britische Kolonialherrschaft mit dem Einfluß des Sklavenhandels und den überlebenden afrikanischen Traditionen. Die Macht der europäischen Religionen formte nach der Emanzipation der Sklaven eine gesunde und vornehme Gesellschaft, die für ihr hohes Bildungsniveau bekannt ist. Die politische Stabilität einer demokratischen Regierung und das äußert angenehme Klima haben unter anderem zu der Entwicklung eines selbstbewußten und kultivierten Volks beigetragen, das es genauso wie Sie genießt, Spaß auf seiner Insel zu haben.

Sogar die englische Sprache, die überall auf der Insel gesprochen wird, weist einen besonders sympathischen Akzent auf. Für diejenigen, die kein Englisch sprechen, gibt es Inselführer, die fließend Deutsch, Spanisch, Französisch und Italienisch sprechen. Diese Einführung soll Ihnen dabei helfen, sich auf das einzigartige Erlebnis, das Barbados Ihnen bieten wird, vorzubereiten, und möchte Sie mit dieser besonderen Karibischen Insel bekannt machen - einer Insel, die jenseits Ihrer Vorstellungskraft liegt.

Was Sie brauchen

KLEIDUNG: Da das Klima in Barbados das ganze Jahr über warm und sonnig ist, ist die weitgehend akzeptierte Bekleidung für Mahlzeiten

274

BARBADOS - PIU' DI QUANTO IMMAGINATE

Se non avete ancora visitato le Barbados, speriamo che le informazioni che seguono vi possano essere utili. Se per caso state leggendo questo libro mentre siete già sul posto è probabile che abbiate già verificato alcune delle informazioni fornite da questa guida, che ci auguriamo possa costituire un valido punto di riferimento.

Sin dal vostro primo giorno nell'isola vi sentirete in un'altra dimensione. Mentre vi state rilassando sotto il sole e cominciate ad apprezzare lo stile di vita locale la vostra curiosità verrà stimolata dalla cordialità dell'ambiente che vi circonda e dai segreti che quest'isola nasconde. Quei fiori vividi e splendenti dal profumo tanto delicato che fiori sono?

E che cosa ci fa lì quel mulino a vento? Procuratevi una mappa e chiedete in giro. State cominciando un viaggio di esplorazione, un'avventura affascinante che potete vivere solo a Barbados.

Nel caldo abbraccio del clima esotico delle Indie Occidentali, Barbados è sbocciata come un fiore eccezionale nel giardino delle Isole Caraibiche. La sua attrattiva non consiste soltanto nella particolare posizione geografica ma anche nella rilassata ospitalità dei suoi abitanti, un popolo intelligente e fiero che accoglie con gioia visitatori provenienti da ogni parte del mondo.

Le gradevoli brezze marine contribuiscono a spazzar via la tensione e le preoccupazioni della vita di ogni giorno. Barbados vi sta invitando e vi offre un contrasto eclatante: due coste completamente diverse e distanti solo pochi chilometri: da una parte la costa orientale spettacolarmente frastagliata, i cui faraglioni fronteggiano i marosi dell'Atlantico, e sul lato occidentale il Mar dei Caraibi, calmo e tranquillo.

La cultura di Barbados si è sviluppata nel corso di trecento anni e riunisce in sé il retaggio coloniale britannico, la schiavitj negra e le tradizioni africane sopravvissute. Dopo l'Emancipazione, l'influsso delle religioni europee ha contribuito alla formazione di una società civile ed equilibrata, ove le strutture scolastiche e l'istruzione ricoprono un ruolo importante. Grazie ad un governo democratico che garantisce la stabilità politica e ad un clima particolarmente felice la popolazione locale, colta e sicura di sé, sa godersi la propria isola, proprio come farete voi.

Persino la lingua inglese, qui universalmente parlata, ha una cadenza isolana piena di colore. Per chi non parla l'inglese, vi sono nell'isola guide di lingua tedesca, spagnola, francese e italiana.

Questa introduzione vuole esservi di aiuto nel preparare la vostra grande vacanza alle Barbados, facendovi conoscere questa isola veramente speciale dei Caraibi dove troverete tutto quanto immaginate, ed anche di più.

Quello di cui avete bisogno

VESTIARIO. Il vestiario deve essere adatto a un clima caldo ed assolato durante tutto l'anno. E' consigliabile adottare un abbigliamento "Casual-Elegante", che vi permetterà di entrare nella maggior parte degli alberghi e dei ristoranti per il pranzo, e che per gli uomini consiste semplicemente in calzoni lunghi, camicia a manica corta o lunga (niente T-shirt) e scarpe chiuse (purché non di tela). Le donne dovrebbero invece evitare shorts o abiti corti. Se avete in programma la spiaggia, non dimenticate costume da bagno, occhiali da sole, lozione abbronzante a protezione UV, cappello e calzature

BARBADOS - MÁS DE LO QUE PUEDA IMAGINARSE

Si todavía no ha visitado Barbados, la información que sigue a continuación le será muy beneficiosa. Si por casualidad estuviera usted leyendo este libro en Barbados, puede que ya haya experimentado o se haya enfrentado con algunos de los puntos que se tratan en el mismo. Esperamos que esta introducción le resulte valiosa y de gran ayuda.

Desde el primer día de su estancia en la isla notará la diferencia. Mientras se relaja al maravilloso calor del sol y se siente como en casa con nuestro estilo de vida, su curiosidad se verá estimulada por el ambiente amistoso que le rodea. Los secretos de la isla le atraerán. ¿Cuales son las flores de brillantes y vívidos colores cuyo aroma perfuma delicadamente el aire?

¿Y qué hace ahí un molino de viento? Agarre un mapa y pregunte. Se encuentra en camino para realizar un viaje de descubrimientos: una fascinante aventura que sólo Barbados le puede proporcionar.

En el seno del exótico clima de las Antillas, Barbados ha prosperado hasta convertirse en una flor extraordinaria que ocupa su lugar en el jardín de las Islas del Caribe. Su belleza no sólo reside en su ubicación especial, sino también en la hospitalidad relajada de las gentes de Barbados: gentes inteligentes y orgullosas que comparten con alegría su isla con visitantes procedentes de todo el mundo.

La refrescante brisa marina ayuda a aliviar el estrés y olvidarse de las preocupaciones características de la vida cotidiana. Barbados atrae con una diferencia relumbrante: dos costas distintivas y en amplio contraste, separadas por tan sólo unas millas. La costa oriental, escarpada de manera dramática, cuyas murallas se tensan ante las ensordecedoras olas del Atlántico; y el suave y calmo Mar Caribe de la costa occidental.

Las raíces culturales de Barbados se desarrollaron a lo largo de trescientos años, combinando el patrimonio colonial británico con el impacto de la esclavitud y las tradiciones africanas todavía vivas. Tras su emancipación, el poder de las religiones occidentales modelaron una sociedad rica y distinguida, reconocida por su alto nivel de educación. Un Gobierno democrático que proporciona estabilidad política y un clima apropiado, constituyen dos elementos que han contribuido a que un pueblo cultivado y seguro de sí mismo disfrute de su isla tanto como lo hará usted.

Incluso el idioma inglés, hablado aquí de manera universal, presenta una colorida cadencia isleña. Para aquéllos que no hablen inglés hay guías isleños que dominan el alemán, el español, el francés y el italiano.

La presente introducción tiene como objetivo ayudarle a prepararse para su gran evasión a Barbados, familiarizándole con esta isla tan especial del Caribe donde encontrará más de lo que pueda imaginarse.

Lo que necesitará

ROPA. Al considerar las prendas requeridas en un clima cálido y soleado durante todo el año, el código mayormente aceptado en la mayoría de los hoteles y restaurantes a la hora de cenar es "*sport* elegante". Esto simplemente significa pantalones de vestir largos para los varones, con camisa de manga larga o corta (no se admiten camisetas) y zapatos cerrados (no se admiten playeras ni calzado de deporte). Para las mujeres, normalmente no se aceptan pantalones o trajes de chaqueta cortos. No se olvide de los bañadores si planea ir a la playa, e incluya también gafas de sol, crema bronceadora, protección para rayos ultravioletas, un sombrero y calzado de playa.

ELECTRICIDAD. En Barbados la corriente eléctrica es de 110V/50 períodos, y los hoteles cuentan con adaptadores para aparatos eléctricos tales como maquinillas de afeitar, radios y secadores.

275

maillot de bain et ajoutez-y vos lunettes de soleil, filtre solaire, protection U.V., un chapeau et des chaussures de plage.

BRANCHEMENT ÉLECTRIQUE. A La Barbade la tension est 110 volts/50 cycles et les hôtels ont des adaptateurs et transformateurs pour des appareils comme les rasoirs, les radios et les sèche-cheveux.

DOCUMENTS. Vous n'aurez sans doute pas besoin d'autres documents que ceux que contient votre portefeuille. Si vous avez l'intention de conduire une voiture à La Barbade, il vous suffira de présenter votre permis de conduire national ou international et, pour BDS$ 10,00, vous obtiendrez un permis de conduire provisoire aux postes de police de Hastings, Worthing ou Holetown et auprès de l'Office des Permis, qui a des bureaux à Oistins, Christ Church; The Pine, St Michael; et Folkstone, St James. De nombreuses sociétés de location de voitures peuvent également prendre les dispositions nécessaires et émettre des permis de conduire provisoires pour les visiteurs.

PASSEPORTS/FORMALITÉS D'ENTRÉE. Les ressortissants des Etats-Unis ou du Canada venant directement de ces pays à La Barbade **peuvent** être admis à entrer sans passeport pour une période n'excédant pas trois mois. Un document d'identité avec photo indiquant leur nationalité, un certificat de naissance et un billet de retour valide doivent être présentés.

Tous les autres visiteurs doivent détenir un passeport valide. Des visas sont exigés pour les ressortissants des pays d'Europe de l'Est, de la République Populaire de Chine, de Taiwan, de l'Inde, du Pakistan, des pays d'Afrique n'appartenant pas au Commonwealth et de tous les pays d'Amérique du Sud, à l'exception de l'Argentine, du Brésil, de la Colombie et du Venezuela. Les demandes de renseignements doivent être adressées à: Immigration and Passport Department, Careenage House, The Wharf, Bridgetown - Téléphone (246) 426-9912 - ou, à l'étranger, aux Ambassades, Hauts Commissariats et Consulats de La Barbade.

DEVISES. Le dollar de La Barbade est lié au dollar américain. Toutes les autres monnaies varient chaque jour par rapport à cet étalon. Quelle que soit la devise utilisée, les banques accordent généralement un meilleur taux de change que si vous utilisez de l'argent étranger pour vos achats. Les chèques de voyage sont aussi acceptés dans la plupart des établissements.

CARTES DE CRÉDIT. Elles sont acceptées à peu près partout et sont un moyen pratique et sûr de gestion de vos dépenses de vacances. Des dizaines d'hôtels, de restaurants et de magasins acceptent les cartes American Express, Carte Blanche, Diners Club International, En Route, Eurocard, MasterCard, Barclaycard et Visa.

Comment venir à La Barbade

PAR AVION. Un grand nombre de compagnies aériennes offrent des vols réguliers vers La Barbade, y compris American Airlines, Air Canada, British Airways, British West Indian Airways et Canadian Airlines International. Le Concorde supersonique dessert aussi La Barbade une fois par semaine.

Plus de douze compagnies de charters aériens fonctionnent à partir des Etats-Unis, du Canada, de l'Europe et du Royaume-Uni de manière régulière. En outre, plusieurs compagnies aériennes locales et régionales plus petites comme LIAT relient La Barbade avec ses voisins des Caraïbes.

Vous pouvez en conséquence venir par avion sans escale depuis les villes d'accès suivantes: 1 heure 30 depuis San Juan, Porto Rico; 3 heures 40 depuis Miami; 4 heures 20 depuis New York; 5 heures depuis Toronto et Montréal; 9 heures depuis Francfort, Bruxelles et Londres; 9 heures 15 depuis Zurich.

EN BATEAU. La Barbade est inscrite au programme de la plupart des lignes internationales proposant des croisières dans les Caraïbes, le port de Bridgetown étant l'une des escales les plus fréquentes sur leur route. Les paquebots arrivent habituellement tôt le matin et repartent tard le soir, laissant tout la journée pour faire du shopping, du tourisme et se détendre à La Barbade.

Le port de Bridgetown est un mouillage moderne, en eaux profondes, situé à environ un kilomètre du centre de la ville. Il peut recevoir en

in den meisten Hotels und Restaurants 'elegante Freizeitkleidung'. Das bedeutet lange Hosen, kurz- oder langärmlige Hemden (keine T-Shirts) und geschlossene Schuhe (keine Turnschuhe) für Herren. Für Damen sind Shorts oder kurze Hosenanzüge in der Regel ebenfalls nicht angemessen. Falls Sie die Absicht haben, sich am Strand aufzuhalten, vergessen Sie nicht, Ihre Badesachen, Sonnenbrille, Sonnenlotion, UV-Schutz, einen Sonnenhut und Fußbekleidung für den Strand mitzunehmen.

ELEKTRIZITÄT: In Barbados beträgt die Spannung 110 Volt/50 Hertz. Hotels stellen Adapter und Umsetzer für Geräte wie Rasierapparate, Radios und Föns zur Verfügung.

DOKUMENTE: In der Regel brauchen Sie außer dem, was Sie ohnehin in Ihrer Brieftasche mit sich herumtragen, keine besonderen Papiere. Falls Sie die Absicht haben, in Barbados Auto zu fahren, benötigen Sie nur Ihren gültigen nationalen oder internationalen Führerschein. Für nur BDS$10,00 können Sie einen zeitlich begrenzten Führerschein von den Polizeistationen in Hastings, Worthing oder Holetown und bei der Konzessionsbehörde mit Büros in Oistins in Christ Church, the Pine in St. Michael und Folkstone in St. James erhalten. Viele Autovermieter können Ihnen ebenfalls behilflich sein und die Ausstellung eines zeitlich begrenzten Führerscheins arrangieren oder selbst vornehmen.

PÄSSE / EINREISEBEDINGUNGEN: Staatsangehörige der USA oder Kanada, die direkt aus diesen Staaten nach Barbados reisen, brauchen für einen Aufenthalt von höchstens drei Monaten zuweilen keinen Paß für die Einreise. Ein mit einem Lichtbild versehener Nachweis der Personalien und Nationalität, die Geburtsurkunde und eine gültige Rückfahrkarte müssen jedoch vorgelegt werden.

Alle anderen Besucher benötigen einen gültigen Paß für die Einreise. Für Staatsangehörige osteuropäischer Länder, der Republik China, Taiwan, Indien, Pakistan, der afrikanischen Länder, die nicht zum Commonwealth gehören, und aller südamerikanischer Länder außer Argentinien, Brasilien, Kolumbien und Venezuela ist ein Einreisevisum erforderlich. Fragen können gerichtet werden an: Immigration and Passport Department, Careenage House, The Wharf, Bridgetown - Telefon: (246) 426 9912 oder an die Botschaften von Barbados, die Hohen Kommissionen und Konsulate im Ausland.

WÄHRUNG: Der Barbados Dollar ist mit dem US Dollar gekoppelt. Sonstige Auslandswährungen fluktuieren täglich. Es ist für Sie im allgemeinen günstiger, Ihr Geld in die lokale Währung über Handelsbanken umzutauschen, als Ihre eigene Währung für Einkäufe zu verwenden. Travellerschecks werden ebenfalls fast überall akzeptiert.

KREDITKARTEN: Kreditkarten werden fast überall angenommen und sind für die Bezahlung Ihrer Reiseausgaben praktisch und sicher. Viele Hotels, Restaurants und Geschäfte akzeptieren als Bezahlung American Express, Carte Blanche, Diners Club International, EnRoute, Eurocard, Mastercard, Barclaycard und Visa.

Wie man die Insel erreicht

FLUGLINIEN: Eine Anzahl von internationalen Fluglinien bietet Linienflüge nach Barbados, einschließlich American Airlines, Air Canada, British Airways, British West Indian Airways und Canadian Airlines International. Supersonic Concorde fliegt Barbados einmal wöchentlich an. Über zwölf Charterunternehmen fliegen regelmäßig aus den USA, Kanada, Europa und Großbritannien nach Barbados. Zusätzlich dazu gibt es eine Anzahl von kleineren, lokalen und regionalen Fluglinien wie LIAT, die Barbados mit den benachbarten Karibischen Inseln verbinden.

Sie können daher nonstop von den folgenden Abflugstädten nach Barbados reisen: 1 Stunde und 30 Minuten von San Juan in Puerto Rico; 3 Stunden und 40 Minuten von Miami; 4 Stunden und 20 Minuten von New York, 5 Stunden von Toronto und Montreal; 9 Stunden von Frankfurt, Brüssel und London; 9 Stunden und 15 Minuten von Zürich.

KREUZFAHRTLINIEN: Barbados ist Reiseziel der meisten internationalen Kreuzfahrtlinien, die Kreuzfahrten in der Karibik anbieten. Der Hafen von Bridgetown ist auf diesen Reiserouten einer der beliebtesten Haltepunkte. Schiffe kommen im allgemeinen früh am Morgen an und fahren wieder spät in der Nacht ab, wodurch Passagieren ein

da spiaggia.

ELETTRICITÀ. A Barbados è di 110 volt/50 cicli e gli alberghi possiedono gli adattatori e I trasformatori necessari ad apparecchi come rasoi, radio e asciugacapelli.

DOCUMENTI. Probabilmente non avrete bisogno di alcun documento speciale oltre a quello che già possedete. Se avete in programma di guidare mentre siete a Barbados vi servirà soltanto un documento valido (patente nazionale o internazionale) e, per soli BDS$10.00, potete ottenere una licenza di guida provvisoria dalle Stazioni di Polizia di Hastings, Worthing o di Holetown o presso gli uffici delle autorità competenti di Oistins a Christ Church, di The Pine a St. Michael o di Folkstone a St.James. Molte agenzie di noleggio autovetture sono anche in grado di rilasciare patenti di guida provvisorie ai visitatori.

PASSAPORTI/REQUISITI D'ENTRATA. I cittadini di nazionalità statunitense o canadese in arrivo direttamente dai paesi d'origine possono essere ammessi senza passaporto per un periodo non superiore ai tre mesi. E' sufficiente esibire un documento di identità fotografico con indicazione della nazionalità, un certificato di nascita e un biglietto di andata e ritorno valido.

Tutti gli altri visitatori devono essere in possesso di un passaporto valido, mentre i cittadini dei paesi dell'Europa Orientale, della Repubblica Popolare Cinese, Taiwan, India, Pakistan, dei paesi africani non appartenenti al Commonwealth e di tutti i paesi del Sud America, ad eccezione di Argentina, Brasile, Colombia e Venezuela hanno bisogno del visto d'entrata. Per ulteriori informazioni è possibile rivolgersi direttamente all'Immigration and Passport Department, Careenage House, The Wharf, Bridgetown - Telefono (246) 426-9912 o alle Ambasciate, agli Alti Commissariati o ai Consolati esteri delle Barbados.

VALUTA. Il dollaro delle Barbados è indicizzato al dollaro US, mentre i cambi delle altre valute straniere oscillano in base alla quotazione giornaliera del dollaro. Per cambiare valuta straniera conviene in genere rivolgersi alle banche commerciali, che offrono tassi di cambio migliori rispetto a quelli che potrebbero farvi nei negozi. La maggior parte degli esercizi commerciali accetta comunque travellers cheques.

CARTE DI CREDITO. Sono accettate in molti posti e rappresentano un mezzo conveniente e sicuro per far fronte alle spese della vacanza. Numerosi alberghi, ristoranti e negozi accettano American Express, Carte Blanche, Diner Club International, En Route, Eurocard, MasterCard, Barclaycard e Visa.

Come arrivarci

LINEE AEREE. Diverse linee aeree internazionali offrono voli di linea per Barbados, tra cui la American Airlines, la Air Canada, la British Airways, la British West Indian Airways e la Canadian Airlines International. La Supersonic Concorde ha in programma un volo settimanale.

Pij di dodici compagnie di voli charter operano su base regolare da Stati Uniti, Canada, Europa e Regno Unito, inoltre vi sono numerose linee aeree più piccole, locali e regionali, come ad esempio la LIAT, che collegano Barbados alle vicine isole caraibiche.

E' quindi possibile arrivare senza scali intermedi direttamente dagli aereoporti di San Juan, Portorico (1 ora e 30 minuti), Miami (3 ore e 40 minuti), New York (4 ore e 20 minuti) Toronto e Montreal (5 ore), Francoforte, Bruxelles e Londra (9 ore), Zurigo (9 ore e 15 minuti)

COMPAGNIE DI NAVIGAZIONE MARITTIMA (CROCIERE). Barbados è una delle tappe in programma nelle crociere offerte da diverse compagnie di navigazione marittima che organizzano crociere nel Mar dei Caraibi, dato che il porto di Bridgetown è una delle tappe favorite degli itinerari previsti. Di solito le navi arrivano al mattino presto e ripartono la sera tardi, lasciando un'intera giornata a disposizione per lo shopping, i giri turistici e il relax.

Il Porto di Bridgetown è una struttura moderna costruita su acque profonde e situato a circa mezzo miglio di distanza dal centro della cittB. Vi possono attraccare contemporaneamente fino a cinque navi

DOCUMENTACIÓN. Casi con toda probabilidad no necesitará ninguna otra documentación que la que lleva normalmente en la cartera. Si tiene la intención de conducir durante su estancia en Barbados, lo único que necesita presentar es un carnet de conducir nacional o internacional que no esté caducado y, por 10 dólares BDS, puede conseguir una matrícula temporal en las comisarías de policía de Hastings, Worthing o Holetown o en las oficinas de las Autoridades de Permisos (*Licencing Authority*) en Oistins, Christ Church; The Pine, St Michael; y Folkstone, St James. Gran número de compañías de alquiler de coches también pueden realizar los trámites necesarios y expedir carnets de conducir provisionales a los visitantes.

PASAPORTES/REQUISITOS PARA LA ENTRADA EN BARBADOS. Los ciudadanos procedentes de los Estados Unidos y Canadá que viajen directamente desde estos países, **podrán** ser admitidos sin necesidad de presentar el pasaporte por un período de tiempo que no supere los tres meses. Se deberá presentar prueba de identificación fotográfica en la que se establezca la identidad y nacionalidad, así como certificado de nacimiento y un billete de vuelta válido.

Todos los demás visitantes deberán ser portadores de un pasaporte válido. Se requieren visados para los visitantes procedentes de países de la Europa del Este, la República Popular China, Taiwan, India, Pakistán, los países africanos que no formen parte de la Commonwealth, así como todos los paísessudamericanos con la excepción de Argentina, Brasil, Colombia y Venezuela. Diríjase toda pregunta a: Immigration and Passport Department, Careenage House, The Wharf, Bridgetown; teléfono: (246) 426-9912, o a cualquier Embajada, Alto Comisariado o Consulado de Barbados en el extranjero.

DIVISA. El dólar Barbados está ligado al dólar USA. Otras divisas extranjeras fluctúan diariamente con respecto a este estándar. Generalmente los bancos comerciales ofrecen un mejor índice de cambio de cualquier divisa que si se realizan las compras utilizando divisas extranjeras. En la mayoría de los establecimientos se aceptan cheques de viaje.

TARJETAS DE CRÉDITO. Casi todos los sitios las aceptan, constituyendo un medio seguro y conveniente de organizar sus gastos vacacionales. Innumerables hoteles, restaurantes y tiendas aceptan American Express, Carte Blanche, Diners Club International, EnRoute, Eurocard, MasterCard, Barclaycard y Visa.

Cómo llegar

LÍNEAS AÉREAS. Una serie de líneas aéreas internacionales ofrecen vuelos regulares a Barbados, incluyendo American Airlines, Air Canada, British Airways, British West Indian Airways y Canadian Airlines International. El Concorde supersónico realiza un vuelo semanal a Barbados.

Más de doce compañías de vuelos chárter operan de modo regular desde los Estados Unidos, Canadá, Europa y el Reino Unido. Además, existen diversas líneas aéreas más pequeñas, locales y regionales, tales como LIAT, que enlazan Barbados con sus vecinos en el Caribe.

Por lo tanto puede usted volar sin escala desde las siguientes ciudades de entrada: San Juan, Puerto Rico (una hora y media); Miami (3 horas y 40 minutos); Nueva York (4 horas y 20 minutos; Toronto y Montreal (5 horas); Frankfurt, Bruselas y Londres (9 horas); Zurich (9 horas y 15 minutos).

LÍNEAS DE CRUCEROS. Barbados constituye una escala de la mayoría de las líneas de cruceros internacionales que ofrecen cruceros por el Caribe, siendo el Puerto de Bridgetown una de las escalas más populares de sus itinerarios. Las embarcaciones llegan normalmente por la mañana temprano y parten tarde por la noche, permitiendo a los pasajeros disfrutar de un día entero para el ir de compras, hacer turismo y relajarse en Barbados.

El Puerto de Bridgetown es un puerto moderno y profundo, situado a media milla aproximadamente del centro de la ciudad. Hasta cinco cruceros de los más grandes del mundo pueden atracar al mismo tiempo. Existe un complejo ultramoderno de tiendas libres de impuestos en los muelles, donde se pueden comprar productos de lujo de las marcas más conocidas del mundo.

ADUANAS. Los visitantes que lleguen a la isla estarán sujetos a derechos de importación, con la excepción de efectos personales, incluyendo cámaras y equipo deportivo. También se permiten 26 onzas (735 gramos) de licores, 1/2 libra (0,23 kilos) de tabaco o cincuenta puros o un cartón de

même temps jusqu'à cinq des plus grands navires de croisière du monde. Sur le quai, on trouve un complexe de magasins de produits hors taxe ultramoderne où l'on peut acheter les produits de luxe des marques les plus prestigieuses du monde.

DOUANES. Les visiteurs qui arrivent peuvent se voir imposer des droits d'importation, sauf pour leurs effets personnels, y compris les appareils photo et équipements de sport. Vous avez droit également à 735 grammes d'alcool, 0,23 kg de tabac ou cinquante cigares ou une cartouche de cigarettes. Si vous projetez d'apporter du matériel de conférence ou des cadeaux à La Barbade, vous devez les faire dédouaner. Ce service peut être fourni par avance. Des règles strictes s'appliquent à l'importation d'animaux familiers. La Barbade ne connaissant pas la rage et souhaitant perpétuer cette situation. Des permis doivent être obtenus auprès du Ministère de l'Agriculture, Graeme Hall. Christ Church. Téléphone: (246) 428 4150. Il sera fait réponse volontiers à toutes vos autres questions par les bureaux du Service du Tourisme de La Barbade à travers le monde, lesquels sont énumérés dans cette brochure.

TRANSPORTS. Lorsque vous avez passé la Douane, peut-être souhaiterez-vous connaître le large choix de moyens de transport dont vous pouvez disposer. Des taxis sont disponibles partout à des tarifs raisonnables. Louer votre propre véhicule (avec ou sans chauffeur) est un autre moyen de déplacement très apprécié. Il est également possible de louer des scooters et des bicyclettes. Les moyens de transport publics sont parmi les meilleurs de la région, équipés de minibus jaunes privés, bleus publics ou de petites camionnettes de transport à dix places desservant régulièrement tout le réseau de routes pavées du pays.

ROUTES. Conduisez à gauche à la mode britannique. La vitesse est limitée à 60 km/h ou 80 km/h sur certaines routes.

Où vous loger

LOGEMENT. La diversité des lieux d'hébergement est telle à La Barbade que vous pouvez projeter des vacances correspondant à vos besoins. Quelques cent quarante établissements vous offrent 12.000 lits. La gamme des tailles allant de dix chambres à plus de trois cents et les catégories d'immeubles incluant des hôtels luxueux, auberges, meublés, pensions et un bon choix de villas et de cottages meublés à louer. Vous pouvez obtenir les tarifs des hôtels auprès des Offices du Tourisme, soit dans votre pays, soit à La Barbade. Le personnel de l'Office du Tourisme, dans le hall d'arrivée de l'aéroport et des ports maritimes se fera un plaisir d'aider les personnes qui arrivent sans réservations. Les tarifs sont établis pour la saison d'hiver (du 16 décembre au 15 avril) et pour la saison d'été (du 16 avril au 15 décembre), où les prix sont considérablement réduits.

Une gamme de centres de réunions et de conférences de première classe sont disponibles pour recevoir tous types de groupes dans le style chaleureux de La Barbade. Pour obtenir un guide complet de tous les hôtels de La Barbade vous pouvez également prendre contact avec: Barbados Hotels and Tourism Association, 4th Avenue, Belleville, St Michael, Barbados, W.1 Tél. (246) 426 5041 Télex: 2314WB HOBARS. Fax: 246 429 2845.

La Barbade offre toute l'année un superbe choix de sports, excursions, activités culturelles et distractions modernes pour meubler vos soirées.

Une saine détente

La Barbade baigne littéralement toute l'année dans le soleil tropical avec plus de 3000 heures d'ensoleillement, tempéré par des vents alizés de nord-est au souffle modéré (16 km/h). Ces atouts naturels, associés à sa situation unique dans la mer des Caraïbes, ont modelé sa culture et constitué un climat sans égal pour une saine détente.

Par 13,4 degrés nord et 59,37 degrés ouest, La Barbade est la plus orientale des îles Caraïbes et la première à subir les assauts de l'Océan Atlantique, dont les énormes vagues viennent s'écraser de façon spectaculaire contre les côtes nord et est. Pendant ce temps, à courte distance, dans la partie "sous le vent" de l'île, les côtes ouest et sud

ganzer Tag für Einkaufsbummel, Besichtigungstouren und Entspannung in Barbados zur Verfügung steht.

Der Hafen von Bridgetown ist eine moderne Einrichtung für Schiffe mit großem Tiefgang und liegt ungefähr eine halbe Meile vom Stadtzentrum entfernt. Bis zu fünf der größten Schiffe der Welt können zur gleichen Zeit im Hafen anlegen. Am Kai befindet sich eine sehr moderne zollfreie Einkaufsanlage, wo Luxusgüter der führenden Weltmarken gekauft werden können.

ZOLL: Ankommende Besucher können außer für persönliche Gegenstände einschließlich Kameras und Sportausrüstung Einfuhrabgaben unterliegen. Sie dürfen 26oz (735 Gramm) alkoholische Getränke, ½ Pfund (0.23 Kilo) Tabak oder 50 Zigarren oder eine Stange Zigaretten einführen. Sollten Sie die Absicht haben, Konferenzunterlagen oder Geschenke nach Barbados zu bringen, benötigen Sie eine Zollabfertigungserklärung. Dies kann bequem im voraus erledigt werden. Es herrschen strenge Vorschriften über die Einfuhr von Haustieren, da die Insel frei von Tollwut ist und dies auch so bleiben soll. Genehmigungen für die Einfuhr von Haustieren werden vom Landwirtschaftsministerium, Graeme Hall, Christ Church erteilt. Tel: (246) 428 4150. Sonstige Fragen können von den weltweiten Tourismusbehörden von Barbados beantwortet werden, die in diesem Führer angeführt sind.

TRANSPORTSYSTEM: Wenn Sie die Zollabfertigung passiert haben, möchten Sie vielleicht mehr über die große Vielfalt der verfügbaren Transporteinrichtungen erfahren. Taxis sind zu angemessenen Preisen überall erhältlich. Das Mieten eines eigenen Fahrzeuges (mit oder ohne Fahrer) ist ebenfalls eine sehr beliebte Fortbewegungsmöglichkeit. Auch Mopeds und Fahrräder können gemietet werden. Das öffentliche Transportsystem mit privaten gelben Minibussen, öffentlichen blauen, oder kleinen Transportbussen mit 10 Sitzen, welches das landesweite asphaltierte Straßennetz mit regelmäßigen Fahrzeiten bedient, ist eines der besten in der Karibik.

STRAßEN: Wie in Großbritannien wird auf der linken Seite der Straße gefahren. Die Höchstgeschwindigkeit liegt bei 60 km/h bzw. 80 km/h auf bestimmten Bundesstraßen.

Unterkunftsmöglichkeiten

UNTERKUNFT: Die Vielfältigkeit der Unterkünfte in Barbados ermöglicht es Ihnen, Ihren Urlaub nach Ihren Erfordernissen zu planen. Es gibt über hundertvierzig Hotels und Pensionen, die insgesamt über 12.000 Betten anbieten. Die Größe der Hoteleinrichtungen reicht von zehn bis zu über dreihundert Zimmern, und Sie können zwischen Luxushotels, Herbergen, Apartments mit Selbstversorgung, Gästehäusern und einer guten Auswahl von Villen und Ferienhäusern zum Mieten wählen. Preislisten sind vom Büro der Touristenbehörde entweder in Ihrem eigenen Land oder in Barbados erhältlich. Das Personal des Büros der Touristenbehörde in der Ankunftshalle des Flughafens und des Hafens ist gerne dazu bereit, Gästen, die ohne Reservierung ankommen, behilflich zu sein. Preislisten geben Preise für die Wintersaison (16. Dez. bis 15. April) und für die Sommersaison (16. April bis 15. Dez.) an, in der die Preise erheblich reduziert sind.

Es gibt eine erstklassige Auswahl von Einrichtungen für Kongresse und Versammlungen, die alle Arten von Gästegruppen auf die herzliche Art der Bewohner von Barbados willkommen heißt. Für ein vollständiges Hotelverzeichnis von Barbados wenden Sie sich an: Barbados Hotel and Tourism Association, 4th Avenue, Belleville, St. Michael, Barbados, W.1 Tel (246) 426 5041 Telex: 2314WB HOBARS Fax: 246 429 2845.

Barbados bietet Ihnen das ganze Jahr über eine hervorragende Auswahl an verschiedenen Sportarten, Besichtigungstouren des Kulturguts und kultureller und moderner Unterhaltung für den Abend.

Gesunde Entspannung

Barbados badet buchstäblich in der tropischen Sonne. Die sanften Passatwinde aus dem Nordosten (10mph =16km/h) mildern das Klima mit über 3000 Stunden Sonnenschein pro Jahr. Diese natürlichen Kräfte zusammen mit der einzigartigen Lage der Insel im Karibischen Meer haben deren Kultur geformt und bieten ein Klima, das für eine gesunde

da crociera, fra le più grandi del mondo. Sul molo si trova un complesso ultramoderno dove si possono acquistare articoli "duty free" di lusso delle migliori marche del mondo.

DOGANA. All'arrivo i visitatori possono essere soggetti al pagamento di una tassa d'importazione che però non si applica ai beni classificati comei effetti personali, tra cui sono comprese macchine fotografiche e attrezzature sportive. E' consentito importare 26 once (735 grammi) di alcol, 1/2 libbra (0,23 Kg) di tabacco ovvero cinquanta sigari oppure una stecca di sigarette. Se dovete portarvi dietro materiali per convegni o regali è necessario procedere allo sdoganamento, formalità che può essere sbrigata anche anticipatamente.

L'importazione di animali domestici è invece soggetta a norme molto rigide per evitare la possibilità che si sparga il contagio portato da animali infetti da rabbia, che sull'isola non esiste. I permessi devono essere ottenuti dal Ministero dell'Agricoltura, Graeme Hall, Christ Church, Tel.: (246) 428 4150. Gli Uffci Turistici di Barbados sparsi nel mondo ed elencati in questo libro saranno lieti di rispondere a qualsiasi ulteriore vostra domanda.

TRASPORTI. Una volta superato il controllo doganale, probabilmente vorrete sapere come spostarvi sull'isola. I taxi si trovano ovunque e hanno tariffe fisse molto convenienti. Se volete, però, potete anche prendere a noleggio un'autovettura (con o senza chauffeur). E' anche possibile noleggiare moto, motorini o biciclette. I trasporti pubblici sono tra i più efficienti della regione: vi sono minibus privati gialli, minibus pubblici blu, o piccoli minifurgoni a dieci posti che servono la rete nazionale su strade asfaltate con orari regolari.

STRADE. La guida è a sinistra, come in Inghilterra; il limite di velocità è di 60 km/ora, oppure, su alcune strade principali, 80 km/ora

Dove Alloggiare

SISTEMAZIONE. L'ampia scelta di alloggi a Barbados vi consente di programmare una vacanza adatta alle vostre esigenze. I centri alberghieri sono circa centoquaranta ed offrono oltre 12.000 posti letto. Le dimensioni variano dalle dieci ad oltre trecento stanze e comprendono sia alberghi di lusso, che locande, appartamenti con uso cucina, pensioni ed una vasta scelta di ville e villini ammobiliati da affittare. Depliant con le tariffe alberghiere possono essere richiesti all'Ufficio del Turismo del vostro paese o a Barbados. Il personale dell'Ufficio del Turismo (Tourism Authority Visitors' Bureau) che potete trovare nella sala Arrivi dell'aeroporto e dei porti marittimi sarà lieto di assistere coloro che arrivano senza alcuna prenotazione. I prospetti delle tariffe indicano i prezzi per la stagione invernale (dal 16 dicembre al 15 aprile) e per la stagione estiva (dal 16 aprile al 15 dicembre), durante la quale vengono praticati forti sconti.

Barbados possiede una serie di strutture accoglienti e confortevoli per ospitare convegni e riunioni organizzate da qualsiasi gruppo. Per una guida completa di tutti gli alberghi di Barbados potete inoltre contattare il Barbados Hotel and Tourism Association, 4th Avenue, Belleville, St.Michael, Barbados, W.1 Tel.: (246) 426 5041 Telex: 2314 WB HOBARS. Fax: 246 429 2845.

Barbados offre, durante tutto l'anno, un'ampia scelta di attività sportive, escursioni turistiche ed intrattenimenti culturali e leggeri per riempire le vostre serate.

Un salutare relax

A Barbados è possibile crogiolarsi letteralmente al sole tropicale. Il sole splende per più di 3.000 ore all'anno e il clima è mitigato dalla fresca brezza degli alisei nord-orientali (venti costanti che soffiano a 16 km/ora). Le condizioni naturali e l'invidiabile posizione geografica dell'isola, situata nel Mar dei Caraibi, hanno contribuito a formare la cultura locale ed offrono un clima impareggiabile per un salutare relax.

Le coordinate dell'isola, situata a 13,4 gradi nord e 59,37 gradi ovest, fanno di Barbados l'isola caraibica più orientale e la prima a subire l'impeto dell'Oceano Atlantico, le cui onde si infrangono

cigarrillos. Si tiene intención de traer a Barbados material para conferencias o regalos, deberá obtener despacho de aduanas. Este servicio puede obtenerse con antelación. Se aplican normas muy estrictas con respecto a la importación de animales de compañía, puesto que no hay caso alguno de rabia en Barbados y se quiere mantener esta situación. Se pueden obtener permisos del Ministerio de Agricultura: *Ministry of Agriculture*, Graeme Hall, Christ Church; teléfono (246) 428 4150. Las Oficinas de Turismo de Barbados en todo el mundo, que se enumeran en este libro, se complacerán en responder a cualquier pregunta que desee dirigirles.

MODO DE TRANSPORTE. Una vez que haya pasado por Aduanas, puede que desee obtener mayor información sobre la amplia gama de servicios de transporte a su disposición. Hay taxis disponibles en todos los sitios y sus tarifas son razonables. Otro método de transporte popular consiste en el alquiler de coches (con o sin chófer). `

También pueden alquilarse motocicletas y bicicletas. El sistema de transporte público es uno de los mejores de la región, contando con minibuses privados amarillos, públicos azules, o mini-furgonetas de diez plazas que operan en toda la red nacional de carreteras pavimentadas con horarios regulares.

CARRETERAS. Conduzca por la izquierda, como en Gran Bretaña; el límite de velocidad en determinadas autopistas es de 60 u 80 kilómetros por hora.

Dónde alojarse

ALOJAMIENTO. La gran variedad de tipos de alojamiento de que dispone Barbados le permite planear las vacaciones de manera que se ajuste a sus necesidades. Existen unos 140 establecimientos que disponen de más de 12.000 camas. El tamaño de los establecimientos varía de tres a más de trescientas habitaciones, y las propiedades incluyen hoteles de lujo, hostales, apartamentos sin servicio de comidas, casas de huéspedes y una buena selección de chalets y casas de campo amuebladas para alquilar. Las oficinas de turismo de su país o de Barbados disponen de listas de las tarifas de los hoteles. El personaldel *Tourism Authority Visitors' Bureau*, ubicado en la sala de llegadas del aeropuerto y los puertos, se complacerán en proporcionar asistencia a aquellos pasajeros que lleguen sin haber reservado alojamiento. Las listas de tarifas indican los precios durante la temporada de invierno (16 de diciembre a 15 de abril) y la temporada de verano (16 de abril a 15 de diciembre), cuando los precios bajan considerablemente.

Se dispone también de una gama de salas para reuniones y convenciones de primera clase, que pueden recibir a todo tipo de grupos en el cálido estilo característico de Barbados. Para obtener una lista completa de todos los hoteles de Barbados puede también ponerse en contacto con: Barbados Hotel and Tourism Association, 4th Avenue, Belleville, St. Michael, Barbados, Las Antillas; teléfono: (246) 426 5041, télex: 2314WB HOBARS, facsímil: 246 429 2845.

Barbados ofrece durante todo el año una estupenda gama de deportes, visitas turísticas a elementos importantes de su patrimonio, entretenimientos modernos y culturales para que usted disfrute por las noches.

Relajación sana

Barbados se deja literalmente acariciar por el sol tropical. Las más de 3.000 horas de sol al año se ven suavizadas por los ligeros vientos alisios del nordeste, que alcanzan unas velocidad de 10 millas por hora (16 km/h). Estas fuerzas de la naturaleza, combinadas con la extraordinaria ubicación de la isla en el Mar Caribe, han modelado su cultura, y proporcionan un clima ideal para relajarse de manera sana que no tiene parangón.

Situada a 13,4° al norte y 59,37° al oeste, Barbados es la isla caribeña más oriental, y la primera en experimentar el poderío del Océano Atlántico, cuyas olas rompen dramáticamente contra las costas oriental y septentrional. Al mismo tiempo, a poca distancia, en el «sotavento» de la isla, las costas occidental y meridional albergan aguas calmas y suaves y playas de arena blanca.

El sol sale normalmente alrededor de las 5:30 a.m., y la puesta de sol fluctúa entre las 6:00 - 6:30 p.m. durante el transcurso del año.

Debido a la influencia refrescante de los vientos alisios, Barbados disfruta

abritent des eaux calmes et accueillantes et des plages de sable blanc. Le soleil se lève en général vers 5 heures 30 et l'heure de son coucher varie entre 6 heures et 6 heures 30 au cours de l'année.

Grâce à l'influence rafraîchissante des alizés, qui soufflent en permanence, La Barbade bénéficie d'un faible taux d'humidité même pendant les mois d'été. Les pluies tombent dans la juste proportion nécessaire pour maintenir la flore verte et luxuriante. Toutefois, la saison des pluies se situe officiellement entre juin et novembre.

PLAGES. Enfoncez vos pieds dans le sable chaud, allongez-vous et détendez-vous sous le ciel bleu et vous commencerez à savourer le genre de vie spécial de La Barbade. Plus de cent dix kilomètres de plages sont prêtesà vous accueillir, dans des paysages allant du rose délicat au blanc le plus pur. Choisissez le décor qui convient le mieux à votre humeur: les vagues vivifiantes de la côte est de l'île ou la mer des Caraïbes, qui vient lécher doucement l'autre côte.

SANTÉ. Partout dans l'île l'eau est saine et rafraîchissante à boire, car elle est filtrée par un substrat géologique de calcaire et de corail et ensuite pompée pure et propre jusqu'au robinet avec un traitement chimique minimum. Les fondations de corail de La Barbade, dont l'épaisseur atteint par endroits 90 mètres, filtrent l'eau de pluie dans des ruisseaux souterrains et des grottes et réduisent le risque d'obtenir une eau impure. C'est là une autre raison pour laquelle La Barbade est connue comme l'un des endroits les plus sains du monde. George Washington, le futur président des Etats-Unis, vint ici en 1751 pour y soigner son demi-frère, Lawrence, qui souffrait d'une grave infection pulmonaire.

La Barbade peut s'enorgueillir de posséder également des services sanitaires de haut niveau. L'hôpital principal, équipé de 600 lits est le Queen Elizabeth Hospital de Bridgetown, qui dispense des services de soins 24 heures sur 24. Il existe également plusieurs cliniques bien équipées réparties à travers l'île. Le corps médical est composé de spécialistes formés aux Etats-Unis, au Royaume-Uni, au Canada et en Europe.

POPULATION. La population totale compte environ 267.000 habitants, l'espérance de vie moyenne étant de 70,5 ans. Soixante pour cent environ de la population vit dans une conurbation qui s'étend le long de la mer des Caraïbes, du côté protégé, depuis Speightown au nord jusqu'à Oistins, au sud, et à St. Philip au sud-est. Le reste de la population vit dans de nombreux villages éparpillés à travers toute la campagne, allant de 100 à 3000 habitants. Près de 100.000 personnes habitent la paroisse de St Michael, la majorité étant domiciliée à Bridgetown, la capitale.

Bref aperçu historique

Un rapide coup d'oeil sur l'histoire de La Barbade est essentiel pour bien comprendre notre style de vie actuel. Les premiers habitants de l'île étaient de paisibles Arawaks et d'aventureux Caraïbes, qui ont donné leur nom à la région. On pense que les Caraïbes ont chassé les Arawaks de l'île, mais ont abandonné eux-mêmes cette dernière au début du XVIIème siècle.

Nul ne connaît la raison exacte de leur départ. Peut-être les Espagnols les ont-ils emmenés comme esclaves ou peut-être ont-ils émigré vers le nord et le sud. Certains habitants se trouvaient sur l'île lorsque les Portugais, en route pour le Brésil, y ont fait escale vers 1537. Les marins ont appelé l'île "Los Barbados", en hommage aux figuiers dont les racines aériennes ressemblaient à des barbes.

Lorsque le capitaine anglais John Powell arriva en 1625 il trouva l'île inhabitée et la revendiqua pour le Roi Jacques 1er d'Angleterre. Powel repartit en Angleterre avec son employeur anglais, Sir William Courteen, donnant de l'île une description enthousiaste. Quatre-vingt colons furent envoyés par la suite et débarquèrent à La Barbade en février 1627, en un lieu appelé aujourd'hui Holetown.

Au cours des deux décennies suivantes la population a connu une croissance spectaculaire pour deux raisons. Lapremière était l'instabilité politique en Angleterre, résultant de la lutte entre Oliver Cromwell et le Roi Charles 1er, qui entraîna l'arrivée de nombreux colons anglais, irlandais et écossais fuyant les persécutions et les exécutions.

Entspannung unübertroffen ist.

Mit 13.4 Grad Nord und 59.37 Grad West ist Barbados die östlichste der Karibischen Inseln und die erste, die am Atlantischen Ozean liegt, dessen Wellen dramatisch gegen die nördlichen und östlichen Küsten schlagen. In kurzer Entfernung davon und im Schutz der Insel befinden sich die westlichen und südlichen Küsten, die ein ruhiges, sanftes Meer und weiße Sandstrände bieten. Die Sonne geht normalerweise um 5:30 morgens auf und abhängig von der Jahreszeit zwischen 18:00 und 18:30 am Abend wieder unter.

Aufgrund der kühlenden Auswirkungen der Passatwinde auf das Klima herrscht in Barbados, sogar in den Sommermonaten, eine durchschnittlich geringe Luftfeuchtigkeit. Es regnet gerade oft genug, um die Vegetation grün und üppig zu erhalten. Die offizielle Regenzeit ist jedoch zwischen Juni und November.

STRÄNDE: Graben Sie Ihre Zehen in den warmen Sand, lehnen Sie sich zurück, entspannen Sie sich unter dem blauen Himmel und genießen Sie das Leben in Barbados in all seiner Einzigartigkeit. Über siebzig Meilen Strand, der in Farbtönen von sanftem rosa bis zu reinem weiß reicht, heißt Sie in Barbados willkommen. Wählen Sie eine Landschaft nach Ihrer Laune: die dramatischen Wellen des Atlantiks an der Ostküste oder das ruhig plätschernde Meer an der anderen Seite der Insel.

GESUNDHEIT: Das Trinkwasser ist auf der ganzen Insel genießbar und erfrischend als Getränk, da es durch eine geologische Grundlage von Kalkstein und Koralle gefiltert und danach pur und sauber und mit einem Minimalausmaß an chemischer Behandlung zum Wasserhahn gepumpt wird. Die Korallenfundamente von Barbados, die zuweilen über dreihundert Fuß (90m) in die Tiefe reichen, filtern das Regenwasser in unterirdischen Wasserläufen und Höhlen und reduzieren somit das Risiko unreinen Wassers. Dies ist ein weiterer Grund dafür, daß Barbados als eines der gesündesten Gebiete der Welt bekannt ist. George Washington, der später Präsident der Vereinigten Staaten wurde, besuchte Barbados im Jahr 1751, um seinem Halbbruder Lawrence im Kampf gegen eine schwerwiegende Lungeninfektion beizustehen.

Barbados hat ebenfalls einen hohen Standard in der Gesundheitsfürsorge vorzuweisen. Das größte Krankenhaus ist das Queen Elisabeth Hospital in Bridgetown mit 600 Betten, das einen 24-stündigen Apothekenservice bietet. Darüber hinaus gibt es etliche gut ausgestattete Polikliniken auf der ganzen Insel. Das medizinische Personal umfaßt Spezialisten, die in den USA, Großbritannien, Kanada und Europa ausgebildet wurden.

BEVÖLKERUNG: Die Gesamtbevölkerung beträgt 267.000 mit einer Lebenserwartung von 70.5 Jahren. Ungefähr 60% der Bevölkerung lebt in städtischen Ansiedlungen, die sich über die geschützte Karibische Seite der Insel, von Speightstown im Norden bis zu Oistins im Süden und St. Philip im Südosten, erstrecken. Der Rest der Bevölkerung lebt in einer Vielzahl von Dörfern, die sich über die ganze Insel verstreuen und jeweils 100-3.000 Einwohner haben. Ungefähr 100.000 Menschen wohnen in der Gemeinde von St. Michael, der Großteil davon in der Hauptstadt Bridgetown.

Kurze Geschichte der Insel

Eine kurze Übersicht über die Geschichte von Barbados ist unerläßlich, um unseren heutigen Lebensstil zu verstehen. Die ersten Inselbewohner waren friedvolle Arawaken und abenteuerlustige Kariber, nach denen dieses Gebiet benannt wurde. Man vermutet, daß die Kariber die Arawaken von der Insel vertrieben, jedoch dann selbst die Insel am Anfang des 16. Jahrhunderts verließen.

Niemand kennt den genauen Grund für die Abwanderung der Kariber. Es könnte sein, daß die Spanier sie zu Sklaven machten, oder daß sie einfach in den Norden und Süden abwanderten. Einige Inselbewohner waren noch da, als die Portugiesen ungefähr um 1537 auf ihrem Weg nach Brasilien in Barbados landeten. Die Segler benannten die Insel nach dem 'Ficus' Baum Los Barbados, dessen Luftwurzeln wie Bärte aussahen.

Als der englische Kapitän John Powell 1625 auf der Insel landete, fand er die Insel unbewohnt und beanspruchte sie für König James I. von England. Powell kehrte mit dem in seinen Diensten stehenden Kaufmann Sir William Courteen nach England zurück und erzählte von der Insel mit großer Begeisterung. Daraufhin wurden achtzig Siedler nach Barbados

impetuosamente contro le coste settentrionali e orientali. Frattanto, a breve distanza, al "riparo" dell'isola, le coste occidentali e meridionali offrono acque calme e spiagge di sabbia bianca.

Durante il corso dell'anno il sole sorge in media verso le 5 .30 della mattina e tramonta verso le 18-18.30 della sera.

Grazie agli alisei l'umidità dell'aria si mantiene a livelli bassi persino nei mesi estivi. La pioggia cade in giusta misura, in modo da mantenere la vegetazione verde e lussureggiante. La stagione ufficiale della pioggia inizia comunque a giugno e termina a novembre.

SPIAGGE. Affondate i piedi nella sabbia calda, distendetevi, rilassatevi sotto il cielo blu e cominciate ad assaporare l'inimitabile stile di vita delle Barbados. Più di settanta miglia di spiagge sabbiose con colori dal rosa pallido al bianco candido vi aspettano per darvi il benvenuto. Scegliete il panorama che meglio si addice al vostro stato d'animo: le inebrianti onde dell'Atlantico sulla costa orientale dell'isola o il calmo del Mar dei Caraibi sul lato opposto.

SALUTE. L'acqua dolce dell'isola è salubre e rinfrescante in quanto viene filtrata da uno strato geologico di calcare e corallo. La distribuzione avviene attraverso il sistema idrico dell'acquedotto locale, con minimo trattamento chimico. Il fondale corallino di Barbados, che in aluni punti si inabissa oltre i trecento piedi (90 metri), filtra la pioggia in rivoli e grotte nel sottosuolo e riduce i rischi di contaminazione. Tuttavia vi è anche un'altra ragione per cui Barbados è nota come uno dei luoghi più salubri del mondo. George Washington, che in seguito divenne il primo Presidente degli Stati Uniti, si recò in visita all'isola nel 1751 per accompagnare il fratellastro Lawrence che soffriva di una grave forma di infezione polmonare ed aiutarlo a rimettersi in salute.

Barbados vanta inoltre ottimi servizi sanitari. L'ospedale principale è il Queen Elizabeth Hospital a Bridgetown, con 600 letti e un dispensario in funzione 24 ore su 24. Vi sono inoltre numerose cliniche sanitarie ben attrezzate situate in ogni parte dell'isola. La comunità medica include specialisti che hanno fatto tirocinio negli Stati Uniti, nel Regno Unito, in Canada e in Europa.

POPOLAZIONE. La popolazione totale è di circa 267.000 abitanti e la vita media di settant'anni e mezzo. Circa il 60 per cento della popolazione vive nelle cittadine che si susseguono senza soluzione di continuità lungo il lato riparato dell'isola, che si affaccia sul Mar dei Caraibi e va da Speighstown al nord a Oistins al sud e St.Philip nella parte sud-orientale. Il resto della popolazione vive nei numerosi villaggi sparsi in ogni parte del territorio, che contano dai 100 ai 3.000 abitanti. Circa 100.000 persone risiedono nel distretto di St. Michael, di cui la maggior parte nella capitale, Bridgetown.

Cenni storici

Una breve occhiata alla storia di Barbados è essenziale per aiutare a comprendere l'attuale stile di vita. I primi abitanti dell'isola furono i pacifici Arawaks e gli avventurosi Caraibi, dai quali la regione ha preso il nome. Si sospetta che i Caraibi spinsero gli Arawaks fuori dall'isola, che essi stessi poi abbandonarono agli inizi del 1600.

Nessuno conosce il vero motivo della loro partenza. Gli spagnoli potrebbero averli catturati come schiavi o forse emigrarono verso nord o verso sud. Alcuni abitanti si trovavano nell'isola quando i portoghesi, diretti verso il Brasile, fecero sosta a Barbados attorno all'anno 1537. I marinai chiamarono l'isola Los Barbados, dal nome degli alberi di ficus le cui radici esposte sembrano barbe.

Quando il Capitano inglese John Powell arrivò nel 1625, trovò l'isola disabitata e la reclamò per James I, Re d'Inghilterra. Powell ritornò in Inghilterra insieme a Sir William Courteen, il mercante per conto del quale operava, riportando entusiastiche descrizioni dell'isola. In seguito vennero inviati ottanta coloni che approdarono a Barbados nel febbraio del 1627, nella località ora nota con il nome di Holetown.

Nel corso dei successivi vent'anni la popolazione aumentò a dismisura essenzialmente per due ragioni. Innanzitutto le sommosse politiche inglesi dovute alla lotta fra Oliver Cromwell e Re Carlo I causarono l'arrivo di molti coloni inglesi, irlandesi e scozzesi che

de una humedad baja como promedio, incluso en los meses de verano. Las precipitaciones de lluvia se producen justo en la cantidad adecuada para mantener la isla verde y frondosa. No obstante, la estación pluviosa oficial comprende de junio a noviembre.

PLAYAS. Sumerja los dedos de los pies en la cálida arena, túmbese y relájese bajo el cielo azul para comenzar a saborear el estilo de vida tan especial de Barbados. Más de setenta millas de playa esperan acogerle, ofreciéndole vistas que varían de un rosa delicado a un blanco purísimo. Elija el paisaje que más se acomode a su estado de ánimo: las tonificantes olas del Océano Atlántico en la costa este de la isla o el Mar Caribe, que besa suavemente la costa opuesta.

SALUD. El agua dulce de la isla se puede beber y resulta muy refrescante, puesto que se filtra mediante una base geológica de piedra caliza y coral, y se bombea, limpia y pura, a los grifos utilizando un tratamiento químico mínimo. Los cimientos de coral de Barbados, que a veces sobrepasan los trescientos pies (90 m), filtran el agua de lluvia hasta hacerla llegar a cuevas y cauces subterráneos, reduciendo la posibilidad de contaminación del agua. Ésta es otra de las razones por las que se considera a Barbados como uno de los lugares más sanos del mundo. George Washington, quien más tarde llegara a ser presidente de los Estados Unidos, visitó la isla en 1751 para intentar que mejorara la salud de su hermanastro, Lawrence, en su lucha contra una seria infección pulmonar.

Barbados también se enorgullece de los altos niveles de sus servicios de sanidad. El hospital principal es el Queen Elizabeth, situado en Bridgetown, que cuenta con 600 plazas y opera un servicio de enfermería durante las 24 horas del día. Existen también diversas clínicas muy bien equipadas, distribuidas por toda la isla. La comunidad médica incluye diversos especialistas que realizaron su período de formación en los Estados Unidos, Reino Unido, Canadá y Europa.

POBLACIÓN. La población total es de unos 267.000 habitantes, siendo la esperanza de vida media de 70,5 años. Alrededor del 60% de la población vive en una secuencia urbana continua, que se extiende a lo largo de la costa resguardada de la isla, la costa caribeña, desde Speightstown, en el norte, hasta Oistins, en el sur, y St. Phillips, en el sudeste. El resto de la población vive en los numerosos pueblos dispersos por todo el campo, y que varían en tamaño, de 100 a 3.000 habitantes. Casi 100.000 personas habitan el distrito de St Michael, viviendo la mayoría de los mismos en Bridgetown, la capital.

Breve recopilación histórica

Es esencial considerar brevemente la historia de Barbados para poder comprender nuestro modo de vida actual. Los primeros habitantes de la isla fueron los pacíficos Arawaks y los aventureros Caribs, de loscuales recibe la región su nombre. Se sospecha que los Caribs expulsaron a los Arawaks de la isla, pero ellos mismos la abandonaron a principios del siglo XVII.

Nadie conoce la verdadera razón por la que abandonaron la isla. Puede que los españoles los utilizaran como esclavos o puede que emigraran al norte y al sur. Algunos habitantes moraban todavía en la isla cuando los portugueses hicieron escala en la misma alrededor de 1537 de camino a Brasil. Los marineros llamaron la isla Los Barbados, debido a los ficus, cuyas raíces aéreas semejan barbas.

Cuando el Capitán inglés John Powell llegó a la isla en 1625, la encontró deshabitada, y la reclamó para el rey Jaime I de Inglaterra. Powell volvió a Inglaterra junto con su patrono mercante, Sir William Courteen, dando descripciones entusiastas de la isla. A partir de este momento se envió a ochenta colonos, que llegaron a Barbados en febrero de 1627, al lugar conocido en la actualidad con el nombre de Holetown.

Durante las dos décadas siguientes la población aumentó enormemente por dos razones: en primer lugar, los disturbios políticos que acaecían en Inglaterra debido a la lucha entre Oliver Cromwell y el Rey Carlos I, ocasionaron la llegada a la isla de más colonos ingleses, irlandeses y escoceses que huían de las persecuciones y ejecuciones.

En segundo lugar, la introducción de la caña de azúcar como cultivo intensivo más importante de Barbados, dependía totalmente de un abastecimiento constante de mano de obra barata. Los nuevos colonos europeos no podían adaptarse a las arduas condiciones y el duro trabajo

La seconde raison est l'introduction de la culture de la canne à sucre avec son énorme besoin de main d'oeuvre, qui a créé à La Barbade, dont c'était le produit agricole de base, un besoin constant de main d'oeuvre bon marché. Les nouveaux colons européens étaient incapables de supporter la dureté et le caractère accablant des tâches imposées dans les champs de canne à sucre. Les propriétaires de plantation ont donc introduit sans concessions l'esclavage à La Barbade.

Le droit et les traditions anglaises se sont implantés si rapidement que, bientôt, l'île a été appelée "Petite Angleterre". Le premier Parlement s'est réuni en 1639, ce qui en a fait le plus ancien du Commonwealth, après la Chambre des Communes britannique et la Chambre des Représentants des Bermudes. D'une grande loyauté envers la Couronne, les habitants de l'île ont été assiégés par les forces de Cromwell en 1651 et se sont rendus en 1652, en signant les Articles de Capitulation dans la ville appelée aujourd'hui Oistins, dans la paroisse de Christ Church. Les Articles sont devenus la Charte de La Barbade et, paradoxalement, lui ont valu une certaine indépendance de la monarchie anglaise, lorsque celle-ci a été restaurée.

Au cours des années qui suivirent La Barbade a évolué vers la constitution d'une société indépendante avec l'Emancipation des esclaves en 1834, le vote des femmes en 1944 et le suffrage universel des adultes en 1951. Avec l'émergence d'un système politique bipartite et d'un gouvernement par cabinet ministériel au cours des années 1950, La Barbade était bien préparée à l'indépendance, qui lui a été accordée le 30 novembre 1966.

GOUVERNEMENT. La Reine d'Angleterre est aussi Reine de La Barbade et un gouverneur général la représente. Le parlement à deux chambres se compose de la Chambre des Représentants, qui compte vingt-huit membres élus, et du Sénat comportant vingt et un membres désignés. Le premier ministre est ordinairement le leader du parti majoritaire à la Chambre des Représentants et il choisit un ministère au sein de son parti au cours d'une législature.

La Barbade constitue un cas unique parmi les îles Caraïbes, car elle a été gouvernée sans interruption par les britanniques depuis son origine. Ceci lui a permis d'asseoir un fondement favorisant la stabilité dans un pays où se mêlent diverses races et croyances.

RELIGION. L'unité sociale a été préservée depuis l'Emancipation grâce au rôle important joué par la religion dans la vie des habitants de La Barbade. Bien que la population soit en majorité anglicane (70 pour cent environ), il existe une centaine de dénominations et de sectes religieuses. Parmi les autres 30 pour cent, les plus nombreux sont les Méthodistes, les Moraves et les Catholiques Romains. En explorant La Barbade pour en débrouiller les mystères, vous découvrirez presque partout des preuves de notre nature éprise de religion.

Beaucoup à faire et beaucoup à voir

LE MUSÉE DE LA BARBADE. Situé dans la Garrison Historic Area, il contient une superbe collection de peintures, de maquettes, d'antiquités et de souvenirs, ainsi que des renseignements sur le passé géologique, social, économique et politique de ce pays. Une flânerie à travers les édifices publics de Bridgetown, la capitale, où se trouve le troisième plus ancien Parlement du Commonwealth, permettra au mordu d'histoire de se faire une excellente idée de cette nation profondément enracinée dans la tradition.

L'OBSERVATOIRE HARRY BAYLEY. Construit en 1963, c'est le siège de la Société d'Astronomie de La Barbade, fondée en 1956. Cet Observatoire, unique dans les Caraïbes Orientales, est situé juste en bordure de la Route 6 à Clapham, St Michael. L'Observatoire est équipé d'un télescope à réflecteur de 14 pouces et il est ouvert au public tous les vendredis, de 20 heures 30 à 23 heures 30.

POUR LES AMOUREUX DE LA NATURE. Aux amoureux de la nature ou à ceux qui apprécient les beautés naturelles, la beauté taillée à coups de serpe des côtes septentrionales et orientales offre des grottes et des arches érodées par les vagues, des falaises élancées, de minuscules criques désertes et des kilomètres de plage.

Une marche dans les grands ravins à l'ombre des arbres portant épices et fruits (dont certains sont très rares) vous conduira à l'endroit

geschickt, die dort im Februar 1627 an dem Ort, der heute als Holetown bekannt ist, ankamen.

Während der nächsten zwei Jahrzehnte wuchs die Bevölkerung aus zwei Gründen erheblich. Erstens führte die politische Unruhe in England aufgrund der Auseinandersetzung zwischen Oliver Cromwell und König Charles I. dazu, daß sich viele Engländer, Iren und Schotten, die vor Verfolgung und Hinrichtung flohen, auf der Insel ansiedelten.

Zweitens war die Einführung des arbeitsintensiven Zuckerrohrs als wichtigstem Agrarprodukt von Barbados von einer konstanten Bereitstellung billiger Arbeitskräfte abhängig. Die europäischen Siedler konnten die in den Zuckerfeldern herrschenden harten Bedingungen körperlicher Arbeit nicht bewältigen, und so führten die Plantagenbesitzer die afrikanische Sklavenarbeit im großen Stil auf der Insel ein.

Englisches Recht und englische Traditionen setzten sich so schnell durch, daß die Insel bald 'Little England' genannt wurde. Das erste Parlament wurde 1639 einberufen und es ist somit nach dem britischen Unterhaus und dem Bermuda House of Assembly das drittälteste im Commonwealth. Die Inselbewohner waren der englischen Krone gegenüber sehr loyal, wurden jedoch von Cromwells Armee im Jahr 1651 belagert und kapitulierten im Jahr 1652, indem sie den Kapitulationsvertrag in der Stadt, die heute als Oistins in der Gemeinde Christ Church bekannt ist, unterschrieben. Der Vertrag wurde zur Charter von Barbados und brachte den Inselbewohnern ironischerweise ein bestimmtes Maß an Unabhängigkeit von der englischen Monarchie, als diese wieder eingesetzt wurde.

In den folgenden Jahren entwickelte sich Barbados zunehmend zu einer unabhängigen und eigenständigen Gesellschaft mit der Emanzipation der Sklaven im Jahr 1834, der Einführung des Wahlrechts für Frauen im Jahr 1944 und dem allgemeinen Wahlrecht für alle Erwachsenen im Jahr 1951. Barbados war auf seine Unabhängigkeit, die die Insel am 30. November 1966 erlangte, durch die Entwicklung eines politischen Systems von zwei Parteien und einer Kabinettsregierung in den 50er Jahren, gut vorbereitet.

REGIERUNG: Die britische Königin ist auch die Königin von Barbados und wird vom Generalgouverneur repräsentiert. Das legislative Zweikammersystem besteht aus dem House of Assembly mit achtundzwanzig gewählten Mitgliedern und dem Senat mit einundzwanzig ernannten Mitgliedern. Der Premierminister ist gewöhnlich der Vorsitzende der Mehrheitspartei im House of Assembly und ernennt ein Kabinett aus dem Kreis seiner Fraktion.

Barbados ist im Vergleich zu anderen Inseln in der Karibik einzigartig, da die Insel von Anfang an ununterbrochen unter britischer Herrschaft stand. Dieser Umstand trug nicht zuletzt zur Entwicklung einer grundlegenden Stabilität für ein Land bei, in dem Angehörige von unterschiedlichen Rassen und Religionen zusammenleben.

RELIGION: Seit der Emanzipation wurde soziale Einheit aufgrund der bedeutenden Rolle, die die Religion in Barbados spielt, aufrecht gehalten. Obwohl der Großteil der Bevölkerung der Anglikanischen Kirche (ungefähr 70 Prozent) angehört, gibt es darüber hinaus über hundert weitere Glaubensgemeinschaften und Sekten. Unter den nicht anglikanischen 30 Prozent sind Methodisten, Moravianer und Römisch Katholische am stärksten repräsentiert. Bei Ihrem Eindringen in die Geheimnisse der Insel werden Sie fast überall Zeugnis unseres engagierten religiösen Lebens finden.

Viel zu sehen und zu tun

BARBADOS MUSEUM ist im historischen Teil von Garrison gelegen und bietet eine ausgezeichnete Sammlung von Gemälden, Kunstgegenständen, Antiquitäten und Memorabilien, sowie Informationen über die geologische, soziologische, wirtschaftliche und politische Geschichte dieses Landes. Schon durch einen bloßen Spaziergang entlang der öffentlichen Gebäude in der Hauptstadt Bridgetown, in der auch das drittälteste Parlament der Commonwealth liegt, kann man einen ausgezeichneten Eindruck über diese traditionsreiche Nation gewinnen.

DAS HARRY BAYLEY OBSERVATORIUM wurde 1963 erbaut und ist der Hauptsitz der Astronomischen Gesellschaft von Barbados, die 1956 gegründet wurde. Das in der östlichen Karibik einzigartige

cercavano scampo alle persecuzioni e alla morte.

In secondo luogo, con l'introduzione della della canna da zucchero, che in breve divenne la coltura principale dell'isola ma che richiedeva ingenti quantità di manodopera, l'economia locale venne a dipendere esclusivamente dal costante approvvigionamento di forza lavoro a basso costo. I coloni europei, che non potevano sostenere le dure condizioni e il lavoro massacrante dei campi di canna da zucchero vennero soppiantati dagli schiavi africani, introdotti su larga scala a Barbados dai proprietari di piantagioni.

La legge e le tradizioni inglesi presero piede così rapidamente che ben presto all'isola venne dato il nome di 'Piccola Inghilterra'. Il primo Parlamento venne eletto nel 1639 ed è il terzo per antichità nel Commonwealth dopo la Camera dei Comuni Britannica e l'Assemblea di Bermuda. Leali alla Corona inglese, gli abitanti dell'isola vennero assediati dalle forze di Cromwell nel 1651e si arresero nel 1652. Gli Articoli di Capitolazione vennero firmati in quella che è oggi la città di Oistins, nel distretto di Christ Church. Gli Articoli divennero lo Statuto di Barbados e, ironicamente, servirono a garantire all'isola un certo grado d'indipendenza dalla monarchia inglese dopo la sua restaurazione.

Negli anni che seguirono Barbados cominciò a trasformarsi in una società indipendente grazie all'Emancipazione degli schiavi del 1834, all'emancipazione delle donne del 1944 ed al suffragio universale adulto del 1951. Con l'emergenza di un sistema politico bipartitico e la nomina di un consiglio dei ministri durante gli anni '50, Barbados si era dimostrata ormai pronta all'indipendenza, che venne concessa il 30 novembre 1966.

GOVERNO. La Regina d'Inghilterra è anche la Regina di Barbados. Il suo rappresentante è il Governatore Generale. L'assemblea legislativa bicamerale è costituita da un parlamento di ventotto membri eletti e da una camera del Senato di ventun membri nominati. Il primo ministro è di norma il leader del partito di maggioranza parlamentare, a cui spetta la nomina del consiglio dei ministri che vengono scelti fra i membri del partito.

Barbados è l'unica tra le isole caraibiche ad essersi trovata sin dall'inizio ed ininterrottamente sotto la dominazione britannica. Ciò ha contribuito a gettare le basi della stabilità politica in un paese composto da razze e religioni diverse.

RELIGIONE. L'unità sociale è stata preservata sin dall'Emancipazione tramite il significativo ruolo che la religione occupa nella vita degli abitanti di Barbados. Sebbene la popolazione sia in prevalenza anglicana (circa il 70 per cento), esistono cento o più confessioni e sette religiose. Del restante 30 per cento, la maggioranza sono Metodisti, Moravi e Cattolici. Esplorando Barbados per svelarne i misteri troverete quasi ovunque traccia della fede e delle tradizioni religiose della popolazione indigena.

Cose da fare e da vedere

IL MUSEO DI BARBADOS. Situato nell'Area Storica del Presidio (Garrison Historic Area), esso offre una superba collezione di dipinti, oggetti d'arte, pezzi d'antiquariato e oggetti di interesse storico e culturale, come pure informazioni sulla formazione geologica, sociale, economica e politica di questo paese. Passeggiando tra gli edifici pubblici di Bridgetown, la capitale, dove si trova il terzo Parlamento del Commonwealth in ordine cronologico, l'appassionato di storia può immergersi a fondo nella stora di questa nazione ricca di tradizione.

L'OSSERVATORIO HARRY BAYLEY. Costruito nel 1963, è la sede della Società d'Astronomia di Barbados, che venne fondata nel 1956. L'Osservatorio, di per sé unico nei Caraibi Orientali, si trova appena fuori la Highway 6 a Clapham, St. Michael. L'Osservatorio è dotato di un telescopio a riflessione da 14 pollici ed è aperto al pubblico ogni venerdì dalle 8.30 della mattina fino alle 23.30 di notte.

ATTRAZIONI NATURALI. A chi ama la natura o apprezza le bellezze naturali l'aspro panorama delle costa settentrionali ed orientali offre grotte e arcate marine erose dalle onde, scogliere altissime, piccole insenature deserte e spiagge lunghe chilometri.

que exigía el cultivo de la caña de azúcar, de modo que los propietarios de las plantaciones introdujeron la esclavitud general de africanos en Barbados.

La legislación y tradiciones inglesas se arraigaron tan rápidamente que pronto se comenzó a llamar a la isla "la Pequeña Inglaterra". La primera sesión del Parlamento tuvo lugar en 1639, lo que lo convierte en el tercero más antiguo de los países de la Commonwealth, tras la Cámara de los Comunes británica y la Asamblea de las Bermudas. Muy leales a la corona, los isleños se vieron asediados por los ejércitos de Cromwell en 1651, rindiéndose en 1652 mediante la firma de los Autos de Capitulación en la ciudad conocida en la actualidad como Oistins, situada en el distrito de Christ Church. Dichos Autos se convirtieron en los Estatutos de Barbados e, irónicamente, proporcionaron a la isla cierta medida de independencia con respecto a la monarquía británica tras la restauración de la misma.

Durante los años siguientes, Barbados evolucionó para constituir una sociedad independiente, con la emancipación de los esclavos en 1834, la concesión del derecho al voto a las mujeres en 1944, y el sufragio universal de los adultos en 1951. Con la aparición en la década de los cincuenta de un sistema político bipartidista y un gobierno constituido por un gabinete ministerial, Barbados se hallaba muy bien preparada para la independencia, que le fue concedida el 30 de noviembre de 1966.

GOBIERNO. La Reina de Gran Bretaña lo es también de Barbados, y se halla representada por un Gobernador General. La legislatura bicameral comprende la Asamblea, compuesta por 28 miembros electos, y el Senado, constituido por 21 miembros designados. Normalmente, el Primer Ministro es el líder del partido que cuenta con la mayoría en la Asamblea, y elige a su gabinete de entre los miembros de su partido en la legislatura.

Barbados es única entre las islas del Caribe puesto que ha contado con gobierno británico ininterrumpido desde sus comienzos. Esto ha contribuido a la formación de una base estable en un país compuesto de diversas razas y credos.

RELIGIÓN. La unidad social se ha mantenido desde los tiempos de la Emancipación debido al importante papel que la religión ha tenido en la vida de los habitantes de Barbados. A pesar de que la población sea predominantemente anglicana (alrededor del 70%), existen cien o más denominaciones y sectas religiosas. Del 30% restante de la población, las religiones más representadas son los metodistas, moravios y católicos romanos. Cuando explore Barbados para desentrañar sus misterios, se dará usted cuenta de que hay evidencia en casi todas partes de nuestra naturaleza religiosa comprometida.

Mucho que ver y hacer

MUSEO DE BARBADOS. Situado en la zona histórica de Garrison, ofrece una soberbia colección de pinturas, artefactos, antigüedades y objetos de interés, así como información sobre la historia política, económica, social y geológica de este país. El aficionado a la Historia podrá llegar a conocer de modo excelente esta nación inmersa en la tradición, paseando simplemente por los edificios públicos de Bridgetown, la capital, donde se encuentra ubicado el tercer Parlamento más antiguo de la Commonwealth.

OBSERVATORIO HARRY BAYLEY. Construido en 1963, constituye la oficina central de la Sociedad Astronómica de Barbados, establecida en 1956. El Observatorio, único en todo el Caribe oriental, está situado a poca distancia de la Autopista 6, en Clapham, St. Michael. Está equipado con un telescopioreflector de 14 pulgadas, y abierto al público todos los viernes de 8:30 p.m. a 11:30 p.m.

AMANTES DE LA NATURALEZA. Para los amantes de la Naturaleza o aquellos que aprecian la belleza natural, las costas septentrional y oriental, toscamente labradas, ofrecen cuevas y arcos como resultado de la erosión marina, acantilados vertiginosos, pequeñas calas desiertas y playas que se extienden por millas.

Avance por las anchas gargantas bajo la sombra de árboles frutales y especieros (siendo algunos de ellos ejemplares muy raros) hasta encontrar el lugar perfecto para ir de *picnic*. Para los más enérgicos, hay expediciones con guías muy capacitados. Se pueden incluir almuerzos preparados y

rêvé pour un pique-nique. Pour les plus énergiques, des excursions à pied sont organisées à travers la campagne, sous la conduite de guides expérimentés. Paniers de pique-nique et boissons sont aussi disponibles.

L'EXPLORATION des mangroves et la plongée sous-marine dans des grottes ou des épaves dans nos parcs sous-marins ajoutent un attrait pour les plus aventureux. Vous pouvez même faire la connaissance de notre monde sous-marin sans vous mouiller. Des sorties de jour et de nuit sont possibles en sous-marin ou en bateau à fond vitré.

WELCHMAN HALL GULLY. Les amoureux de la nature apprécieront également plusieurs endroits magnifiques, comme Welchman Hall Gully, un large et profond ravin, couvert de bosquets produisant épices et agrumes, et de nombreux autres arbres rares. Cette ravine, où l'on peut voir un pilier de calcaire massif de plus de quatre pieds de diamètre, était un endroit sauvage et inaccessible, jusqu'à ce que, dans les années 1960, elle ait été intelligemment transformée en un lieu de randonnée superbe protégé, sous l'égide de la Conservation des Sites.

HARRISON'S CAVE. Tout près, reliée au système géophysique naturel de Welchman Hall Gully, on trouve Harrison's Cave, un site sous-marin habilement mis en valeur, présentant des stalactites et des stalagmites cristallines, des ruisseaux, des bassins et une chute d'eau. On accède par un train électrique à cette grotte profonde et impressionnante.

ANIMAL FLOWER CAVE. La grotte des fleurs animales est un autre objet d'émerveillement. Tirant son nom de minuscules anémones de mer, que l'on dit ressembler à des fleurs car elles ouvrent et referment leurs tentacules en réponse à la sollicitation des vagues, la grotte s'ouvre sur le violent Océan Atlantique. Les vagues de l'océan ont sculpté les rochers jusqu'à modeler cette grotte fascinante située à la pointe la plus septentrionale de l'île dans laparoisse de St. Lucy.

LES MAISONS DOMANIALES. Pour ceux qui recherchent l'opulent style de vie des grands barons du sucre, diverses Maisons Domaniales de plantation sont ouvertes au public, entièrement garnies de leur mobilier et des objets domestiques, qui sont aujourd'hui devenus des antiquités hors de prix. Il en est ainsi de St. Nicholas Abbey à St. Peter et de Francia Plantation à St. George.

FARLEY HILL. Pour jouir d'un décor exquis ou simplement organiser un pique-nique dans des jardins ombreux et verdoyants entourés de fleurs aux couleurs éclatantes, choisissez Farley Hill National Park à St. Peter, avec son magnifique panorama sur la côte est déchiquetée.

THE FLOWER FOREST AND ANDROMEDA GARDENS - La Forêt fleurie et les Jardins d'Andromède, situés tous deux à St. Joseph, sont deux autres modèles de beauté de la nature sur la côte est.

VISITES ORGANISÉES - Il existe des possibilités de visite organisée d'une sucrerie moderne en plein travail de mouture pendant la saison de la récolte (de février au 15 mai), complétée par le tour d'une rhumerie, où les techniques de mélange et de vieillissement sont démontrées au milieu des vapeurs entêtantes et des dégustations encore plus entêtantes des différents rhums produits.

Pour les amis des animaux, des excursions sont organisées à dos de cheval à travers les vallées verdoyantes ou le long des plages de sable de corail isolées. Des réserves de singes, des parcs d'oiseaux, ainsi que des mini zoos sont également prêts à vous accueillir.

Festivals

FESTIVALS. Sept festivals annuels passionnants ponctuent le calendrier pour les Barbadiens, les touristes et les visiteurs qui aiment se distraire. Ils sont les bienvenus et invités à participer. Ces événements culturels sont particuliers à notre île et offrent au visiteur une occasion de prendre part aux activités qui révèlent la nature des habitants de l'île.

FESTIVAL DE JAZZ. Les passionnés de musique à travers le monde reconnaissent que, juxtaposés, les mots "janvier" et "jazz" évoquent irrésistiblement La Barbade. Cette exaltante manifestation attire une pléiade de maîtres de la musique, parmi lesquels certains des musiciens de jazz les plus talentueux des scènes mondiales. Cet événement annuel est un grand moment de l'art musical, qui se déroule sur la fascinante toile de fond de la vie tropicale de La Barbade.

Observatorium, befindet sich in unmittelbarer Nähe des Highway 6 in Clapham, St. Michael. Es ist mit einem 14-inch (35,56 cm)Reflektor-Teleskop ausgestattet und ist jeden Freitag von 20:30 Uhr bis 23:30 Uhr für die Öffentlichkeit zugänglich.

NATURFREUNDE: Dem Naturfreund oder Naturgenießer bietet die Schönheit der Nord- und Ostküste eine Vielzahl von Attraktionen: die von den Wellen durchspülten Meereshöhlen und Gewölbe, steil aufragende Klippen, winzige verlassene Buchten und kilometerlange Strände.

Ein Spaziergang durch die großen Schluchten im Schatten von Gewürz- und Obstbäumen (einige davon sind sehr selten) kann Sie zu einem perfekten Ort für ein Picknick führen. Für die sportlicheren Gäste gibt es Wandertouren durch das Land, die von erfahrenen Führern begleitet werden. Nach Wunsch wird auch für das leibliche Wohl auf diesen Touren gesorgt.

DIE ERKUNDUNG von Mangrovenbaum-Sümpfen und das Tauchen zu Unterwasserhöhlen oder Schiffswracks in unseren Unterwasserparks zieht die abenteuerlustigeren Gäste an. Sie können sogar die Meereswelt unter Wasser genießen, ohne dabei naß zu werden. Tages- und Nachttouren in U-Booten oder Glasrumpfbooten sind im Angebot.

WELCHMAN HALL GULLY: Naturfreunde werden auch Naturschönheiten wie Welchman Hall Gully genießen, eine tiefe breite Schlucht, die mit Wäldchen von Zitrusbäumen, Gewürzbäumen und vielen anderen seltenen Bäumen überwachsen ist. Der Gully, der eine riesige Kalksteinsäule mit einem Durchmesser von vier Fuß besitzt, wuchs bis in die 60er Jahre wild. Danach wurde er zu einer wunderschönen Attraktion der nationalen Einrichtung für Naturschutz und Denkmalpflege vorsichtig umgestaltet.

HARRISON'S CAVE ist mit dem natürlichen geophysischen System der Welchman Hall Gully verbunden und liegt in dessen unmittelbarer Nähe. Die Höhle ist eine geschickt entwickelte unterirdische Attraktion mit Kristallstalaktiten und Stalagmiten, Wasserläufen, Teichen und Wasserfällen. Eine elektrische Bahn eröffnet den Zugang zu dieser beeindruckenden tiefen Höhle.

ANIMAL FLOWER CAVE ist ebenfalls ein Naturwunder. Diese Höhle wurde nach winzigen Meeresanemonen benannt, von denen behauptet wird, daß sie Blumen ähnlich sind, wenn sich ihre Tentakel in Reaktion auf die Wellenschläge öffnen und schließen. Die Höhle öffnet sich zum wilden Atlantischen Ozean hin. Die Wellen des Ozeans haben die Felsen modelliert, die diese faszinierende Höhle bilden, die auf dem nördlichsten Gipfel der Insel in der Gemeinde von St. Lucy gelegen ist.

HERRSCHAFTLICHE ANWESEN: Für diejenigen, die einen Eindruck über den feudalen Lebensstil der Zuckerbarone gewinnen wollen, sind einige 'Plantation Great Houses' für die Öffentlichkeit komplett mit Möbel und Haushaltseinrichtungen, die jetzt unschätzbare Antiquitäten sind, geöffnet. Beispiele sind St. Nicholas Abtei in St. Peter und Francia Plantation, St. George.

FARLEY HILL: Für eine wunderschöne Landschaft oder einfach ein Picknick in den schattigen, grünen Gärten, die von prachtvollen Blumen umgeben sind, gibt es den Nationalpark Farley Hill in St. Peters, der Ihnen einen wunderbaren Blick über die zerklüftete Ostküste bietet.

DER BLUMENWALD UND DIE ANDROMEDA GÄRTEN sind beide in St. Joseph gelegen und sind weitere Beispiele für die Naturschönheit des Gebietes an der Ostküste.

TOUREN zu einer modernen Zuckerfabrik, in der während der Erntezeit (Februar bis Mitte Mai) Zucker gemahlen wird, werden mit einem Abstecher zu einer Brennerei für eine Rum-Mischung vervollständigt, wo die Techniken des Mischens und Alterns des Alkohols zwischen berauschenden Dämpfen und noch berauschenderen Proben der hergestellten Rumsorten demonstriert werden.

Für Tierfreunde gibt es Führungen zu Pferd durch grüne Täler oder entlang der Korallensandstrände. Naturschutzgebiete für Affen, Vogelparks und auch Minizoos können besichtigt werden.

Feste

FESTE: Sieben aufregende jährliche Feste sind im Kalender der amüsierfreudigen Bevölkerung von Barbados eingetragen, bei denen Touristen und Besucher herzlichst willkommen sind und zur Teilnahme

Una camminata attraverso ampie gole sotto alberi ombrosi di spezie e di frutta (tra cui figurano anche esemplari piuttosto rari) vi condurrà al luogo perfetto per un picnic. Per i più allenati vi sono itinerari a piedi attraverso la campagna, accompagnati da guide esperte. A richiesta nelle escursioni sono incluse colazioni al sacco e bevande.

ESPLORAZIONE. I più avventurosi possono esplorare gli acquitrini di mangrovie, immergersi in grotte o alla scoperta di relitti sottomarini nei nostri parchi subacquei. E' possibile persino sperimentare il mondo subacqueo senza bagnarsi sia di giorno che di notte, con escursioni in sottomarino o in barche dal fondo trasparente.

WELCHMAN HALL GULLY. Gli amanti della natura apprezzeranno anche molti luoghi famosi per la loro bellezza quali ad esempio la Welchman Hall Gully, una gola ampia e profonda ricoperta da vegetazione lussureggiante, da piantagioni di agrumi, alberi di spezie e molte altre specie rare. Questa gola, in cui si trova un imponente pilastro naturale di calcare del diametro di oltre quattro piedi, rimase allo stato selvaggio fino agli anni '60, quando venne intelligentemente trasformata dal National Trust in una meravigliosa attrazione naturale.

GROTTA HARRISON. Collegata al naturale sistema geofisico della Welchman Hall Gully vi è la vicina Harrison's Cave, una grotta naturale sotterranea in cui si trovano stalattiti e stalagmiti cristalline, corsi d'acqua, piscine e una cascata. L'accesso a questa profonda e maestosa grotta è garantito da una piccola ferrovia elettrica.

ANIMAL FLOWER CAVE. E' un'altra meraviglia della natura. Chiamata con il nome di minuscoli anemoni di mare che si dice assomiglino a fiori perché aprono e chiudono i loro tentacoli seguendo il ritmo delle onde, la caverna si apre sul fragoroso Oceano Atlantico. Le onde dell'oceano hanno scolpito le rocce formando questa grotta incantevole, situata all'estremità più settentrionale dell'isola nel distretto di St. Lucy.

GRANDI CASE. Per chi desidera osservare da vicino l'opulenza dei grandi piantatori di zucchero è possibile visitare le Grandi Case ora aperte al pubblico, complete di arredamento e suppellettili domestiche che oggi sono divenute pezzi d'antiquariato d'inestimabile valore. Gli esempi più importanti si trovano a St.Nicholas Abbey a St.Peter e alla Francia Plantation di St.George.

FARLEY HILL. Per godere di un paesaggio incantevole o semplicemente per un picnic in giardini verdi e ombreggiati, circondati da fiori brillanti, ci si può recare a Farley Hill National Park a St. Peter, da cui si gode una fantastica vista dell'aspra costiera orientale.

LA FORESTA DI FIORI E I GIARDINI ANDROMEDA. Entrambi a St. Joseph, sono altri luoghi di grande bellezza naturale situati sulla costa orientale.

ESCURSIONI. Si possono prenotare visite ad uno zuccherificio moderno in piena attività durante la stagione del raccolto (da febbraio a metà maggio), completate dalla visita ad una distilleria per la miscelazione di rum dove, fra vapori inebrianti, vengono dimostrate le varie tecniche di miscelazione e invecchiamento e si possono degustare le diverse qualità di rum prodotte.

Per chi ama gli animali vi sono escursioni a cavallo guidate, attraverso vallate verdi o lungo isolate spiagge di sabbie coralline. Se preferite potete visitare le riserve dove vivono le scimmie, i parchi di uccelli esotici o i mini-zoo.

Festival

FESTIVAL. A Barbados vengono organizzati sette eccitanti festival all'anno. Gli abitanti dell'isola amano divertirsi e turisti e visitatori sono benvenuti ed incoraggiati a partecipare. Gli eventi culturali di quest'isola sono unici nel loro genere e offrono ai visitatori l'occasione di prender parte alle attività e di conoscere il vero carattere degli abitanti dell'isola.

FESTIVAL DEL JAZZ. Gli appassionati di musica di ogni parte del mondo sanno che ogni gennaio si tiene a Barbados uno dei più importanti appuntamenti di questo genere musicale. L'entusiasmante

refrescos.

LA EXPLORACIÓN de manglares y el submarinismo en cuevas o restos de naufragios en nuestros parques submarinos añaden otro incentivo para los más osados. Podrá incluso disfrutar de la experiencia de nuestro mundo submarino sin mojarse: tenemos a su disposición excursiones en embarcaciones con fondo de cristal, tanto durante el día como por la noche.

WELCHMAN HALL GULLY. Los amantes de la naturaleza también apreciarán diversos lugares de gran belleza, tales como el Welchman Hall Gully, una garganta ancha y profunda cubierta de árboles cítricos y especieros, así como otros muchos ejemplares raros de árboles. El Gully, que posee un pilar de caliza de más de cuatro pies de diámetro, creció en estado salvaje hasta la década de los 60, cuando fue transformado de manera sensible en una hermosa atracción del National Trust, una organización no gubernamental protectora del patrimonio arquitectónico y espacios naturales.

HARRISON'S CAVE. Vinculada al sistema geofísico natural del Welcham Hall Gully, esta cueva se encuentra en su proximidad, constituyendo una atracción subterránea desarrollada de modo sutil, que contiene estalactitas y estalagmitas cristalinas, arroyos, estanques y una cascada. El acceso a esta impresionante y profunda cueva es mediante un tren eléctrico.

LA ANIMAL FLOWER CAVE (Cueva de las flores animales) es otra maravilla de la naturaleza. Recibe su nombre de las minúsculas anémonas que, se dice, parecen flores puesto que abren y cierran sus tentáculos en respuesta a los movimientos marinos. Esta cueva se abre al feroz Océano Atlántico. Las olas del océano han cincelado estas rocas para formar esta fascinante cueva, situada en la punta más norteña de la isla, en la parroquia de St. Lucy.

GREAT HOUSES (Mansiones). Para aquellos que buscan el estilo de vida opulento de los magnates del azúcar, están abiertas al público una serie de mansiones situadas en las plantaciones, completas con mobiliario y utensilios domésticos que constituyen ahora antigüedades de incalculable valor. Ejemplos de estas mansiones son St. Nicholas Abbey, en St. Peter, y Francia Plantation, en St. George.

FARLEY HILL. Para gozar de un panorama exquisito o simplemente ir de *picnic* a unos jardines verdes y frondosos, rodeados de flores brillantes, el Parque Nacional de Farley Hill, en St. Peter, es el lugar ideal, puesto que se enorgullece de contar con unas magníficas vistas de la escarpada costa oriental.

EL BOSQUE DE FLORES Y LOS JARDINES ANDRÓMEDA, ambos en St Joseph, constituyen otros lugares de belleza natural situados en la costa oriental.

EXCURSIONES. Se pueden realizar excursiones a una fábrica de azúcar moderna a pleno funcionamiento durante la época de la cosecha (de febrero a mediados de mayo), complementadas con una excursión a una destilería de ron, en la que se demuestran las técnicas de mezcla y envejecimiento del ron mientras se ve usted envuelto en los embriagadores vapores y las aún más embriagadoras muestras de los distintos tipos de ron que se producen. Para los amantes de los animales hay giras a caballo con guía a través de los verdes valles o a lo largo de playas de arena coralina. También pueden disfrutarse reservas de monos, parques de aves y zoos en miniatura.

Festivales

FESTIVALES. Siete emocionantes festivales anuales marcan el calendario de los habitantes de Barbados, amantes de la diversión, así como de los turistas y visitantes que son acogidos afablemente y a los que se insta a participar. Estos acontecimientos culturales son únicos de nuestra isla, y proporcionan al visitante una oportunidad especial para tomar parte en actividades reveladoras de la naturaleza de los isleños.

FESTIVAL DE JAZZ. Los entusiastas de la música de todo el mundo reconocen que, cuando se yuxtaponen las palabras jazz y enero, quiere decir Barbados. Este acontecimiento jubiloso atrae a toda una serie de maestros de la música, que representan a los mejores talentos del mundo del jazz y hacen honor a los escenarios. Este acontecimiento anual constituye una obra de arte musical que tiene como telón de

FESTIVAL DE HOLETOWN. Cette manifestation commence en février, époque anniversaire de l'arrivée des premiers colons anglais, le 17 février 1627. Le site de leur débarquement, aujourd'hui Holetown, accueille une semaine de réjouissances. Des chansons médiévales sont chantées dans les églises et sur les terrains de foire on peut entendreles rythmes les plus modernes. L'atmosphère ancienne et nouvelle se combinent avec des chants folkloriques et des danses, du sport et des jeux, des parades dans les rues, des marchés en plein air, des foires et des étals offrant les produits d'alimentation locaux traditionnels.

FESTIVAL DU POISSON D'OISTINS. Le week-end de Pâques est une occasion de se distinguer pour les habitants qui concourent entre eux pendant ces deux jours de fête célébrant l'habilité des pêcheurs de l'île. Les pêcheurs, hommes et femmes, montrent leurs aptitudes à la pêche, à la découpe du poisson, dans des courses de bateaux et même des courses de crabes et les spectateurs se réjouissent en dansant au son des steel bands et en s'intégrant aux foules grouillantes sur les plages, au marché et dans les pittoresques "rum shops", qui bordent les routes. Des étals de nourriture, d'objets d'art et de l'artisanat et une exposition organisée par les Garde-côte terminent les festivités.

GOSPELFEST. Le Gospel (chanson inspirée des Evangiles) est une célébration spirituelle utilisée par les Barbadiens depuis des générations pour exprimer en musique leur héritage africain. Cet ensemble de chants est repris pendant trois jours en mai, lorsque des artistes de gospel locaux, caraïbes et internationaux, se réunissent pour un des concerts les plus passionnants de ce type. La Gospelfest est un événement familial, qui comporte quantité d'attractions, avec une succession continue des chanteurs de gospel les plus divers.

CROP OVER FESTIVAL. Le festival de la fin des récoltes est le clou de l'été, une réjouissance à laquelle toute l'île participe de la mi-juillet au début d'août. Crop Over célèbre la fin de la récolte de canne à sucre. Les "Tentes" vibrent du féroce combat des chanteurs de calypso luttant pour la récompense, le titre convoité de Roi du Calypso et l'air est rempli des odeurs de la cuisine barbadienne pendant la foire en plein air, le grand "Bridgetown Market". Riche de l'esprit de la culture locale, "The Cohobblopot" mélange de théâtre, de danse et de musique, qui voit le couronnement du Roi et de la Reine des "costume bands" (orchestres costumés) . Une passionnante soirée est occupée par le "Pic-O-de-Crop Show", pendant laquelle le Roi du Calypso est couronné. L'apogée du festival est "Kadooment Day", jour de fête nationale, pendant lequel les costume bands remplissent les rues des rythmes barbadiens vibrants, tandis que le soir, des feux d'artifice embrasent le ciel.

NATIONAL INDEPENDENCE FESTIVAL OFTHE CREATIVE ARTS. Le festival de l'indépendance nationale et des arts créatifs se déroule en novembre. Les Barbadiens de tous âges y confrontent leurs talents dans les domaines de la musique, du chant, de la danse, du théâtre et de l'écriture. Puis, le Jour de l'Indépendance, le 30 novembre, les manifestations finales ont lieu avec des expositions photographiques, artistiques et artisanales.

CONGALINE CARNIVAL ET HOLDER'S OPERA SEASON. Le Carnaval de Congaline dure neuf jours. Il a lieu à la fin avril. Le village de Congaline est le coeur et l'âme du Carnaval de Congaline et offre un lieu quotidien d'exposition et de marché à une myriade de libres réjouissances, d'artisanat et de culture locaux. Il est surnommé "La plus grande fête de rue du monde" lorsqu'il culmine dans sa parade d'un jour des orchestres en T-shirt. La Holder's Opera Season, fondée en 1993, a lieu en mars et s'est déjà imposé comme le premier événement culturel des Caraïbes. Célébrée au plan national comme international, la saison est une remarquable manifestation d'opéra, de musique et de théâtre, un événement important dans le calendrier culturel mondial, dont le haut niveau artistique attire des publicsvenus du monde entier.

Le monde du sport de La Barbade

Sports nautiques

La mer est notre terrain de jeu et il est toujours possible de participer à des sports aquatiques partout disponibles, accessibles et source d'enrichissement.

ermutigt werden. Diese kulturellen Veranstaltungen sind für unsere Insel einzigartig und bieten den Besuchern eine besondere Gelegenheit, an den Aktivitäten, die das Wesen der Inselbewohner verdeutlicht, teilzunehmen.

JAZZ FESTIVAL: Musikbegeisterte der ganzen Welt wissen, daß Januar und Jazz zusammen Barbados bedeutet. Diese hervorragende Veranstaltung zieht eine Vielzahl von Virtuosen an, darunter einige der besten Talente des Jazz, die sich jährlich in Barbados die Ehre geben. Diese jährliche Veranstaltung stellt ohne Zweifel einen der Höhepunkte des musikalischen Lebens dar und erweist sich auf dem Hintergrund des tropischen Barbados als besonders reizvoll.

HOLETOWN FESTIVAL: Die Festlichkeiten beginnen im Februar mit dem Jahrestag der Ankunft der ersten englischen Siedler am 17. Februar 1627. Das heutige Holetown, wo jene Siedler seinerzeit landeten, ist Gastgeber einer ganzen Festwoche. Lieder aus dem Mittelalter werden in den Kirchen gesungen, und auf den Festplätzen kann man sich modernerer Rhythmen erfreuen. Diese Atmosphäre des Alten und Modernen wird durch das Singen von Volksliedern, sowie durch Tanz, Sport und Spiel, Straßenparaden, Straßenmärkte, Ausstellungen und Imbißstände mit traditionellen lokalen Speisen unterstrichen.

OISTINS FISH FESTIVAL: Das Osterwochenende erfüllt die Ortsbewohner, die während dieses zweitägigen Festes zu Ehren der Fischer der Insel miteinander wetteifern, mit Stolz. Die lokalen Fischer und Fischerinnen demonstrieren ihre Fertigkeiten beim Fischen, Entgräten, Bootsrennen und sogar Krabbenrennen, während sich die Zuschauer beim Tanz zu Steelbands und in den Menschenmengen auf den Stränden, auf dem Marktplatz und in den eigentümlichen Rumgeschäften am Straßenrand amüsieren. Imbißstände, das Kunstgewerbe und eine Ausstellung der Küstenwache vervollständigen die Festlichkeiten.

GOSPELFEST: Gospel ist eine spirituelle Feier, die von den Bewohnern von Barbados seit Generationen gefeiert wird, um ihr afrikanisches Kulturgut durch Musik auszudrücken. Gospellieder werden drei Tage lang im Mai aufgeführt, wenn internationale Gospelsänger sich für eines der aufregendsten Konzerte dieser Art zusammenfinden. Das Gospelfest ist ein Familienereignis, auf dem man sich mit unzähligen Attraktionen und Konzerten verschiedener Gospelsänger vergnügen kann.

CROP OVER FESTIVAL: Der Höhepunkt des Sommers ist das 'Crop Over Festival', ein Fest auf der ganzen Insel, das von Mitte Juli bis Anfang August stattfindet. 'Crop Over' markiert das Ende der Zuckerrohrernte. Im Wettspiel 'Tents' gibt es einen erbitterten Wettkampf zwischen den Kalypsonianern um den Preis des Kalypso-Königstitels. Die Luft auf dem großen 'Bridgetown Markt' ist erfüllt von den Gerüchen der Küche von Barbados. Ganz im Geiste der lokalen Kultur verbindet 'der Cohobblopot' Drama, Tanz und Musik mit der Krönung des Königs und der Königin der Karnevalsvereine. Die 'Pic-O-de-Crop Show' ist ein aufregender Abend, an dem der Kalypsokönig gekrönt wird. Der Höhepunkt des Festes ist der 'Kadooment Tag', ein nationaler Feiertag, an dem Karnevalsumzüge die Straßen mit den pulsierenden Rhythmen von Barbados füllen. Feuerwerke bringen Licht in den dunklen Abendhimmel.

NATIONAL INDEPENDENCE FESTIVAL OFTHE CREATIVE ARTS: Im November messen Inselbewohner jeden Alters ihre Talente im Bereich der Musik, des Gesangs, beim Tanz, dem Schauspiel und der Kunst des Schreibens. Am nationalen Unabhängigkeitstag, dem 30. November, finden schließlich die Abschlußaufführungen zusammen mit Foto- und Kunstausstellungen, statt.

CONGALINE CARNIVAL UND HOLDERS OPERNSAISON: Der Congaline Carnival ist ein neuntägiger Karneval, der Ende April stattfindet. Das Congaline Dorf ist das Herzstück des Congaline Karnevals und bietet ein tägliches Ausstellungsforum und einen Marktplatz für unzählige kostenlose Veranstaltungen, lokales Kunstgewerbe und Kultur. Dieser Karneval wird 'die größte Straßenparty der Welt' genannt und findet seinen Höhepunkt in dem eintägigen 'T-Shirt Umzug'.

Die Holders Opernsaison, die im Jahr 1993 gegründet wurde, findet im März statt und hat sich bereits zum wichtigsten Kulturereignis in der Karibik entwickelt. Die Saison ist national und international anerkannt und ist ein einzigartiges Festival der Oper, der Musik und des Theaters.

290

avvenimento attrae sul podio un vasto numero di musicisti di alto livello e i più grandi talenti del jazz internazionale. Questo evento annuale è un capolavoro di arte musicale che ha come sfondo l'incantevole paesaggio tropicale di Barbados.

FESTIVAL DI HOLETOWN. I festeggiamenti hanno inizio a febbraio per commemorare l'arrivo dei primi coloni inglesi avvenuto il 17 febbraio 1627. La località del loro approdo, ora Holetown, ospita attività che durano una settimana. Nelle chiese vengono tenuti concerti di canti medievali mentre i gruppi moderni suonano alle fiere. Questa manifestazione, ove si fondono il vecchio e il nuovo, combina canto, danze folcloristiche, sport e giochi, sfilate e mercati, fiere e bancarelle ove è possibile assaggiare i piatti della cucina tipica dell'isola.

FESTIVAL DEL PESCE DI OISTINS. Il fine settimana di Pasqua, nel corso del festival di due giorni organizzato in onore dei pescatori dell'isola, vengono tenute delle gare a cui partecipano gli abitanti della località. I pescatori e le donne del luogo dimostrano la loro abilità nella pesca, nello spinare il pesce, in gare fra imbarcazioni e persino in corse di granchi, mentre gli spettatori si divertono ballando al suono di bande improvvisate e mescolandosi alla folla che si accalca sulle spiagge, sulla piazza del mercato e nei caratteristici spacci di rum che fiancheggiano la strada. Bancarelle che offrono cibo, arte e artigianato e una mostra della Guardia Costiera completano le attrazioni di questa festa.

GOSPELFEST. Il Gospel è una celebrazione spirituale che gli abitanti di Barbados usano da generazioni per esprimere attraverso la musica il loro retaggio africano. Questo programma di canzoni ha luogo in maggio e dura tre giorni, durante i quali la popolazione locale ed artisti internazionali di gospel si uniscono per creare uno dei più eccitanti concerti di questo genere. Il Gospelfest è un evento familiare caratterizzato da miriadi di attività e da una serie ininterrotta di esibizioni da parte di vari cantanti gospel.

FESTIVAL DI FINE RACCOLTO. L'apice dell'estate è costituita dal festival che celebra la fine del raccolto (Crop Over Festival), un'esultanza che si estende a tutta l'isola e che dura da metà luglio fino ai primi di agosto. Il Crop Over celebra la fine del raccolto della canna da zucchero. Nei padiglioni di gara risuonano la musica e le grida dell'accanita lotta tra danzatori di calipso per ottenere l'ambito titolo di Re del Calipso, mentre durante la grande fiera del mercato di Bridgetown nell'aria si spandono gli invitanti odori della cucina tipica di Barbados. Ricco dello spirito della cultura locale, 'Il Cohobblopot' mescola teatro, danza e musica all'incoronazione del Re e della Regina delle bande in costume. Una serata particolarmente eccitante è quella del 'Pic-O-de-Crop Show', durante la quale viene incoronato il Re del Calipso. L'apice del festival è 'Kadooment Day', giorno di festa nazionale in cui bande in costume si riversano nelle strade al suono dei pulsanti ritmi di Barbados mentre il cielo notturno è illuminato da fuochi d'artificio.

FESTIVAL INDIPENDENZA NAZIONALE PER LE ARTI CREATIVE. Durante il mese di novembre, gli abitanti di Barbados di ogni età misurano il proprio talento nel campo della musica, della danza, della recitazione e dell'opera letteraria. Il 30 novembre, giorno dell'Indipendenza, i festeggiamenti si concludono con le esibizioni finali e con mostre fotografiche, d'arte e d'artigianato.

CARNEVALE CONGALINE E STAGIONE DELL'OPERA Il Carnevale Congaline dura nove giorni ed ha luogo alla fine di aprile. il Villaggio di Congaline è l'epicentro del Carnevale e funge da tribuna per mostre giornaliere e un mercato con innumerevoli intrattenimenti, prodotti dell'artigianato e della cultura locale. E' stato soprannominato "La Miglior Festa su Strada del Mondo", e culmina nella sfilata di una banda in T-shirt che dura tutto un giorno. La Stagione dell'Opera, fondata nel 1993, ha luogo nel mese di marzo e si è già affermata come l'evento culturale più importante dei Caraibi. Acclamata in campo nazionale e internazionale, la stagione è una celebrazione di per se unica di opera, musica e teatro, un avvenimento importante nel calendario culturale internazionale, il cui elevato livello artistico attira pubblico da ogni parte del mondo.

fondo la fascinante vida de Barbados.

FESTIVAL DE HOLETOWN. Las celebraciones comienzan en febrero, cuando se conmemora el aniversario de la llegada de los primeros colonos ingleses el 17 de febrero de 1627. El lugar en el quedesembarcaron dichos colonos, conocido en la actualidad como Holetown, constituye el marco en el que se celebra una semana de actividades. En las iglesias se cantan canciones medievales, mientras que los ritmos más modernos se pueden oír en las ferias. Este ambiente de lo antiguo y lo nuevo combina cantos y bailes folclóricos, deportes y juegos, desfiles callejeros, mercadillos, ferias y puestos de comida en donde se pueden degustar los platos típicos locales y tradicionales.

FESTIVAL DE PESCADO DE OISTINS. El fin de semana de Pascua les confiere honor a las gentes locales que compiten en el festival de dos días en el que se rinde homenaje a las habilidades de los pescadores de la isla. Los pescadores y pescadoras locales demuestran sus habilidades pescando, quitándole las espinas al pescado, realizando carreras de barcos e incluso carreras de cangrejos, mientras que los espectadores disfrutan bailando al ritmo de las *steel bands* (bandas de percusión típicas del Caribe) e interrelacionándose con las muchedumbres que abarrotan las playas, el mercado y los curiosos establecimientos de ron que se alinean en la acera. Para poner el broche de oro a estas actividades hay puestos de comida, artes y manualidades, y una demostración de los Guardacostas.

GOSPELFEST. El *gospel* es una celebración espiritual que los habitantes de Barbados han utilizado durante generaciones para expresar su patrimonio africano mediante la música. Este cuadro de canciones se captura durante tres días en el mes de mayo cuando artistas de *gospel* locales e internacionales se reúnen para dar uno de los conciertos más emocionantes de los de su clase. El Gospelfelt es un acontecimiento familiar que incluye miríadas de atracciones y actuaciones consecutivas de toda una serie de cantantes de *gospel*.

FESTIVAL DEL FINAL DE LA COSECHA (CROP OVER FESTIVAL). El punto culminante del verano lo constituye el *Crop Over Festival*, una celebración jubilosa que tiene lugar en toda la isla desde mediados de julio a principios de agosto. En este Festival se celebra el fin de la cosecha de la caña de azúcar. Las "Carpas" de competición resuenan con la feroz batalla de entusiastas del Calypso por obtener el codiciado título de Monarca del Calypso, y el aire está cargado de los aromas procedentes de la cocina típica de Barbados durante la masiva feria callejera del "Mercado de Bridgetown". Lleno del espíritu de la cultura local, el "Cohobblopot" mezcla drama, baile y música con la coronación del Rey y la Reina de las *custom bands* (bandas de carnaval). Una noche emocionante es la de "Pic-O-de-Crop Show", en la que se corona al Rey del Calypso. El clima del festival lo constituye "Kadooment Day" (día festivo a nivel nacional), en el que las *custom bands* impregnan las calles con los latentes ritmos de Barbados y los fuegos artificiales prenden fuego al cielo nocturno.

FESTIVAL DE LA INDEPENDENCIA NACIONAL DE LAS ARTES CREATIVAS. Durante noviembre los habitantes de Barbados de todas las edades comparan sus talentos en los campos de la música, la canción, la danza, la interpretación y la literatura. Más tarde, el día de la Independencia (30 de noviembre), tienen lugar las presentaciones finales al mismo tiempo que se muestran exposiciones fotográficas, de artes y manualidades.

CARNAVAL DE CONGALINE Y TEMPORADA DE ÓPERA DE HOLDER. El Carnaval de Congaline tiene una duración de nueve días y se celebra a finales de abril. El pueblo de Congaline es el centro y alma del Carnaval de Congaline, y ofrece un foro de exposiciones diarias y un mercado para una miríada de entretenimientos gratuitos, artesanía y cultura locales. Se le denomina "la Fiesta Callejera más Grande del Mundo", puesto que culmina con un desfile de *T-shirt bands* de un día.

La Temporada de Ópera de Holder, fundada en 1993, tiene lugar en marzo, y ya se ha establecido como el principal acontecimiento cultural del Caribe. Aclamada tanto a nivel nacional como internacional, la temporada es una celebración extraordinaria de la Ópera, la música y el teatro; un acontecimiento importantísimo en el calendario cultural internacional cuyos altos niveles artísticos atraen a audiencias de todas las partes del mundo.

PLANCHE À VOILE ET SURF. Grâce aux vents constants et à l'ensoleillement permanent les conditions propices à la planche à voile à La Barbade sont parmi les meilleures du monde. Les vagues puissantes et provocantes de la côte atlantique à l'est constituent un vrai paradis pour les véliplanchistes.

YACHTING. Dans les eaux qui entourent La Barbade, les conditions pour faire de la voile dans les alizés sont à présent universellement vantées. Il est possible de louer de grands catamarans et des yachts pour des croisières guidées. Sur les plages, on peut louer des bateaux plus petits, comme les Hobie Cats. Pour la plongée et l'exploration, des bateaux de tous types sont disponibles.

PLONGÉE. Les amateurs de plongée en apnée seront étonnés par la variété de la faune sous-marine tropicale qui existe autour des rochers de corail et des épaves gisant sur le fond: le cargo *Stavronikita*, juste au large de la côte de St. James (dans le parc sous-marin de Folkestone); l'épave d'un vieux remorqueur dans la Baie de Carlisle, avec l'*Eillon Kingston* qui a récemment sombré; le *Frair's Craig*, un petit paquebot, dans les eaux juste à l'Est du Barbados Hilton. Le Park sous-marin de Folkestone est une réserve marine, divisée en quatre zones, pour la recherche et la protection de la vie marine ainsi que les loisirs. Un équipement de plongée et des instructions pour plongeurs débutants sont disponibles à Folkestone Park, au Sandy Lane Hotel, au Coral Reef Club et au Dive Boat Safari, au Dive Shop, au Barbados Hilton International, à l'Explore Sub Barbados et aux Divi Southwinds.

SKI NAUTIQUE ET PARASAILING. Les eaux bleues et calmes du littoral de la côte ouest procurent d'excellentes conditions pour les fanatiques du ski nautique. Quant aux plus hardis, pourquoi ne pas se munir d'un parachute et de voler dans le ciel, loin au-dessus de la plage pour jouir du panorama spectaculaire de la ligne côtière?

Sports terrestres

Sur terre, les sports sont encore plus variés et nombreux, soit que vous recherchiez l'excitation de la difficulté, soit que vous vous détendiez comme spectateur.

CRICKET: Le cricket est le sport national. Le batteur marque un point et les applaudissements retentissent à travers toute l'île. Des milliers de gens se pressent aux matches de classe mondiale à Kensington Oval ou restent près de leur poste de radio pour encourager leurs favoris. La Barbade est l'une des capitales du cricket et contribue toujours un large contingent à l'équipe des Antilles britanniques.

Notre Sir Garfield Sobers national, le plus grand touche-à-tout mondial, a été fait chevalier par Sa Majesté la Reine Elisabeth II en personne, au Garrison Savannah, à La Barbade, pour sa contribution à ce jeu.

En toute saison, vous pourrez assister à un bon match de cricket à La Barbade, qu'il s'agisse d'un match Test international auquel participe l'élite, et qui se joue ordinairement entre janvier et avril, un passionnant match de club dans le concours de Première Division local (de mai au 15 décembre) ou à un match amical joué sur la plage, sur un quelconque carré d'herbe ou sur le terrain du village.

COURSES DE CHEVAUX - EQUITATION . Si vous voulez vous distraire et vous passionner tout à la fois, consacrez votre après-midi au sport des rois, les courses de chevaux. Les pistes de Garrison Savannah attirent des foules, qui assistent aux efforts des pur-sang de haute qualité pour atteindre la ligne d'arrivée. Le Turf Club de La Barbade organise vingt réunions au cours de l'année: dix un samedi sur deux, entre janvier et avril, et dix d'août à novembre. Le Polo est aussi pratiqué à un haut niveau à La Barbade. Si c'est l'équitation qui vous attire, enfourchez votre monture. Cinq écuries au moins fournissent des chevaux pour des randonnées à cheval à travers les collines ondulantes et les plages isolées.

COURSE À PIED - Les courses de longue distance, bien qu'elles ne s'adressent qu'à ceux qui sont en parfaite forme physique, éveillent un tel enthousiasme dans l'île qu'une grande épreuve appelée Run Barbados International Road Race Series est organisée le premier week-end de décembre. Le marathon de 42,195 kilomètres, courue sur des routes pavées le long des rivages et le parcours de 10 km à travers et autour de Bridgetown, attirent des concurrents hommes et femmes du

Sie ist eine wichtige im Kulturkalender der Welt eingetragene Veranstaltung, deren hoher künstlerischer Standard Zuschauer aus der ganzen Welt anzieht.

Die Welt des Sports in Barbados

Wassersportarten

Das Meer ist unser Spielplatz und die Teilnahme an Wassersportarten ist immer möglich, leicht zugänglich und macht Spaß.

WINDSURFEN UND SURFEN: Aufgrund der konstanten Brise und des ständigen Sonnenscheins sind die Wetterbedingungen für das Windsurfen in Barbados eine der besten in der Welt. Die starken und hohen Wellen des Atlantiks an der Ostküste bieten ein absolutes Paradies für Wellensurfer.

SEGELN: Die guten Segelbedingungen in den Meeren, die Barbados umgeben, sind auf der ganzen Welt bekannt. Es ist möglich, große Katamarane und Jachten für Kreuzfahrten mit Führer zu chartern. An den Stränden können kleinere Boote, wie 'Hobie Cats' gemietet werden. Zum Tauchen und zur Erkundung der Insel sind alle Arten von Booten erhältlich.

TAUCHEN: Taucher werden über die Vielfältigkeit der tropischen Meeresflora und -fauna, die im Umfeld unserer Korallenriffe und gesunkenen Wracks zu sehen ist, erstaunt sein. Beispiele von vorhandenen Schiffswracks sind das Frachtschiff *Stavronikita*, das gleich in der Nähe der St. James Küste (im Folkstone Unterwasserpark) gesunken ist, das Wrack eines alten Schleppers in Carlisle Bay zusammen mit *Eillon Kingston*, das vor kurzem sank, und der *Friar's Craig*, ein kleiner Dampfer, der im Meer rechts von Barbados Hilton zu finden ist. Der Folkstone Unterwasserpark ist ein Meeresschutzgebiet, das für die Forschung und den Schutz der Meeresflora und -fauna sowie zur Besichtigung und Freizeitgestaltung in vier Bereiche eingeteilt ist. Tauchausrüstungen und Anleitung für Tauchanfänger sind in Folkstone Park, Sandy Lane Hotel, Coral Reef Club und dem Dive Boat Safari, dem Dive Shop, Barbados Hilton International, Explore Sub Barbados und Divi Southwinds erhältlich.

WASSERSKI UND PARA-SAILING: Das ruhige Meer an der Westküste bietet ausgezeichnete Bedingungen für enthusiastische Wasserskifahrer. Wie wäre es mit dem Anschnallen eines Fallschirmes und dem Para-sailing am Himmel für die Abenteuerlustigeren - hoch über dem Strand, mit einem spektakulären Blick über die Küste?

Landsportarten

Am Land sind die Sportmöglichkeiten noch vielfältiger, ganz gleich ob Sie den Nervenkitzel einer sportlichen Herausforderung spüren oder als Zuschauer entspannt zusehen wollen.

KRICKET: Kricket ist ein Nationalsport. Der Schlagmann schlägt durch die Deckung und überall auf der Insel hört man Beifallsrufe. Tausende Fans strömen zu Weltklasse-Spielen nach Kensington Oval oder hören sich das Spiel im Radio an, um ihre Lieblingsspieler anzufeuern. Barbados ist eine der internationalen Kricket-Hauptstädte und stellt regelmäßig eine beachtliche Anzahl von Spielern für das westindische Team.

Unser Spieler Sir Garfield Sobers, das weltbeste Allroundtalent, wurde von Ihrer Majestät, Königin Elisabeth II persönlich am Garrison Savannah in Barbados für seinen Beitrag zum Spiel geadelt. Sie können fast jederzeit ein gutes Kricket Match in Barbados sehen, ob es nun ein erstklassiges internationales Test Match ist, das im allgemeinen zwischen Januar und April gespielt wird, ein spannendes Club Match im lokalen Wettkampf der ersten Division (Mai bis Mitte Dezember) oder ein Freundschaftsspiel, das am Strand, auf einer offenen Wiese oder in einem Dorffeld gespielt wird.

PFERDERENNEN: Für den hohen Unterhaltungswert und die große Spannung, die diese Sportart bietet, sehen Sie sich einen Nachmittag lang den Sport der Könige an - das Pferderennen. Die Rennbahn bei Garrison Savannah zieht Scharen von Menschen an, die den ausgezeichneten reinrassigen Pferden bei deren Versuch, die Ziellinie zu erreichen, zusehen. Der Barbados Turf Club organisiert zwanzig Rennen pro Jahr: zehn an jedem zweiten Samstag zwischen Januar und April und zehn zwischen August und November. Auch Polo wird mit hohem

Il mondo dello sport di Barbados

Sport Acquatici

Il mare è il nostro campo da gioco e non vi è nulla di più facile, accessibile e gratificante che prendere parte agli sport acquatici.

WINDSURF E SURFING. Grazie alle brezze costanti e all'eterno bel tempo, Barbados possiede condizioni ideali per il windsurf. Le possenti e stimolanti onde della costa orientale dell'Atlantico rappresentano invece il paradiso dei surfisti.

YACHTING. Nelle acque che circondano Barbados, i venti costanti forniscono le condizioni più adatte allo yachting, per cui l'isola è internazionalmente rinomata. E' possibile noleggiare grandi catamarani e yacht per crociere guidate. Nelle spiagge si possono noleggiare imbarcazioni più piccole, come gli Hobie Cats. Inoltre si può trovare qualsiasi tipo di imbarcazione per immersioni subacquee ed esplorazioni marine.

ATTIVITÀ SUBACQUEE. I subacquei si stupiranno della varietà della vita marina tropicale che esiste attorno alle barriere di corallo ed ai relitti dei fondali oceanici: la nave mercantile *Stavronikita*, appena al largo della costa di St.James (entro il Parco Subacqueo Folkstone); un vecchio relitto di rimorchiatore nella Baia Carisle unitamente a *Eillon Kingston,* affondato di recente; *Frair's Craig,* un piccolo vaporetto nelle acque ad est di Barbados Hilton. Il Parco Subacqueo di Folkstone è una riserva marina suddivisa in quattro aree di ricerca e protezione nonché ricreazione. Il Parco di Folkstone, il Sandy Lane Hotel, il Coral Reef Club, il Dive Boat Safari, il Dive Shop, il Barbados Hilton International, l'Explore Sub Barbados e il Divi Southwinds noleggiano attrezzature subacquee e organizzano corsi per principianti.

SCI ACQUATICO E PARA-VELA. Le tranquille acque blu della costa occidentale offrono condizioni eccellenti agli appassionati di sci acquatico. Chi se la sente può infilarsi un paracadute e farsi trascinare con il paracadute veleggiando alto nel cielo, sopra la spiaggia. Cosa c'è di meglio per godersi una veduta spettacolare della costa?

Sport di terra

Sulla terraferma, gli sport sono persino più svariati e numerosi, sia che cerchiate il brivido della sfida o il relax dello spettacolo.

CRICKET. Il cricket è lo sport nazionale. Durante le partite, dappertutto nell'isola si alzano gli evviva dei tifosi quando il battitore riesce a lanciare la palla tra le difese. Migliaia di persone affollano i campionati mondiali che si tengono al Kensington Oval oppure stanno incollate alla radio per fare il tifo per i propri favoriti. Barbados è una delle capitali internazionali del cricket e contribuisce sempre con un vasto contingente al team delle West Indies.

Al nostro Sir Garfield Sobers, giudicato il miglior atleta del mondo, è stato conferito il titolo di cavaliere per il suo contributo al gioco del criket personalmente da Sua Maestà la Regina Elisabetta II presso la Garrison Savannah di Barbados. A Barbados è possibile assistere ad una buona partita di cricket pressoché in qualsiasi momento, sia si tratti di un importante incontro internazionale, che di solito hanno luogo fra gennaio e aprile, di un'eccitante partita fra i club della Serie A locale (da maggio a metà dicembre), o di un'amichevole giocata sulla spiaggia, su un terreno da pascolo o sul campo di un villaggio.

GARE IPPICHE. Per un pomeriggio di grande eccitazione e divertimento scegliete lo sport dei re - le corse dei cavalli. La pista di Garrison Savannah attrae vaste folle ad osservare gli sforzi dei purosangue in gara. Il Barbados Turf Club organizza venti corse durante l'anno: dieci a sabati alternati fra gennaio e aprile e dieci fra agosto e novembre. A Barbados si gioca anche il polo, ed a grande livello. Se poi volete provare a montare a cavallo, non avete che l'imbarazzo della scelta. Vi sono almeno cinque scuderie per escursioni a cavallo su sentieri che attraversano colline ondulate e costeggiano spiagge deserte.

PODISMO. Il podismo su percorsi lunghi, anche se consigliabile solo a chi è fisicamente in forma, suscita localmente tanto entusiasmo da giustificare l'organizzazione di una serie di gare internazionali di

El mundo deportivo de Barbados

Deportes acuáticos

El mar es nuestro campo de recreo, y siempre se puede participar en deportes acuáticos que resultan accesibles y gratificantes.

WINDSURFING Y SURFING. Gracias a las brisas constantes y al sol que brilla siempre, las condiciones de Barbados para el surfing se encuentran entre las mejores del mundo. Las poderosas y desafiantes olas del Atlántico, en la costa oriental, proporcionan un refugio absoluto para los surfistas.

NAVEGACIÓN A VELA. Las condiciones para la navegación a vela en las aguas que rodean a Barbados, con los vientos alisios constantes, se han hecho conocidas a nivel internacional. Es posible fletar catamaranes grandes y yates para realizar cruceros con guía. En las playas se pueden alquilar embarcaciones más pequeñas, como es el caso de los Hobie Cats. Disponemos de todo tipo de embarcaciones para practicar el submarinismo y realizar expediciones.

SUBMARINISMO. Los submarinistas quedarán asombrados ante la gran variedad de vida marina tropicalexistente alrededor de nuestros arrecifes de coral y los restos de naufragios: el carguero *Stavronikita*, muy cerca de la costa de St. James (en el Parque Submarino de Folkestone); los restos del naufragio de un antiguo remolcador en la Bahía de Carlisle junto al *Ellion Kingston*, que se hundió recientemente; el *Frair's Craigh*, un pequeño barco a vapor que se encuentra en las aguas al este del Barbados Hilton. El Parque Submarino de Folkestone es una reserva marina dividida en cuatro áreas, para la investigación y protección de la vida marina, que tiene también fines recreativos. Se pueden obtener equipos de submarinismo e instrucciones para los principiantes en el Parque de Folkestone, el Hotel Sandy Lane, el Coral Reef Club y el Dive Boat Safari, la Dive Shop, el Barbados International Hilton, Explore Sub Barbados y Divi Southwinds.

ESQUÍ ACUÁTICO Y "PARA-SAILING". Las tranquilas aguas azules de la costa oeste proporcionan unas excelentes condiciones para los entusiastas del esquí acuático. Para los más osados, ¿por qué no ajustarse un paracaídas y practicar "para-sailing" en el cielo, por encima de la playa, para disfrutar de unas vistas espectaculares de la costa?

Deportes en tierra

En tierra los deportes son aún más variados y abundantes, ya busque usted la emoción de los desafíos o prefiera relajarse como espectador.

CRICKET. Se trata del deporte nacional. El bateador lanza a través de las lonas y en todas las partes de la isla se eleva un clamor. Miles de personas se abarrotan en Kensington Oval para presenciar partidos de clase mundial o permanecen cerca de la radio para animar a sus favoritos. Barbados es una de las capitales internacionales de cricket, y siempre contribuye al equipo de las Antillas con un gran número de jugadores.

Su Majestad la Reina Isabel II concedió personalmente el título de caballero (*Sir*), a nuestro jugador Garfield Sobers, el mejor jugador del mundo en todas las posiciones, en Garrison Savannah, Barbados, por su contribución a este deporte.

En Barbados puede presenciar un buen partido de cricket casi en cualquier época, ya se trate de un partido internacional de élite (que se juegan normalmente entre enero y abril), un emocionante partido entre clubes locales que están en la Primera División (de mayo a mediados de diciembre) o un partido amistoso en la playa, unos prados al aire libre o el campo de un pueblo.

CARRERAS DE CABALLOS. Para pasar una tarde entretenida y llena de emociones decídase por el deporte de los reyes: las carreras de caballos. El hipódromo de Garrison Savannah atrae a multitudes para presenciar los esfuerzos por alcanzar la meta que realizan los caballos pura sangre de gran calidad. El Barbados Turf Club organiza veinte carreras al año: diez en sábados alternados entre enero y abril, y diez de agosto a noviembre. En Barbados también se juega al polo a un alto nivel. Y si uno de sus placeres consiste en montar su propia maravilla equina, ¡ensille el caballo! Cinco establos como mínimo ofrecen caballos para realizar paseos panorámicos por las onduladas colinas y playas aisladas.

ATLETISMO. El atletismo a larga distancia, aunque sólo sea para aquellos que estén en perfecta forma física, es acogido localmente con

monde entier. Parmi les premiers prix pour les participants étrangers, sont offerts des billets d'avion et des chambres d'hôtel pour revenir participer l'année suivante.

TENNIS - Le tennis est largement pratiqué à La Barbade sur un grand nombre de cours appartenant aux hôtels, ou sur des cours publics au Park Folkestone à Holetown.

GOLF - Le beau temps ensoleillé toute l'année à La Barbade fait la joie des amateurs de golf. Quatre beaux terrains sont à leur disposition. Deux parcours à 18 trous, à Sandy Lane et Royal Westmoreland, et deux parcours à 9 trous, au Club Rockley et Almond Beach Village.

SQUASH - Si vos faveurs vont au squash, il existe dix endroits différents où il peut être pratiqué à La Barbade.

Autres sports

Vous pouvez aisément occuper vos journées avec le football, la bicyclette, le basket-ball, le volley-ball, le hockey et le rugby. Les visiteurs passionnés de tir trouveront toujours un ball-trap ou un tir au pistolet.

Des jeux qui se jouent normalement à l'intérieur, comme le bridge, les échecs, le billard et les fléchettes, peuvent être pratiqués ici à l'extérieur. Le jeu de table national, les dominos, se joue avec un tel enthousiasme que le claquement des dominos sur la table peut vous faire sursauter. Mais, bien sûr, il ne s'agit que d'un jeu. Le climat presque parfait et la passion des gens pour le jeu font de La Barbade un lieu de vacances paradisiaque pour lesvoyageurs à l'esprit sportif.

Sur le marché

La Barbade offre des occasions uniques de shopping, que vous soyez attirés par les marchés locaux, un souvenir d'artisanat authentique ou des économies sur les achats de produits détaxés.

MARCHÉS - Une promenade sur l'un des marchés est toujours très distrayante. Ils regorgent de produits alimentaires frais locaux et fournissent un cadre idéal pour rencontrer les habitants de l'île. Les marchés de Cheapside et de Fairchild Street, à Bridgetown, sont remarquables, de même que le marché aux poissons d'Oistins. En outre, des dizaines de supermarchés, épiceries fines et mini-marchés ponctuent l'île et vendent viandes, fruits, légumes, vins, spiritueux et d'autres produits.

BOUTIQUES D'ARTISANS - Pelican Village, sur la Princess Alice Highway, près du port de Bridgetown, est la principale vitrine de l'île pour les produits de l'artisanat. Les visiteurs peuvent y voir les artisans travailler et c'est l'endroit idéal pour acheter le cadeau parfait.

Il existe également plusieurs boutiques de produits de l'artisanat à Bridgetown, où sont présentés des articles comme des accessoires en coque de noix de coco, des éventails en paille et khus-khus, des paniers à bouteille et des articles en acajou, tels que des porte-clés, des boîtes à bijoux, des cendriers, des dessous de verre et des boîtes à lettres. Des poteries, des objets à pendre au mur, des paniers tissés de toutes formes, des nattes, des carpettes et des bijoux en coquillage et en corail sont également vendus. De nombreuses boutiques souvenirs présentent également les travaux des artistes locaux.

LES ACHATS DE PRODUITS HORS-TAXE - Le shopping hors-taxe dans plusieurs magasins climatisés et bien aménagés peut permettre des économies importantes. Les visiteurs sont simplement tenus de présenter leurs documents de voyage et la transaction hors-taxe se fait sans problème. Certaines catégories de marchandises peuvent être emportées lors de leur achat, d'autres sont livrées à l'aéroport pour être récupérées avant de monter à bord ou au port pour être récupérées avant l'embarcation. Les produits exemptés bénéficiant de la détaxe sont les alcools, les vins, le tabac, les cigarettes, les cigares, les magnétoscopes et les jeux vidéo, les disques, les autoradios, les postes de télévision et les PC. Les boutiques à l'aéroport et dans le port vendent une grande variété d'articles détaxés.

Les rythmes de la nuit

Lorsque les couchers de soleil dorés marquent la fin du jour, des rythmes envoûtants viennent donner le tempo de la nuit tropicale. Tout

Niveau in Barbados gespielt. Und wenn Sie gerne selbst reiten - satteln Sie eines unserer schönen Pferden. Ungefähr fünf Ställe versorgen Sie mit Pferden für festgelegte Routen in den sanften Hügeln und auf den abgelegenen Stränden.

LAUFEN: Langstreckenlauf, wenn auch nur für die körperlich fitten Menschen geeignet, wird mit solch großem Enthusiasmus lokal betrieben, daß ein jährliches Rennen, die 'Barbados International Road Race Series', am ersten Wochenende im Dezember abgehalten wird. Der 26 Meilen 385-Yard lange Marathonkurs (42,195 Kilometer) , der auf gepflasterten Küstenstraßen und den 10km in und um Bridgetown gelaufen wird, zieht sowohl männliche als auch weibliche Teilnehmer aus der ganzen Welt an.

Zu den Spitzenpreisen für Teilnehmer aus dem Ausland gehören die bezahlten Flugkosten und Hotelunterkunft für die Teilnahme am Rennen des folgenden Jahres.

TENNIS: Tennis wird in ganz Barbados sowohl auf einer Anzahl von zu Hotels gehörenden Tennisplätzen als auch auf öffentlichen Tennisplätzen in Folkstone Park in Holetown gespielt.

GOLF: Das schöne sonnige Wetter, das Barbados das ganze Jahr über verwöhnt, begeistert Golfspieler. Es gibt vier sehr gute Golfplätze, zwei Golfplätze mit 18 Löchern in Sandy Lane und Royal Westmoreland und zwei mit 9 Löchern im Club Rockey und in Almond Beach Village.

SQUASH: Wenn Sie gerne Squash spielen, bietet Ihnen Barbados zehn verschiedene Sqash-Anlagen.

Sonstige Sportmöglichkeiten

Sie können leicht Ihren Tag mit Fußball, Radfahren, Basketball, Volleyball, Landhockey und Rugby verbringen. Beim Schießsport werden interessierte Besucher so gut wie jederzeit auf ihre Kosten kommen, sei es im Tontaubenschießen, Skeet- oder Pistolenschießen.

Spiele, die im allgemeinen nicht im Freien gespielt werden (in Barbados jedoch auch draußen beliebt sind), sind Bridge, Schach, Billard und Würfelspiele.

Das nationale Tischspiel Dominos wird mit so viel Begeisterung gespielt, daß das Geräusch der auf den Tisch geknallten Dominos Sie erschrecken könnte. Aber es ist alles nur Spaß. Das fast perfekte Klima von Barbados und seine sich für Spiele begeisternden Inselbewohner machen die Insel zu einem Urlaubsparadies für sportlich aktive Urlauber.

Auf dem Markt

Barbados bietet einzigartige Einkaufsmöglichkeiten, ob Sie sich nun für die Geheimnisse des lokalen Marktplatzes, ein authentisches handgemachtes Souvenir oder die Ersparnis durch den zollfreien Einkauf interessieren.

MÄRKTE: Ein Ausflug auf einem der Märkte ist immer unterhaltsam. Frische, lokale Köstlichkeiten sind dort reichlich vorhanden, und der Marktplatz bietet einen idealen Rahmen, um einheimische Bewohner kennenzulernen. Die Cheapside und Fairchild Straßenmärkte in Bridgetown sind ausgezeichnet, wie auch der Fischmarkt in Oistins. Zusätzlich dazu gibt es Dutzende Supermärkte, Delikatessengeschäfte und Minimärkte auf der Insel, die Fleisch, Obst, Gemüse, Wein, Spirituosen und sonstige Lebensmittel verkaufen.

KUNSTHANDWERKSBETRIEBE: Pelican Village am Princess Alice Highway in der Nähe des Hafens in Bridgetown ist das wichtigste Zentrum für Kunsthandwerk auf der Insel. Besucher sind herzlichst dazu eingeladen, Kunsthandwerkern bei der Arbeit zuzusehen. Pelican Village ist der ideale Ort, um das 'perfekte' Geschenk zu erwerben.

Es gibt auch etliche Kunsthandwerksgeschäfte in Bridgetown, die Waren wie Accessoires aus Kokosnußschalen, Stroh-und Khus-Khus-Fächer, Flaschenkörbe und Artikel aus Mahagoni wie Schlüsselringe, Schmuckschatullen, Aschenbecher, Untersetzer und Briefkästen verkaufen. Keramiken, Wandbehänge, geflochtene Körbe aller Art, Matten, kleine Teppiche und Schmuck aus Muscheln und Korallen können auch erstanden werden. In vielen Souvirgeschäften finden Sie auch Kunstwerke von lokalen Künstlern.

ZOLLFREIES EINKAUFEN: Beim zollfreien Einkauf in etlichen gut gelegenen klimatisierten Geschäften sparen Sie viel Geld. Besucher brauchen nur ihre Reisedokumente vorzulegen, und der Einkauf kann ganz

corsa su strada che si tiene a Barbados nel primo week-end di dicembre. Le più importanti sono la maratona di 42 Km e 195 metri che si svolge su strada asfaltata lungo il litorale e la corsa di 10 km a Bridgetown che attraggono partecipanti di ogni sesso da ogni parte del mondo. Fra i primi premi per i partecipanti provenienti dall'estero sono in palio biglietti aerei e sistemazioni alberghiere per prendere parte alla corsa dell'anno successivo.

TENNIS. Il tennis viene giocato in ogni parte dell'isola nei numerosi campi da tennis degli alberghi come pure nei campi pubblici del Parco di Folkstone a Holetown.

GOLF. Il cielo sempre sereno delle Barbados è una vera e propria benedizione per i giocatori di golf. Sono disponibili quattro ottimi campi: due da 18 buche a Sandy Lane e a Royal Westmoreland e due da 9 buche al Club Rockley e ad Almond Beach Village.

SQUASH. Se lo squash è il vostro gioco, a Barbados potete praticarlo in dieci centri diversi.

Altri sport

Potete facilmente riempire le vostre giornate giocando a calcio, facendo ciclismo, pallacanestro, pallavolo, hockey su prato e rugby. Gli amanti delle armi sportive hanno a disposizione sia il tiro al piattello che lo skeet e la pistola.

I giochi che si svolgono di norma al chiuso (qui però li trovate anche all'aperto) sono il bridge, gli scacchi, il biliardo e le freccette.

Il gioco nazionale da tavola - il domino - viene giocato con tanto entusiasmo che le tessere sbattute sul tavolo potrebbero farvi sobbalzare. Ma, naturalmente, è tutto per gioco. Un clima quasi perfetto e gente che ama divertirsi fanno di Barbados un santuario per la vacanza ideale del visitatore sportivo.

Al mercato

Barbados offre opportunità eccezionali per lo shopping, sia che vi attirino gli intriganti mercati locali, i prodotti dell'artigianato locale o i risparmi del duty free shop.

MERCATI. La visita a uno dei mercati è sempre divertente. Troverete cibi freschi e prodotti tipici in abbondanza, inoltre è un posto ideale per incontrare la gente del luogo. I mercati di Cheapside e Fairchild Street di Bridgetown sono eccezionali, come pure il mercato del pesce della città di Oistin. Inoltre vi sono decine di supermercati, negozi di gastronomia e mini-centri commerciali sparsi nell'isola ove si vendono carni diverse, frutta, verdure, vini, alcol ed altri prodotti tipici.

NEGOZI D'ARTIGIANATO. Il villaggio di Pelican, sulla strada principale Princess Alice, vicino al Porto di Bridgetown, rappresenta la principale vetrina dell'artigianato locale. I visitatori possono osservare gli artigiani al lavoro, ed è un ottimo posto per acquistare il regalo ideale.

Vi sono inoltre numerosi negozi d'artigianato a Bridgetown, dove si possono trovare accessori ricavati da gusci di noce di cocco, ventagli di paglia e khus-khus, cestelli per bottiglie e articoli di mogano quali portachiavi, astucci per gioielli, set di sottobicchieri e cassette per le lettere. Inoltre si possono acquistare ceramiche, arazzi, cesti intrecciati di ogni forma, stuoie, tappetini e gioielli di conchiglie e di corallo. Molti negozi di souvenir hanno anche opere di artisti locali.

DUTY FREE SHOPPING. Nei negozi duty free, numerosi, ben attrezzati e dotati di sistema di condizionamento d'aria, è possibile realizzare notevoli risparmi. Per acquistare al duty free basta esibire un documento di viaggio. Alcuni tipi di merci possono essere ritirate subito, altre vengono consegnate all'aeroporto o al porto d'imbarco prima della partenza. Gli articoli esentasse venduti senza restrizioni comprendono alcol, vini, tabacco, sigarette, sigari, videogiochi video, dischi, stereo per auto, televisori e home computer. I negozi all'aeroporto e del porto offrono una vasta scelta di articoli.

I ritmi della notte

Quando i tramonti dorati segnano la fine della giornata, il tempo

---

tanto entusiasmo que, en el primer fin de semana de diciembre de cada año se celebran una serie de maratones internacionales, los *Run Barbados International Road Race Series*. El circuito del maratón, de 26 millas y 385 yardas (42.195 metros), que corre a través de carreras asfaltadas a lo largo de la costa, y los 10 km que se corren en Bridgetown y alrededor de la misma, atraen a competidores masculinos y femeninos procedentes de todo el mundo. Entre los principales premios para los participantes extranjeros se incluye el alojamiento en hotel y la tarifa aérea para que regresen el año siguiente para la carrera.

TENIS. En Barbados se juega mucho al tenis en una serie de pistas pertenecientes a hoteles, así como en pistas de tenis públicas en Folkstone Park y Holetown.

GOLF. El buen tiempo soleado de que se disfruta en Barbados tiene extasiados a los golfistas. Disponemos de cuatro campos de golf muy buenos: dos campos de 18 hoyos en Sandy Lane y Royal Westmoreland, y dos campos de 9 hoyos en el Club Rockeley y Almond Beach Village.

SQUASH. Si el squash es su deporte preferido, puede practicarlo en diez sitios diferentes durante su estancia en Barbados.

Otros deportes

Puede pasar el día fácilmente jugando al fútbol, practicando ciclismo, baloncesto, voleibol, hockey sobre hierba y rugby. Y los cazadores pueden practicar el tiro, ya sea tiro al pichón, tiro al plato o con pistola.

Los juegos de mesa en los que normalmente se participa a cubierto (aquí podrá jugar también al aire libre) son el bridge, el ajedrez, el billar y los dardos.

El juego de mesa nacional, el dominó, se juega con tanto vigor que le podrá sorprender los golpes conlos que se ponen las fichas sobre la mesa. Por supuesto, todo se hace con el ánimo de divertirse. El clima casi perfecto y las gentes, amantes de los juegos y deportes, hacen de Barbados un refugio para los viajeros que disfrutan de los deportes.

El mercado

Barbados ofrece unas oportunidades únicas para ir de compras, ya le apetezcan las intrigas de los mercados locales, un recuerdo auténtico hecho a mano, o el ahorro que supone realizar compras libres de impuestos.

MERCADOS. Siempre resulta entretenido visitar uno de los mercados. Ofrecen productos alimenticios locales frescos en abundancia, y proporcionan un marco ideal para conocer a más gente. Los mercados de Cheapside y Fairchild Street, en Bridgetown, son excepcionales, como también lo es el mercado de pescado de la ciudad de Oistins. Además, docenas de supermercados, tiendas especializadas y mini-mercados salpican la isla y venden carne, fruta, verduras, vinos, licores y víveres en general.

TIENDAS DE ARTESANÍA. Pelican Village, situado en la Autopista Princess Alice, cerca del puerto de Bridgetown, es el principal escaparate de artículos de artesanía de la isla. Se recibe con mucho gusto a los visitantes para que vean a los artesanos realizando su labor, y resulta un buen lugar para comprar ese regalo perfecto.

También existen diversas tiendas de artesanía en Bridgetown, que ofrecen artículos tales como accesorios realizados con cáscara de coco, abanicos de paja y *khus-khus*, cestos para el vino, y artículos de ébano tales como llaveros, joyeros, ceniceros, juegos de posavasos y buzones. También se puede comprar cerámica, colgantes para las paredes, cestas entretejidas de todas las formas, esterillas, alfombras y joyas de coral y conchas. Muchas tiendas de recuerdos también ofrecen trabajos de artistas locales.

COMPRAS LIBRES DE IMPUESTOS. Se puede ahorrar considerablemente comprando artículos libres de impuestos en diversas tiendas bien designadas y con aire acondicionado. Sólo se requiere que los visitantes presenten sus documentos de viaje para que se pueda realizar de modo fácil la transacción libre de impuestos. En el momento de la compra se pueden recoger determinadas categorías de artículos, mientras que otros le serán entregados en el aeropuerto para que los recoja antes de subir al avión o en el puerto para que los recoja al embarcar. Los artículos libres de impuestos que no se pueden comprar de modo directo son licores, vino, tabaco, cigarrillos, puros, vídeos, videojuegos, discos, radios para coches,

un choix de distractions est possible: dîners dansants, spectacles de variété, disco et night-clubs ou un paisible dîner aux chandelles dans un beau restaurant du bord de mer.

CROISIÈRES-RÉCEPTIONS - Un grand nombre de grands navires de croisière sont disponibles, assurant des croisières-réceptions de quatre ou cinq heures le long de la côte ouest de l'île, avec orchestre à bord. Ou bien l'on peut choisir des croisières plus détendues à bord de toute une variété de catamarans.

DISTRACTIONS - La plupart des hôtels offrent des spectacles de variété locaux en semaine, basés sur les expressions culturelles des Caraïbes, telles que le limbo, les mangeurs de feu, le steel band, le calypso et la danse du ventre. Magie, mystère, romantisme et excitation s'emparent de l'imagination.

NIGHT-CLUBS - Il existe de nombreux night-clubs et boîtes de nuit à la disposition des fêtards noctambules. Il y a aussi Baxters Road, "la rue qui ne dort jamais", offrant ses plats locaux et ses boissons agréables pour les après-réception.

ALIMENTS ET BOISSONS - Si explorer l'univers culinaire à la recherche de fumets et de goûts originaux est l'un de vos passe-temps favori, vous découvrirez que La Barbade possède une énorme variété de délices gastronomiques. Les restaurants offrent une large gamme de menus, allant des plats continentaux aux aliments locaux les plus exotiques.

LE POISSON VOLANT est une spécialité et il est si populaire qu'il est virtuellement devenu un symbole national. On le trouve partout depuis les plats raffinés jusqu'aux sandwichs sur la plage. D'autres délicieux produits de la mer, qui arrivent frais pêchés dans les eaux entourant l'île, comprennent le homard, les crevettes, le coryphène, la tortue de mer, le lutjanide rouge, le thon, le lampris tacheté et le maquereau, pour n'en citer que quelques-uns. Le Crane Chubb et les sea eggs (oeufs d'oursins grillés, fortement poivrés, ou panés ou préparés à votre goût) sont des spécialités.

Notre sol tropical fournit en abondance les fruits et légumes frais. Au nombre des fruits on trouve les mangues, les papayes, les bananes, les goyaves, les avocats et les noix de coco, à côté d'autres plus exotiques comme les cachimans et les cerises de La Barbade. Parmi les légumes fraîchement cueillis, le fruit à pain, les yams, les ignames, les taros, les christophènes, l'aubergine, l'okra, le potiron, les bananes des Antilles et le patisson. On trouve également à La Barbade la plupart des légumes pour salades les plus courants.

Certaines spécialités valent d'être essayées comme le cou-cou, un plat fait de farine de maïs et d'okra; le jug-jug, un mélange de Guinea corn et de petits pois; le pepperpot, un ragoût, assaisonné de poivre de Cayenne, avec diverses viandes; le roti, un plat caraïbes/antillais se compose de viandes au curry, enveloppées dans un chipatee, et les conkies, un mélange de farine de maïs, de noix de coco, de potiron, de raisins secs, de patates douces et d'épices, cuit à la vapeur dans une feuille de bananier.

A La Barbade, "boisson" signifie le plus souvent "rhum". Les marques locales comptent au nombre des meilleures du monde et sont servies sous la forme de nombreux délicieux mélanges.

SERVICE/POURBOIRE - Dans la plupart des hôtels, une taxe de service de 10 pour cent et une Taxe Gouvernementalede 5 pour cent sont ajoutées à la note. Sinon, un pourboire volontaire de 10 pour cent est le taux courant.

La Barbade aujourd'hui

BANQUES - Les banques ayant une agence permanente à La Barbade sont: Barbados National Bank, Caribbean Commercial Bank, Barclays Bank plc, CIBC Caribbean Ltd, Royal Bank of Canada et la Bank of Nova Scotia. Leurs sièges locaux sont à Bridgetown.

La plupart sont ouvertes de 8 h. à 15 h., du lundi au jeudi. Le vendredi, la plupart des banques demeurent ouvertes de 8 h. à 17 h. La Barbados National Bank a un bureau de change à l'aéroport, ouvert de 8 h. à minuit tous les jours.

ECONOMIE - L'économie de la Barbade repose sur quatre secteurs d'activité principaux: le tourisme, les services financiers off-shore,

leicht erledigt werden. Bestimmte Kategorien von Waren können beim Einkauf mitgenommen und andere wiederum zum Flughafen oder Hafen für eine Entgegennahme vor dem Boarding geliefert werden. Waren, die vom zollfreien Kauf in Barbados ausgeschlossen sind, sind Spirituosen, Weine, Tabak, Zigaretten, Zigarren, Videogeräte, Videospiele, Platten, Autoradios, Fernseher und Heimcomputer. Geschäfte auf dem Flugplatz und im Hafen bieten Ihnen eine breitgefächerte Auswahl an zollfreien Waren.

Rhythmen der Nacht

Wenn der goldene Sonnenuntergang das Ende des Tages kennzeichnet, beginnt sich das Leben der tropischen Nächte auf aufregende Rhythmen vorzubereiten. Das Nachtleben von Barbados bietet Ihnen Theatervorstellungen mit Abendessen, Shows, Tanz in Discos und Nachtclubs oder einen ruhigen Abend bei Kerzenlicht in einem guten Restaurant an der Küste.

PARTYFAHRTEN: Es gibt eine Anzahl von großen Kreuzfahrtschiffen, die an der Westküste der Insel vier oder fünf Stunden lange Partyfahrten bieten, bei denen Bands live an Bord auftreten. Sie können auch ruhigere Fahrten an Bord einer Auswahl von Katamaranen unternehmen.

UNTERHALTUNG: Viele Hotels bieten an Wochentagen Shows, die auf traditionellen Ausdrucksformen karibischen Kulturguts basieren, wie Limbo Tanzen, Feuerschlucken, Steelbands, Kalypso und Bauchtanzen. Die Magie, das Geheimnisvolle, die Romantik und Aufregung dringen in die Phantasie ein.

NACHTKLUBS: Für die Unterhaltung der Nachtschwärmer unter Ihnen öffnen viele Nachtklubs ihre Türen. Dann gibt es auch noch Baxters Road, 'die Straße, die niemals schläft', wo Sie sich nach dem Nachtklub bei einheimischen Speisen und erfrischenden Getränken entspannen können.

ESSEN UND GETRÄNKE: Wenn die Erkundung der verschiedenen Düfte und Geschmäcker der Welt zu Ihren Lieblingsbeschäftigungen gehört, finden Sie in Barbados eine große Vielfalt an gastronomischen Freuden. Restaurants bieten Ihnen eine große Auswahl von Menüs, die von kontinentalen Gerichten bis zu den exotischeren einheimischen Speisen reichen.

FLIEGENDER FISCH: Dieser Fisch ist eine Delikatesse und so beliebt, daß er praktisch ein Nationalsymbol darstellt. Der fliegende Fisch wird in Feinschmeckergerichten wie auch in Sandwiches am Strand gegessen. Sonstige köstliche Meeresfrüchte, die täglich frisch aus den umliegenden Wassern gefischt werden, sind unter anderem Hummer, Krabben, 'Dorado', Meeresschildkröte, roter 'Snapper', Thunfisch, Königsfisch und Makrele. Einzigartig sind der 'Crane Chubb' und die Meereseier (weißer Seeigelrogen kleingehackt und scharf gewürzt gebraten, paniert oder nach Ihrem Geschmack zubereitet).

Unsere tropische Erde bringt einen Reichtum an frischem Obst und Gemüse hervor. Typische Früchte der Insel sind z.B. Mangos, Paws-Paws (Papayas), Bananen, Guava, Avocado und Kokosnüsse und die etwas exotischeren Früchte 'Soursops' und Barbados Kirschen. In unserem Korb von frisch gepflücktem Gemüse finden Sie unter anderem Brotfrucht, Jamswurzel, weiße 'Eddoes', 'Christophenes', Auberginen, Okra, Kürbis, Kochbananen und Speisekürbis. Das etwas vertrautere Salatgemüse wächst ebenfalls auf Barbados.

Spezialitäten, die Sie ausprobieren sollten, sind 'cou-cou', ein Gericht aus Mais und Okra, 'jug-jug', eine Mischung von Guinea Mais und grünen Erbsen, 'pepperpot', ein würziger Eintopf mit verschiedenen Fleischsorten, 'roti', eine karibische/ostindische Speise, die aus mit Curry mariniertem Fleisch in einer 'Chipatee' besteht, und 'conkies', eine Mischung aus Maismehl, Kokosnuß, Kürbis, Rosinen, süßen Kartoffeln und Gewürzen, die in einem Bananenblatt gedünstet wird.

Trinken in Barbados bedeutet im allgemeinen Rum. Die lokalen Rummarken gehören zu den weltbesten und werden in verschiedenen ausgezeichneten Zubereitungen serviert.

TRINKGELD: In den meisten Hotels wird ein Trinkgeld von 10 Prozent und eine 5 prozentige Verkaufssteuer der Regierung automatisch auf die Rechnung aufgeschlagen. Wenn nicht, ist ein Trinkgeld von 10 Prozent angemessen.

musicale della notte tropicale è animato da ritmi eccitanti. Fra gli intrattenimenti a disposizione vi sono cene animate da spettacoli teatrali, spettacoli di varietB, discoteche e night -club oppure una tranquilla serata al lume di candela in un buon ristorante della costa.

CROCIERE PER PARTY. Vi è un certo numero di grandi imbarcazioni da crociera che offre crociere di quattro o cinque ore lungo la costa occidentale dell'isola per party con musica dal vivo. Potete anche scegliere crociere più rilassanti a bordo dei più piccoli catamarani.

INTRATTENIMENTI. Molti alberghi offrono durante la settimana programmi di spettacoli ispirati alle espressioni culturali dei Caraibi quali danza limbo, mangiatori di fuoco, bande di strumenti a percussione, calipso e danza del ventre. Magia, mistero, avventura ed eccitazione catturano la fantasia.

NIGHT-CLUB I numerosi night-club e locali notturni offrono tutto quanto può servire a divertire e stimolare che vuole star fuori la sera. Vi è poi Baxters Road, 'la strada che non dorme mai' per gli spuntini e i drink del dopo-party.

CIBI E BEVANDE. Se esplorare il mondo della gastronomia per scoprire sapori e gusti diversi è uno dei vostri passatempi preferiti, scoprirete che Barbados offre un'enorme varietà di delizie gastronomiche. Le trattorie offrono un'ampia gamma di menù, dalla cucina europea a cibi locali più esotici.

PESCE VOLANTE. E' una ghiottoneria ed è così richiesto da essere diventato un vero e proprio simbolo nazionale. Si trova ovunque, dai piatti dei buongustai ai sandwich della spiaggia. Tra i frutti di mare, deliziosi e freschi perchè pescati ogni giorno dalle acque circostanti ricordiamo le aragoste, i gamberetti, le corifene ed inoltre tartarughe, pesce serra rosso, tonno, pesce re e sgombri, per menzionarne solo alcuni. Eccezionali sono il *Crane Chubb* e le uova marine (uova bianche di riccio di mare con spezie, impanate o preparate secondo i vostri gusti).

Nell'isola crescono inoltre frutta fresca e verdure in abbondanza, tra cui mango, paw-paw (papaya), banane, guava, avocado e noci di cocco, insieme ai più esotici soursop e alle ciliege di Barbados. Le primizie includono i frutti dell'albero del pane, le patate dolci, il taro bianco, il christophene, le melanzane, il gombo, la zucca, la piantaggine e le zucchine. Sull'isola si coltivano anche la maggior parte delle verdure per insalata più comuni.

Alcune specialità che vale veramente la pena di assaggiare sono il cou-cou, un piatto di cereali e gombo ; il jug-jug, una miscela di cereale della Guinea e piselli verdi; la pepaiola, uno stufato piccante fatto con diversi tipi di carne; il roti, un cibo dei Caraibi/India Orientale che consiste in carni cucinate col curry e avvolte in chipatee; e i conkies, una miscela di cereali, noce di cocco, zucca, uva passa, patate dolci e spezie che viene cotta a vapore in una foglia di palma.

Bere a Barbados significa di solito bere rum. Le marche locali sono fra le migliori del mondo e vengono servite in una varietà di deliziose miscele.

MANCIA. In molti alberghi viene aggiunto al conto un 10 per cento per il servizio e un 5 per cento per Imposte Governative sulle vendite. Altrimenti, si consiglia di lasciare una mancia del 10 per cento.

Barbados oggi

BANCHE. Tra le banche che operano a Barbados le maggiori sono la Barbados National Bank, la Caribbean Commercial Bank, la Barclays Bank plc, la CIBC Caribbean Ltd., la Royal Bank of Canada e la Bank of Nova Scotia. Tutte le sedi principali si trovano a Bridgetown.

La maggior parte delle banche è aperta dalle 8 di mattina fino alle 15 del pomeriggio da lunedì a giovedX. Il venerdX, molte banche rimangono aperte dalle 8 alle 17. La Barbados National Bank ha un'agenzia di cambio all'aeroporto che rimane aperta tutti i giorni dalle 8 di mattina a mezzanotte.

ECONOMIA. L'economia di Barbados è basata su quattro principali attivitB: turismo, servizi finanziari offshore, agricoltura (inclusa la pesca) e industria leggera. Il turismo è quello che realizza

televisores y ordenadores personales para uso doméstico. Las tiendas del aeropuerto y el puerto presentan una amplia gama de artículos libres de impuestos.

Los ritmos de la noche

Cuando las doradas puestas de sol marcan el final del día, el tempo de la noche tropical se alegra al son de los emocionantes ritmos. Entre la selección de entretenimientos de que disponemos, se cuentan las salas de espectáculos con servicio de restaurante, espectáculos de cabaret, discotecas y clubes nocturnos, o una cena tranquila a la luz de las velas en un restaurante de la playa.

CRUCEROS DE FIESTA. Existe toda una serie de cruceros grandes que ofrecen fiestas de cuatro o cinco horas mientras navegan por la costa occidental de la isla, contando con bandas de música que actúan en vivo a bordo de la embarcación. También se pueden elegir cruceros más relajantes a bordo de una amplia gama de catamaranes que tenemos a su disposición.

ENTRETENIMIENTOS. La mayoría de los hoteles cuentan con espectáculos de cabaret de lunes a viernes, basados en expresiones culturales caribeñas tales como limbo, tragafuegos, *steel band*, calypso y danza del vientre. Magia, misterio, romance y emociones invaden la imaginación.

CLUBES NOCTURNOS. Existen numerosos clubes y locales nocturnos para entretener y estimular al juerguista nocturno. Y también contamos con Baxter Road, "la calle que nunca duerme", para disfrutar de comidas locales y agradables bebidas tras la diversión.

COMIDA Y BEBIDA. Si uno de sus pasatiempos favoritos consiste en explorar el mundo de la cocina para descubrir diferentes sabores y aromas, descubrirá que Barbados cuenta con una extensísima variedad de delicias gastronómicas. Los locales que ofrecen comida cuentan con una amplia gama de menús, desde platos continentales hasta los platos locales más exóticos.

EL PEZVOLADOR resulta un manjar tan popular, que es prácticamente un símbolo nacional. Puede encontrarlo en todas partes, desde platos de alta cocina hasta emparedados en la playa. Otros deliciosos pescados y mariscos que se pueden saborear frescos a diario, procedentes de las aguas costeras, incluyen langosta, camarones, doradas, tortuga, pargos, atún, *king fish* y caballa, entre otros. *Crane Chubb* y *sea egges* son algo único (huevas de erizo de mar blanco con salsa picante, rebozadas o cocinadas al gusto del comensal).

Nuestra tierra tropical produce verduras y frutas frescas en abundancia. Entre las frutas se incluyen mangos, *paw-paws* (papayas), bananas, guayabas, aguacates y cocos, así como las más exóticas guanábanas y cerezas de Barbados. Las verduras recién recogidas pueden incluir los frutos del árbol del pan, ñames, *eddoes* blancos, *christophenes*, berenjenas, calalúes, calabazas, los frutos del llantén y zapallos. También se cultivan en Barbados las verduras para ensalada más conocidas.

Algunas especialidades que merece la pena probar son *cou-cou*, un plato hecho con harina de maíz y calalúes; *jug-jug*, una mezcla de guisantes verdes y maíz de Barbados; *pepperpot*, un guiso de diferentes tipos de carne con especias; *roti*, un plato Caribeño/de las Indias orientales que consiste en diversas carnes al curry envueltas en *chipatee* (pan ácimo); y *conkies*, una mezcla de harina de maíz, coco, calabaza, uvas pasas, boniatos y especias, cocinada al vapor en una hoja de bananero.

Beber en Barbados normalmente quiere decir "ron". Las marcas locales se encuentran entre las mejores del mundo, y se sirven en gran variedad de deliciosos brebajes.

PROPINAS. En la mayoría de los hoteles se añaden a la factura un 10% de servicio y un 5% a título de Impuestos gubernamentales sobre las ventas. De no ser así, una propina del 10% es lo normal.

Barbados en la actualidad

BANCOS. Los bancos que operan en la actualidad en Barbados incluyen: el Banco Nacional de Barbados, Banco Comercial del Caribe, Barclays Bank plc, CIBC Caribbean Ltd, Royal Bank de Canadá y el Banco de Nueva Escocia. Todas las sucursales principales se hallan en Bridgetown.

La mayoría de ellos permanecen abiertos de 8:00 a.m. a 3:00 p.m., de

l'agriculture (y compris la pêche) et l'industrie légère. Le tourisme est le principal fournisseur de devises et assure un emploi à près de 13 pour cent de la main-d'oeuvre locale.

L'industrie participe à hauteur de 12 pour cent au Produit National Brut.

Le secteur industriel inclut actuellement des sociétés produisant des vêtements, des meubles, des produits et équipements électroniques et des fournitures médicales pour les marchés régionaux et nord-américains. Ce secteur représente environ 10 pour cent du Produit National Brut.

L'agriculture représente presque 7 pour cent du Produit National Brut de l'île. La canne à sucre est la culture la plus rentable et apporte une saine contribution au gain à l'exportation de l'île. Au cours de ces dernières années, le Gouvernement a lancé une vigoureuse politique de diversification agricole, qui a entraîné une augmentation de la production de légumes, de volailles, de viandes et de fruits.

L'industrie de la pêche a également connu une expansion récente avec l'amélioration des installations du port de pêche principal d'Oistins, engendrant une grande augmentation du volume de poisson disponible pour la consommation locale. Le gouvernement a également adopté des lois facilitant les opérations de sociétés internationales, de banques off-shore, de compagnies d'assurance et de compagnies de navigation exonérées, ainsi que d'enregistrement de navires sous pavillon de La Barbade.

La Barbade est considéré comme un lieu d'investissement sûr en raison de sa bonne stabilité politique et sociale, de la main-d'oeuvre disponible, des communications, de l'enseignement, des services sanitaires et médicaux.

COMMUNICATIONS ET MÉDIAS - La Barbade est le principal centre d'opération régional pour Cable et Wireless (West Indies) Ltd, qui assure des communications par télégraphe, téléphone, télex et télécopie dans le monde entier. Les télégrammes et télécopies sont envoyés directement de votre hôtel ou de la plupart des bureaux de poste ou du Bureau des Télécommunications Extérieures de La Barbade à Wildey, St Michael.

La Barbade possède un service de téléphone avec composition du numéro direct vers la plupart des lieux du monde et ses services sont fournis à travers tout le monde par Bartel Co Ltd. grâce à un central moderne à Bridgetown. Tous les appels téléphoniques locaux sont gratuits.

TV/RADIO - La Barbade possède sa propre station de télévision, la Caribbean Broadcasting Television, qui émet sur la Chaîne 8. CBC offre également un service de télévision par abonnement avec cinq chaînes internationales.

Sept stations de radio émettent dans l'île: (Caribbean Broadcasting Corporation) CBC 900 AM, Liberty 98,1 FM, (The voice of Barbados) VOB 790 AM, YESS 104 FM, (Barbados Broadcasting Service) BBS 90,7 FM et FAITH FM 102,1 et une station de câble appelée Star Radio.

JOURNAUX - La Barbade a deux journaux quotidiens, l'"Advocate" et la "Nation". Il existe, par ailleurs, un certain nombre de journaux, magazines gratuits destinés aux touristes, ainsi que d'autres publications régionales et internationales à acheter.

CLUBS DE SERVICES - Bien représentés à La Barbade on trouve le Lions Club, le Rotary Club, le Soroptimists, le Kiwanis, le Jaycees et Jaycettes et les Toastmasters et les Toastmistresses. En outre, il existe plusieurs organisations fraternelles, y compris les Francs-Maçons, The Mechanics, The Shepherds et The Foresters, The Elks et The Gardeners et Odd Fellows.

Services divers

LAVERIE - Des services spéciaux de laverie dans l'heure ou le même jour sont disponibles. Il existe aussi un certain nombre de laveries automatiques dans les secteurs hôteliers, tels que Oistins, Worthing et Hastings à Christ Church; Bridgetown et Black Rock à St Michael et Sunset Crest à St. James.

PHOTOGRAPHIE - Un service de développement photographique dans l'heure est disponible, avec des laboratoires offrant des services

Barbados heute

BANKEN: Zu den gegenwärtig in Barbados tätigen Banken gehören Barbados National Bank, Carribean Commercial Bank, Barclays Bank plc, CIBC Carribean Ltd, Royal Bank of Canada und die Bank of Nova Scotia. Die Hauptbüros aller dieser Banken sind in Bridgetown.

Die meisten Banken sind zwischen 8:00 Uhr und 15:00 Uhr von Montag bis Donnerstag geöffnet. Am Freitag bleiben die meisten Banken von 8:00 Uhr bis 17:00 Uhr geöffnet. Die Barbados National Bank betreibt ein Wechselbüro am Flughafen, das täglich von 8:00 Uhr bis 24:00 Uhr geöffnet ist.

WIRTSCHAFT: Die Wirtschaft von Barbados basiert auf vier Hauptsektoren: Tourismus, Auslandsfinanzleistungen, Landwirtschaft (einschließlich Fischerei) und Leichtindustrie. Tourismus ist die Haupteinnahmequelle von Devisen und beschäftigt 13 Prozent der Arbeitskräfte mit Arbeit.

Die 'Tourismusindustrie' trägt zu 12 Prozent des Bruttoinlandproduktes bei.

Der Produktionssektor umfaßt im Moment Unternehmen, die Kleidungsstücke, Möbel, elektronische Produkte und deren Montage und Produkte der medizinischen Versorgung für den regionalen und den nordamerikanischen Markt herstellen. Dieser Sektor stellt ungefähr 10 Prozent des Bruttoinlandsproduktes dar.

Die Landwirtschaft nimmt fast 7 Prozent des Bruttoinlandsproduktes ein. Zuckerrohr ist das Agrarprodukt, das am meisten Ertrag bringt und einen gesunden Beitrag zu den Exportverdiensten der Insel leistet. Die Regierung hat in den letzten Jahren eine wirkungsvolle Politik der landwirtschaftlichen Streuung eingeführt, die zu einer Produktionssteigerung von Gemüse, Geflügel, anderen Fleischsorten und Obst führte.

Die Fischindustrie hat sich in letzter Zeit ebenfalls mit verbesserten Einrichtungen am Hauptfischhafen von Oistins vergrößert, was zu einer großen Steigerung der Menge von gefangenen Fischen, die für den örtlichen Konsum bestimmt sind, führte. Die Regierung hat darüber hinaus Gesetze verabschiedet, die die Geschäfte von internationalen Unternehmen, Auslandsbanken, freigestellten Versicherungsgesellschaften und Schiffahrtsgesellschaften wie auch die Resignation von Schiffen unter der Fahne von Barbados erleichtern sollten.

Barbados wird aufgrund seiner soliden politischen und gesellschaftlichen Lage, seines Arbeitskräftepotentials, seiner Kommunikation, seines Schulwesens, Gesundheitsdienstes und ärztlichen Dienstes als ein sicherer Platz für Investitionen angesehen.

KOMMUNIKATION UND MEDIEN: Barbados ist das wichtigste regionale Betriebszentrum für Cable and Wireless (West Indies) Ltd. Dieses Unternehmen bietet Kommunikation weltweit in Form von Telegraphen, Telefon, Telex und Fax. Telegramme und Faxe können von Ihrem Hotel aus, den meisten Postämtern oder dem externen Telekommunikationsbüro von Barbados (Barbados External Telecommunications) in Wildey, St. Michael gesendet werden.

Barbados verfügt über einen Telefonservice mit Direktwahl in fast alle Teile der Welt. Diese Dienstleistungen werden im ganzen Land von Bartel Co Ltd. über deren modernes Fernsprechamt in Bridgetown bereitgestellt. Alle Ortsgespräche sind kostenlos.

TV/RADIO: Barbados hat seine eigene Fernsehstation, die 'Carribean Broadcasting Corporation', die auf Kanal 8 sendet. Die CBC bietet auch einen Subskriptionsfernsehservice, der fünf internationale Fernsehkanäle offeriert. Sieben Radiostationen senden auf Barbados: (Carribean Broadcasting Corporation) CBC 900 AM, Liberty 98.1 FM, (The Voice of Barbados) VOB 790 AM, YESS 104 FM, (Barbados Broadcasting Service) BBS 90.7 FM und FAITH FM 102.1. Darüber hinaus gibt es einen Kabelsender, der unter dem Namen Star Radio sendet.

ZEITUNGEN: Barbados hat zwei Tageszeitungen, den "Advocate" und die "Nation". Eine Anzahl von kostenlosen Touristenzeitungen und -zeitschriften sind ebenfalls erhältlich. Daneben gibt es eine Anzahl von zu bezahlenden lokalen, regionalen und internationalen Publikationen.

SERVICE CLUBS: Der Lions Club, Rotarier Club, die Soroptimisten, Kiwanis, Jacees und Jacettes und die Toastmasters und Toastmistresses sind in Barbados stark repräsentiert. Zusätzlich dazu gibt es einige Logen einschließlich der Freimaurer, der Mechanics, der Shepherds, Foresters,

i maggiori guadagni nel settore del cambio estero e fornisce occupazione a circa il 13 per cento della forza lavoro.

L'industria è responsabile del 12 per cento del Prodotto Interno Lordo.

Il settore manifatturiero attualmente comprende fabbriche di abbigliamento, mobili, prodotti e componenti elettronici e forniture mediche per i mercati regionali e del Nord America. Questo settore rappresenta approssimativamente il 10 per cento del Prodotto Interno Lordo.

L'agricoltura è responsabile di circa il 7 per cento del Prodotto Interno Lordo dell'isola. La canna da zucchero è il maggior prodotto di esportazione e rappresenta un notevole contributo alla bilancia delle esportazioni. Negli ultimi anni, il Governo ha intrapreso una vigorosa politica di diversificazione agricola che ha determinato l'aumento della produzione di verdure, pollame, carne e frutta.

Anche il settore della pesca ha subito di recente un'espansione grazie al miglioramento delle infrastrutture del principale porto peschereccio di Oistins e la quantità del pescato per consumo locale è di conseguenza notevolmente aumentata. Il Governo ha inoltre approvato un insieme di leggi per facilitare le operazioni di società commerciali internazionali e banche off-shore, garantendo facilitazioni fiscali alle compagnie d'assicurazione e alle società di spedizione, come pure alle imbarcazioni che battono la bandiera delle Barbados.

Barbados è considerata una località sicura per gli investimenti grazie alla stabilità politica e sociale, alla disponibilità di manodopera, comunicazioni, educazione scolastica, servizi sanitari e medici.

COMUNICAZIONI E MEDIA. A Barbados ha sede il maggior centro regionale operativo della Cable and Wireless (West Indies) Ltd., che assicura i collegamenti telegrafici, telefonici, telex e fax in ogni parte del mondo. Telegrammi e fax possono essere spediti dal vostro albergo, dall'ufficio postale o dall'ufficio della Barbados External Telecommunications di Wildey a St. Michael.

Barbados ha un servizio telefonico in teleselezione per molte località internazionali e i servizi di telefonia vengono forniti su tutta l'isola dalla Bartel Co. Ltd. tramite la moderna centrale telefonica di Bridgetown. Tutte le telefonate locali sono gratuite.

TV/RADIO. Barbados possiede la propria stazione televisiva, la Caribbean Broadcasting Corporation, che trasmette sul Canale 8. La CBC fornisce inoltre un servizio Tv in abbonamento che offre in visione cinque canali internazionali.

Sul posto operano sette stazioni radio: CBC (Caribbean Broadcasting Corporation) 900 AM, Liberty 98.1 FM, (The Voice of Barbados) VOB 790 FM, YESS 104 FM, (Barbados Broadcasting Service) BBS 90.7 FM e FAITH FM 102.1 e una stazione via cavo chiamata Star Radio.

GIORNALI. Barbados ha due quotidiani, l'"Advocate" e il "Nation". Vengono pubblicati diversi giornali e riviste per i turisti, alcune gratuite, ed altre locali, regionali e internazionali, a pagamento.

CLUB Ben rappresentati a Barbados sono il Lions Club, il Rotary Club, il Soroptimists, il Kiwanis, lo Jaycees e Jaycettes, e il Toastmasters e Toastmistresses.

Vi sono inoltre numerose confraternite tra cui The Free Masons, The Mechanics, The Shupherds e The Foresters, The Elks e The Gardners e Odd Fellows.

Infornazioni di carattere generale

LAVANDERIA. Sono disponibili servizi di lavanderia express di un'ora o con ritiro in giornata. Esistono inoltre lavanderie self-service a gettone nei complessi alberghieri di Oistins, Worthing e Hastings a Christ Church; Bridgetown e Black Rock a St.Michael e Sunset Crest a St. James.

FOTOGRAFIA. Lo sviluppo delle pellicole viene effettuato in un'ora e alcuni studi offrono servizi gratuiti di ritiro e consegna in albergo.

POSTE. Barbados possiede un servizio e strutture postali estremamente efficienti. La sede del nuovo General Post Office a Cheapside, Bridgetown, comprende un servizio di trasporto di pacchi

lunes a jueves. Los viernes abren de 8:00 a.m. a 5:00 p.m. El Banco Nacional de Barbados opera una oficina de cambio de divisas situada en el aeropuerto, que permanece abierta diariamente de ocho de la mañana a media noche.

ECONOMÍA. La economía de Barbados se basa en cuatro secciones principales: turismo, servicios financieros extraterritoriales, agricultura (incluyendo la pesca) e industria manufacturera ligera. El turismo constituye la mayor fuente de ingresos en divisas extranjeras, y proporciona empleo a un 13% de la mano de obra.

La industria contribuye con un 12% del producto interior bruto.

El sector de la industria manufacturera incluye en la actualidad compañías fabricantes de prendas de vestir, mobiliario, montajes y productos electrónicos, y suministros médicos para los mercados regional y norteamericano. Este sector representa aproximadamente un 10% del producto interior bruto.

La agricultura representa casi un 7% del producto interior bruto de la isla. El cultivo de la caña de azúcar constituye la principal fuente de ingresos, y contribuye de manera substancial a los ingresos de exportación de la isla. En los últimos años, el Gobierno se ha embarcado en una vigorosa política de diversificación agrícola, que ha tenido como resultado el crecimiento en la producción de verduras, aves, carnes y frutas.

La industria pesquera también se ha expandido recientemente con la mejora de los servicio del principal puerto pesquero, el de Oistins, lo que ha tenido como resultado un gran crecimiento en el volumen de pescado disponible para el consumo local. El Gobierno también ha aprobado determinada legislación para facilitar la operación de compañías comerciales internacionales, bancos extraterritoriales, compañías de seguros exentas y compañías de fletes, así como la inscripción de buques con la bandera de Barbados.

Barbados se considera como un lugar seguro para inversiones, debido a su gran estabilidad socio-política, abastecimiento de mano de obra, comunicaciones, escolaridad y servicios médicos y sanitarios.

MEDIOS DE COMUNICACIÓN. Barbados constituye el centro operativo principal a nivel regional de Cable and Wireless (West Indies) Ltd, que proporciona medios de comunicación con todo el mundo mediante telegramas, teléfono, télex y facsímil. Puede usted enviar telegramas y facsímiles desde su hotel, la mayoría de las oficinas de correos y la oficina de Telecomunicaciones Externas de Barbados, ubicada en Wildey, St. Michael.

Barbados cuenta con un servicio de telefonía directa a casi todas las partes del mundo, siendo proporcionados estos servicios en todo el país por Bartel Co Ltd. mediante una moderna central telefónica ubicada en Bridgetown. Todas las llamadas telefónicas locales son gratuitas.

TELEVISIÓN/RADIO. Barbados cuenta con su propia emisora de televisión, la Caribbean Broadcasting Corporation, que emite su programación en el Canal 8. La CBC también ofrece un servicio de subscripción de televisión que proporciona acceso a cinco canales internacionales.

En Barbados operan siete emisoras de radio: (Caribbean Broadcasting Corporation) CBC 900 AM, Liberty 98.1 FM, (The Voice of Barbados) VOB 790 AM, YESS 104 FM, (Barbados Broadcasting Service) BBS 90.7 FM y FAITH FM 102.1, así como una emisora por cable llamada Star Radio.

PERIÓDICOS. Barbados cuenta con dos periódicos diarios, el "Advocate" y el "Nation". Existe toda una serie de revistas y periódicos gratuitos como guía para el turista, así como otras publicaciones locales, regionales e internacionales pagadas por el interesado.

ASOCIACIONES. El *Lions Club*, el *Rotary Club*, los *Soroptimists*, los *Kiwanis*, los *Jaycees* y las *Jaycettes*, y los *Toastmasters* y las *Toastmistresses* están ampliamente representados en la isla. Además existen diversas fraternidades, incluyendo los Francmasones, los *Mechanics*, los *Shepherds* y *Foresters*, los *Elks* y los *Gardeners* y *Odd Fellows*.

Servicios diversos

LAVANDERÍA. Disponemos de servicios de lavandería especiales de lavado en una hora o en el mismo día. También existe una serie de lavanderías de autoservicio en las zonas hoteleras tales como Oistins,

de collecte et livraison gratuits aux hôtels.

COURRIER - La Barbade possède des services et équipements postaux exceptionnels. Le nouveau centre de la Poste à Cheapside, Bridgetown, comporte un service de colis et des services de livraison expresse à Londres et New York, avec livraison garantie dans les quarante-huit heures. Un service de courrier recommandé assure l'expédition garantie de courrier dans des conditions de grande sécurité. Un Bureau Philatélique offre les émissions premier jour de La Barbade, qui interviennent quatre fois par an. Les collectionneurs peuvent organiser des comptes de dépôt grâce auxquels les nouvelles émissions peuvent leur être envoyées partout dans le monde.

Il existe des Bureaux de Poste dans chaque Paroisse. Les boîtes à lettres rouges sont situées au bord des rues dans toute l'île. La distribution du courrier se fait deux fois par jour à Bridgetown et dans les faubourgs et une fois par jour dans les districts ruraux.

RÈGLEMENTS CONCERNANT LE MARIAGE - Une demande de licence de mariage doit être présentée par les deux parties en personne au bureau du Ministère de l'intérieur. Les documents exigés sont (a) un passeport valide ou l'original des copies certifiées des certificats de naissance des demandeurs; (b) si l'une des parties a déjà été mariée et est veuve, des copies certifiées du certificat de mariage et du certificat de décès concernant l'époux décédé; (c) si l'une des parties a divorcé, un jugement définitif de divorce ou une copie certifiée du jugement définitif, est exigée, et non le jugement provisoire. Tous les documents qui ne sont pas en anglais doivent être accompagnés d'une traduction certifiée par un Notaire autorisé. Frais: si aucune des parties n'est citoyen ou résident de La Barbade, un paiement de BDS$ 100,00 et un timbre de $25,00 pour obtenir la licence. Si l'une des parties est citoyen de La Barbade, lesfrais sont BDS$35,00 et BDS$10,00 de timbrage.

Les arrangements peuvent être faits auprès d'un officier de l'état civil (un juge ou un prêtre autorisé à jouer le rôle d'officier de l'état civil pour les mariages) avant de remplir un formulaire de demande de licence. Une lettre de l'officier de l'état Civil qui a accepté de célébrer la cérémonie de mariage doit être présentée au moment de remplir la demande. Un mariage peut être célébré immédiatement après l'émission de la licence - laquelle est disponible le même jour. Les deux intéressés doivent aller chercher leur licence ensemble.

INSTALLATIONS SPORTIVES ET LIEUX DE CONFÉRENCE - Le Complexe Sportif Sir Garfield Sobers est un gymnase polyvalent conçu pour permettre douze disciplines sportives. Situé de façon idéale, l'établissement est très proche des services de communications, des banques et des magasins. Les équipements nécessaires aux diverses manifestations sportives sont disponibles sans problème et font partie du service fourni. Au nombre des autres aménités, on compte une salle d'échauffement pour les athlètes avec des appareils d'exercice polyvalents, des salles de sauna et de massage, un cabinet médical et deux tableaux d'affichage électroniques. Le Sir Garfield Sobers Sports Complex, Wildey, St. Michael, La Barbade, Antilles, Tél. (246) 437 6016, Télécopie (246) 437 3358. Le Centre Aquatique de La Barbade est situé tout près du Complexe Sportif Sir Garfield Sobers et est conçu pour permettre des épreuves de natation et de sports aquatiques de compétition, ainsi que d'autres activités de détente en piscine. Les installations comprennent deux piscines. La piscine principale mesure 50 mètres sur 25, ce qui fournit vingt couloirs pour les courses courtes et dix couloirs pour les longs parcours. On trouve aussi dans ces installations pour sports aquatiques un centre de tennis équipé de quatre cours opérationnels.

Le complexe de Wildey a été utilisé pour y donner des concerts et séries de manifestations importantes. Pour plus de renseignements, veuillez prendre contact avec: The Manager, Aquatic Centre, Wildey, St. Michael, Barbados, West Indies, Tél.(246) 429 7946, Télécopie: (246) 436 2272.

Le nouveau Sherbourne Centre est le plus récent des établissements de conférences qu'offre La Barbade. Le Centre est entièrement climatisé et, outre les conférences, il est équipé pour accueillir des foires commerciales, des séminaires et expositions. Le hall principal du Centre comporte 800 places assises de style théâtre et 400 places style salle de classe. Des services de traduction sont disponibles en six langues

Elks und der Gardeners und Odd Fellows.

Sonstige Dienstleistungen

WÄSCHE: Ein besonderer einstündiger Waschservice und ein Waschservice, bei dem die Wäsche am gleichen Tag fertig ist, steht zur Verfügung. Es gibt auch eine Anzahl von SB-Waschsalons in den Hotelgebieten wie Oistins, Worthing und Hastings in Christ Church, Bridgetown und Black Rock in St. Michael und Sunset Crest in St. James.

FOTOGRAFIE: Ein einstündiger Filmentwicklungsservice ist erhältlich; einige Fotolabore bieten einen kostenlosen Abhol- und Zustellservice zu Hotels.

POST: Barbados verfügt über einen außerordentlich guten Postdienst und Posteinrichtungen. Die neue Zentrale des Hauptpostamtes in Cheapside, Bridgetown, bietet einen Paketpostdienst und Eilzustellungsservice nach London und New York mit einer garantierten Zustellung innerhalb von achtundvierzig Stunden. Ein Einschreibedienst garantiert einen zuverlässigen Postversand zu sicheren Bedingungen. Ein philatelistisches Büro bietet Ersttagsstempel, die nur viermal im Jahr herausgebracht werden. Sammler können sich ein Einlagekonto anlegen, das es ermöglicht, sich neue Ausgaben weltweit zusenden zu lassen.

Es gibt Bezirkspostämter in jeder Gemeinde. Die roten Briefkästen sind an Straßenrändern überall auf der Insel zu sehen. Zustellungen erfolgen zweimal täglich in Bridgetown und dessen Vororten und einmal täglich in ländlichen Gebieten.

VORSCHRIFTEN FÜR DIE EHESCHLIEßUNG: Anträge auf eine Ehegenehmigung müssen von beiden Parteien persönlich im Büro des Innenministeriums gestellt werden. Die dafür erforderliche Dokumente sind: (a) ein gültiger Paß oder die Originalkopie oder beglaubigte Kopie der Geburtsurkunden der Antragsteller; (b) falls eine der beiden Parteien zuvor verheiratet war und verwitwet ist, sind die beglaubigten Kopien der Heiratsurkunde und Sterbeurkunde des/r verstorbenen Gatten/in erforderlich; (c) wenn eine der beiden Parteien geschieden ist, ist das originale Scheidungsurteil oder rechtskräftige Urteil erforderlich und nicht das vorläufige Scheidungsurteil. Allen Dokumenten, die nicht in englisch abgefaßt sind, muß eine beglaubigte Übersetzung eines bevollmächtigten Notars beigelegt sein. Falls keiner der beiden Antragsteller Bürger oder Einwohner von Barbados ist, wird eine Gebühr von BDS$100,00 Bargeld und $25,00 Stempelgebühr für die Erteilung einer Ehegenehmigung erhoben. Wenn einer der Antragsteller Bürger von Barbados ist, betragen die Gebühren BDS $35,00 und BDS $10,00 Stempelgebühr.

Vor der Antragstellung auf Ehegenehmigung sollten Sie die notwendigen Vereinbarungen mit einem Standesbeamten oder einem für Eheschließungen autorisierten Pastor oder Pfarrer treffen. Ein Brief des Standesbeamten oder Pastors, der eingewilligt hat, die Eheschließung durchzuführen, sollte Ihrem Antrag beigelegt sein. Nach Erteilen der Ehegenehmigung, die noch am gleichen Tag des Antrags ausgestellt wird, kann das Paar sofort getraut werden. Das Paar muß seine Ehegenehmigung gemeinsam abholen.

SPORT- UND KONFERENZEINRICHTUNGEN: Der Sir Garfield Sobers Sports Complex ist ein Vielzweck-Fitneßzentrum, in dem zwölf Sportarten betrieben werden können. Das Sportzentrum befindet sich idealerweise in unmittelbarer Nähe von Kommunikationseinrichtungen, Banken und Geschäften. Die Sportausrüstung, die Sie möglicherweise benötigen, ist komplett erhältlich und gehört zum gebotenen Service. Darüber hinaus bietet der Sir Garfield Sobers Sportkomplex einen Warm-Up-Raum für die Athleten mit Vielzweck-Fitneßeinrichtungen, Saunas und Massageräumen, sportmedizinischer Betreuung und zwei elektronischen Anzeigetafeln. Sir Garfield Sobers Sports Complex, Wildey, St. Michael, Barbados, West Indies, Tel: (246) 437 6016, Fax: (246) 437 3358.

Das Barbados Aquatic Centre ist neben dem Sir Garfield Sobers Complex gelegen und ist so gestaltet, daß Schwimmwettkämpfe und Wassersport wie auch Freizeitaktivitäten im Pool stattfinden können. Die Anlage besteht aus zwei Swimmingpools. Der größere Swimmingpool ist 50 x 25 Meter groß und verfügt über zwanzig Bahnen für Kurzstreckenveranstaltungen und zehn Bahnen für Veranstaltungen im Langstreckenschwimmen. Darüber hinaus ist die Sportanlage auch mit einem Tenniszentrum ausgestattet, das über vier einsatzbereite

postali e consegna espresso garantita entro quarantotto ore a Londra e New York. Un servizio di posta raccomandata permette di spedire in tutta tranquillità tutta la vostra posta, con la certezza che verrà puntualmente recapitata. Un Bureau Filatelico offre serie speciali emesse soltanto quattro volte all'anno. I collezionisti possono predisporre conti deposito in base ai quali le nuove emissioni possono essere loro inviate in qualsiasi parte del mondo.

Vi sono Uffici Postali Distrettuali in ogni distretto. Per strada si trovano le cassette postali rosse dove imbucare le lettere. Le consegne vengono effettuate due volte al giorno a Bridgetown e nei sobborghi, e una volta al giorno nei distretti rurali.

REGOLE PER CONTRARRE MATRIMONIO. La richiesta di una licenza di matrimonio deve essere fatta da ambedue le parti di persona presso il Ministero dell'Interno (Ministry of Home Affairs). I documenti necessari sono (a) Passaporto valido o originale o copie autenticate dei certificati di nascita dei richiedenti; (b) se l'una o l'altra parte è stata coniugata in precedenza ed è rimasta vedova, copie autenticate del certificato di matrimonio e del certificato di morte relativo al coniuge deceduto; (c) se l'una o l'altra parte ha divorziato, è necessaria la sentenza definitiva in originale o una copia autenticata della sentenza definitiva di divorzio, ma non della sentenza provvisoria. Tutti i documenti non in inglese devono essere accompagnati da una traduzione autenticata da un Notaio. L'onorario, se nessuna delle parti ha la cittadinanza o risiede a Barbados, è di BDS$100.00 in contanti più spese di bollo pari a $25.00 per il rilascio della licenza. Se l'una o l'altra parte ha cittadinanza di Barbados l'onorario è di BDS$35.00 e il bollo costa BDS $10.00.

Bisogna prendere accordi con un funzionario di stato civile (un magistrato o un sacerdote autorizzato ad agire come tale) e quindi compilare un modulo di richiesta per la licenza. Alla presentazione della richiesta va esibita anche una lettera del funzionario di stato civile che ha consentito a celebrare la cerimonia di matrimonio. Il matrimonio può essere solennizzato subito dopo il rilascio della licenza - che è disponibile in giornata. Gli sposi devono recarsi insieme a ritirare la licenza.

STRUTTURE SPORTIVE E STRUTTURE PER CONVEGNI. Il Sir Garfield Sobers Sports Complex è una palestra multifunzionale progettata per dodici diverse discipline sportive. Situata in una posizione ideale, è vicina a servizi di comunicazione, banche e negozi. Le attrezzature necessarie per i diversi eventi sportivi sono facilmente disponibili e fanno parte del servizio. Altre strutture comprendono una stanza per il riscaldamento degli atleti con macchine di allenamento multifunzionali, sauna e salette per i massaggi, una saletta medica e due tabelloni segnapunti elettronici. Il Sir Garfield Sobers Sports Complex, si trova a Wildey, St.Michael, Barbados, West Indies. Tel.: (246) 437 6016, Fax (246) 437 3358.

Il Centro Acquatico di Barbados si trova vicino al Sir Garland Sobers Sports Complex ed è stato progettato in modo da ospitare nuoto e sport acquatici competitivi oltre ad altre attività ricreative da piscina. La struttura è composta da due piscine. La piscina principale è di 50 metri x 25. Sono disponibili venti corsie per eventi di breve durata e dieci corsie per eventi di lunga durata. Presso il complesso per sport acquatici vi è anche un centro per il tennis attrezzato con quattro campi. Il complesso Wildey viene impiegato per mettere in scena concerti importanti e vari eventi ricreativi.

Per maggiori informazioni si prega di contattare: The Manager, Aquatic Centre, Wildey, St. Michael, Barbados, West Indies. Tel.: (246) 429 7946. Fax: (246) 436 2272.

Il nuovo Sherbourne Centre è il più recente fra un certo numero di strutture per convegni offerte da Barbados. Il Centro è equipaggiato con un sistema di condizionamento d'aria e, oltre a convegni, può ospitare mostre commerciali, seminari ed esposizioni. La sala principale del Centro ha un anfiteatro con 800 posti a sedere ed un'aula di 400 posti. Sono disponibili servizi di traduzione in sei lingue ed altri servizi tra cui sale riunioni, servizi medici, servizi stampa, sportelli bancari, postali, ristoranti e tavole calde. Per ulteriori informazioni si prega di contattare: The Manager, Sherbourne Conference Centre, Two Mile Hill, St. Michael, Barbados, West Indies.

Worthing y Hastings en Christ Church; Bridgetown y Black Rock en St. Michael, y Sunset Crest en St. James.

FOTOGRAFÍA. Disponemos de servicios de revelado de fotos en una hora, y algunos de los laboratorios fotográficos ofrecen servicios gratuitos de recogida y entrega a los hoteles.

CORREO. Barbados goza de unas facilidades y un servicio de correos excepcionales. La nueva oficina principal de Correos, situada en Cheapside, Bridgetown, incluye un servicio de envío de paquetes y correo expreso a Londres y Nueva York con entrega garantizada en el plazo de 48 horas. El servicio de correo certificado asegura el despacho garantizado de correo en condiciones de alta seguridad. La Oficina Filatélica ofrece sobres del día de emisión de sellos, que se expiden sólo cuatro veces al año. Los coleccionistas pueden concertar cuentas de depósito, de manera que se les puedan enviar las nuevas ediciones a cualquier parte del mundo.

Existen oficinas de correos en todos los distritos. Los buzones, de color rojo, están situados al borde de la carretera por toda la isla. Hay reparto de correos dos veces al día en Bridgetown y los barrios residenciales de las afueras, y una vez al día en los distritos rurales.

REGULACIONES MATRIMONIALES. Ambas partes deben solicitar personalmente una licencia matrimonial en la oficina del Ministerio del Interior. Los documentos necesarios son: (a) Pasaporte válido o los originales o copias certificadas de las partidas de nacimiento de los solicitantes; (b) si cualquiera de las partes hubiera estado casada anteriormente y hubiera enviudado, copias certificadas del certificado de matrimonio y el de defunción del cónyuge fallecido; (c) si cualquiera de las partes se hubiera divorciado, el original de una sentencia de divorcio firme o una copia certificada de la sentencia definitiva, pero no el fallo de divorcio condicional. Todos los documentos que no estén redactados originalmente en lengua inglesa habrán de acompañarse de una traducción certificada realizada por un Notario Público autorizado. Los honorarios, si ninguna de las partes tuviera ciudadanía de Barbados o fuera residente en la isla, son de 100 dólares BDS al contado y un sello de 25 dólares BDS para obtener la licencia. Si cualquiera de las partes tuviera ciudadanía de Barbados, los honorarios son de 35 dólares BDS y 10 dólares BDS de timbre.

Se deberán realizar los trámites con un funcionario de matrimonios (un magistrado o autoridad religiosa) antes de completar el impreso de solicitud de la licencia. En el momento de rellenar la solicitud se deberá presentar una carta del funcionario de matrimonios o autoridad religiosa que haya consentido en llevar a cabo la ceremonia. Todo matrimonio ha de solemnizarse de manera inmediata tras la expedición de la licencia, lo que se puede realizar el mismo día . La pareja habrá de acudir conjuntamente para obtener la licencia matrimonial.

FACILIDADES DEPORTIVAS Y PARA CONFERENCIAS. El complejo polideportivo Sir Garfield Sobers es un gimnasio multi-usos diseñado para satisfacer las necesidades de doce disciplinas deportivas. Contando con una ubicación ideal, se halla en la próxima vecindad de instituciones de comunicaciones, bancarias y de compras. El equipo necesario para los diferentes acontecimientos deportivos está disponible fácilmente y forma parte del servicio que ofrece este complejo. Otras características incluyen una sala para que los atletas realicen ejercicios de calentamiento, con máquinas de ejercicios multi-uso, sauna y salas de masaje, una sala médica y dos marcadores electrónicos. Dirección: Sir Garfield Sobers Sports Complex, Wildey, St. Michael, Barbados, Antillas; teléfono: (246) 437 6016, facsímil: (246) 437 3358.

El Centro Acuático de Barbados se encuentra junto al complejo polideportivo Sir Garfield Sobers, y ha sido diseñado para acoger competiciones de natación y deportes acuáticos, así como otras actividades recreativas relacionadas con las piscinas. Este centro cuenta con dos piscinas. La piscina principal tiene unas dimensiones de 50 x 25 metros, ofreciendo veinte calles para competiciones que requieran poca longitud, y diez calles para competiciones que requieran mayores longitudes. También, en las facilidades para deportes acuáticos, existe un centro tenístico equipado con cuatro pistas a pleno funcionamiento. El complejo Wildley se utiliza como escenario de espectáculos de entretenimiento organizados y conciertos importantes. Para obtener más información, sírvase ponerse en contacto con: The Manager, Aquatic Centre, Wildey, St. Michael, Barbados, Las Antillas; teléfono: (246) 429 7946, facsímil: (246) 436 2272.

El nuevo Sherbourne Centre es la más nueva de una serie de facilidades

ainsi que d'autres aménités comme des salles de réunion, des services médicaux, de presse, de banque, postaux, de restaurants et cafétérias. Pour plus de renseignements, veuillez prendre contact avec: The Manager, Sherbourne Conference Centre, Two Mile Hill, St. Michael, Barbados, West Indies, Tél.: (246) 431 7600; Télécopie: (246) 437 8859.

RÉSIDENCES PERMANENTES. Les personnes qui souhaitent résider de façon permanente à La Barbade doivent fournir une preuve tangible de ce qu'elles ne risquent pas de devenir une charge pour la nation. Les demandes doivent être adressées au Chief Immigration Officer, Immigration and Passeport Department, Careenage House, The Wharf, Bridgetown, Tél.: (246) 426 1011.

PROPRIÉTÉ IMMOBILIÈRE - De nombreuses occasions de propriétés résidentielles attrayantes, allant de luxueuses demeures et villas à des copropriétés et immeubles en ville, sont disponibles. Plusieurs sociétés de gestion d'immeubles assurent la surveillance des propriétés. Terrains et immeubles sont disponibles aux étrangers sans restriction. Un impôt de 10 pour cent est appliqué sur les achats étrangers, plus 3 pour cent de frais juridiques.

GALERIES D'ART - La Barbade possède un certain nombre de galeries d'art, où l'on peut voir les oeuvres d'artistes locaux et, dans la plupart des cas, les acheter.

Bibliothèque - La Bibliothèque Publique Centrale est située dans Coleridge Street, près du Palais de Justice, Bridgetown. Des services modernes comportent un département de référence, un département des jeunes et une division itinérante opérant à travers l'île. Il existe des succursales dans les paroisses de Christ Church, St. George, St. James, St. Peter, St. Philip, St. Joseph, St. Michael et St. Thomas. Tous les services sont accessibles aux visiteurs. Une caution remboursable est demandée si des livres sont empruntés à la bibliothèque. Tél. (246) 426 1744.

BABY SITTING - Des arrangements fiables pour prendre soin des enfants peuvent être organisés dans la plupart des grands hôtels.

DIVERS - Un service de location de magnétoscope et télévision, des instituts de beauté et des salons de coiffure, des gymnases et centres de danse aérobic sont tous aisément disponibles.

JOURS FÉRIÉS - Les jours fériés normaux sont Noël, le 26 décembre, le Premier Janvier, le Vendredi Saint, le lundi de Pâques et le lundi de Pentecôte. L'île célèbre aussi le Errol Barrow Day (21 janvier), May day (Premier Mai), Kadooment Day (premier lundi d'août), United Nations Day (premier lundi d'octobre) et Independence Day (30 novembre).

Tennisplätze verfügt.

Der Wildey Complex wird als Veranstaltungsort für wichtige Konzerte und verschiedene Unterhaltungsveranstaltungen verwendet.

Für weitere Informationen nehmen Sie bitte Kontakt auf mit: dem Manager, Aquatic Centre, Wildey, St. Michael, Barbados, West Indies. Tel: (246) 429 7946, Fax: (246) 436 2272.

Das neue Sherbourne Zentrum ist das jüngste einer Anzahl von Konferenzeinrichtungen, die Barbados bietet. Das Zentrum ist voll klimatisiert und veranstaltet, abgesehen von Konferenzen, auch Handelsmessen, Seminare und Ausstellungen. Die Haupthalle des Zentrums ist mit 800 Hörsaalplätzen und 400 Sitzplätzen im Schulklassenstil ausgestattet. Ein Übersetzungsservice ist in sechs Sprachen erhältlich. Darüber hinaus verfügt das Zentrum über Sitzungsräume, einen medizinischen Service, Presse-, Bank-, Postservice, ein Restaurant und Café. Für weitere Informationen wenden Sie sich bitte an: den Manager, Sherbourne Conference Centre, Two Mile Hill, St. Michael, Barbados, West Indies, Tel: (246) 431 7600, Fax: (246) 437 8859.

DAUERNDER AUFENTHALT: Sollten Sie die Absicht haben, Ihren ständigen Wohnsitz nach Barbados zu verlegen, müssen Sie stichhaltig nachweisen, daß Sie als Einwohner von Barbados dem Staat nicht zu Last fallen werden. Anträge müssen an den Hauptimmigrationsbeamten gerichtet werden, Immigration and Passport Department, Careenage House, The Wharf, Bridgetown, Tel: (246) 426 1011.

IMMOBILIEN: Viele attraktive Immobilien, die von Luxushäusern und Villen zu Appartementhäusern und Stadthäusern reichen, sind erhältlich. Einige Immobilienmakler bieten Ihre Dienste als Verwalter von Eigentum an. Land und Eigentum sind ohne Einschränkungen für Ausländer erhältlich. Bei Auslandskäufen muß eine Steuer von 10 Prozent und Rechtsgebühren von ungefähr 3 Prozent bezahlt werden.

KUNSTGALERIEN: Barbados verfügt über eine Anzahl von Kunstgalerien, wo die Arbeiten von einheimischen Künstlern ausgestellt und in den meisten Fällen auch verkauft werden.

BIBLIOTHEK: Die Central Public Library befindet sich in der Coleridge Street neben den Gerichtshöfen in Bridgetown. Der aktuelle Service umfaßt eine Referenzabteilung, Jugendabteilung und eine inselweite mobile Abteilung. Zweigstellen der Bibliothek befinden sich in den Gemeinden von Christ Church, St. George, St. James, St. Peter, St. Philip, St. Joseph, St. Michael und St. Thomas. Alle Dienstleistungen sind auch für Besucher zugänglich. Für entliehene Bücher ist eine rückzahlbare Kaution zu hinterlegen. Tel: (246) 426 1744.

BABYSITTEN: Zuverlässige Betreuung von Kindern kann in allen größeren Hotels arrangiert werden.

SONSTIGES: Ein Service für das Mieten von Videogeräten und Fernsehern, Schönheitssalons und Friseurläden, Fitneßzentren und Aerobic-Zentren stehen Ihnen problemlos zur Verfügung.

FEIERTAGE: Gesetzliche Feiertage sind der 1. und 2. Weihnachtstag, Neujahrstag, Karfreitag, Ostermontag und Pfingstmontag. Ansonsten werden in Barbados auch der Errol Barrow Tag (21. Januar), Maitag (1. Mai), Kadooment Tag (erster Montag im August), Tag der Vereinten Nationen (erster Montag im Oktober) und Unabhängigkeitstag (30. November) als Feiertage begangen.

Tel.: (246) 431 600. Fax: (246) 437 8859.

RESIDENZA. Le persone che desiderino ottenere la residenza permanente alle Barbados devono fornire prova che è improbabile che possano divenire in futuro un onere per lo stato. Le richieste devono essere trasmesse al Chief Immigration Officer, Immigration and Passport Department, Careenage House, The Wharf, Bridgetown. Tel.: (246) 426 1011.

IMMOBILI. Sono attualmente offerte in vendita diverse proprietà imobiliari, sia case e ville di lusso che condomini e case di città. Esistono inoltre numerose agenzie immobiliari che si occupano della gestione degli immobili. Anche chi non ha la cittadinanza può investire in terreni e proprietà senza alcuna restrizione. Vi è una tassa del 10 per cento su acquisti da parte di stranieri, più circa il 3 per cento per spese legali.

GALLERIE D'ARTE. Barbados possiede diverse gallerie d'arte presso le quali è possibile ammirare e, nella maggioranza dei casi, anche acquistare, le opere di artisti locali.

BIBLIOTECA. La Central Public Library si trova a Coleridge Street, vicino alla Corte di Giustizia di Bridgetown. I servizi includono una sezione di consultazione, una sezione per giovani e una divisione mobile che si estende su tutta l'isola. Ulteriori sedi di consultazione si trovano anche nei distretti di Christ Church, St.George, St.James, St.Peter, St.Philip, St.Joseph, St.Michael e St.Thomas.Tutti i servizi sono a disposizione dei visitatori. Viene richiesto un deposito rimborsabile per l'asporto dei libri. Tel.: (246) 426 1744.

BABYSITTER Presso tutti i maggiori alberghi è possibile prenotare i servizi di persone di fiducia a cui affidare i bambini.

ALTRI SERVIZI. Si possono inoltre noleggiare videoregistratori e televisori e si trovano a portata di mano negozi di parrucchieri da uomo e signora, istituti di bellezza, palestre e centri di danza aerobica.

FESTE NAZIONALI. Le feste nazionali sono il giorno di Natale, Santo Stefano, Capodanno, Venerdì Santo, Lunedì di Pasqua e Lunedì di Pentecoste. L'isola festeggia inoltre Errol Barrow Day (21 gennaio), Calendimaggio (1 maggio) Kadooment Day (il primo lunedì d'agosto), la Giornata delle Nazioni Unite (il primo lunedì d'ottobre) e il Giorno dell'Indipendenza (30 novembre).

para conferencias de que dispone Barbados. El centro cuenta con aire acondicionado en su totalidad y está equipado, además de para conferencias, para ferias de muestras, seminarios y exposiciones. La sala principal del Centro puede acomodar a 800 personas en estilo de teatro y a 400 en estilo de clase. Se dispone de servicios de traducción para seis idiomas, y otras características incluyen salas para comités, servicios médicos, de prensa, bancarios y postales, así como restaurante y cafetería. Para obtener mayor información, sírvase ponerse en contacto con: The Manager, Sherbourne Conference Centre, Two Mile Hill, St. Michael, Barbados, Las Antillas; teléfono: (246) 431 7600, facsímil: (246) 437 8859.

RESIDENCIA PERMANENTE. Aquellas personas que deseen convertirse en residentes permanentes de Barbados deberán proporcionar evidencia tangible de que no es probable que se conviertan en una carga para la nación. Las solicitudes han de enviarse al Chief Immigration Officer, Immigration and Passport Department, Careenage House, The Wharf, Bridgetown; teléfono: (246) 426 1001.

BIENES INMUEBLES. Disponemos de numerosas y atractivas oportunidades para adquirir propiedades residenciales, desde mansiones de lujo hasta chalets, pasando por condominios y viviendas unifamiliares construidas en hilera. Disponemos de tierras y propiedades sin restricción alguna para ciudadanos de otros países. Existe un impuesto sobre las ventas extranjeras del 10%, además de un 3% de costas legales.

GALERÍAS DE ARTE. Barbados cuenta con una serie de galerías de arte, en las que se pueden admirar y, en muchos casos comprarse, las obras de los artistas locales.

BIBLIOTECA. La Biblioteca Pública Central se encuentra situada en Coleridge Street, junto a los Tribunales, en Bridgetown. Los servicios, muy actualizados, incluyen un departamento de referencia, otro juvenil, y una división móvil por toda la isla. Se mantienen sucursales de la misma en los distritos de Christ Church, St. George, St. James, St. Peter, St. Phillip, St. Joseph, St. Michael y St. Thomas. Todos los servicios están a disposición de los visitantes. Se exige un depósito reembolsable para sacar libros de la biblioteca. Teléfono: (246) 426 1744.

BABY SITTING. Se pueden concertar servicios de confianza para el cuidado de niños en todos los hoteles más importantes.

INFORMACIÓN ADICIONAL: Se pueden obtener fácilmente servicios de alquiler de vídeos y televisores, peluquerías y salas de belleza, gimnasios y centros de aerobic.

DÍAS FESTIVOS. Los días festivos oficiales son el día de Navidad, el 26 de diciembre, el día de Año Nuevo, el Viernes Santo, Lunes de Pascua y el día de Pentecostés. La isla también celebra Errol Barrow Day (21 de enero), May Day (uno de mayo), Kadooment Day (primer lunes de agosto), el Día de las Naciones Unidas (primer lunes de octubre) y el Día de la Independencia (30 de noviembre).

Barbados Directory

INTERNATIONAL DIALING CODE: 246

The Government

Ministries

Office of the Prime Minister, Government Headquarters, Bay Street, St Michael. Tel: 436-6435 Fax: 436-9280

Ministry of Agriculture and Rural Development, Graeme Hall, PO Box 505, Christ Church. Tel: 428-4061 Fax: 420-8444

Ministry of Defence, Security and Information, Government Headquarters, Bay Street, St Michael. Tel: 436-6435

Ministry of Education, Youth Affairs and Culture, Jemmot's Lane, St Michael. Tel: 426-5416

Ministry of Finance and Economic Affairs, Government Headquarters, Bay Street, St Michael. Tel: 426-2814 Fax: 429 4032

Ministry of Foreign Affairs, Foreign Trade and International Business, 1 Culloden Road, St Michael. Tel: 436-2990 Fax: 429-6652

Ministry of Health, Jemmott's Lane, St Michael. Tel: 426-4669 Fax: 426-5570

Ministry of Home Affairs, Government Headquarters, Bay Street, St Michael. Tel: 431-7600

Ministry of Industry, Commerce and Business Development, Reef Road, Fontabelle, St Michael. Tel: 426-4452 Fax: 431-0056

Ministry of Justice, Marine House, Hastings, Christ Church. Tel: 427-0622

Ministry of Labour, Community Development and Sports: National Insurance Building, 5th Floor, Fairchild Street, Bridgetown. Tel:426-2888 Fax: 426-8959

Ministry of Public Works, Transport and Housing: Marine House, Hastings, Christ Church. Tel: 427-5420

Ministry of Tourism, International Transport and the Environment: Herbert House, Reef Road, Fontabelle, St Michael. Tel: 427-5777 Fax: 431-0121

Political Organisations

Barbados Labour Party, Grantley Adams House, 111 Roebuck Street, Bridgetown. Tel: 426-2274

Democratic Labour Party, George St, Belleville, St Michael. Tel: 429-3104

National Democratic Party, Suenos', 3 Sixth Ave, Belleville. Tel: 429-6882

People's Pressure Movement, Bridgetown

Workers' Party of Barbados, Bridgetown. Tel: 425-1620

Embassies and High Commissions in Barbados

Brazil: Sunjet House, Independence Square, Bridgetown. Tel: 427-1735

Canada:Bishops Court Hill, St Michael. Tel: 429-3550 Fax: 429-3780

China People's Republic: 17 Golf View Terrace, Rockley, Christ Church. Tel: 435-6890 Fax: 435-8300

Colombia: 'Rosemary', Dayrells Road, Rockley, PO Box 37W Christ Church. Tel: 429-6821 Fax: 429-6830

Costa Rica: Golden Anchorage House, Sunset Crest, St James. Tel: 432-0194 Fax: 432-5566

United Kingdom: Lower Collymore Rock, PO Box 676, St Michael. Tel: 436-6694 Fax: 436-5398

USA: Canadian Imperial Bank of Commerce Bldg, Broad Street. PO Box 302, Bridgetown.

Tel: 436-4950 Fax: 429-5246

Venezuela: Hastings, Christ Church. Tel: 435-7619 Fax: 435-7830

Religion

More than 100 religious denominations and sects are represented in Barbados, but the vast majority of the population profess Christianity. According to the 1980 census, there were 6,894 Anglicans (or some 40 percent of the total population), while the Pentecostal (eight percent) and Methodist (seven percent) churches were next in importance. The regional Caribbean Conference of Churches is based in Barbados. There are also small groups of Hindus, Muslims and Jews.

The Anglican Community

Anglicans in Barbados are adherents of the Church in the Province of the Westindies, comprising eight dioceses. The Archbishop of the Province is the Bishop of the North Eastern Caribbean and Aruba, resident at St John's,

Antigua. In Barbados there is a Provincial Office (St George's Church, St George) and an Anglican Theological College (Codrington College, St John).

Bishop of Barbados, Diocesan Office, Mandeville House, Bridgetown. Tel: 426-2761 Fax: 427-5867

The Roman Catholic Church

Barbados comprises a single diocese (formed in January 1990, when the diocese of Bridgetown-Kingstown was divided), which is suffragan to the archdiocese of Port of Spain (Trinidad and Tobago). At 31 December 1992 there were an estimated 10,500 adherents in the diocese. The Bishop participates in the Antilles Episcopal Conference (currently based in Port of Spain, Trinidad and Tobago).

Bishop of Bridgetown, St Patrick's Cathedral, Jemmott's Lane, PO Box 1223, Bridgetown. Tel: 426-3510 Fax: 429-6198

Protestant Churches

Baptist Churches of Barbados, National Baptist Convention. Tel: 429-2697

Church of God (Caribbean Atlantic Assembly), St Michael's Plaza, St Michael's Row, PO Box 1, Bridgetown. Tel: 427-5770

Church of Jesus Christ of Latter-day Saints (Mormons) - West Indies Mission, Carleigh House, 3 Golf Club Road, Bridgetown. Tel: 435-7853

Church of the Nazarene, District Office, Eagle Hall, Bridgetown. Tel: 425-1067

Methodist Church, Bethel Church Office, Bay Street, Bridgetown. Tel: 426-2223

Moravian Church, Roebuck Street, Bridgetown. Tel: 426-2337

Seventh-Day Adventists (East Caribbean Conference), Brydens Avenue, Brittons Hill, PO Box 223, St Michael. Tel: 429-7234

Wesleyan Holiness Church, General Headquarters, Bank Hall. Tel: 429-4864

Other denominations include the Apostolic Church, the Assemblies of Brethren, the Salvation Army, Presbyterian Congregations, the African Methodist Episcopal Church, the Mount Olive United Holy Church of America and Jehovah's Witnesses.

Islam

Islamic Teaching Centre, Harts Gap, Hastings. Tel: 427-0120

Judaism

Nidhe Israel and Shaara Tzedek Synagogue, Rockley New Road, PO Box 651, Bridgetown. Tel: 427-0703

Caribbean Jewish Congress, PO Box 1331, Bridgetown.

Hinduism

Hindu Community, Bridgetown.

Publishing & Broadcasting

The Press

Barbados Advocate, Fontabelle, PO Box 230, St Michael. Tel: 426-1210 Fax: 429-7045

The Beacon, 111 Roebuck Street, Bridgetown; organ of the Barbados Labour Party

Caribbean Week, Lefferts Place, River Road, St Michael. Tel: 436-1902 Fax: 436-1904

The Nation, Nation House, Fontabelle, St Michael. Tel: 436-6240

The New Bajan, Nation House, Fontabelle, St Michael. Tel: 436-6240 Fax: 427-6968

Official Gazette, Government Printing Office, Bay Street, St Michael. Tel: 436-6776

Sunday Advocate, Fontabelle, PO Box 230, St Michael; Tel: 426-1210 Fax: 429-7045

The Sunday Sun, Fontabelle, St Michael. Tel: 436-6340 Fax: 427-6968

Free Tourist Publications

The Ins & Outs of Barbados, Miller Publishing Co. Ltd., Prior Hill, St James. Tel: 421-6700 Fax: 421-6707

Simply Barbados, Peter J Sassman Publishing Co., Letchworth Complex, The Garrison, St Michael. Tel: 430-9075 Fax: 430-9077

The Barbados SUNSEEKER, The Advocate Company Limited, Fontabelle, St Michael. Tel: 426-1210

Visitor, The Nation Publishing Co Ltd., Fontabelle, St Michael. Tel: 436-6240

News Agencies

Caribbean News Agency (CANA): Culloden View, Beckles Road, St Michael. Tel: 429-2903 Fax: 429-4355

Foreign Bureaux

Agencia EFE (Spain): 48 Gladioli Drive, Husbands, St James. Tel: 425-1542

Inter Press Service (IPS) (Italy): PO Box 697, Bridgetown. Tel: 426-4474

United Press International (UPI) (USA): Bridgetown. Tel: 436-0465

Xinhua (New China) News Agency (People's Republic of China): 29 Newton Terrace, PO Box 22A, Christ Church.

Agence France-Presse (AFP) is also represented.

Publishers

Caribbean Publishing Co Ltd: Nation House, Fontabelle, St Michael.Tel: 436 5889

Nation Publishing Co Ltd: Nation House, Fontabelle, St Michael. Tel: 436-6240 Fax: 436-0849

Television

Caribbean Broadcasting Corporation (CBC): The Pine, PO Box 900, Bridgetown.Tel: 429-2041 Fax: 429-4795

Channel Eight is the main national service, broadcasting 24-hours daily. Five cabled subscription channels are available.

Radio

Barbados Broadcasting Service Ltd, Astoria Street, St. George. Tel: 437-9550 Fax: 437-9554

Barbados Rediffusion Service Ltd; River Road, St Michael. Tel: 426-0820 Fax: 429-8093

Rediffusion Star Radio, at River Road, St Michael - commercial wired service island-wide coverage.

Voice of Barbados, at River Road, St George - commercial station covering Barbados and Eastern Caribbean.

YESS Ten-Four FM, at River Road, St George, is a commercial station.

CBC Radio: PO Box 900, Bridgetown. Tel: 429-2041 Fax: 429-4795

Radio Liberty FM, Drydock Lounge & Restaurant, Bridgetown. Tel: 431-0482

Financial & Investment Services

Banks

Central Bank of Barbados, Church Village, PO Box 1016, St Michael. Tel: 436-6870 Fax: 427 9559

Caribbean Commercial Bank Ltd, Broad Street , PO Box 1007c, Bridgetown. Tel: 431-2500 Fax: 431-2530

Caribbean Development Bank, Wildey, PO Box 408, St Michael. Tel: 431-1600 Fax: 426-7269

Barbados Development Bank, Central Bank Bldg, Level 7, Church Village, PO Box 50, St Michael. Tel: 436-8870 Fax: 429-2391

Barbados National Bank, 1 Broad Street, PO Box 1002, Bridgetown. Tel: 431-3000 Fax: 429 2606

Foreign Banks

Bank of Nova Scotia (Canada), Broad Street, PO Box 202, Bridgetown. Tel: 431-3000 Fax: 426-0969. Haggatt Hall branch open Saturday.

Barclays Bank Plc (United Kingdom), Broad Street, PO Box 301, Bridgetown. Tel: 431 5151 Fax: 436-7957

Canadian Imperial Bank of Commerce, Broad Street, PO Box 405, Bridgetown. Tel: 426-0571

Royal Bank of Canada, Trident House, Broad Street, PO Box 68, Bridgetown. Tel: 431-6580

Post Office

Central Post Office Cheapside, Bridgetown. Tel: 436-4800

Branches are located throughout the island and at Grantley Adams International Airport.

Trust Companies

Bank of Commerce Trust Co Barbados Ltd, PO Box 503, Bridgetown. Tel: 426-2740

Bank of Nova Scotia Trust Co (Caribbean) Ltd, Bank of Nova Scotia Bldg, Broad Street, PO Box 1003B, Bridgetown. Tel: 431-3120 Fax: 426-0969

Barbados International Bank and Trust Co Ltd, Bissex Hill, St Joseph. Tel: 422-9417 Fax: 422-9903

Barclays Bank Trust Company, Roebuck Street, PO Box 180, Bridgetown. Tel: 426 1608

Caribbean Commercial Trust Co Ltd, White Park Road, Bridgetown. Tel: 431-4719 Fax: 431-2530

Royal Bank of Canada Financial Corporation,

Royal Bank House, Bush Hill, Garrison, PO Box 48B, St Michael. Tel: 431-6580 Fax: 426-4139

Stock Exchange

Securities Exchange of Barbados (SEB): Central Bank Bldg, 6th Floor, Church Village, St Michael. Tel: 436-9871 Fax: 429-8942. In 1989 the governments of Barbados, Trinidad and Tobago and Jamaica agreed to combine their national exchanges into a regional stock exchange; cross-trading began in April 1991.

Insurance

The leading British and a number of US and Canadian companies have agents in the territory. Local insurance companies include the following:

Barbados Commercial Insurance Co Ltd, Harrison's Bldg, 1 Broad St, Bridgetown. Tel: 436-6560

Barbados Fire & General Insurance Co, Beckwith Place, Broad Street, PO Box 150, Bridgetown. Tel: 426-4291 Fax: 426-0752

Barbados Mutual Life Assurance Society, Collymore Rock, St Michael. Tel: 431-7000 Fax: 436-8829

Insurance Corporation of Barbados, Roebuck Street, Bridgetown. Tel: 427-5590 Fax: 426-3393

Life of Barbados Ltd, Wildey, PO Box 69, St Michael. Tel: 426-1060 Fax: 436-8835

United Insurance Co Ltd, Cavan House, Lower Broad Street, PO Box 1215, Bridgetown. Tel: 436-1991

Insurance Association

Insurance Association of the Caribbean, IAC Bldg, Melrose, Lower Collymore Rock. Tel: 427-5608

Barbados Investment and Development Cooperation, Pelican House, Princess Alice Highway, Bridgetown. Tel: 427-5350, Fax: 426-7802

New York. Barbados Investment and Development Corporation, 800 Second Avenue, New York, NY 10017 USA. Tel: (212) 867-6420 Fax: (212) 682-5496. e mail:bidc@interport.net

Toronto. Barbados Investment and Development Corporation, 5160 Yonge Street, Suite 1800 North York, Ontario, M2N 6L9 Canada. Tel: (416) 512-0700 Fax: (416) 512-6580

London. Barbados Investment and Development Corporation, Commercial Section, Barbados High Commission, 1 Great Russell Street, London WC1B 3JY England. Tel: (0171) 580-6077 Fax: (0171) 323-6872

Miami. Barbados Investment and Development Corporation, Consulate General of Barbados, 150 Alhambra Circle, Suite 1270, Coral Gables, Florida 33134 USA. Tel: (305) 442-1994 Fax: (305) 567-2844. Website: http://www.bidc.com

Trade and Industry

Barbados Chamber of Commerce Inc, Nemwill House, 1st Floor, Lower Collymore Rock, PO Box 189, St Michael. Tel: 426-2056 Fax: 429-2907

Development Organisations

Agricultural Venture Trust, 'Hillcarr', Worthing, Christ Church. Tel: 435-8990 Fax: 435-8895.

Barbados Agriculture Development and Marketing Corp, Fairy Valley, Christ Church. Tel: 428-0250

Barbados Investment and Development Corporation, Pelican House, Princess Alice Highway, Bridgetown. Tel: 427-5350 Fax: 426-7802

British Development Division in the Caribbean, Collymore Rock, PO Box 167, St Michael. Tel: 436-9873 Fax: 426-2194

State-Owned Companies

Arawak Cement Co Ltd., Checker Hall, St Lucy. Tel: 439-9880 Fax: 439-7976

Barbados Agricultural Management Co Ltd., Warrens, PO Box 719c, St Michael. Tel: 425-0010 Fax: 425-3505

Barbados National Oil Company Ltd., Woodbourne, St Philip. Tel: 423-0918 Fax: 423-0166

Barbados Sugar Industry Ltd., PO Box 719c, Warrens, St Thomas. Tel: 425-0010 Fax: 425-3505

Professional Associations

Barbados Agricultural Society, The Grotto, Beckles Road, St Michael. Tel: 436-6680

Barbados Association of Medical Practitioners, Ellna House, Spring Garden, St Michael. Tel:429-7569

Barbados Association of Professional Engineers, PO Box 666, Bridgetown. Tel: 425-9879

Barbados Builders' Association, Bridgetown. Tel: 437 8383

Barbados Hotel & Tourist Association, Fourth Ave, Belleville, St Michael. Tel: 426-5041

Barbados Manufacturers' Association, Harbour Road, Fontabelle. Tel: 426-4474

Barbados National Association of Co-operative Societies, James Street, Bridgetown. Tel: 436-2270

Police Association. Tel: 428-937

West India Sea Island Cotton Association (Inc), c/o Barbados Agriculture Development and Marketing Corporation, Fairy Valley, Christ Church. Tel: 428-0250

Employers' Organization

Barbados Employers' Confederation, Nemwil House, Lower Collymore Rock, St Michael. Tel: 426-1574

Main Trade Unions

Barbados Industrial and General Workers' Union, Bridgetown.

Barbados Secondary Teachers' Union, Eighth Ave, Belleville, St Michael. Tel: 429-7676

Barbados Union of Teachers, Welches, PO Box 58, St Michael. Tel: 436-6139

Barbados Workers' Union, Solidarity House, Harmony Hall, PO Box 172, St Michael. Tel: 426-3492

Caribbean Association of Media Workers, Bridgetown.

National Union of Public Workers, Dalkeith Road, PO Box 174, Bridgetown. Tel: 426-1764

National Union of Seamen, 34 Tudor Street, Bridgetown. Tel: 436-6137

Transportation

Roads

Ministry of Public Works, Transport and Housing, Marine House, Hastings, Christ Church. Tel: 427-5420

Shipping

Inter-island traffic is catered for by a fornightly service of one vessel of the West Indies Shipping Corporation (WISCO), the regional shipping company, based in Trinidad and Tobago, in which the Barbados government is a shareholder, operating from Trinidad as far north as Jamaica. The CAROL container service consortium connects Bridgetown with western European ports and several foreign shipping lines call at the port. Bridgetown Harbour has berths for eight ships and simultaneous bunkering facilities for five.

Shipping Companies

Barbados Port Authority, University Row, Bridgetown Harbour. Tel: 436-6883 Fax: 429-5348

Barbados Shipping and Trading Co Ltd., Musson Bldg, Hincks Street, PO Box 1227c, Bridgetown. Tel: 426-3844 Fax: 427-4719

Booth Steamship Company (Barbados) Ltd., Cockspur House, 1st Floor, Nile Street, PO Box 263, Bridgetown. Tel: 427-5131 Fax: 426-0484

DaCosta Ltd., Carlisle House, Hincks Street, PO Box 103, Bridgetown. Tel: 426-0850 Fax: 431-0051

Hassell, Eric and Son Ltd., Carlisle House, Hincks Street Bridgetown. Tel: 436-6102 Fax: 429-3416

Shipping Association of Barbados, Cockspur House, 1st Floor, Nile Street, Bridgetown. Tel: 427- 9860 Fax: 426-8392

Tore Torsteinson, Fairfield House, St Philip. Tel: 423-6125 Fax: 423-4664

Windward Lines Ltd., Fairfield House, St Philip. Tel: 431-0449

Civil Aviation

Grantley Adams International Airport, at Seawell, 18 km (11 miles) from Bridgetown. Tel: 428-7107

Aero Ambulance Services, Grantley Adams International Airport, Seawell. Tel: 435-2820

EC Air, jointly-owned by Air Martinique .Daily services between Barbados, Martinique, Dominica, St Lucia and St Vincent and the Grenadines.

Consulates & Embassies Overseas

Consulates in the United States

These offices may be closed on National and US holidays.

California. San Francisco: Honorary Consulate, 442 Post Street, San Francisco, Calif. 94102, (415) 421-8789. Hours: 9.00 am - 5.00 pm; Sat closed

Washington DC. Washington: Embassy, 2144 Wyoming Ave. NW, Washington, DC 20008, (202) 939-9202; Fax (202) 332-7467. Hours 9.00 am - 5.00pm; Sat closed.

Florida. Miami: Honorary Consulate, Airport Business Centre, 7504 NW 54th Street, Miami, Fla. 33166, (305) 599-1310.

Illinois. Chicago: Honorary Consulate, 220 S.State Street, Suite 2200, Chicago, Ill. 60624, (312) 922-7757; Fax: (312) 922-4093. Hours: By appointment only.

Louisiana. New Orleans: Honorary Consulate,

321 St. Charles Ave., 10th Floor, New Orleans, La. 70130, (504) 586-1979. Hours: 8:30 am - 4:30 pm; Sat closed.

Massachusetts. Boston: Honorary Consulate, 26 School Street, Lexington, Mass 02173, (617) 862-5042.

Michigan. Detroit: Honorary Consulate, 11012 E. Thirteen Mile Road, Suite 208, Warren, Mich. 48093, (313) 751-8840. Hours: By appointment only.

New York. New York: Consulate General, 800 Second Ave., 18th floor, New York, N.Y. 10017. (212) 867 8435. Hours: 9.00 am - 5.00 pm; Sat closed.

Ohio. Toledo: Honorary Consulate, 723 Phillips Ave., Toledo, Ohio 43612, (419) 476-5461. Hours: 1.00 -5.00 pm ; Sat closed.

Oregan. Milwaukee: Honorary Consulate, 10202 SE 32nd Ave., Suite 601, Milwaukee, Ore. 97222, (503) 659-0283.

Accommodation & Real Estates

Hotels

Abbeville Hotel, Rockley, Christ Church. Tel: 435-7924 Fax: 435-8502

Accra Beach Hotel, Rockley, Christ Church. Tel: 435-8920 Fax: 435-6794

Almond Beach Village, Christ Church. Tel: 422-4900

Andrea On Sea, St Lawrence Gap, Christ Church. Tel: 428-6021

Apple Experience, Hastings, Christ Church. Tel: 436-7604

Asta, Hastings,Christ Church. Tel: 427-2541 Fax: 426-9566

Atlantis Hotel, Bathsheba, St Joseph. Tel: 433-9445

Bagshot House, St Lawrence, Christ Church. Tel: 435-6956

Barbados Beach Village, Fitts Village, St James.Tel: 425-1440 Fax: 424-0996

Barbados Hilton Hotel, Needhams Point, St Michael. Tel: 426-0200 Fax: 436-8946

Bella Beach Tropicana, Lower Carlton, St James. Tel: 422-2277

Blue Horizon, Rockley, Christ Church. Tel: 435-8916 Fax: 435-8153

Bresmay, St Lawrence Gap, Christ Church.Tel: 428-6131 Fax: 428-7722

Buccaneer Bay Hotel, Paynes Bay, St James. Tel: 432-7981 Fax: 432-7230

Caribbee Beach Hotel, Hasting, Christ Church. Tel: 436-6232 Fax: 436-0124

Casuarina Beach Club, Dover, Christ Church.Tel: 428-3600 Fax: 428-1970

Cobblers Cove Hotel, Speightstown, St Peter. Tel: 422-2291 Fax: 422-1460

Coconut Court Beach, Hastings, Christ Church. Tel: 427-1655 Fax: 429-8198

Coconut Creek Club Hotel, Derricks, St James. Tel: 432-0803 Fax: 422-1726

Colony Club Hotel, Porters, St James. Tel: 422-2335 Fax: 422-1726

Coral Reef Club, Holetown, St James.Tel: 422-2372 Fax: 422-1776

Crane Beach Hotel, Crane, St Philip.Tel: 423-6220 Fax: 423-5343

Cunard Paradise Village & Beach Club, Black Rock, St Michael.Tel: 424-0888 Fax: 424-0889

Discovery Bay Hotel, Holetown, St James. Tel: 432-1301 Fax: 432-2553

Divi Southwinds Hotel & Beach Club, St Lawrence, Christ Church. Tel: 428-7181 Fax: 428-4674

Dover Beach Hotel, Dover, Christ Church. Tel: 428-8076 Fax: 428-2122

Eastry House, Gibbs, St Peter. Tel: 422-2021 Fax: 422-2202

Edgewater Hotel, Bathsheba, St Joseph. Tel: 433-9900 Fax: 433-9900

Fairholme Hotel, Maxwell, Christ Church. Tel: 428-9425

Ginger Bay Beach Club, Crane, St Philip.Tel: 423-5810 Fax: 423-6629

Glitter Bay Hotel, Porters,St James. Tel: 422-4111 Fax: 422-3940

Golden Beach Apartel, Hastings, Christ Church. Tel: 429-5818 Fax: 429-2845

Golden Sands Hotel, Maxwell,Christ Church.Tel: 428-8051/56 Fax: 428-3897

Grand Barbados Beach Resort, Aquatic Gap, St Michael. Tel: 426-0890 Fax: 436-9833

Half Moon Beach Hotel, St Lawrence, Christ Church.Tel: 428-7131 Fax: 428-6089

Heywoods Hotel, St. Peter. Tel: 422-4900 Fax: 422-1581

Inn On The Beach, Holetown, St. James. Tel: 432-0385 Fax: 432-2440

Island Inn Hotel, Aquatic Gap, St Michael. Tel: 436-6393 Fax: 437-8035

Kings Beach Hotel, Road View, St Peter. Tel: 422-1690 Fax: 422-1691

Kingsley Club, Cattlewash, St Joseph. Tel: 433-9422 Fax: 433-9226

Little Bay Hotel, St Lawrence, Christ Church. Tel: 435-7246/8574 Fax: 428-7705

Long Beach Club, Chancery Lane, Christ Church. Tel: 428-6890

Sam Lords Castle, Long Bay, St Philip.Tel: 423-7350 Fax: 423-5918

Ocean View Hotel, Hastings, Christ Church. Tel: 427-7821 Fax: 427-7826

Peach and Quiet Hotel, Inch Marlow, Christ Church. Tel: 428-5682

Pineapple Beach Club, Vauxhall, St James. Tel: 432-7840 Fax: 432-2115/2542

Rainbow Reef Hotel, Dover, Christ Church. Tel: 428-5710 Fax: 428-5395

Regency Cove Hotel, Hastings, Christ Church, Tel: 435-8924 Fax: 426-9010

Riviera Beach Hotel, Rockley, Christ Church. Tel: 435-8970

Robin's Nest Hotel, Long Bay, St Philip. Tel: 423-6088

Rockley Resort And Beach Club, Rockley, Christ Church. Tel: 435-7880 Fax: 435-8015

Royal Pavilion Hotel, Porters,St. James. Tel: 422-4444 Fax: 422-3940

San Remo Hotel, Maxwell, Christ Church. Tel: 428-2822

Sand Acres Hotel, Christ Church. Tel: 428-7234 Fax: 428-2525

Sandpiper Inn, St James. Tel: 422-2251 Fax: 422-1776

Sandridge Beach Hotel, St Peter.Tel: 422-2361 Fax: 422-1965

Sandy Beach Hotel, Worthing, Christ Church. Tel: 435-8000 Fax: 435-8053

Sandy Lane Hotel And Golf Club, St James.Tel: 432-1311 Fax: 432-2954

Sea Breeze Beach Hotel, Maxwell, Christ Church. Tel: 428-2825 Fax: 428-2733

Seaview Hotel, Hastings, Christ Church. Tel: 426-1450 Fax: 436-1333

Settlers Beach Hotel, Holetown, St. James.Tel: 422-3052 Fax: 422-1937

Sichris Hotel, Rockley, Christ Church.Tel: 435-7930 Fax: 435-8232

Silver Sands Resort, Christ Church.Tel: 428-6001 Fax: 428 3758

Smugglers Cove Hotel, Paynes Bay, St. James.Tel: 432-1741/44 Fax: 432-1749

Southern Palms Beach Club, St Lawrence Gap, Christ Church.Tel: 432-1741 Fax: 428-7175

Sugar Cane Club, Maynards, St. Peter.Tel: 422-5026 Fax: 422-0522

Sunhaven Beach Hotel, Hastings, Christ Church. Tel: 435-8905 Fax: 435-6621

Tamarind Cove Hotel, Paynes Bay, St James.Tel: 432-1332 Fax: 422-1726

Treasure Beach Hotel, Paynes Bay, St James.Tel: 432-1346 Fax: 432-1740

Welcome Inn Hotel, Maxwell, Christ Church. Tel: 428-9900 Fax: 428-8905

Worthing Court Apartment Hotel, Worthing, Christ Church.Tel: 435-7910 Fax: 435-7374

Yellow Bird Hotel, St Lawrence Gap, Christ Church. Tel: 435-7107 Fax: 435-8522

Guest Houses

Bona Vista, Christ Church. Tel: 435-6680

Crystal Waters, Worthing, Christ Church. Tel: 435-7514

Pegwell Inn, Welches, Christ Church. Tel: 428-6150

Rio Guest House, St Lawrence Gap, Christ Church. Tel: 428-1546

Rydal Waters, Worthing, Christ Church. Tel: 435-7433

Shonlan Inn, Christ Church. Tel: 428-0039

Summer Place Summer Home On Sea, Worthing, Christ Church. Tel: 435-7424

Woodbine, Rockley, Christ Church. Tel: 427-7627

Apartments

Adulo, Rockley, Christ Church. Tel: 426-6811

Angler Apartments, Derricks, St James. Tel: 432-0817

Beachcomber Apartments, Paynes Bay, St James. Tel: 432-0489

Bernita Apartments, Maxwell, Christ Church. Tel: 428-9115

Blythwood Beach Apartments, Worthing, Christ Church. Tel: 437-7712

Cacrabank Beach Apartments, Worthing, Christ Church.Tel: 435-8057/60

Carib Blue, Dover Terrace, Christ Church. Tel: 428-2290

Carib Caban,Worthing, Christ Church. Tel: 435-7423

Chateau Blanc, Worthing, Christ Church. Tel: 435-7423

Coral Sands, Worthing, Christ Church. Tel: 428-9828

Dorisville &Goldwater, Dover, Christ Church. Tel: 428-8686

Flamboyant, Hastings, Christ Church. Tel: 427-5588

Four Aces, St Lawrence Gap, Christ Church. Tel: 428-9441

Fred La Rose Bonanza, Dover, Christ Church.Tel: 428-9097

Gibbs Gardens, Gibbs, St Peter. Tel: 422-4211

Golden Palm Beach, Sunset Crest, St James. Tel: 432-6666

Homer Rentals, Sunset Crest, St James. Tel: 432-6750

Inchcape, Silver Sands, Christ Church. Tel: 428-9476

Kingsway Apartment Hotel, Maxwell, Christ Church. Tel: 428-8202

Leeton-On-Sea Apartments, Maxwell. Christ Church.Tel: 428-4500

Magic Isle Beach, Rockley, Christ Church. Tel: 435-6760

Maresol Beach, St Lawrencce Gap, Christ Church. Tel: 428-9300

Melrose Beach,Worthing, Christ Church. Tel: 435-7984

Meridian Inn, Dover, Christ Church.Tel: 428-4051

Miami Beach, Christ Church. Tel: 428-5387

Monteray Apartments Hotel, Dover, Christ Church.Tel: 428-9152

Myosotis, Dover, Christ Church.Tel: 428-3517

Na-Diesie Apartment Hotel, Holetown, St James. Tel: 432-0469

Nautilus Beach, Bay Street, St Michael. Tel: 426-3541

New Haven Mansion, Gibbs, St Peter. Tel: 422-1828

The Nook, Rockley, Christ Church. Tel: 436-6494

Paradise Villas, Black Rock, St Michael. Tel: 424-4581

Pirates Inn, Hastings, Christ Church. Tel: 426-6273

Romans Beach, Christ Church. Tel: 428-7635

Round Rock Apartments On Sea, Silver Sands, Christ Church. Tel: 428-7500

Salt Ash, St Lawrence Gap, Christ Church. Tel: 428-8753

Sandrift Paradise Beach Apartments, Black Rock, St Michael. Tel: 424-2062

Sandy Cove Apartments, Christ Church. Tel: 428-4358

Sea Foam Haciendas, Worthing, Christ Church. Tel: 435-7380

Shangri-La Apartment Hotel, Maxwell, Christ Church. Tel: 428-9112

Southern Surf Beach, Rockley, Christ Church. Tel: 435-6672

Summerset Apartments, Dover, Christ Church. Tel: 428-7936

Sunshine Beach, Hastings, Christ Church. Tel: 427-1234

Travellers Palm, Sunset Crest, St James. Tel: 432-7722

Walmer Lodge, Black Rock, St Michael. Tel: 425-1026

White Sands, St Lawrence Gap, Christ Church.Tel: 435-6694

Woodville Beach, Hastings, Christ Church. Tel: 435-6693

Real Estate Agents

Alleyne Aguilar and Altman, Derricks, St James. Tel: 432-0840

Armstrong Martin Realty Ltd, Sunset Crest, St James. Tel: 432-754

Bajan Services Ltd, Gibbs Beach, St Peter. Tel: 422-2618

Big Mac Enterprises, Rockley, Christ Church. Tel: 435-8148

John M Bladon & Co. Ltd, Hastings, Christ Church. Tel: 426-4640

F. Pitcher Realty, Upper Atlantic Shores, Christ Church. Tel: 428-1523

Realtors Ltd., River Road, St Michael. Tel: 426-4900

Ronald Stoute & Sons Ltd. Sam Lord's Castle, St Philip. Tel: 423-6800

Sunset Crest Resort Ltd. St James. Tel: 432-6666

Conference Facilities

Barbados Hilton Hotel, Needham's Point, St Michael. Tel: 426-0200 Fax: 436-8946. Six conference rooms.

Caribbee Beach Hotel, Hastings, Christ Church. Tel: 436-6232 Fax: 436-0130. Three air-conditioned rooms.

Coral Reef Club, St James. Tel: 422-2372 Fax: 422-1776. One room.

Cunard Paradise Village and Beach Club, Black Rock, St Michael. Tel: 424-0888 Fax: 424-0889. One conference room.

Discovery Bay Hotel, Holetown, St James. Tel: 432-1301 Fax: 432-2553. One room, with seating capacity for 40.

Divi Southwinds, St Lawrence, Christ Church.Tel: 428-7181 Fax: 428-4674. One room with the capacity for 100 persons theatre style.

Dover Convention Centre, Dover Beach, Christ Church.Tel: 428-5980/1 Fax: 428-9271. Can accommodate 120-750.

Grand Barbados, Aquatic Gap, St Michael. Tel: 426-0890 Fax: 436-9823. Three rooms, with seating for up to 120 people.

Heywoods, St Peter.Tel: 422-4900 Fax: 422-1581. The Meeting Hall can accommodate up to 250 people.

King Beach Hotel, St Peter.Tel: 422-1690 Fax: 422-1691. Can accommodate 70 people.

Rockley Resort and Beach Club. Tel: 435-7880 Fax: 435-8015. Can accommodate 170 people, theatre style.

Sam Lord's Castle, St Philip. Tel: 423-7350 Fax: 423-5918. Can accommodate 500 people.

Sandy Lane Hotel and Golf Club, St James. Tel: 432-1311 Fax: 432-2954. Can accommodate 40 people.

Tamarind Cove Hotel, St James.Tel: 432-1332 Fax: 422-1726. Can accommodate up to 48 people.

Restaurants

Andy-Anns, Collymore Rock, St Michael. Tel: 436-2098

Ali Baba's Restaurant, Rockley, Christ Church. Tel: 435-8249

A & D's Bar & Restaurant, Christ Church. Tel: 426-0617

Ambrosia Restaurant, Maxwell, Christ Church. Tel: 428-6854

Angie's Restaurant & Beach Bar, Maxwell, Christ Church. Tel: 428-5380

Angry Annie's Restaurant, Prospect, St James. Tel: 424-0425

Apple Experience, Hastings, Christ Church. Tel: 436-7604

Arfer's English Pub & Restaurant, Maxwell, Christ Church. Tel: 428-4613

Bagatelle, St Thomas. Tel: 425-0666

Bajan Cuisine Restaurant, Ivy, St Michael. Tel: 427-6579

Bajan Deli, Bay Street, St Michael. Tel: 426-0685

The Bajan Orchard Restaurant, Speightstown, St Peter. Tel: 422-1847

Balcony Restaurant, Broad Street, St Michael. Tel: 431-2088

Bamboo Beach Bar & Restaurant, Paynes Bay, St James. Tel: 432-0910

Barclay Park, Beach Bar, East Coast Road, St Andrews. Tel: 422-9213

Barker's Twilight, Oistins, Christ Church. Tel: 428-3289

Bistro Italia, Rockley, Christ Church. Tel: 435-8114

The Boatyard (Knowles Marine), Bay Street, St Michael. Tel: 436-2622

Bombas Beach Bar & Restaurant, St James. Tel: 432-0569

Black Rock Grill, Black Rock, St Michael. Tel: 424-7859

Blakey's Bar & Restaurant, St Lawrence Gap, Christ Church. Tel: 428-1933

Bongo Light Ital Shop, Bridgetown, St Michael. Tel: 426-0718

Bonito Bar & Restaurant, Bathsheba, St Joseph. Tel: 433-9034

Boomers Restaurant & Lounge, St Lawrence Gap, Christ Church. Tel: 428 8439

The Brig Bar & Restaurant, Sunset Crest, St James. Tel: 432-1103

Brown Sugar, Bay Street, St Michael. Tel: 426-7684

Cafe Musee, St Michael. Tel: 427-1713

Callaloo Restaurant, Rockley, Christ Church. Tel: 435-8204

Canton Restaurant & Bar, Paynes Bay, St James. Tel: 432-7285

Capricorn Restaurant, Bridgetown. Tel: 426-2727

Captain's Carvery, St Lawrence Gap, Christ Church. Tel: 435-6961

Carambola, Derricks, St James. Tel: 432-0832

Carib Beach Bar, Worthing, Christ Church. Tel: 435-8540

The Caribbean Castle, Maxwell, Christ Church. Tel: 428-55870

Catamara Ltd, Holetown, St James. Tel: 432-0125

Cat's Bar & Restaurant, Bridgetown. Tel: 436-2507

Chateau Creole, Porters, St James. Tel: 422-4116

Char-B-Que, Rockley, Christ Church. Tel: 435-8427

Chossels Beach Bar & Restaurant, Rockley, Christ Church. Tel: 435-8074

Chrizel's Garden, Gibbs, St Peter. Tel: 422-2403

Clarke's Dinery, Bridgetown. Tel: 426 6072

Coach House, Paynes Bay, St James. Tel: 432-1163

Coco Banana Bar & Restaurant, St Peter. Tel: 422-0640

Coconuts Restaurant & Bar, Worthing, Christ Church. Tel: 435-7314

Colonade Restaurant & Bar, Dover, Christ Church. Tel: 428-8091

Courtyard Cafe, Bridgetown. Tel: 436-5261

Da Luciano, Hastings, Christ Church . Tel: 427-5518

David's Place, St Lawrence, Christ Church. Tel: 435-6550

The Drydock Lounge & Restaurant, Bridgetown. Tel: 431-0482

Encore Restaurant Ltd, Bridgetown. Tel: 429-8284

Excuses Pub, Worthing, Christ Church. Tel: 435-7338

The Fathoms, Paynes Bay, St James. Tel: 432-2568

The Fiesta Restaurant, Prospect on Sea, St James. Tel: 425-1107

Flash In Restaurant, Pilgrim Place, Christ Church. Tel: 428-0122

Frankie's Canteen & Bar, Christ Church. Tel: 428-1764

Fisherman's Wharf, Bridgetown. Tel: 436-7778

Flamboyant, Hastings, Christ Church. Tel: 427-558

Fortune Cookie, Rockley, Christ Church. Tel: 435-8124

Ginger Restaurant, The Crane, St Philip. Tel: 423-5810

Granny's Restaurant, Bridgetown. Tel: 436-2727

The Great Escape, St Michael. Tel: 436-3554

Guang Dong Chinese Restaurant & Bar, Worthing, Christ Church. Tel: 435-7387

Habitt's Restaurant & Lounge, Maxwell, Christ Church. Tel: 428-9525

Havana Restaurant, Bridgetown, St Michael. Tel: 427-5861

Higher Level, Bridgetown. Tel: 436-7455

H J Restaurant & Bar, Collymore Rock, St Michael. Tel: 427-7103

Home Cookin', Hastings, Christ Church. Tel: 436 5367

Hot Corner Snackette & Bar, Bridgetown. Tel: 426-1392

Ideal Restaurant, Bridgetown. Tel: 431-2118

Ile De France, Hastings, Christ Church. Tel: 435-6869

Jade Garden Chinese Restaurant, St Lawrence Gap, Christ Church. Tel: 428-2759

Josef's, St Lawrence Gap, Christ Church. Tel: 435-6541

Kensington Kings Restaurant, Bridgetown. Tel: 436-5290

King Chicken, St Lawrence Gap, Christ Church. Tel: 428-6768

Koko's, Prospect, St James. Tel: 424- 4557

La Cage Aux Folles, Prospect, St James. Tel: 424-2424

La Maison, Holetown, St James. Tel: 432-1156

The Legend Restaurant, Mullins Bay, St Peter. Tel: 422-0631

Limers Bar & Restaurant, St Lawrence Gap, Christ Church. Tel: 435-6554

Look-Out Restaurant & Bar, Bridgetown. Tel: 426-4399

Luigi's, Dover, Christ Church. Tel: 428 9218

Mal's Refreshments, Bridgetown.Tel: 427-3699

The Mango Cafe, Speightstown, St Peter. Tel: 422-0704

Marcy's Canteen, St Michael. Tel: 425-7313

Margo's Munchies Restaurant & Bar, St Michael. Tel: 424-9381

Mariner's Restaurant, St Lawrence Gap, Christ Church. Tel: 435-7246

Mayflower Ltd, Bridgetown. Tel: 426-4734

Melting Pot Restaurant, St Lawrence, Christ Church. Tel: 428-3555

Mermaid Restaurant, Maxwell, Christ Church. Tel: 428-4116

Mullins Beach Bar & Restaurant, Mullins Bay, St Peter. Tel: 422-1878

Nico's Champagne Wine Bar, Holetown, St James. Tel: 432-6386

One Love Bar & Restaurant, Bridgetown. Tel: 436-0251

The Open Gallery, Bridgetown.Tel: 436-4703

Orchid Restaurant, Dover, Christ Church. Tel: 428-7584

Overtime Restaurant, Brandons, St Michael. Tel: 425-8508

Paolo's Italian Cuisine, Prospect, St James. Tel: 424-0425

Pebble Restaurant & Bar, Aquatic Gap, St Michael. Tel: 436-8399

Pelican Restaurant, Bridgetown. Tel: 427-9481

Pink Star Bar & Restaurant, Bridgetown. Tel: 436-1612

Pisces, St Lawrence Gap, Christ Church. Tel: 435-6564

The Plantation Restaurant, St Lawrence, Christ Church. Tel: 428-5048

Police Cafeteria, Bridgetown. Tel: 429-2281

The Posse Restaurant, Sargeant's Village, Christ Church. Tel: 437-2055

Queen's Park Restaurant, Bridgetown. Tel: 427-9481

Raffle's, Holetown, St James. Tel: 432-1280

Rain Rama Bar & Restaurant, Collymore Rock, St Michael. Tel: 429-5688

Reid's, Derricks, St James. Tel: 432 7623

The Roadhouse Restaurant, Hastings, Christ Church. Tel: 435-8509

Ron's Green House, Worthing, Christ Church. Tel: 435-8000

Rosebud Restaurant, Worthing, Christ Church. Tel: 435-7377

The Rose & Crown, Prospect, St James. Tel: 425-1074

The Roti Hut, Worthing, Christ Church, Tel: 435-7362

Rumours Beach Bar & Restaurant, Holetown, St James. Tel: 432-5294

Sam's Lantern Restaurant & Bar, Long Bay, St Philip. Tel: 423-5674

Sandy Bank Beach Bar & Restaurant, Hastings, Christ Church. Tel: 435-6689

Seaway Restaurant, St Lawrence Gap, Christ Church. Tel: 428-6768

Secret's Restaurant, Bagshot House, Worthing, Christ Church. Tel: 435-9000

September's Restaurant, Bridgetown. Tel: 429-5574

Ship Inn, St Lawrence Gap, Christ Church. Tel: 435-6961

Shirley's Reddy Dun Food Restaurant, Speightstown, St Peter. Tel: 422-1316

Snackles Restaurant, Vauxhall, Christ Church. Tel: 437-2075

The Steak House, St Lawrence Gap, Christ Church. Tel: 428-7152

Steve's Cafe, Bridgetown. Tel: 429-6930

Stowaways Restaurant & Bar, Maxwell, Christ Church. Tel: 420-6101

Sugar Cane Club, Maynards, St Peter. Tel: 422-5026

Super Q Restaurant, Bridgetown. Tel: 436-5641

Surfside Restaurant & Bar, Holetown, St James. Tel: 432-2104

Sylvester's Restaurant, St Michael. Tel: 436-0488

Taj Restaurant & Bar, Bridgetown. Tel: 427-4521

Tallies Bajan Bar, St James. Tel: 422-0092

Tony's Snack Bar, Clapham Park, St Michael. Tel: 436-0240

Tyrone's Restaurant & Lounge, St Lawrence Gap, Christ Church. Tel: 435-6531

Upper Deck Chinese Restaurant, Bridgetown. Tel: 436-2268

Venus Bar & Restaurant, Oistins, Christ Church. Tel: 428-7509

Voyager Restaurant, Grantley Adams Int. Airport, Christ Church. Tel: 428-7101

Waterfront Cafe, Bridgetown, St Michael. Tel: 427-0093

Where the Rum Comes From, St Michael. Tel: 435-6900

Whitey's Restaurant & Bar, Worthing, Christ Church. Tel: 435-9044

Wildey Conference Centre Restaurant, St Michael. Tel: 429-8799

Witch Doctor, St Lawrence Gap, Christ Church. Tel: 435-6581

Wok Chinese Take Out, Bridgetown. Tel: 431-0110

Young Roy's Restaurant & Bar, Bridgetown. Tel: 427-4735

Fastfoods

Beefeater, Sargeants Village, Christ Church. Tel: 427-5466

Kentucky Fried Chicken:
  West Coast: Speightstown. Tel: 422-5827
  Black Rock. Tel: 424-9268
  KFC Delivery. Tel: 424-8888
  In the City: Trident House. Tel: 429-8520
  Fairchild Street. Tel: 436-9342
  South Coast: Hastings. Tel: 435-8185
  KFC Delivery. Tel: 435-8888
  Out of City: Collymore Rock. Tel: 437-3791
  KFC Delivery. Tel: 435-8888

Chefette:
  Rockley, Christ Church. Tel: 435-6709
  Broad Street, St Michael. Tel: 436-6381
  Marhill Street, St Michael. Tel: 429-5216
  Harbour Road, St Michael. Tel: 426-3043
  Oistins, Christ Church. Tel: 428-2223
  Holetown, St James. Tel: 432-0430

Barbados Pizza House:
  Holetown. Tel: 432-0227
  Worthing. Tel: 437-2980
  Fontabelle. Tel: 429-6228

Nightclubs

After Dark, St Lawrence Gap, Christ Church. Tel: 435-6547

Apple Experience, Hastings Christ Church. Tel: 436-7604

Club Miliki, Heywoods Hotel, St Peter, Tel: 422-4900

The Coach House, Paynes Bay, St James, Tel: 432-7604

The Dry Dock, Cavans Lane, Bridgetown. Tel: 431-0482

Harbour Lights, Bay Street, St Michael, Tel: 436-7225

Hippo Disco, Beach Village, St James, Tel: 425-1440

Rat Trap Night Club, Rices, St Philip. Tel: 423-6552

September's, Lower Bay Street, St Michael. Tel: 429-5574

Sandy Night Club Bank, Hastings, Tel 435-1234

The Ship Inn, St Lawrence Gap, Christ Church, Tel: 428-5777

The Warehouse, Cavans Lane, Bridgetown. Tel: 436-2897

Tourist Facilities

Barbados Tourism Authority: Harbour Road, PO Box 242, Bridgetown. Tel: 427-2623 Fax: 426-4080

Bicycle Rentals

Fun Seekers Inc, Rockley Main Rd, Christ Church. Tel: 435-8206

William M.A.Bicycle Rentals, Hastings, Christ Church. Tel: 427-3955

Crafts shops

Antiquaria, Garden Highway, Bridgetown, Tel: 426-0635

Best of Barbados, Gift Shop, Welches, St Thomas. Tel: 421-6900

Earthworks Pottery, St Thomas. Tel: 425-0223

Fairfield Pottery & Gallery, St Michael, Tel: 424-3800

The Fred Art Gallery, Tel: 430-9322

Golfing

Golf Club, Sandy Lane, St James. Tel: 432-1145

Heywoods Golf Club, St Peter. Tel: 422-4900

Rockley Resort Golf Club, Christ Church. Tel: 435-7880

Hiking

The Barbados National Trust, Ronald Tree House, Belleville. Tel 436-9033

Horse Riding

Beau Geste Farm, St George. Tel: 429-0139

Brighton Riding Stables, Brighton, Black Rock, St Michael. Tel: 425-9381

Caribbean International Riding Centre, Auburn, St Joseph. Tel 423-0186

Tony's Riding Stables, Gibbes, St Peter. Tel: 422-1549/1465

Ye Old Congo Road Stables, St Philip, Tel: 423-6180

Judo

Classes at the National Stadium, Christ Church. Tel: 437-0601

Karate

Avalon Karate Club, George Street, Belleville, St Michael. Tel: 427-0410

Barbados Shotokan Karate Club, Hastings, Christ Church. Tel: 428-2674

Tae Kwon Do, The Foundation School, Christ Church. Tel: 436-4459

Tiger System Karate, Speightstown Community Centre, St Peter. Tel: 422-2424

Universal Kempo Karate School, St James. Tel: 432-7608

Motor Scooter Rentals

Fun Seekers Inc, Rockley Main Rd, Christ Church. Tel: 435-8206

Lynn's Rental, Hastings, Christ Church. Tel: 435-8585

Photograph Services

Photo Finish, One Hour Labs, Sunset Crest, Westcoast, Tel: 432-6167

Shopping Malls

Cave Shepherd Store, Broad Street, Bridgetown. Tel: 431-2121

Sheraton Centre, Seargents Village, Christ Church. Tel: 437-0970

Tours

Animal Flower Caves, St Lucy, opens daily and by arrangement. Tel: 439 8797

Andromeda Botanic Gardens, open daily 9.00 am - 5.00 pm except public holidays. Tel: 433-9384

Flower Forest Richmond Plantation, St Joseph, open 7 days 9.00 am - 5.00 pm. Tel: 433-8152

Francia Plantation, Francia, St George, open Mon - Fri except on public holidays. Tel 429-0474

Gun Hill Signal Station, open Mon - Sat 9.00 am - 5.00pm except public holidays. Tel: 429 1358

Harrison's Cave, open 7 days, first tour 9.00 am -last tour 4.00 pm. Tel: 438-6641

Morgan Lewis Sugar Mill, open Mon - Fri 9.00 am - 5.00 pm. Tel: 422-9222

Mount Gay Rum Tour, Exmouth Gap, Brandons, open Mon-Fri 9.00 am - 4.00 pm Tel: 425-9066

The Sugar Museum, open Mon - Sat 9.00 am - 5.00 pm except major holidays. Tel: 432-0100

Tyrol Cottage Heritage Village, open Mon - Fri 9.00 am - 5.00 pm. Tel: 424-2074

Welchman Hall Gulley, open daily 9.00 am - 5.00 pm except public holidays. Tel: 438-6671

Underwater Sports Facilities

Blue Reef Watersports, Glitter Bay, St James. Tel: 422-3133

Dive Shop Ltd, St Micheal. Tel: 426-9947

Exploresub Barbados, St Lawrence Gap, Christ Church. Tel: 435-6542

Sandy Lane WaterSports, Sandy Lane Hotel, St James. Tel: 432-1311

Scuba Barbados, St Lawrence Gap, Christ Church. Tel: 435-6565

Shade of Blue, Coral Reef Club, St James. Tel: 422-3215

Southern Palms Watersports, St Lawrence Gap, Christ Church. Tel: 428-7171

Boat Rental & Charter

Charter Cruises/ Deep Sea Fishing

Barracuda Too, Christ Church. Tel: 426-7252

Blue Jay Charters, St James. Tel: 422-2098

Blue Marlin Cruises. Tel: 435-6669

Dive Boat Safari, Hilton Hotel, Needham 's Point. Tel: 427-4350

The Dive Shop Ltd, Aquatic Gap, St Michael. Tel: 426-9947

The Habour Master, Bridgetown, St Michael. Tel: 430-0900

Heatwave Sailing Cruises, Longbay, St Philip. Tel: 423-7871

Irish Mist Cruises, Bridgetown. Tel: 436-9201 Fax 430-0533

Limbo Lady Sailing Cruises, Chancery Lane, Christ Church. Tel: 420-5418

Seaworld Explorer, Bridgetown. Tel: 436-6426
Tiami Cruises Ltd, Bridgetown. Tel: 427-7245
Why Not Sailing Cruises, Hastings, Christ Church. Tel: 427-1043

Coastal Cruises

Bajan Queen, Deepwater Harbour, Bridgetown. Tel: 436 6424

Bajan Queen Party Cruises, Bridgetown, St Michael. Tel: 436-2149

Jolly Roger, Deepwater Harbour, Bridgetown. Tel: 436 6424

Secret Love, Lancaster Heights, St James. Tel: 432 1972

Car Rental Agencies

A & M Car Rentals, St Michael, Tel: 424-0469

Abbac Rentals, St.Lawrence Gap, Tel: 428-8149

Ace Ltd, Black Rock, Tel: 424-8124

Adam Car Rental, Bridgetown. Tel: 436-0543

Ahmed's Car Rental, Cave Hill, St Michael. Tel: 424-2052

Alleyne Auto Rentals, Holders Hill, St James. Tel: 432-7604

Armel Rentals, Ealing Park, Christ Church. Tel: 428-6689

Auto Rentals Ltd, Top Rock, Christ Church. Tel: 428-9085

Barbados Rent-A-Car, Tudor Bridge, St Michael. Tel: 425-1388

Barbados Rent-A-Car, Airport, Christ Church. Tel: 428-0960

Belmont Taxi Service, St Michael. Tel: 429-2659

Blenman's Garage, St Michael. Tel: 427-3904

Coconut Car Rentals, Christ Church. Tel: 437-0297

Corbins Car Rentals, Collymore Rock, St Michael. Tel: 427-9531

Courtesy Car Rentals, Wildey, St Michael. Tel: 426-5219

Dear's Garage Ltd, St Michael. Tel: 429-9277

Direct Rentals, Christ Church. Tel: 428-3133

Double J Car & Moke Rentals, Bank Hall. Tel: 427-3155

Drive-A-Matic, St Michael. Tel: 422-5017

Eastern Enterprises Ltd, St Peter. Tel: 435-4405

Griffith PM & Sons, St Michael. Tel: 436-2639

Henry's Car Rentals, Church Village, St Joseph. Tel: 433-1270

Hill Bruce, Christ Church. Tel: 428-6657

Johnson Stable & Garage, Upper Collymore Rock, St Michael. Tel: 426-5030

Johnson's Car Rentals, Two Mile Hill, St Michael. Tel: 426-2273

Jones Garage Ltd, St Michael. Tel: 426-5030

Kentruth's Garage, St Michael. Tel: 427-1963

Leisure Rentals Ltd, Hastings, Christ Church. Tel: 426-1452

M A H Car Rentals, St Michael. Tel: 427-1952

M & C Moke Rentals Ltd. Dover, Christ Church. Tel: 428-7845

M Jay's Rentals Ltd, St Lawrence Gap, Christ Church. Tel: 428-7319

Mangera Car Rentals, Welches Main Road, St Michael. Tel: 436-0562

Miramar Rental Ltd, Westmoreland, St James. Tel: 422-3912

Mohammed Car Rentals, Belleville, St Michael. Tel: 426-3073

National Car Rentals Ltd. Strathclyde, St Michael. Tel: 426-0603

Nassi Rentals, Belleville, St Michael. Tel: 436-2019

P & S Car Rentals, Cave Hill, St Michael. Tel: 424-2052

Pandora Rent-A-Car, Belle Gully, St Michael. Tel: 429-4329

Paramont Taxi Service, St Michael. Tel: 429-3718

Patel,Mohammed, St Michael. Tel: 424-0469

Premier Auto Rentals, St Michael. Tel: 424-2277

R P Rentals, St Michael. Tel: 436-6113

Ray's Enterprises, Lakes Folly, St Michael. Tel: 436-3560

Rayside Car Rental, Charnocks, Christ Church. Tel: 428-0264

S.L. Car Rentals, Clapham Main Road, St Michael. Tel: 429-8091

Sand Acres Car Rentals, Maxwell, St Michael. Tel: 428-7141

Sealy's Car Rentals, St Michael. Tel: 429-4627

Smith,L E& Co Ltd, St Michael's Row, Bridgetown. Tel: 436-5895

Sonic Car Rental, St Helen, St George. Tel: 437-9626

Stoute's Car Rental, St Philip. Tel: 435-4456

Sunny Isle Motors Ltd, Worthing, Christ Church. Tel: 435-7979

Sunset Crest Rent-A-Car, Sunset Crest, St James. Tel: 432-1482

Sunset Rent-A-Car, Hastings, Christ Church. Tel: 426-1763

Sunshine Rentals, Hastings, Christ Church. Tel: 427-1234

Thompson Willie B Car & Moke, Silver Sands, Christ Church. Tel: 428-7500

Tropicar Rentals, St James. Tel: 425-5267

Ward Joan, St James. Tel: 424-1043

West Coast Rentals, St James. Tel: 422-2872

William L.E. Tours, Hastings, Christ Church. Tel: 427-1043

Museums & Art Galleries

Barbados has a variety of galleries that range in features from private artists studios to those offering solely temporary exhibitions, and those of a purely commercial nature. This list offers a brief insight to their individual features.

Amandla Gallery, Dayrell's Road, St Michael. Tel: 435-0247. Carries fine art originals; limited edition prints and sculptures. Framing also offered. Hours: Mon - Fri 9.00am - 5.00 pm. Sat 10.00 am - 1.00 pm.

Bagatelle Caribbean Art Gallery, Bagatelle Great House, St Thomas. Tel: 421-6767. Carries a variety of fine art with some craft exhibits. Open primarily during the dinner hour (after 7.00 pm). Call to arrange alternative viewing times.

Barbados Arts Council Gallery, Pelican Village, Bridgetown. Tel: 426-4385. Temporary exhibitions of its members artwork. Hours: Mon - Fri 10.00 am - 5.00 pm. Sat 9.00 am - 1.00pm.

The Barbados Gallery of Art, Bush Hill, Garrison, St Michael. Tel: 228-0149. A permanent display of Barbadian and Caribbean art. Opened October 1996. Call to enquire hours.

Barbados Museum & Historical Society, Garrison, St Michael. Tel: 427-0201. Permanent exhibits featuring the island's natural and social history. Call to enquire about their temporary art exhibitions. Hours: Mon - Sat 9.00 am - 5.00 pm. Sun 2.00 pm - 6.00 pm.

Batik Art Gallery, Cleavers Hill, Bathsheba, St Joseph. Tel: 433-9668. Features the work of local batik artist John Mayers. Hours: Mondays 7.30 am - 4.30 pm.

Creative Expressions, Gingerbread House, Hincks Street, Bridgetown. Tel: 436-0506. A wide selection of fine art and crafts. Hours: Mon - Fri 9.00 am - 6.00 pm. Sat 10.00 am - 1.00 am.

Fine Crafts, Chattel House Shopping Village, St Lawrence Gap. Tel: 428-4289. A variety of quality craft items made locally. Hours: Mon - Fri 9.00 am - 6.00 pm. Saturday 9.00 - 3.00 am.

H P Batic Studio, 2nd Avenue, Newbury, St George. - create batik wall hangings. Artists Patrick Craigwell and Henderson Reece. Mon - Fri. 8.00 am - 5.00 pm.

The Potters House, Edgehill Heights, St Thomas. Tel: 425-0223. Fax: 425-3224. Special one-of-a-kind functional art. Hours: Mon - Fri 9.00 am - 5.00 pm. Sat 9.00 am - 1.00 pm.

Portobello Gallery, Batts Rock & Prospect, St James. Tel: 424-1687. Features a collection of Haitian art. Hours: Mon - Sun 9.00 am - 5.30 pm.

Queen's Park Gallery, Queen's Park, Bridgetown. Tel: 427-2345. Temporary exhibitions by Barbadian, Caribbean and international artists. Hours: Tue - Thur 10.00 am - 6.00 pm. Fri - Mon 10.00 am - 1.00 pm, 2.00 pm - 6.00 pm.

Studio Art Gallery, Speedbird House, Fairchild Street, Bridgetown. Tel: 427-5463. Offers fine art originals and reproductions. However framing is its primary service. Hours: Mon - Fri 8.00 am - 4.00 pm. Sat 8.00 am - 12 noon.

Verandah Art Gallery, Women's Self-Help Building, Broad Street, Bridgetown. Tel: 426-2605. A wide selection of Barbadian and some Haitian art. Sculptures, ceramics and batik also on sale. Hours: Mon - Fri 9.00 am - 4.30 pm. Sat 9.00 am - 1.00 pm.

Several artists welcome visitors to their studios to view their work by appointment. To find out more contact the National Cultural Foundation, West Terrace, St James. Tel: 424-0909.

Other Hansib titles

ANTIGUA & BARBUDA - A Little Bit of Paradise (3rd revised edition). This edition explores in a highly informative and sensitively illustrated way, the history of these idyllic islands from the emergence of the Siboney (stone people) 4,000 years ago to the present day democracy, enjoying one of the highest standards of living in the Caribbean. This edition also includes a German language synopsis. Hardback £25/US$45

GRENADA, CARRIACOU & PETIT MARTINIQUE: Spice Island of the Caribbean This unique country profile presents a complete view of Grenada, Carriacou and Petit Martinique - combining historical and modern photographs with authoritative commentary on social and economic history and the country's abundant natural assets. Hardback. £25/US$45

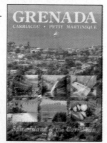

DOMINICA - Nature Island of the Caribbean. This 320 page book, richly illustrated in full colour, captures the beauty of this Caribbean country and offers a brief account of its sometimes turbulent history and rich culture. Hardback £19.95 /US$40

FROM COLONY TO NATION: THE RISE OF WESTINDIAN CRICKET. by Frank Birbalsingh. Mixing historical reflection with cricket reminiscence to conjure up the magical evocation of the events, issues, attitudes and personalities central to the evolution of Westindian cricket in its most critical years, from the 1920s to the 1960s. Paperback £12.95/US$18

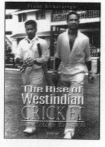

PRIDE OF BLACK BRITISH WOMEN by Deborah King A book which provides young people, particularly young black people who were born in Britain, with positive images and role models of women who they can relate to, identify with and aspire to emulate. Paperback £5.95/US$8.50

INDO-WESTINDIAN CRICKET. By Professor Frank Birbalsingh and Clem Shiwcharan. Two brilliant essays on Westindian cricket by two of the region's leading cultural historians. Hardback £7.95/US$15

100 GREAT WESTINDIAN TEST CRICKETERS. By Bridgette Lawrence with Reg Scarlett. Through the eyes of the leading players of the last 60 years, Bridgette Lawrence traces the rise of Westindian Test cricket from its beginnings at Lord's in 1928 to the triumphs of the last two decades. Hardback £14.95 /US$22

CHEDDI JAGAN: SELECTED SPEECHES 1992-1994 Edited by David Dabydeen A volume containing the recent speeches the Guyanese President, one of the oustanding leaders of the developing world. They testify to his vision, integrity and eloquent concern for the potential as well as the plight of the Guyanese people. Paperback £6.95/US$8.50

THE OTHER MIDDLE PASSAGE - Journal of a Voyage from Calcutta to Trinidad, 1858. Introduction by Ron Ramdin This book reproduces, in facsimile, the Journal of the Captain of the Salsette, a ship carrying Indian indentured labourers from Calcutta to Trinidad in 1858. A detailed introductory analysis by Ramdin, puts in context the significance of this document for the better understanding of this little known mass migration. Paperback £3.95/US$6

RASTA AND RESISTANCE - From Marcus Garvey to Walter Rodney. By Dr Horace Campbell. Tracing the cultural, political and spiritual sources of this movement of resistance, highlighting the quest for change among an oppressed people. Paperback £8.95/US$14

SPEECHES BY ERROL BARROW. Edited by Yussuff Haniff. A collection of speeches made by the late Barbadian Prime Minister, showing Barrow as a true Caribbean man, fighting for the region's independent identity. This book is now recommended reading in most Barbadian schools. Hardback £10.95/US$17

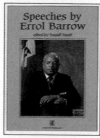

A NEW SYSTEM OF SLAVERY - The Export of Indian Labour Overseas 1830-1920. By Hugh Tinker. The first comprehensive historical survey of a hitherto neglected and only partially known migration- the export of Indians to supply the labour needed in producing plantation crops all over the world. Paperback £11.99/US$18

INDIA IN THE CARIBBEAN. Edited by Dr David Dabydeen and Dr Brinsley Samaroo. A collection of essays, poems and prose by leading Indo-Caribbean scholars and writers, on East Indian history and culture in the Caribbean. Paperback £8.95. Hardback £11.95/US$18

PROSPERO'S RETURN? Historical Essays on Race, Culture and British Society. By Paul Rich. In this wide-ranging collection of essays, exploring the nature and meaning of race and racism in British society and the nature of British and English national identity. Paperback £8.95/US$14

INSEPARABLE HUMANITY. Inseparable Humanity is an anthology of reflections by one of the world's leading thinkers, Shridath S Ramphal - the former Commonwealth Secretary-General. Hardback £14.95/US$20

KING OF THE CARNIVAL AND OTHER STORIES. By Willi Chen. A unique collection of short stories from the Caribbean, capturing the violence, trickery, pathos and racial comedy of Trinidadian society. Paperback £5.95/US$9

THE OPEN PRISON. A novel by Angus Richmond. The story of Angela, a sensitive and disturbed child, growing up on the estate of her white guardian in British Guiana, is slowly and painfully awakened to a society in turmoil, in which both black and white are struggling to reassert their roles during the First World War. Paperback £4.95/US$7.50

THE REGGAE FILES. By Gordon C. A collection of interviews with reggae superstars from Jamaica and Britain who speak about the influence of Jamaican politics, Rastafarian ideas and the black British experience on the creation of their music. Paperback £6.95/US$10

ENQUIRIES:
UNITED KINGDOM
Readers Book Club, Third Floor, Tower House, 141-149 Fonthill Road, London N4 3HF. Tel: 071-281 1191, Fax: 071-263 9656.
CARIBBEAN
Hansib Publishing (Caribbean) Limited, PO Box 2773, St John's, Antigua, Westindies.
UNITED STATES
Hansib Publishing (USA), 17498 Tuscan Avenue, Granada Hills, California CA 91344.
CANADA
Hansib Publishing (Canada), 22 Gaslight Crescent, Scarborough, Ontario M1C 3S8.